Gay and Lesbian Activism in the Republic of Ireland, 1973–93

Gay and Lesbian Activism in the Republic of Ireland, 1973–93

Patrick McDonagh

BLOOMSBURY ACADEMIC
LONDON • NEW YORK • OXFORD • NEW DELHI • SYDNEY

BLOOMSBURY ACADEMIC
Bloomsbury Publishing Plc
50 Bedford Square, London, WC1B 3DP, UK
1385 Broadway, New York, NY 10018, USA
29 Earlsfort Terrace, Dublin 2, Ireland

BLOOMSBURY, BLOOMSBURY ACADEMIC and the Diana logo are trademarks of
Bloomsbury Publishing Plc

First published in Great Britain 2021
Paperback edition first published 2023

Copyright © Patrick McDonagh, 2021

Patrick McDonagh has asserted their right under the Copyright, Designs
and Patents Act, 1988, to be identified as Author of this work.

Cover image: Robson, Christopher, 1941–2013, photographer, NLGF Float at
St Patrick's Day parade. © Image courtesy of the National Library of Ireland.

All rights reserved. No part of this publication may be reproduced or transmitted
in any form or by any means, electronic or mechanical, including photocopying,
recording, or any information storage or retrieval system, without prior
permission in writing from the publishers.

Bloomsbury Publishing Plc does not have any control over, or responsibility for,
any third-party websites referred to or in this book. All internet addresses given in
this book were correct at the time of going to press. The author and publisher
regret any inconvenience caused if addresses have changed or sites have
ceased to exist, but can accept no responsibility for any such changes.

Every effort has been made to trace copyright holders and to obtain their
permissions for the use of copyright material. The publisher apologizes for any
errors or omissions and would be grateful if notified of any corrections that
should be incorporated in future reprints or editions of this book.

A catalogue record for this book is available from the British Library.

Library of Congress Cataloging-in-Publication Data
Names: McDonagh, Patrick (Patrick J.), author.
Title: Gay and lesbian activism in the republic of Ireland, 1973–93 /
Patrick McDonagh.
Description: London, UK ; New York, NY, USA : Bloomsbury Academic, 2021. |
Includes bibliographical references and index. |
Identifiers: LCCN 2021017353 (print) | LCCN 2021017354 (ebook) |
ISBN 9781350197466 (hardback) | ISBN 9781350197473 (ebook) |
ISBN 9781350197480 (epub)
Subjects: LCSH: Gay rights—Ireland—History—20th century. | Gay men—
Civil rights—Ireland—History—20th century. | Gay men—Political activity—
Ireland—History—20th century. | Lesbians—Civil rights—Ireland—History—
20th century. | Lesbians—Political activity—Ireland—History—20th century. |
Homosexuality—Law and legislation—Ireland—History—20th century.
Classification: LCC HQ76.8.I73 M33 2021 (print) | LCC HQ76.8.I73 (ebook) |
DDC 306.76/6094170904—dc23
LC record available at https://lccn.loc.gov/2021017353
LC ebook record available at https://lccn.loc.gov/2021017354

ISBN:	HB:	978-1-3501-9746-6
	PB:	978-1-3501-9745-9
	ePDF:	978-1-3501-9747-3
	eBook:	978-1-3501-9748-0

Typeset by RefineCatch Limited, Bungay, Suffolk

To find out more about our authors and books visit www.bloomsbury.com
and sign up for our newsletters.

Contents

List of Plates		vi
Acknowledgements		viii
List of Abbreviations		x
Introduction		1
1	Irish Homosexuals are Revolting, 1973–78	13
2	Social Life as Resistance in 1980s Dublin	39
3	1980s Provincial Activism: Cork and Galway	63
4	Gay Rights are not Extravagant Demands	87
5	Ireland was Ill-Equipped to deal with the AIDS Epidemic	111
6	Gay Rights: It's Time	135
Notes		161
Appendix: Glossary of Terms		197
Bibliography		199
Index		207

Plates

1. Members of the Sexual Liberation Movement protesting outside the Department of Justice on 27 June 1974 as part of Gay Pride.
2. Picture of five of the founding members of the Irish Gay Rights Movement. Kenneth F. Jackson is the sixth person.
3. Dublin's Gay Pride protest march, June 1983.
4. Arthur Leahy and Tony O'Regan of Cork Gay Collective handing out leaflets during Gay Pride week on Princes Street, Cork, c. 1982/83.
5. The Quay Co-Op, Sullivan's Quay, Cork. Photo c. 1984 during Lesbian and Gay Pride week.
6. Laurie Steele of Cork Gay Collective lobbying delegates as they arrived for the Irish Congress of Trade Unions annual general congress at Cork City Hall, July 1981.
7. GHA AIDS Information Leaflet, May 1985.
8. GHA Play Safe Card, 1986.

This book has been published with a financial subsidy from the European University Institute, Florence. This publication is based on a revised version of an EUI PhD thesis defended in 2019 in the Department of History and Civilization.

Acknowledgements

From the beginning of this project, I have been fortunate to be surrounded by supportive individuals, without whose advice, guidance and friendship this project would never have seen the light of day. To begin with, I want to thank the team at Bloomsbury Academic, who have been a pleasure to work with over the past two years. During my time at the EUI, I will be forever grateful to my PhD supervisor, Pieter Judson, and second reader, Laura Lee Downs, who have both been a constant source of support throughout the project. I would also like to acknowledge the kind support I received from Lindsey Earner-Byrne. This project owes much to her early support and guidance. A special thanks also to Lucy Riall, Sean Brady and Diarmuid Ferriter.

To all the staff at the EUI, in particular Serge Noiret, Francesca Parenti, Anna Coda and Nicola Hargreaves, thank you all for your assistance. I would like to give a special mention to the late Nicky Owtram, who was a wonderful source of support during my time at the EUI. Thank you also to the staff at the National Library of Ireland, in particular to James Harte; National Archives of Ireland; the Deputy Keeper of the Records, Public Record Office of Northern Ireland; University College Dublin Archives; University College Cork Archives; Trinity College Dublin Archives; Noelle Dowling at the Dublin Diocesan Archives; RTÉ Archives; Gale Primary Sources; Irish Newspaper Archive; *Galway Advertiser*; *The Irish Times*; SAGE Publication; Palgrave Macmillan; University of Texas Press; Firenze University Press; Paul Gouldsbury; Celine Curtin; Eamon Brett; Miriam G. Smith; and especially Orla Egan at the Cork LGBT Archive. Without these individuals and institutions this project would not have been possible.

Throughout this project I had the privilege to meet and talk with individuals involved in gay and lesbian activism in the Republic of Ireland, so thank you to: Edmund Lynch, Cathal Kerrigan, Kieran Rose, Marese Walsh, Tonie Walsh, David Norris, Helen Slattery, Deirdre Walsh, Nuala Ward, Sean Connolly, Clement Clancy and Bill Foley.

To my wonderful friends: Sara, Jennifer, Emma, Carmel, Tasneem, Kathryn, Alexandra, Eva, Dieter, Sebastian, Evair, Anthony, Aoife, Judith, Kate and Adam, thank you for your friendship. My final thanks are for my family. To my husband Breno, your love and support has meant everything to me. To Sarah, Noel, JD, Geni and Osmar (RIP), thanks/obrigado for always being there for me. Finally, for all their sacrifices over the last thirty-two years, I owe everything to my Mam (Bernie) and Dad (Jim). This book is dedicated to them.

The author and publisher gratefully acknowledge the permission granted to reproduce the copyright material in this book. Every effort has been made to trace copyright holders and to obtain their permission for the use of copyright material. The publisher apologizes for any errors or omissions in the above list and would be grateful if notified of any corrections that should be incorporated in future reprints or editions of this book. The third party copyrighted material displayed in the pages of this book is displayed on the basis of 'fair dealing for the purposes of criticism and review' or 'fair use for the purposes of teaching, criticism, scholarship or research' only in accordance with international copyright laws, and is not intended to infringe upon the ownership rights of the original owners.

Abbreviations

AAA	AIDS Action Alliance
AOH	Ancient Order of Hibernians
AAC	Anti-Amendment Campaign
CGC	Cork Gay Collective
CHE	Campaign for Homosexual Equality
CHLR	Campaign for Homosexual Law Reform
CLG	Cork Lesbian Group
CSW	Council for the Status of Women
DGC	Dublin Gay Collective
ESBOA	Electricity Supply Board Officers Association
EEA	Employment Equality Authority
ECHR	European Court of Human Rights
EEC	European Economic Community
FUE	Federated Union of Employers
FWUI	Federated Workers Union of Ireland
FWGH	Federation of Working Groups Homophily
GLEN	Gay and Lesbian Equality Network
GHA	Gay Health Action
HEB	Health Education Bureau
IGA	International Gay Association
ILGA	International Lesbian and Gay Association
ICTU	Irish Congress of Trade Unions
ICCL	Irish Council for Civil Liberties
IDATU	Irish Distributive and Administrative Trade Union
IFUT	Irish Federation of University Teachers

IGRM	Irish Gay Rights Movement
ILGO	Irish Lesbian and Gay Organisation
IMPACT	Irish Municipal, Public and Civil Trade Union
IQA	Irish Queer Archive
LGRW	Lesbian and Gay Rights at Work
LIL	Liberation for Irish Lesbians
LGPSU	Local Government and Public Services Union
NGCOC	National Gay Conference Organising Committee
NGF	National Gay Federation
NLI	National Library of Ireland
NUPE	National Union of Public Employees
NUS	National Union of Students
NUU	New University of Ulster
NICRA	Northern Ireland Civil Rights Association
NIFPA	Northern Ireland Family Planning Association
NIGRA	Northern Ireland Gay Rights Association
PLUTO	People Like Us Totally Outrageous
PRONI	Public Record Office of Northern Ireland
QUB	Queen's University Belfast
RTÉ	Raidió Teilifís Éireann
SHRG	Scottish Homosexual Rights Group
SMG	Scottish Minorities Group
SLM	Sexual Liberation Movement
SRM	Sexual Reform Movement
STDs	Sexually Transmitted Diseases
TAF	Tel-A-Friend
THT	Terrence Higgins Trust
TCD	Trinity College Dublin
UPTCS	Union of Professional and Technical Civil Servants
USI	Union of Students in Ireland

UCC	University College Cork
UCD	University College Dublin
UCG	University College Galway
WRTCC	Women's Right to Choose Campaign

Introduction

In May 2015, in what has been described as a 'social revolution' within Irish society, the Republic of Ireland became the first country in the world to legalise same-sex marriage by popular vote. Forty-one of forty-two constituencies, representing 1,202,198 people, overwhelmingly endorsed the following amendment to *Bunreacht na hÉireann* (Constitution of Ireland): 'Marriage may be contracted in accordance with law by two persons without distinction as to their sex.'[1] Internationally, the Republic of Ireland received widespread praise and admiration as a beacon for LGBT civil rights. The former United Nations Secretary-General, Ban Ki-moon, remarked at the time that 'the result sends an important message to the world: All people are entitled to enjoy their human rights no matter who they are or whom they love.'[2] Such is the image of the Republic of Ireland today as a leading voice for LGBT civil rights, that as recently as September 2020, former Polish Prime Minister Jaroslaw Kaczynski claimed that the Republic of Ireland has become a 'Catholic wilderness with rampant LGBT ideology'.[3]

That it is the Republic of Ireland that is now seen as a beacon for LGBT civil rights internationally is all the more surprising, considering that the country has long been viewed as a socially conservative society dominated by the teachings of the Roman Catholic Church. Moreover, it was only in 1993 that the Irish government decriminalised sexual activity between men, comparatively later than its European counterparts. For example, England and Wales partially decriminalised sexual activity between men in 1967, with Scotland and Northern Ireland following suit in 1981 and 1982 respectively.[4] Yet, despite the recent nature of decriminalisation, within the space of twenty-two years the Republic of Ireland has come to be viewed as a leading light for LGBT civil rights internationally and a sign of hope for oppressed LGBT individuals. Today, the Republic of Ireland uses this newfound reputation on the international stage to strengthen its position as a defender and promoter of human rights. For many, this transformation from decriminalisation in 1993 to same-sex marriage in 2015 has been rapid.

In the immediate aftermath of the 2015 referendum, a number of authors sought to explain how the Republic of Ireland came to be the first country in the world to introduce same-sex marriage by popular vote.[5] For the most part, these books begin by highlighting that sexual activity between men was criminalised until 1993. Reference is made to David Norris' legal battle in the Irish courts to challenge the laws that criminalised sexual activity between men and his subsequent victory at the European Court of Human Rights in 1988, and the amending of those laws in 1993. The narrative then moves onto the early 2000s and the efforts to introduce legislation permitting same-sex marriage. While these accounts provide an impressive forensic analysis of the marriage equality campaign from the early 2000s, little else is learned of gay rights activism in the Republic of Ireland pre-1993. As a result, one is left with the distinct impression that it is only in the post-decriminalisation era that efforts to change mindsets in the Republic of Ireland actually began. Prior to that, the efforts solely revolved around David Norris' legal battle and activities confined to Irish and European courts. It is hardly surprising, therefore, that after the 2015 referendum result a number of Irish politicians signalled Norris out as 'the pathfinder on this human rights issue' and someone who had ploughed 'a lone furrow' in this country for gay rights.[6] There can be no denying the immense role that Norris played in advancing gay rights, but as he himself has often acknowledged, he was *not* alone.

In reality, the history of gay rights activism in the Republic of Ireland dates back to the early 1970s, included much more than a campaign to decriminalise sexual activity between men and involved more individuals than just David Norris. In fact, if we are to truly understand the dramatic changes in recent years, we need to contextualise the efforts dating from the 1970s of gay and lesbian individuals who paved the way for later activism on issues such as civil partnership, marriage equality and gender recognition. In other words, 1993 was not the beginning, but rather an important juncture. Looked at from this perspective, the history of gay rights activism in the Republic of Ireland is much broader and has a longer trajectory.

In recent years scholars have begun to explore the history of gay rights activism in the Republic of Ireland in more depth. New work impressively explores issues such as LGBT activism in Cork; Irish radical gay activism; Irish LGBTQ+ visibility in the Irish media; Ireland's LGBT diaspora; and the gay community's response to AIDS in 1980s Ireland.[7] Despite these important contributions, this history remains in its infancy and there can be no doubt that Irish historians and Ireland's history departments more generally have been slow to explore Ireland's wider queer history in comparison to many of their international counterparts. It was only in 2018 that the first ever degree-level Irish LGBT History module was taught in an Irish university at University College Cork. Writing in 2004, Diarmaid Ferriter argued that into the latter years of the twentieth century in Ireland, 'the unfortunate reality was that the focus of historians remained narrow – republicanism, violence and the continuing fixation with intransigence in the North ...'.[8] While some progress has been made in diversifying Irish history, particularly in the area of Gender (although there is still a long way to go), some may well argue that Ferriter's analysis from 2004 could still be applied to Irish history today.

Ireland has a rich queer history that has yet to be fully uncovered, and as Colm Tóibín stated at the handover of the Irish Queer Archive (IQA) to the National Library of Ireland (NLI) in 2008: 'This [handover of the IQA to NLI] establishes that an understanding of our history, the history of gay women and men's struggle for liberation, is as essential in understanding contemporary Ireland as the history of the women's movement, or the labour movement, or the Fianna Fáil party'. Tóibín further maintained that in acquiring the IQA, the NLI 'understands the importance of our story as part of the national story'.[9]

While the passage of the 2015 marriage equality referendum was a seminal moment in Ireland's queer history, contextualising its passage should not be restricted solely to events post-1993 nor to David Norris' legal battle. Instead, we need to broaden our approach to explore other actors, other factors and the other sites of activism. In particular, we need to explore what took place in the years prior to the decriminalisation and how gay and lesbian individuals fought to bring about not only legal change but also socio-cultural change in the Republic of Ireland with regard to homosexuality. The twenty years prior to 1993 saw considerable advances for Ireland's gay community that have paved the way for subsequent victories in the 1990s and 2000s. Without a broader understanding of what happened prior to 1993, we cannot fully understand events in more recent years. With this in mind, *Gay and Lesbian Activism in the Republic of Ireland, 1973–1993* seeks to expand our understanding of events that transpired in the twenty years preceding the decriminalisation of sexual activity between men.

I do not claim that this book is the definitive history of gay rights activism in the Republic of Ireland during this period; it is not. There are many other stories and events that I have not been able to include in this book, which, if space had permitted, I would have liked to have discussed. Moreover, I have focused exclusively on gay and lesbian individuals, to the exclusion of a broader history on Lesbian, Gay, Bisexual and Transgender (LGBT) activism. It would be disingenuous to suggest that bisexual and transgender individuals were not mobilising during this period, but until more sources on the efforts and activities of bisexual and transgender individuals emerge, a comprehensive account is significantly curtailed. For this reason, the efforts of Sara Phillips to create an Irish Trans Archive, for example, are crucial in helping to document this area of Irish history. Furthermore, while this book does, to some degree, allude to the issue of gay and lesbian emigration/migration, this is certainly one area of Irish history where considerably more research is warranted. However, in saying that, this book does seek to provide a more nuanced and comprehensive account of the activities of gay and lesbian individuals and organisations to fight for their rights in the years between 1973 and 1993. This period represents the first phase of gay rights activism in the Republic of Ireland.

At the heart of this book is an attempt to explore the other sites of gay and lesbian activism in the Republic of Ireland outside the courtroom and beyond Dublin; the efforts of lesbian women, not just gay men; the efforts of provincial gay and lesbian activists; the efforts to win over allies, namely the student movement, trade union movement, and international organisations; the efforts to confront and challenge opponents of gay rights; and the strategies and rhetoric gay and lesbian activists adopted to engage with the wider Irish society in an effort to bring about a change in how the Republic of Ireland treated and viewed its lesbian and gay citizens. Put simply, this book seeks to demonstrate the extent to which a gay rights movement, rather than a small collection of individuals, emerged in the early 1970s to challenge the oppression of Irish gay and lesbian citizens and how it was through these efforts that progressive legislation was introduced in 1989 and 1993 to protect gay and lesbian individuals from discrimination. In the process, they also convinced many in Irish society to adopt a more tolerant and understanding attitude towards homosexuality.

Although the primary focus of this book centres on the efforts to challenge the socio-cultural, political and legal oppression of gay and lesbian individuals in the Republic of Ireland, this story should not be read exclusively as one of repression. This is not to suggest that I am diminishing in any way the oppression faced not just by Irish gay and lesbian individuals, but also those who did not conform to the strict societal norms of twentieth-century Ireland; rather, I am seeking to highlight the extent to which this book also reveals stories that are often ignored, particularly in an Irish context, namely stories of fun and pleasure. In his seminal book on the history of sexuality in Ireland, *Occasions of Sin*, Diarmaid Ferriter argued that 'an over reliance on sources relating to sexual crime also presents the historian with a dilemma. Does the history of sex in Ireland have to be a history of criminal sexual activity? In the absence of accounts of the joys of sex, this remains a problem . . .'.[10] As we shall see in this book, there are glimpses of fun and pleasure and it is hoped that these glimpses will encourage further exploration of the joys of sex in Ireland. One only needs to look at the existence of saunas targeting Dublin's gay community in the 1980s or the personal advertisements in Irish gay magazines to see evidence of gay men and lesbian women looking to meet others to act out their sexual fetishes – no doubt the same applies to their heterosexual counterparts.

Moreover, while I concentrate on the activities taking place within the Republic of Ireland, it must be acknowledged that Irish gay and lesbian activists situated themselves and their struggle within the wider international gay rights movement during this period. In other words, Irish gay and lesbian individuals were not isolated from their international counterparts – quite the contrary. Throughout this book, we will see the extent to which international gay and lesbian organisations lent support to their Irish counterparts. This support can be seen in the rise of a gay rights movement in Ireland, but also in the development of important services for the gay community, most notably and crucially during the height of the AIDS epidemic. There can be no doubt that international gay rights organisations helped sustain their Irish counterparts during challenging periods and that Irish gay and lesbian activists drew inspiration from their international colleagues. This inspiration came not only through direct contact with international gay organisations and the media, but also from those who emigrated from the Republic of Ireland and subsequently returned, bringing with them new ideas and a determination to change Irish society. In saying that, it must be acknowledged that Irish gay and lesbian individuals were also part of shaping the international gay rights movement.

What emerges, therefore, in *Gay and Lesbian Activism in the Republic of Ireland, 1973–1993*, is a story of how Irish gay and lesbian individuals refused to continue to accept the status quo with regard to homosexuality. By challenging the Republic of Ireland's attitudes towards homosexuality, by presenting a different image of and rhetoric on homosexuality, and by forging effective alliances with other social groups, both inside and outside Ireland, Irish gay and lesbian organisations successfully renegotiated Irish perceptions of homosexuality by the early 1990s. They did so by challenging the specific (often unspoken) meanings of what constituted 'Irishness', by coming out publicly discussing their sexuality, by engaging with Irish society through day-to-day interactions, in the media, talks, lobbying, protests, by creating a space for gay and lesbian individuals to become more comfortable in their sexuality, and crucially by confronting those who continued to portray homosexuality as sinful, deviant, perverted and a threat to society. Irish gay and lesbian individuals were unafraid to speak publicly and to articulate their cause, unafraid to confront their opponents and unwilling to succumb to any setback, despite their limited resources. By empowering gay and lesbian individuals to proudly 'come out' and to no longer feel ashamed or isolated and to tell their stories, Irish gay and lesbian organisations convinced Irish society and its policymakers to re-think their attitudes towards homosexuality. In doing so, they successfully presented themselves as ordinary respectable Irish citizens who should not be viewed as deviant, sick or a threat, and their demands as neither extravagant or unique, but rather as basic human rights. In many respects, many of the strategies and rhetoric rightly deemed to have been so successful during the marriage equality campaign had been adopted during the first phase of gay rights activism in the Republic of Ireland. With that being said, this book does not seek to claim that the history of gay rights activism in the Republic of Ireland from 1973–1993 is one of an inevitable march towards liberty or freedom. As we shall see throughout this book, this was certainly not the case – it was anything but. My hope is that this book will encourage further research into Ireland's queer history not only during the period of focus in this book, but both before and after.

Book outline and reflection on sources

This book is thematically structured and is divided into six chapters. Chapter 1 traces the emergence and development of the Republic of Ireland's first gay rights organisation, the Irish Gay Rights Movement (IGRM) between 1973 and 1978. It begins by looking at the events that led to the rise of the IGRM and thereafter how it sought to provide a space and voice for Irish gay and lesbian individuals. Chapter 2 looks at events in 1980s Dublin, in particular the activities of the National Gay Federation (NGF) and Liberation for Irish Lesbians (LIL). Through a focus on the social activities organised by these groups, it charts the rise of a more visible gay community in the Republic of Ireland in the 1980s and demonstrates how these social activities must be viewed as a form of resistance, i.e., they cannot be disregarded as apolitical. Chapter 3 moves outside Dublin to explore the different forms of activism taking place in Cork and Galway in the 1980s, arguing that these areas also played a significant role in championing gay rights and challenging the status quo in the Republic of Ireland.

Chapter 4 discusses the efforts to forge alliances with other organisations in Ireland. It explores the strategies and rhetoric activists engaged when they sought support from others, such as the Student Movement, the Trade Union Movement and the political class, as well as the support they received from their international counterparts. In short, this chapter focuses on the efforts to build up alliances outside the gay rights movement, while at the same time trying to undermine those who opposed any change in attitude towards homosexuality. Chapter 5 looks at the response of the gay rights movement to the AIDS epidemic and how this impacted the movement's activities and public image. Chapter 6 concludes with an examination of the legal changes introduced in 1993. It seeks to move beyond the assumption that the type of change introduced in

1993 was solely a direct result of Norris' legal victory in 1988. While the 1988 ECHR was crucial, it does not alone explain why the Irish government introduced the type of law reform it did, nor why it introduced an amendment to employment legislation that same year outlawing discrimination on the basis of sexual orientation. This chapter looks at the activities of gay and lesbian individuals post-1988 and how these actions influenced the legal reform introduced in 1993.

Primary archival research forms the backbone of this book. In particular, I have made extensive use of the Irish Queer Archive and the Personal Papers of David Norris at the National Library of Ireland; the Northern Ireland Gay Rights Association Archive at the Public Record Office of Northern Ireland; Cork LGBT Archive; National Archives of Ireland; personal papers of individuals involved in gay rights activism; and the archives of national and provincial papers. I am very grateful to all for granting me access to their material. I have also incorporated Oral Interviews into my research methodology. Through interviews I conducted with not only some of the leading activists of this period, but also those less publicly known, and together with 220 interviews conducted by Edmund Lynch, these stories add the personal to the history of gay rights activism in the Republic of Ireland. Since 2013, Lynch has been interviewing LGBT individuals who grew up in the Republic of Ireland pre-decriminalisation, as well as some high-profile individuals who supported gay rights activism, such as former presidents Mary Robinson and Mary McAleese. I am very grateful to Edmund Lynch for granting me full access and use of his interviews.

Suffice to say, Oral Interviews have both strengths and weaknesses. It goes without saying that the period of focus in this book dates back over forty years and there can be no doubt that memory lapses exist, and individuals' recollections of certain events may also have changed over the years. Moreover, while an extensive number of interviews were conducted, many individuals, for their own reasons, chose not to participate, and therefore, their stories have not been recorded. However, Oral Interviews have facilitated telling a broader history of gay rights activism in the Republic of Ireland, which is not exclusively focused on political activities. Instead, these Oral Interviews have enabled me to explore other issues such as: growing up in the Republic of Ireland; how individuals came to learn about gay rights organisations or homosexuality; how individuals came to involve themselves in gay rights activism; and the emotions they experienced both then and looking back at these events. Crucially, they have facilitated uncovering the stories of individuals whose voices hitherto had not been recorded in the archives, namely those involved in provincial activism. This has been especially important in recounting the role of lesbian women in gay rights activism during this period.

Overview of (homo)sexuality in the Republic of Ireland in the twentieth century

Jeffrey Weeks has noted that: '[the] mid-1960s was the golden age of liberal-humanitarian reforms, and of single-issue campaigns, mostly of long standing, to achieve them: the abolition of capital punishment and abortion-law reform and divorce-law reform as well as homosexual-law reform. And this was a European phenomenon.'[11] Weeks only had to look across to the Republic of Ireland to find an exception to this 'European phenomenon'. The Republic of Ireland of the 1960s lagged considerably behind its European counterparts in terms of liberal-humanitarian reforms.

Since the foundation of the Irish Free State in 1922 a strict puritanism had been institutionalised, primarily because of the power that the Roman Catholic Church wielded over Irish society. Chrystel Hug has argued that a Catholic morality 'has been central to the development of state law and state politics as it has been to the personal development of the Irish individual ...'[12] Throughout the twentieth century successive Irish governments sought to maintain, and strengthen, restrictions on the sexual activities of Ireland's citizens. While similar restrictions existed internationally, the difference is that in the Republic of Ireland they remained in force much longer, well into the late twentieth century. A key issue influencing this was what Lindsey Earner-Byrne and Diane Urquhart described as 'a self-conscious narrative of moral superiority [that] emerged to differentiate the fledgling state from its erstwhile coloniser'.[13] An active laity, they argue, along with 'various professional groups, religious leaders and politicians worked hard to shape independent Ireland's society and legislation in accordance with Catholic moral teaching ... In both states [Northern Ireland and Irish Free State] shame and secrecy formed fundamental bulwarks of societies which placed a high premium on sexual "purity".'[14]

While the Free State was keen to distance itself from its colonial oppressor England, it nevertheless was content to retain many of the same laws that Westminster had introduced. For example, the Free State maintained the 1861 Offences Against the Person Act and the 1885 Criminal Law Amendment Act, both of which contained sections that criminalised sexual activity between men (notably, this act did not criminalise sexual activity between women).[15] The 1861 Act also criminalised abortion with a penalty of life imprisonment. Averill Erin Earls has noted the extent to which the Free State was more than willing to enforce these laws. Whereas from 1900 to 1920 eighteen men were arrested for same-sex crimes, in the first twenty years of Irish independence over 200 men were arrested for gross indecency or sodomy with men.[16] These figures continued to increase into the second half of the century, with Hug noting that between 1962 and 1972 there were 455 men convicted.[17] Available statistics from 1979 to 1987 show a further 247 prosecutions under the same laws.[18]

The Free State did not shy away from introducing further restrictions when the opportunity arose. In 1929 the then *Cumann na nGaedheal* government, following recommendations from the Committee of Enquiry on Evil Literature, introduced the 1929 Censorship of Publications Act.[19] This Act prohibited the sale and distribution of 'unwholesome literature'. Two of the first books to fall foul of this law were Radcliffe Hall's *The Well of Loneliness* and Bertrand Russell's *Marriage and Morals*, while books by Dr Marie Stopes on birth control were also censored.[20] Even into the late 1970s, gay rights activists maintained that the Act had resulted in all the major studies on homosexuality going back to Havelock Ellis, Krafft-Ebing and Magnus Hirschfeld being banned.[21]

With the rise of *Fianna Fáil* to power in 1932, the 1930s saw the further strengthening of a Catholic morality in Ireland. This decade saw an amendment to the 1885 Criminal

Law Amendment Act in 1935 prohibiting the sale and importation of contraceptives, while two years later a new constitution, *Bunreacht na hÉireann*, was passed by the Irish electorate. During the drafting of the new constitution, Fr John Charles McQuaid, future Archbishop of Dublin and Primate of Ireland, had sought (successfully) to influence its content and make-up by sending a 'deluge of material' to government officials.[22] Niall O'Dowd has also noted how the then *Taoiseach*, Eamon DeValera, sent a copy of the draft constitution to Pope Pius XI for benediction, but none was forthcoming.[23] Nevertheless, O'Dowd describes the passage of the new constitution as heralding the Republic of Ireland as the 'most ferociously Catholic state on Earth'.[24]

Bunreacht na hÉireann reaffirmed the primacy of Catholicism. Article 44.1.2 stated that the 'State recognises the special position of the Holy Catholic Apostolic and Roman Church as the guardian of the Faith professed by the great majority of the citizens'.[25] The 'special position' of the Roman Catholic Church was most obvious in the educational sphere in the Republic of Ireland, with the overwhelming majority of Irish schools coming under the patronage of the Roman Catholic Church.[26] As a result, the hierarchy enjoyed considerable influence over the education of Irish citizens, with the power to prevent anything they deemed not in-keeping with the religious ethos of the school from entering the classroom. It is hardly surprising then that there was an almost complete lack of sex education within the Irish educational system throughout the twentieth century.

The passage of the constitution had far-reaching implications for many in Ireland, but none more so than for women. Not only did the new constitution outlaw divorce, but it also affirmed that the state would 'endeavour to ensure that mothers shall not be obliged by economic necessity to engage in labour to the neglect of their duties in the home'.[27] The woman's place, therefore, was in the home not the public sphere. These legal restrictions and the social climate they engendered ensured that anyone who failed to conform to societal expectations (i.e., heteronormativity and sex confined to marriage between a woman and man) found themselves alienated and shunned from society, as unmarried mothers and children born outside of wedlock learned. In the last two decades a number of inquiries and commissions have unveiled the sustained abuse and ill-treatment of many women and children who, through no fault of their own, ended up in Magdalen laundries or reformatory and industrial schools operated by religious organisations and funded by the Irish state.[28] Lindsey Earner-Byrne has rightly argued that in Ireland 'there was little room for sexual individualism'.[29] One cohort who could strongly attest to this was homosexuals.[30]

Internationally, the late nineteenth century and early twentieth century saw the rise of individuals and organisations, most notably in Germany and the Netherlands, who began to highlight and confront the oppression of what were then labelled homophiles or homosexuals. These efforts later spread across other western societies in the mid-twentieth century, for example, in the USA, Great Britain and France; however, no such efforts appeared in the Republic of Ireland during this period.[31] For much of the twentieth century, the Republic of Ireland was an unwelcoming society for homosexuals. Notwithstanding the aforementioned laws that criminalised sexual activity between men, there was also considerable ignorance and, oftentimes, hostility towards homosexuals. As was true elsewhere, homosexuals were commonly characterised as being criminal, sinful, promiscuous, effeminate, mentally unwell and un-Irish.[32] The vast majority of Irish citizens grew up in ignorance of homosexuality and regarded homosexuals as deviant outcasts without actually ever knowingly meeting, talking to or even listening to one. One gay man writing in 1986 about his experience of growing up in the Republic of Ireland recalled that:

> Growing up gay is very hard, but more so if you happen to be growing up in rural Ireland. You have a very negative attitude all around you and many people would prefer to lose a gay family member rather than have to face the neighbours ... People saw stereotypes and most articles which appeared in the papers helped to reinforce these stereotyped images. Two of these that my family believed were that all gays were either screaming queens or else they were child molesters.[33]

The conflation of homosexuality with child molestation was, as was the case in other countries, common in the Republic of Ireland and could even be seen in a submission by the Irish government to the European Court of Human Rights (ECHR) in 1987 as part of its defence of the 1861 and 1885 laws. The submission provided a breakdown of what the government labelled 'prosecutions for homosexual offences in Ireland'. However, a closer look at these cases shows that what the government had characterised as homosexual offences were actually sexual acts with minors. Of the 247 prosecutions between 1979 and 1987, 63%, or 156 cases, involved sexual acts with minors 13 years of age or younger.[34] That the government labelled these offences specifically 'homosexual offences' suggests that there was little differentiation in their minds between homosexuality and paedophilia.

There can be no doubt that many Irish homosexuals felt the need to suppress or hide their sexuality. According to Dr James Quinn, a psychiatrist at Belfast City hospital, speaking in 1975, 'Ireland was one of the most difficult societies for homosexuals to live in'.[35] The Samaritans' 1977 annual report supported this view, noting that the largest increase in calls that year had come from individuals affected by loneliness (up 22%), marital problems (up 25%) and homosexuality (up 50%).[36] Most worryingly, the following year's report noted that the highest proportion of suicidal calls came from individuals affected by extramarital issues, girls with unwanted pregnancies and homosexuals.[37]

Many have recalled that the negative attitudes towards homosexuality resulted in them developing anxiety and feelings of loneliness. Theresa Blanche, who was born in Dublin in 1957, recalled that: 'I was sort of coming out at sixteen, but there was nowhere to come out to. Where did my type go? And there was nowhere to go. And there was no one to talk to. You didn't discuss it. You didn't talk. I didn't talk. I had no one. It was a very lonely time, very isolated time.'[38] Tonie Walsh, who was born in Dublin in 1960 but spent his youth growing up in Clonmel, Tipperary, recalls a similar experience during his teenage years:

> The thing that set me apart, I realise now, was my sexuality, although I simply had no understanding of it at the time. And, you know, we're talking about the late 60s in Ireland, in rural Ireland. There was nothing that I could reference at the time.

There was nothing that could tell me this is the person that you are, the person you might be, these are the sort of people you belong to, because, of course, there was no gay civil rights movement or anything, and there was very little talk. And there were no positive role models ... So, what I'm really trying to say here is my teenage years were quite fraught with anxiety – especially as I came face-to-face with dealing with my sexual identity, and, of course, also having to sort of square that up with being Roman Catholic as well.[39]

Often those who did find an outlet with which to discuss their sexuality did not fare any better. One individual revealed in a letter to *OUT* the problems he faced after coming out to his mother. He recounted how after he told her he was gay, she told him she wanted him to have 'aversion treatment [and that] the psychiatrist has told her it will cost £2,800 and there is 85pc cure ...'[40] While acknowledging that this amount of money would be a considerable financial burden on her, she told her son that this was something his late father would have supported. The belief that homosexuality could be cured was not uncommon. In 1973, Dr Austin Darragh, director of the UCD Psycho Endocrine Centre, had called on the Irish government to introduce new laws relating to homosexuality whereby convicted homosexuals would be sent for medical treatment instead of to jail, stating his firm belief that homosexuals could in fact be cured.[41] Speaking to the *Irish Independent*, Dr Darragh warned that 'to legalise it [homosexuality] may be legalising a disease and may stop researchers like us proceeding with our attempts to plum the causes and possible treatment for the condition.'[42] Later in the 1970s and 1980s, the issue of aversion therapy was raised by gay rights activists. David Norris, a founding member of the Irish Gay Rights Movement, for example, called for a public enquiry into the extent to which aversion therapy was being practised in Ireland, telling *The Irish Times* that he knew of 'at least one psychiatrist who was seemingly quite proud of having used electric shock treatment in an attempt to alter homosexual orientation ...'.[43] To this day, the extent and degree to which electric shock treatment was used to try and alter one's sexuality in the Republic of Ireland remains unknown.[44]

This legal and cultural climate placed emotional and oftentimes physical pressures on many homosexuals. In a society with such rigid sexual norms as those in the Republic of Ireland, there existed few outlets in which homosexuals could feel secure and comfortable in openly discussing their feelings with others. For David Norris, who was born in 1944 in Leopoldville before his family moved back to Dublin in 1945, the pressure of concealing his sexuality had implications for his health. In his 2012 autobiography Norris recounted an incident in the late 1960s when he was rushed to Baggot Street Hospital with a suspected heart attack. However, after examinations he was informed that it was an anxiety attack caused by the fact that 'I was homosexual'.[45] Norris was subsequently sent to a psychiatrist, who advised him that 'for the preservation of my health and to forestall a possible nervous collapse, I should leave Ireland and go to live in the south of France, where these matters were better understood under the Code Napoléon'.[46] This advice outraged Norris and rather than leaving, he chose to remain and fight the injustices against homosexuals.

While Norris decided to remain, there can be no doubt that many others felt the need to emigrate from the Republic of Ireland in search of more tolerant societies where their sexuality did not need to be concealed to the same degree as it did back home.[47] Sexuality, of course, was not the only motivating factor behind many leaving; economic factors also played a role. In *Rethinking the Irish Diaspora*, Johanne Devlin Trew and Michael Pierse rightly acknowledged that 'emigration has been an enduring and defining experience for the island of Ireland'.[48] Between 1922 and the end of the twentieth century, 1.5 million people emigrated from the Republic of Ireland, with the 1950s and 1980s witnessing particularly high levels of emigration.[49] Among those who emigrated were many homosexuals. One place in particular that proved to be a popular destination was London. According to Daryl Leeworthy,

> the liberalisation of English law, even on the relatively modest terms of the 1967 Act, encouraged a gay migrant's trail from the island of Ireland to major cities in England – most notably London ... For young gay Irishmen, then, London may have seemed like Nirvana compared with circumstances at home, but it was by no means a hotspot of liberty and free expression.'[50]

One individual who believed that London offered a greater prospect than remaining in the Republic of Ireland did was Colm O'Clubhán. Writing in *Out for Ourselves*, O'Clubhán explains his decision to leave in the early 1970s for London, 'that beacon of lust and potential occasions of sin'.[51] It was London where he decided he would come out, not Dublin: 'No, London was where it was all going to happen. London where they even had a law for doing it. London, of marches and the Gay Liberation Front. London. I was nineteen when I finally got here. I found the number for the Gay Liberation Front (GLF) and rang them. Suddenly I was free. I was gay.'[52]

O'Clubhán's story is just one of many told by gay people who left the Republic of Ireland. Some others who left, however, returned bringing with them ideas and a newfound determination to challenge the oppressiveness of Irish society. In saying that, those who remained abroad also involved themselves in gay rights activism, as Leeworthy's research demonstrates. This can also be seen in New York and no doubt in other parts of the world; however, further research is needed on Ireland's LGBT diaspora.[53] As Róisín Ryan-Flood has recently noted, it is important to uncover the life narratives of Irish LGBT migrants because it 'allows for more nuanced accounts of the Irish diaspora and rectifies the heteronormative focus of much previous writing and research within migration'.[54,55]

As noted previously, the late nineteenth and early twentieth century saw the emergence of individuals and organisations determined to challenge the oppression of homosexuals. These efforts increased in the post-war decades, often met with resistance by state officials, but ultimately led, as Weeks noted, to the introduction of a wide spectrum of liberal humanitarian reforms across Europe in the 1960s. However, this was not the case in the Republic of Ireland, where it was not until the 1960s that sustained efforts emerged to challenge the status quo, in particular with regard to sexuality and women's rights. The late 1960s and early 1970s saw the emergence of influential feminist and civil rights organisations in Ireland, namely the Northern Ireland Civil Rights Association in 1967 and the Irish Women's Liberation Movement in 1970. Both organisations were spurred on by international and domestic events and went on to have a considerable impact on the transformation of Irish society.[56] In particular, their actions and rhetoric helped to create a vacuum for minority groups to emerge and demand their human and civil rights. International events were also filtering through to Ireland, most notably the 1967 Sexual Offences Bill, which partially decriminalised sexual activity between men aged 21 and over in private in England and Wales, the Stonewall Riots in 1969 and the Anti-Apartheid Movement. The Republic of Ireland's decision to join the European Economic Community (EEC) in 1973 also confirmed a desire to move away from years of isolationism. This was a period in which the status quo on the island of Ireland was being challenged and created the space into which minority groups were able to organise and begin a process of seeking change. Linda Connolly has argued that 'the mobilisation of the civil rights movement in Northern Ireland in 1968 and the flowering of Republican, student and left-wing organisations crystallised a social movement sector across Irish society'.[57] It was within this changing domestic and international context that some Irish homosexuals began to meet to discuss gay rights in the early 1970s.

1

Irish Homosexuals are Revolting, 1973–1978

In May 1973, *Gay News* printed a letter from Paddy from Galway.¹ Paddy's letter was in response to a previous article in *Gay News*, 'Breakthrough in Éire', in which it was reported that Alan Crossley, a member of the Campaign for Homosexual Equality (CHE), had travelled to Dublin to meet an existing homophile grouping.² As it transpired, the group that Crossley had met was the Legion of Mary, which had been advertising meetings for homosexuals since 1970 to discuss their problems in an informal and sympathetic manner with the 'view to encouraging them to explore a possible solution'.³ It was this description of the Legion of Mary as an 'existing sympathetic homophile grouping' that led Paddy to write to *Gay News* lambasting the organisation as a group 'confined to Roman Catholics whose near-worship of the "Blessed Virgin" is among the many mediaeval groups contributing to the continuing suppression of gays in Ireland'.⁴ Coincidentally, while Paddy did not consider the organisation a supportive homophile grouping, John Grundy remembers that it was through the Legion of Mary that he and others often met men to 'go off with' in the 1970s.⁵

What was most interesting about Paddy's letter, however, was what he described as his surprise – and that of 'other Irish gays' – at 'the scarcity of articles on the gay scene in Ireland. Surprised, because there is quite an advanced and organised gay scene here – even if it is still ostensibly an underground one.'⁶ Paddy's letter provides an insight into what might be described as a gay subculture in the Republic of Ireland during this period. The letter revealed the extent to which there were not only a number of cottaging areas throughout the country, but also a number of 'gay bars' in Dublin, Cork and Westmeath. In Dublin, Paddy named Bartley Dunne's on 32 Lower Stephen Street and Robert Rice's on the corner of St Stephen's Green as the main 'gay bars'. In Cork, there was the Persian Bar in the Imperial Hotel on Pembroke Street, while the Genoa Bar in Athlone in Westmeath was described as 'worth a try'. Although Paddy did not name any bar in Galway, he did mention that the promenade in Salthill was a popular spot for cottaging. However, he warned against cottaging, particularly in Dublin, as a few gay men had been mugged in recent months. Other popular pubs frequented by homosexuals in the early 1970s, but not listed in Paddy's letter, included Larry Tobin's and Davy Byrne's on Duke Street in Dublin, O'Donovan's Bar, Lower Glenworth Street in Limerick, and La Chateau, Patrick Street in Cork.⁷ Clearly, therefore, despite the social and legal climate, there were certain establishments in the Republic of Ireland that homosexuals frequented. Moreover, Paddy's reference to other 'Irish gays' who he was aware were as surprised as he was also suggests that there was to some degree a network of homosexuals who were in touch with each other and clearly had access to the British magazine, *Gay News*, even in a provincial county like Galway. This is further evidenced by the fact that Paddy, who was based in Galway, was aware of gay men in Dublin who had been mugged in recent months while cottaging.

Although none of the aforementioned bars advertised as 'gay bars' they nevertheless provided a space, albeit a relatively hidden one, for homosexuals. Theresa Blanche described how in Bartley Dunne's there was only a small group of ten lesbian women who regularly visited the establishment, but 'the men numbered in the hundreds'.[8] One of those men was Edmund Lynch (born in 1947 in Dublin), who remembered being nervous at first going into Bartley's in the early 1970s, but soon felt that he had entered a whole new world: 'I had a riot'.[9] The sign of the warmth that many individuals felt towards Bartley Dunne's was evident in 1977, when it was announced that the barman Brian was leaving after fifteen years. Brian was described as a wonderful man who had 'served the gay patrons of B.D.'s with respect and genuine friendliness rare among barmen in any establishment'.[10] Before he departed, a collection was held for him, which raised £131.94 (approximately €881 in today's currency), something that was described as 'one of the loveliest occasions experienced on the scene for a very long time'.[11]

While those frequenting Bartley Dunne's may have felt welcomed, this was not always the case in these establishments. Describing his time attending the Imperial Hotel in the early 1970s, Kieran Rose, who grew up in Cork in the 1950s, recalled that: 'It was all kind of subterfuge, you know a nod and a wink and basically it was just a hotel bar, but you could go in there and you might meet gay people by accident, but it wasn't a very pleasant feeling, because you were there on sufferance.'[12] This is an experience shared by Cathal Kerrigan (who grew up in Cork in the 1950s), who remembered that in 1975 La Chateau barred suspected homosexuals after word reached the owner that his pub was advertised in *Gay News* as a gay-friendly pub. Kerrigan recalled that the owners 'were horrified and convinced we had betrayed them. I mean this is 1975, they did not want to be a gay bar.'[13] That same year, the *Sunday Independent* reported that five Dublin pubs were 'furious about the listing of their premises in a homosexual newspaper [*Gay News*]'.[14] One pub owner told the newspaper that, while accepting their premises did have the reputation of being a gay bar, they strongly objected 'to this being printed' and expressed the view that they would 'prefer that they [homosexuals] did not come in.'[15] On the whole, therefore, the Irish gay pub scene at that time was best described by Paddy as one which depended on 'being unobtrusive rather than being accepted'.[16]

Less than one year after Alan Crossley visited Dublin in the hope of setting up a branch of the CHE, *Gay News* reported on a conference at the New University of Ulster (NUU), Coleraine, Derry, which took place on 3 November 1973. *Gay News* informed readers that:

> for Irish homosexuals the border question has little or no meaning – at least as far as their homosexuality is concerned. For neither the North nor the South allows gays to make love ... It was in acknowledgement of their common problems that the first ever Gay Rights Conference in Ireland was organised by the Sexual Reform Movement on an all-Ireland basis.[17]

While not exclusively a gay rights conference but rather one which discussed more broadly the whole area of sexual oppression and alternative sexuality, it became a critical juncture in Irish queer history. Don Gill, a member of the Sexual Reform Movement (SRM), a student organisation at the NUU, was one of the leading figures behind the organisation of the conference. Northern Ireland, in fact, had seen the first attempts to organise around the issue of gay rights on the island of Ireland, with the establishment of the Belfast Gay Liberation Society at Queen's University Belfast (QUB) in 1971.[18]

The Coleraine conference succeeded in attracting over fifty individuals (one third of whom were women) from Northern Ireland, the Republic of Ireland and Great Britain. These included representatives from: the Exeter Gay Liberation Society; the Society of Friends' Homosexual Fellowship; the National Union of Students (NUS); the Scottish Minorities Group (SMG); the Northern Ireland Civil Rights Association (NICRA).[19] In his address to delegates, Terry Bruton (NICRA) insisted that 'gay rights were a part of civil rights' and it was 'important for as many gays as possible to come out into the open boldly, and seek acceptance ...'.[20] Alastair Stewart (NUS) echoed these sentiments, but suggested they needed 'to treat the problems faced by gays within the wider context of civil rights for all oppressed people, rather than seek change for gays alone'. Meanwhile the SMG's Fred Broughton, who was studying at the NUU, provided an overview of efforts to extend the 1967 Sexual Offences Act to Scotland. Pat Knight (NUU student), the only woman to make an address, concentrated on highlighting the double oppression of gay women, oppressed both as women and as homosexuals, noting that 'contrary to what one would expect, and hope, gay men were no less chauvinistic than heterosexual men.'

It is quite evident then that the issue of gay rights dominated the Coleraine conference. Following the speeches, delegates passed a resolution that committed them:

> to work in the future for the establishment of human rights for the sexually oppressed in society, noting that problems exist in all areas of civil liberties, these liberties being continually ignored and rejected by the authorities at present controlling our society ... We resolve to elect a steering committee of 6 to (a) keep activists aware of developments in Northern Ireland and the Republic of Ireland, (b) organise future meetings and (c) establish firm links with other groups active in gay rights and civil liberties (NICRA, CHE, GLF, NUS, SMG, etc.).[21]

This was the first time in Ireland that individuals north and south of the border had committed themselves to work for the establishment of human rights for the sexually oppressed and to establish firm links with British groups active on the issue of gay rights. It is quite clear from the speeches and the resolution that the context of the period, particularly the international gay rights movement and the campaign for civil rights in Northern Ireland, heavily influenced the rhetoric of those who participated, with considerable emphasis placed on human rights and civil liberties.

In a sign of the commitment to work on these issues on a cross-border basis, the steering committee consisted of individuals from Northern Ireland and the Republic of Ireland: Don Gill (NUU, SRM); Pat Knight (NUU, SRM); Margaret McWilliam (Sappho, Dublin); Edmund Lynch (CHE, Dublin); Maeve Molloy (QUB); Margaret Ward (Belfast); Peter Bradley (Trinity College Dublin, SRM); Hugo MacManus (Trinity College Dublin, SRM). It's interesting to note that both Lynch and McWilliam were listed as Dublin members of two British-based gay/lesbian organisations: CHE and Sappho. Again, this highlights the awareness of some Irish homosexuals of international gay/lesbian organisations and their ability to make contact with them.

The Coleraine conference coincided with events that had taken place at UK universities only a few months prior to its organisation. In April 1973 the NUS had met for its annual conference at the University of Exeter. During the course of this conference a motion was passed that committed the NUS to campaign for an end to sexual inequality and discrimination against homosexuals.[22] The task of following through with this motion fell to Alastair Stewart, who played a central role in the Coleraine conference. Within a few months of the aforementioned motion, almost sixty colleges had established gay societies, including the University of Exeter, another key participant at the Coleraine conference.[23]

As the NUS was the representative body for student unions throughout the UK, we might confidently assume that students in Northern Ireland would have been aware of these developments. It is also possible that Fred Broughton's presence as an SMG member studying at the NUU also influenced the organisation of this historic conference. These transnational influences, interactions, and networks were crucial at an early stage in the emergence of a wider gay rights movement in Ireland. Peter Bradley, a Union of Students in Ireland (USI) delegate to the Coleraine conference, described it as the 'first practical step on the road to lifting sexual oppression in Ireland . . .'.[24]

Following the Coleraine conference, a number of individuals in the Republic of Ireland came together to form the Sexual Liberation Movement (SLM) at Trinity College Dublin (TCD).[25] Although established in TCD, its membership comprised both students and non-students, including Hugo MacManus, Margaret McWilliam, Edmund Lynch, David Norris and Mary Dorcey. As we have seen, MacManus, McWilliam and Lynch had been elected to the steering committee that had emerged from the NUU conference, while David Norris was a lecturer in TCD and Mary Dorcey had recently returned from living in France. In a 2013 interview, Dorcey recalled moving to Paris in the 1960s to live with a French man she had met in Dublin, leaving behind an Ireland that she described as 'so regressive, so conformist, so depressing, in every way damaging to the individual spirt'.[26] In France she recalled:

> Through one of my lecturers in Paris, I went to this wonderful gay nightclub in Paris, which was a huge event, something like 300 gay people in the room, fantastic, beautiful, energetic figures, vital people, like, you know, you've never seen in your life and certainly hadn't seen in Dublin. And I thought these are the people for me, you know. So, that was what it meant for me. It was about excitement; it was about freedom. It was about redefining yourself.[27]

Dorcey's immersion in Parisian life and the more vibrant and open gay scene there clearly had a liberating effect on her, providing her with the confidence to return to the

Republic of Ireland 'determined to find people who were different'. Lynch recalls a number of other individuals who were also involved with the founding of the SLM: Ruth Riddick, Gerry McNamara, Peter Bradley, Irene Brady and Michael Kerrigan.[28]

The SLM mobilised around a broad range of issues such as contraception, divorce and homosexuality. This reflected the mixed configuration of the group, which consisted of both homosexual and heterosexual individuals. By February 1974, Christina Murphy reported that the SLM had close to 100 members.[29] Buoyed by the success of the Coleraine conference, the SLM organised a two-day symposium at TCD from 16 to 17 February 1974. In contrast to the Coleraine conference, the TCD symposium focused exclusively on homosexuality, discussing issues such as the legal situation facing homosexuals in Ireland, the difficulties of being homosexual and the importance of challenging the legal and cultural climate in Ireland.[30] Jeffrey Dudgeon, then a member of the Belfast Gay Liberation Society and later a founding member of the Northern Ireland Gay Rights Association (NIGRA), described the excitement and significance of the TCD symposium, proclaiming, 'Fuck it, this was to be the big coming out event in Irish sexual history.'[31]

The symposium attracted over 300 individuals from Ireland and Great Britain and included speeches from: Dr Noel Browne, a psychiatrist and then an Irish Senator; Rose Robertson, London Parents Enquiry (support group for parents of homosexuals); Ian Dunn, SMG; Babs Todd, CHE; and Fr Enda MacDonagh, a Catholic priest and moral theology lecturer at Maynooth University. Dudgeon later wrote that during the coffee interval after Robertson, Browne and McDonagh had spoken, there was 'bitching about the condescension of the speakers ...'.[32] However, he was more praiseworthy of Ian Dunn and Babs Todd's contributions. While Dunn concentrated his speech on providing lessons learned from his experience of being involved with the SMG, Todd spoke openly and proudly about her sexuality. According to Dudgeon:

> she spoke as if to a gay audience which it largely was, rather than to a symposium of persons, "interested in the homosexual problem". She told of her lover, her children, her double bed and offered a future. The applause and cheering was colossal. At last the audience spoke and it spoke loud. Had Babs continued there could easily have been an outbreak of straight-bashing in Dublin that night, not to mention the birth of gay terrorist groupings.[33]

The novelty of the TCD symposium helped generate media attention. Edmund Lynch, one of the conference organisers and then an employee with RTÉ, recalled how he arranged for Rose Robertson to appear on Ireland's most watched show, *The Late Late Show*, to discuss Parents Enquiry and homosexuality, while Hugo MacManus and Margaret McWilliam appeared on radio on the *Liam Nolan Show*.[34] Journalists with *The Irish Times*, *Irish Farmers Journal* and the *Sunday Independent* also reported on the symposium. Interestingly, these articles presented a more sympathetic image of homosexuals to the one Irish society was more accustomed to. Conor McAnally's article in the *Sunday Independent*, for example, revealed the extent to which he had changed his mind about homosexuals after attending the symposium:

I expected to find a bunch of effeminate caricatures of gay men and a collection of equally obvious lesbian women. I was in for a surprise ... It's amazing how much a person's views can change in five hours ... Four hours later I had a clearer picture as one by one gay men and women contributed to the discussion, questioned speakers and spoke seriously and a little angrily about repressive laws and attitudes such as mine ... Society is altered by a change of attitude. My attitudes to homosexuality and gay people were changed at the meeting.[35]

Mary Dorcey has described the symposium as 'the start of all the changes that have since happened in Ireland and it was the first time publicly in the South that questions of sexual orientation had ever been addressed. We came out of a society that was as repressed as Stalinist Russia.'[36] David Norris likewise wrote how 'the injection of confidence provided by these events confirmed a number of us in the view that it was necessary to emerge from under the comparatively bland umbrella of general liberation and specify an interest in gay liberation as such.'[37] While this did not immediately happen, the seeds were sown for such a move a few months later.

Norris and Edmund Lynch both began to question the extent to which it was wise for a majority of homosexual individuals within the SLM to spend 'their Monday evenings in a Trinity garret writing letters to *The Irish Times* indignantly demanding unrestricted access to contraceptive devices'.[38] According to an interview that Norris gave to *Gay News*, he thought it 'idiotic that gays within SLM were fighting the contraception issue. "First, we must define our own aims, then we can lend our support to other things."'[39] At a meeting in June 1974, which Norris described 'as the gunfight at the K.Y. [sic] Corral', the differences within the SLM became evident.[40] For Norris 'the protective mask of woolly liberal reform should be discarded, and our position publicly announced by the formation of an openly gay movement'.[41]

This June 1974 meeting coincided with an announcement by Kim Friele, general secretary of the Norwegian gay organisation, Det Norske Forbundet, that that year's Gay Liberation Day (27 June) would be dedicated to the people of Ireland in their struggle against Church and State. In doing so, Friele and their Norwegian colleagues spotlighted the situation in Ireland. Demonstrating outside the British Embassy in Oslo, they carried placards with slogans saying: 'Stop the oppression of Irish homosexuals' and 'No to discrimination on the grounds of being different'.[42] Encouraged by their Norwegian counterparts, twelve individuals, including David Norris, Hugo MacManus, Michael Kerrigan, Margaret McWilliam, Joseph Leckey, Jeffrey Dudgeon and Edwin Henshaw picketed outside the British Embassy in Dublin before moving to the Department of Justice, with placards saying: 'Homosexuals are revolting', 'Gay is Good' and 'Lesbian Love'. This was the Republic of Ireland's first gay pride demonstration.

Shortly afterwards another meeting took place at the South County Hotel, in Stillorgan, Dublin, on 7 July at which Norris and Lynch recalled thirty people attended.[43] While Norris and Lynch did not list those in attendance, the meeting did include Clement Clancy, Sean Connolly and Martin Barnes. A note from the personal papers of David Norris states that the topics discussed included the 'conception of IGRM [Irish Gay Rights Movement]' which would have the objective of 'working for gays on gay issues'.[44] Opening the meeting, Edmund Lynch told those in attendance that the

'IGRM was being launched to fight vigorously and actively on homosexual issues only'.⁴⁵ Therefore, between the June and 7 July 1974 meetings, the Republic of Ireland's first gay rights organisation, the Irish Gay Rights Movement (IGRM), was born.

From the beginning, the title the IGRM adopted sent out a strong statement of intent, challenging the assumption that Irish and gay were mutually exclusive. Moreover, it is interesting to note that while the relationship between Ireland's Catholic and Protestant communities was at one of the lowest points in its history, it was in fact the combined efforts of individuals on an all-island basis, with support from their counterparts in Great Britain, that the IGRM had emerged in the Republic of Ireland in 1974. In fact, we cannot underestimate the important role played by British gay rights organisations in the rise of a gay rights movement in Ireland.

Irish Gay Rights Movement

The IGRM described itself as a non-party political, non-sectarian homophile grouping with the following objectives:

1. The improvement in the lifestyle of homosexual men and women.
2. The achievement of equality under the law with heterosexual congress.
3. The promotion of better understanding of homosexuality by the community at large, by education and example.
4. The provision of social amenities and events for members.
5. Befriending.
6. The provision of religious, legal and medical information relating to homosexuality.
7. The acquisition of premises for official and social activities.
8. Any other activity acceptable to the Committee conducive to the furtherance of the main aims and objects [sic] of the IGRM.⁴⁶

Under the IGRM's constitution those wanting to join had to pay an annual membership fee (£3.50 in 1975, £5 in 1976 – approximately €31 and €37 today) and be over 18 years of age. Each year a committee of nine members was elected to serve on the National Executive, which took over the day-to-day running of the IGRM. The first IGRM National Executive comprised: David Norris, who was elected National Chairman with responsibility for the Legal & Educational portfolio; Sean Connolly, General Secretary; Clement Clancy, Finance Controller; Theresa Blanche, Women's Group; Kenneth Watters, Medical; Seamus O'Riain, Social Committee; James Malone, Religion Projects; Martin Barnes, Tel-A-Friend (TAF).⁴⁷

The IGRM prioritised the organisation of social activities from the beginning, placing advertisements in *In Dublin* and *Hot Press* to promote their existence. This reflected two realities: the first being that the IGRM needed the revenue from these social events to survive; second, it recognised that Irish homosexuals were crying out for a space where they could meet others in a safe non-judgemental environment. In its first year, the IGRM's headquarters was a ground floor office at 23 Lower Leeson Street,

Dublin, before moving to a larger venue at 46 Parnell Square, also in Dublin, at the end of 1975, which became known as the Phoenix Club. In effect, the Phoenix Club became the Republic of Ireland's first gay centre. The move from Leeson Street to Parnell Square was seen as a considerable achievement for the IGRM, with *Gay News* remarking that the new club was now in a 'very fashionable part of the city'.[48]

In its formative months, the IGRM's social events revolved around coffee meetings every Saturday afternoon, with Thursday evenings set aside for general enquiries, while on Sunday nights a disco was held outside the Leeson Street venue at an address listed as Petticoat Lane Market, Dublin. Once a month the IGRM also hosted a cheese and wine reception.[49] Towards the end of 1975 the IGRM was hosting a disco every Friday, Saturday and Sunday night, along with a women's only disco once a month and a cheese and wine reception twice a month, while a drama group (Phoenix Players) had been established, along with a library and a Wednesday Forum, where the IGRM invited speakers to give talks on different subjects of interest.

The IGRM discos proved particularly popular, with *Gay News* estimating that the discos attracted an average of 180 people every Friday and Saturday night.[50] The only currently available income and expenditure report for the IGRM dates from 1976–1977 and provides an insight into just how dependant the IGRM was on the revenue from these discos. The total expenditure for the IGRM during this period amounted to £12,797.30 (approximately €85,000 today), while the total income was £13,255.87, of which the disco generated £12,152.19. In contrast the membership fees only generated £433.65.[51] These figures, therefore, demonstrate the high cost of running an organisation like the IGRM and the extent to which it had to operate within a tight fiscal space. The inability to hold discos with regular crowds would have jeopardised the IGRM's agenda.

There can be no doubt that providing these social activities did require effort and sacrifice from a minority of individuals. Aidan Lacey, for example, who held the position of IGRM Social Officer for eight and a half months in 1977, described the experience as an 'onerous task' that demanded 'every moment of your free time'.[52] He advised those who were 'not prepared to yield to this demand [that they would be] better off not being on the Executive Committee'.[53] Those who did volunteer, however, were able to take solace from the fact that their efforts were appreciated. One individual, who spoke to Anthony Redmond for the *Sunday Independent* in 1975, told how he travelled from Navan every Friday to attend the disco, revealing that he had 'made a lot of new friends and can't tell how delighted I am about it all. Never knew what it was really like to enjoy myself until I came here. You can be yourself here without being considered queer.'[54] Another who spoke to Mary Maher in 1977 for *The Irish Times* stated that the Phoenix Club was 'a great thing for gays in rural Ireland to be able to come to a place like this. You can have the freedom to dance, to be yourself for a little while, even if it's within the confines of these walls'.[55] A similar appreciation was expressed by Anna from Cavan in a letter to Theresa Blanche that same year. Anna revealed that it is 'the most important thing in my life to know I can meet people who feel like I do, and to be able to talk to someone who understands my feelings'.[56] This was just one of many letters that the IGRM received. Within just one year of its foundation, Sean Connolly reported that they had received over 400 letters; not a small number for an organisation with limited means of advertising its existence.[57]

Anna was one of the few women who interacted with the IGRM during this period. In reality, the IGRM was an overwhelmingly male-dominated organisation. Joni Crone, who became a leading lesbian activist in the Republic of Ireland, remembered the disappointment she felt when she first entered the Phoenix Club in 1976, 'disappointed because there were no women around'.[58] Crone had recently returned from living in London, where she had 'come out'. In a sign of the hidden nature of the gay scene in the Republic of Ireland at that time, Crone revealed that it was only when she moved to London that she actually learned of the existence of a gay scene in Dublin.[59] The IGRM, in fact, was keenly aware of the existence of many Irish homosexuals living in Great Britain and even sought to appoint an IGRM representative there who could provide details of the organisation's activities on a regular basis. They also noted that there were many Irish in Great Britain who had supported the IGRM financially through donations and subscriptions, a sign of some who had emigrated but were watching events unfolding in the Republic of Ireland and hoping for an improvement in the climate there.[60] Crone was no different, and on her return to the Republic of Ireland she joined the IGRM and teamed up with Theresa Blanche and Phil Carson; both of whom had been leading the efforts to provide a space for women within the IGRM.

One of the first initiatives was the creation of a dedicated women's space within the Phoenix Club, becoming known as the Lavender Room – a possible reference to Betty Friedan's infamous description of lesbian women as the Lavender Menace.[61] The second initiative was the introduction of a women's only disco on the first Thursday of every month, which began in December 1975. On average the women's discos attracted twenty-five women, a much smaller number than the reported 180 who attended the 'mixed' disco nights. Although the number of women visiting the women's disco was small, this number must be put into perspective. It took the IGRM three years to increase its women members from three in 1974 to fifteen in 1977. Moreover, the IGRM only received an average of two phone calls/letters per week from women, many of whom were not willing to visit the Phoenix Club, preferring instead to maintain contact by telephone.[62] Looked at from this perspective, an average of twenty-five was an achievement, particularly when there were so few women actively involved in running the women's events. It was, however, a challenge and the organisers noted that 'the women's area is rather limited in outlets, and so sometimes tends to stagnate.'[63]

The effort to attract women was just one of a number of challenges that the IGRM encountered; another was trying to reach homosexuals outside Dublin. Under its constitution, the IGRM was a national rather than Dublin-only organisation. In an article on gay rights in the *Sunday Press* in 1975, Hugh Lambert noted that 'there are 200 fully paid-up regulars [discussing the IGRM], most of them surprisingly living in rural Ireland. This is not so surprising, however, when one considers the much more furtive atmosphere which must cloak a homosexual's life in small towns.'[64] While we have seen that some homosexuals from provincial Ireland did visit the Phoenix Club, for the vast majority it remained off limits. In an attempt to support these individuals, the IGRM had established a confidential telephone befriending service for homosexuals, Tel-A-Friend (TAF), in 1974.

TAF was modelled on the London Gay Switchboard, but unlike its equivalent in Northern Ireland, CARA-friend, which received an annual grant of £750 from the Department of Health and Social Services, TAF received no funding from the Irish state.[65] In 1970s Ireland, contacting TAF was the first step for many in coming to terms with their sexuality and the first opportunity to talk to another homosexual. TAF acted as an important link between those who were confident in their sexuality and those who were struggling to come to terms with their sexuality. Whereas a large city like Dublin offered greater freedom, most towns in the Republic of Ireland did not. Des Fitzgerald, a TAF volunteer, remembers the isolation and nervousness of those who called:

> It was very interesting for me because quite a lot of people were ringing from rural areas, from country areas. And they were really very isolated. They really didn't have any place to go or any place to meet people, and very often you were the first person they talked to. So, we always operated on the principle that for the first 10 minutes they probably don't hear a word you're saying because they're so wound up and nervous. So, the first part would be really calming people down and then just getting to talk to them.[66]

Between 1975 and 1980 annual calls to TAF increased from 136 to 1,024 respectively, reflecting the demand for such a service.[67]

TAF was complemented in its efforts by the IGRM organising trips to different parts of Ireland to meet homosexuals who had contacted them but had no outlet to meet others. Quite often, these meetings took place in hotels under a pseudonym, which allowed closeted homosexuals to attend without arousing any suspicion. From as early as 1975, the IGRM had organised these outings to Cork, Limerick, Galway, Waterford, Kilkenny, Roscommon, Athlone, Longford, Drogheda, Sligo, Letterkenny and Mullingar. Through these, which became known as branch promotion meetings, the IGRM built up contacts with individuals in these locales, who in turn acted as local representatives for the organisation. Although the vast majority of these counties did not see the emergence of an organised local group, the existence of an IGRM representative in many ensured that anyone who contacted the IGRM could be put in contact with some in their locality.

Some areas like Cork and Waterford, however, did see the emergence of local groups which took on responsibility for organising events in their respective regions. The numbers in these regions were naturally much smaller than in Dublin and therefore, local groups like those in Cork and Waterford were dependant on a small cohort of dedicated individuals for their survival. This brought with it both pros and cons. For example, in Waterford four dedicated men organised the local Waterford group, which the IGRM described as 'one of our most progressive groups'. However, the Waterford IGRM had barely developed this reputation when the IGRM sadly announced in 1976 that the group had been 'depleted due to the emigration of Dermot, John, Tony and Noel'. It would seem that once these four men had left, there was nobody to step in to take over the running of the Waterford IGRM. The IGRM even stated that they had 'got reports that things are on a very low key since their departure'.[68]

Cork, on the other hand, enjoyed more success than Waterford. In 1976, Bert Meany, Oliver Cogan, Cathal Kerrigan, Denis Hyland and Pat O'Mahony-Rysh became the first Cork IGRM committee members.[69] The biggest challenge that local groups faced was securing a venue from which they could organise. At a Cork IGRM meeting in December 1976, attended by Michael Bergin (Dublin IGRM), a 'firm and committed agreement was taken to organise an official premises in Cork, to provide the gay community with amenities such as in Dublin'.[70] This was something the Dublin IGRM strongly supported, even providing financial funding towards this endeavour.[71] In a letter sent one month after the December 1976 meeting, Bert Meany announced that the Cork IGRM was operating out of a suitable temporary premises, but that he would ask 'each member to be continuously on the look-out for the ideal more permanent premises as this is essential to continue our work ...'.[72] Despite the temporary nature of their premises, Meany revealed that the Cork IGRM was already organising events for homosexuals in Cork. Each Saturday their temporary premises was open to those who wanted to come in and have a 'cuppa and a chat', while they had also scheduled a 'musical appreciation afternoon' for 16 January 1977, where members were encouraged to let the Cork IGRM know if they had a particular record they wanted played.[73]

The Cork IGRM did not take too long to secure a more permanent premises. In July 1977 it began renting 4 MacCurtain Street in the heart of Cork City, which became known as the Phoenix Centre.[74] Cathal Kerrigan recalls that the only reason the Cork IGRM was able to obtain this building was because of its poor condition:

> It was a firetrap. It was filthy. So, we had to go in with gloves and masks and clean the dirt. But it was good, it was community building, because everybody came on board, so some people were carpenters, some were in the drinks trades etc. So, we set up a little [coffee] bar and that's how it began. There is no better way than creating something like that, to create a sense of community and sense of ownership.[75]

Within the Cork Phoenix Centre social gatherings took place every Monday, Wednesday and Saturday, as well as discos every Saturday and Sunday night. One notable visitor to the Phoenix Centre in 1977 was Alan Amsby, aka Mr Pussy – Ireland's foremost drag queen during this period.[76] The Cork IGRM also published a series of publications – albeit short-lived ones – including four issues of *Corks Crew* in 1977, which was subsequently replaced with *Sapphire* in 1978. Both publications gave the Cork IGRM a greater voice within the wider IGRM, while also providing an insight into the organisation's development and activities. For example, in 1978 *Sapphire* advertised the first women's meeting in the Phoenix Centre on the 30 January 1978.[77] This meeting was organised by Marian Barry, who had secured the use of the centre for women only once a week. Orla Egan notes in *Queer Republic of Cork* that 'the meetings continued for some time, with women meeting at the No. 4 Centre and then going to The Metropole for a drink and then on up to The Steeple Bar'.[78] That same issue of *Sapphire* also noted that the TAF service was now operating in Cork. Whereas the Dublin IGRM had a telephone line, contact with the service in Cork was only available through its P.O. box number (64). This in itself was a considerable achievement for the Cork IGRM, which had struggled to acquire a P.O. box number throughout 1977. Now those living outside Dublin who were looking to use the TAF service could avail of the opportunity to meet or make contact with individuals in Cork, rather than having to make the journey to Dublin.

1978 was a year in which the Cork IGRM was growing in confidence. On 8 January 1978, the Cork IGRM held its first annual general meeting at the Metropole Hotel, at which thirty-five men and four women attended.[79] During the course of his opening remarks, Bert Meany, chairman of the Cork IGRM, reminded delegates of the successes they had enjoyed since the group's foundation, noting in particular the organisation of social events and the publication of four issues of *Corks Crew*. Not unlike other smaller groups, however, concern was raised at the meeting about the lack of individuals going forward for election to the executive committee of the Cork IGRM. In fact, only four names were put forward, thereby negating, to the disappointment of Meany, the need to hold an election that year. This was despite a plea from Meany for others to put their names forward. The four individuals who were elected without a contest were: Bert Meany, David Good, Sean Savage and Oliver Cogan.[80]

Following their election to the executive committee of the Cork IGRM, Cogan and Meany sought to further raise the profile of the Cork IGRM and homosexuals. Together with Anne Philpott, who was described as a 'heterosexual involved in a gay group', Cogan and Meany took part in an RTÉ *Cork-about* radio programme on 'Homosexuals in Cork'.[81] The programme was divided into two segments and broadcast on 20 January 1978. The first segment included pre-recorded interviews with Meany, Cogan and Philpott about the legal, religious, social and personal aspects of gay life in Cork, while the second segment consisted of a live discussion with contributions from a psychiatrist, a priest and a solicitor, who focused respectively on the medical, religious and legal aspects of homosexuality. Pre-recorded interviews with people on the streets of Cork to get their views on homosexuality were also played throughout the programme, which Cogan reported 'were quite favourable and encouraging to the Movement'. According to a report on the programme, 'the phones in RTE [sic] were litterally [sic] "hopping". Listeners' comments ranged from "take that rubbish off the air" to complete support for the contributors and the organisation. Whatever the general consensus of opinion, the programme certainly stimulated discussion.'[82] While Cogan expressed disappointment that the first segment was edited so much, 'leaving out many important points which had been made' such as the 'aims and activities of the organisation', he nevertheless described it as 'one of the most significant milestones in the history of the Cork Branch of IGRM'.[83]

The Cork IGRM's establishment, particularly the opening of the Phoenix Centre on MacCurtain Street, demonstrated the success the IGRM was enjoying in a relatively short period of time and provided encouragement and hope to the movement, and to Irish homosexuals more generally, that change was happening. It is clear, therefore, that within the space of a few years, the IGRM had succeeded in achieving some of its key objectives, namely the provision of social amenities and events for members, befriending and the acquisition of premises. But what of its other objectives?

'The perverts are not the homosexuals but the bigots'

The IGRM was keenly aware that it needed to present homosexuals in a different image than the negative one Irish society was accustomed to; hence why one of its key objectives was 'the promotion of [a] better understanding of homosexuality by the community at large, by education and example'. To this end, the Irish media, namely television, print media and radio, became central to the IGRM's efforts to reinvent the image of the homosexual in the Republic of Ireland and to shift the rhetoric on homosexuality in a direction that emphasised the extent to which homosexuals were much the same as heterosexuals.[84] What emerged in the 1970s, therefore, was an active campaign by the IGRM to challenge the stereotypes surrounding homosexuality and to confront those who spoke negatively about it, while simultaneously presenting a more positive narrative about homosexuals. To do so, members of the IGRM made themselves available to the Irish media, while also monitoring extensively any reference to homosexuality in the media and, when necessary, submitting a rebuttal. In fact, IGRM members were prolific letter writers to all of Ireland's newspapers.

In July 1975, within just one year of the IGRM's foundation, it got the opportunity to speak directly to an Irish audience about homosexuality when its chairman, David Norris, was invited to appear on RTÉ's (*Raidió Teilifís Éireann*) *Last House*. Edmund Lynch, who was working as a sound engineer on *Last House*, played a central role in Norris' appearance on the show. Norris later recalled that it was suggested to him that he do the interview with Áine O'Connor in the shadow with his back to the camera, but he refused because 'I told them the whole point I wanted to make was that I was a perfectly normal, ordinary person ...'.[85] The assertion that homosexuals were normal, ordinary people was at the crux of the IGRM's argument and Norris did not shy away from making this point throughout the interview. Therefore, rather than turning his back to the camera, Norris appeared front and centre dressed smartly in a three-piece suit.

Before introducing Norris, the segment began with a short cameo from Franklin Kameny, a founding member of the Washington Mattachine Society, who explained that homosexuality was simply 'a preference for entering into close, intimate, affectional sexual relationships with persons of the same sex'.[86] Páraic Kerrigan, in his impressive study of LGBTQ+ media visibility in Ireland, has rightly argued that the inclusion of Kameny was aimed at demonstrating the extent to which there was an international gay community, but also the IGRM's efforts to 'appeal to notions of respectability, inclusion, cooperation and engagement with the dominant culture ...'.[87] Immediately after Kameny concluded, O'Connor then gave a brief overview of the legal context relating to homosexuality, noting that Ireland was the only sovereign country in the EEC to retain criminal sanctions for sexual activity between men, before asking Norris 'are homosexuals sick people?' O'Connor's early questions focused specifically on the many stereotypes related to homosexuality, also asking if homosexuals were perverted or immoral persons and if homosexuality could be cured.

Throughout the interview Norris spoke confidently about the normality of homosexuality, often using 'we' as a means of emphasising the extent to which there were many thousands of homosexuals in Ireland. Replying to O'Connor's question on whether or not homosexuals were sick, Norris responded that:

> No, indeed they're not. We're neither sick, ill, pathological, neurotic or any of these emotive terms that are occasionally used by people who are not well informed on the subject to conceal their own prejudices and to allege that we are ill. I don't feel ill, I hope I don't look it. We are, of course, subject, as ordinary people are, to head-colds, influenza, hangover, these kind of things. In the basic sense we are not sick.

Norris sought to present those who condemned homosexuality as those who were actually the problem. When asked, for example, were homosexual persons perverted, Norris insisted that those who labelled homosexuals perverted or immoral were doing so to 'project their own feeling or dislike of the homosexual which is irrational and emotional and is not in fact a scientific or clinical way of looking at things at all …'. These people, who Norris labelled homophobes, were in fact 'those who are really ill, not us …'. During one of the rare moments when Norris used 'I' rather than 'we', he explained to O'Connor how difficult it was growing up in 'ignorance of the facts of my true nature … I was brought up in Ireland to believe that I was possibly the only homosexual in Ireland'. While the Irish constitution claimed to cherish all the children of Ireland equally, Norris told O'Connor that 'I can tell you from my experience it did not cherish me as I was growing up …'.[88]

Although Norris' interview only lasted nine minutes, it did generate a reaction from viewers and the Irish media. A report compiled by the IGRM showed that a number of callers contacted RTÉ to complain about the interview, with one caller stating that 'he was not paying a licence to see a programme like this'.[89] Another described the interview as 'propaganda for homosexuality', while one 'very angry gentleman from Castlebar objected to this discussion on homosexuality and said he would keep ringing RTÉ until he could speak to somebody in authority. His wife also objected'.[90] One viewer, Maire Breathnach, went a step further and submitted a complaint to RTÉ's Complaints Advisory Committee, insisting that it was 'improper for RTE [sic] to present anything which could be reasonably regarded as encouragement or advocacy of homosexual acts, as homosexual practices, even between consenting adults, are a criminal offence in Ireland'.[91] Breathnach's complaint was upheld, with the committee ruling that the programme was in breach of the Public Affairs Broadcasting Code and 'could have been offensive to the majority of Irish citizens …'[92]

The response from media critics, however, would suggest that the programme may not have been as offensive to Irish citizens as the committee believed. In fact, these positive reactions demonstrated the powerful impact such media appearances could have on changing mindsets and opening up a discussion on homosexuality. In one of the first reviews to appear after Norris' interview, Tony Wilson commended Norris, who he believed did 'a lot to dispel the myths and shibboleths surrounding homosexuality'.[93] Wilson's sentiments were shared by Pearse Hutchinson and Val Mulkerns in *The Irish Times* and *Evening Press* respectively. Hutchinson described Norris as being 'determined without being vehement. No camp, completely relaxed, as convincing and quietly eloquent a spokesman as any persecuted group could wish for ... As he pointed out, the perverts are not the homosexuals but the bigots.'[94] Norris' rhetoric had clearly won Hutchinson over, but so too had his demeanour and appearance. It is evident from Hutchinson's comments that the image and manner in which homosexuals appeared was equally as important as was what they were saying. In this instance, the fact that Norris was not 'camp' had helped him with viewers such as Hutchinson. Mulkerns concluded her review of the *Last House* interview by remarking that 'if anything could help towards getting a square deal in Ireland for responsible adult homosexuals, this must have been it'.[95]

One of the rare media critics to condemn the interview was Peter Cleary. In the *Sunday Independent*, Cleary was unforgiving in his criticism of RTÉ and the subject of homosexuality. RTÉ, he maintained, should have given advance notice of what the programme was about as some viewers 'find that homosexuality is a disgusting subject'.[96] So disgusted was Cleary with homosexuality that he told readers he 'switched off "Last House" because I'm not prepared to listen and to watch programmes about the perversions of my fellowmen'.[97] In what would be a common approach by the IGRM and later gay rights organisations, the IGRM decided that the nature of Cleary's review could not go unchallenged. In a letter to the *Sunday Independent*, Sean Connolly condemned Cleary's 'scurrilous attack on homosexuality' and insisted he must be 'suffering from an advanced stage of Homophobia – that irrational fear of homosexuals akin to a child's unreasonable fear of the dark, except that children grow up. Not so Peter Cleary'.[98] Connolly took the opportunity to inform readers that homosexuality was 'a naturally occurring, healthy variation of the common sexual capacity'. In a defiant conclusion to his letter, Connolly declared that 'we will be seen again on TV, and in other media, despite the witch-hunt mentality of Peter Cleary. Truth and honesty will prevail.'[99]

Despite the mixed response to Norris' interview, what is clear nonetheless is that his appearance had brought the issue of homosexuality much more out into the open and into the homes of many Irish citizens. In doing so, he had helped start a process of opening up a conversation with the wider Irish society on that very issue. The extent to which these efforts were having an impact was evident only a few weeks after the *Last House* interview, when the *Longford Leader* noted that 'The Gay Rights Association (homosexuals) are really getting on the ball these days. Wonder will it ever catch on in Ireland where queers are still frowned upon. Is it natural? Should they be allowed to practise their relationships? What do you readers out there think?'[100]

The *Longford Leader* did not have to wait long to hear what readers' opinions were. In fact, it received a barrage of letters condemning the language it used and expressing support for homosexuals. Throughout October, November, and even into December 1975, the *Longford Leader* received a high volume of letters condemning their choice of language. The sheer number even took the newspaper by surprise, with one journalist remarking: 'so we thought there were no homosexuals in Longford. The place it seems is crawling with them.'[101] Individuals such as: Paddy Horan; 'One of Longford's many gays'; 'Gay and Proud'; 'Gay Christian' – and the IGRM itself, criticised the use of the word *queer* and the ignorance surrounding homosexuality. In his contribution, Horan argued that 'the first lesson one must learn in trying to understand the position of some of our fellow men is that they are not abnormal or queer as you put it, but quite the opposite. They are just ordinary, everyday people who live, work and worry the same as everyone else.'[102] Once more, Sean Connolly took the opportunity presented by the *Longford Leader* to educate, explaining that homosexuals now adopted the term 'gay' because 'it is a short positive word used by us to describe a lifestyle, not a clinical term like heterosexual or homosexual, there is more to life, you'll agree than sex. Gay now has international status, being equally applied to men and women.'[103] Again, like with Kameny, Connolly was situating efforts in Ireland within the wider international gay rights movement, specifically adopting the terminology of the gay liberation movement that had emerged following the Stonewall Riots in 1969.

While the *Longford Leader* did not apologise for using the term queer and maintained that homosexuality was an unusual habit, it agreed that since homosexuals did not like the term queer, they would drop it – a victory for the IGRM.[104] It is perhaps quite ironic that while the *Longford Leader* recognised that the gay rights association was 'really getting on the ball', its journalists failed to appreciate what this actually meant for them; that they could no longer afford to use their accustomed derogatory terms to describe homosexuals without facing the wrath of the so-called 'on the ball' gay rights movement now present in the Republic of Ireland. The reaction to their piece clearly took the *Longford Leader* by surprise, but it demonstrated the extent to which such comments would no longer go unchallenged. The IGRM was not willing to ignore any negative comment published or spoken about homosexuality. Instead, its strategy was to confront negative comments, while at the same time using them as an opportunity to reshape the discourse and narrative on homosexuality.

The degree to which the IGRM's efforts were also not going to go unchallenged was evident in some of the reactions to Norris' appearance on *Last House*. Opponents of homosexuality were not going to shy away from condemning it or the actions of the IGRM. This was made clear to the IGRM in November 1976, when it found itself at the centre of a public controversy following its invitation to the London-based theatre group, Gay Sweatshop, to perform *Any Woman Can* and *Mister X* at the Project Arts Centre in Dublin.[105] Prior to the Gay Sweatshop's performance, *Scene Magazine* mused that 'it'll be interesting to see whether or not traditional guardians of the moral fibre of the nation like the Irish Family League and the *Irish Independent* will step out for the occasion. It's unlikely that a more controversial exploration of the whole question of sexual roles and attitudes has ever been staged in this country before, so there's meat for their kind of politics here.'[106] This comment proved prophetic.

While the *Sunday Independent* noted that Gay Sweatshop played to a crowded house, the Project Arts Centre came in for criticism from some sectors of Irish society.[107] Councillor Ned Brennan, a member of the Dublin City Council Corporation Culture Committee, reportedly fumed that 'ratepayers did not elect me to subsidise that kind of filth. I will oppose any further grants to this theatre unless they give an assurance that the quality of their productions will not be obscene.'[108] A fellow committee member, Sean D. Loftus, was quoted as saying that a Christian society like Ireland should not be subjected to 'this sort of stuff'.[109] Desmond Rushe, reviewing the production for the *Irish Independent*, described Gay Sweatshop as 'propagandist' and the production as one that 'was more geared to repulsing the heterosexual and making the homosexual with a tittle of sensitivity cringe with shame.'[110] Rushe even questioned if the grant given by Dublin City Council to the Project Arts Centre was intended to support such productions.[111] Despite this high-profile criticism, there was some reprieve for the IGRM, Gay Sweatshop and the Project Arts Centre, as critics with the *Cork Examiner*, *Evening Herald*, *The Irish Times*, *Hibernia* and the *Irish Press* all praising the production. Elgy Gillespie, for example, commended the production in *The Irish Times*, believing it was a good idea for 'the Irish Gay Rights Movement to bring Gay Sweatshop into Dublin since they are still battling away to beat that same old 1867 [sic] law which bothered Wilde.'[112]

Although criticism was levelled at Gay Sweatshop and the Project Arts Centre, the controversy had clearly erupted because homosexuality was presented in a positive light. This was something opponents were not willing to tolerate on an Irish stage and as a result had significant consequences for the Project Arts Centre. Therefore, while it may well have been a good idea for the IGRM, the Project Arts Centre's reputation and very survival came under attack. Shortly after Gay Sweatshop concluded their appearance at the Project Arts Centre, a debate emerged over whether or not Dublin City Council should continue to award the Project Arts Centre its grant for the upcoming year. Numerous newspaper articles and letters appeared both in support of and against the continued awarding of a grant to the centre. In one such letter, Nial MacDara, Chairman of the Society to Outlaw Pornography, wrote to remind the 'Cultural Committee of Dublin Corporation that to give a grant of £6,000 from the rates to the Project Arts Centre, after the disgraceful "Gay Sweatshop Production", would be tantamount to a rejection of the deeply-held religious convictions of the vast majority of ratepayers of this city and a vote of confidence in amoralism [sic] and a society holding no bars to vice.'[113] When Dublin City Council met to decide, a majority voted against awarding a future grant to the Project Arts Centre, citing its failure to secure security of tenure rather than its hosting Gay Sweatshop's productions.[114] This was something the Project Arts Centre insisted was only an excuse and the real reason was because 'councillors had set themselves up as censors and had more objections to the kind of shows being put on at the centre, particularly those by Gay Sweatshop'.[115]

The fallout from Gay Sweatshop's performance was a stark reminder to the IGRM that there were forces in the Republic of Ireland who were not going to support their efforts. Gay Sweatshop was later reported to have described their trip to Dublin 'as a visit to a "repressive society"'.[116] Ironically, the attempts to censor Gay Sweatshop resulted in a much greater discussion on homosexuality than would have likely occurred had the council and opponents said nothing. David Norris stated that it had 'brought into open some of the uncomfortable realities with which as homosexuals we have to live and from which too many uncaring and unconcerned fellow citizens are content to avert their gaze.'[117] John O'Shaughnessy, writing in the *Limerick Leader*, believed that 'in the light of the Project controversy, the Gay Sweatshop are probably the most talked about outfit now on the theatre scene.'[118] Therefore, what started out as an invitation to Gay Sweatshop to perform at the Project Arts Centre resulted in a much broader debate around homosexuality and its place in Irish theatre and Irish society.

That there was a growing awareness and interest in this issue was evident in February 1977, when RTÉ's *Tuesday Report* aired a documentary on homosexuality in

Ireland. The impact that the IGRM had in the space of just three years could be seen in Cathal O'Shannon's preview of his documentary for the *RTÉ Guide*. Explaining why he had come to explore this topic, O'Shannon stated that he wanted to 'examine the reasons why homosexuals themselves have become so vocal, so open in recent years. By this I don't mean that homosexuality is on the increase – there is no evidence that it is; but what has happened is that more and more homosexuals are joining the various Gay Rights Movements and are unafraid to state quite openly that they are homosexual.'[119]

Tuesday Report was a wide-ranging documentary that sought to explore questions such as: how should we treat them [homosexuals]? Should we fear them? Are they like lepers, to be avoided, and maybe cured of some loathsome disease? And, as Christians, should we shun them as appalling sinners?[120] For the IGRM it provided another opportunity to challenge the myths surrounding homosexuality and speak up for themselves. Whereas the *Last House* interview only featured David Norris, *Tuesday Report* saw a number of IGRM members participate, including Norris, Sean Connolly, James Malone, Clement Clancy, Phil Carson and Tony O'Connell.

The *Tuesday Report* documentary aired on 22 February 1977 and began with a short introduction by Nancy Diuguid, who had travelled over to Dublin to perform with Gay Sweatshop in November 1976. One of the first questions posed by O'Shannon was, what is a homosexual? Replying, Norris explained that a 'homosexual is a human being like anybody else who needs affection, needs love, needs friends, needs companionship, needs a social life, needs the reinforcing power of the social structures of powers which heterosexuals accept as their due but something homosexual people have only had in limited form'.[121] Norris also told O'Shannon that homosexuals were not child molesters, monsters, corrupters of youths, sick people, unhappy people, people who have no future, alcoholics or derelicts. In his interaction with O'Shannon, Sean Connolly, responding to a question on how he realised he was homosexual, explained that 'that's much the same as asking how I came to first realise I was Irish . . . I discovered that my orientation was towards members of my own same sex, for the same reasons as anybody else, for companionship, emotional stimulation and the usual things one forms a relationship for.'

Those who participated in the documentary focused on emphasising the extent to which homosexuality did not mean a life of despair, loneliness or unhappiness, but rather that homosexuals could live fulfilling lives if society altered its attitude towards them. When asked if she wished 'at any time that you were like the girls you work with, out chasing fellas at dances', Phil Carson told O'Shannon: 'No not at all. I wouldn't change my life or myself for anything. I am happy the way I am, in everything in life.' This positive embracement of her sexuality helped to counteract the belief that homosexuality was an affliction.

The oppression many faced, however, was also highlighted in the documentary, with the interview touching on an issue not as yet articulated by the IGRM; that of the many Irish men and women emigrating due to society's hostility towards homosexuality. In statements by the IGRM, they often highlighted how there were an estimated 200,000 homosexuals in Ireland, yet this figure ignored the many more who had emigrated, one of whom spoke to O'Shannon about his experience. Reg spoke about how he had moved to England for more freedom, explaining how difficult he found it to come to terms with his sexuality: 'The reasons were within me. Having been brought up to hate homosexuality, to fear and to loathe particularly homosexuals, I found it very difficult once I realised I was one to do otherwise than to continue to hate them, which I did for about ten years. It was very difficult to admit I was a homosexual.'

Significant at this early stage for the IGRM was the appearance of supportive heterosexual allies. The IGRM was joined by Rose Robertson (Parents Enquiry), who turned the tables on heterosexual viewers by asking them to imagine how they would feel if their sexuality was not socially accepted like homosexuality was? Dr Noel Browne also participated, telling O'Shannon that homosexuality was as normal as heterosexuality, it was just a different side of human sexuality. Perhaps, however, the biggest surprise in the documentary was the appearance of a Catholic priest, Fr Michael Cleary, who told O'Shannon 'that people fear homosexuals, I don't know why they fear them, they are normal people. Their sexual desire and urges are in a different direction to others.'[122] Preceding his appearance on *Tuesday Report*, Cleary had taken to the *Catholic Standard* on a number of occasions to defend homosexuals. As a result, he had developed a reputation for being what one Mayo priest described as the 'national chaplain to homosexuals'.[123]

Just as the *Last House* interview generated reaction, so too did *Tuesday Report*. Of the forty calls that RTÉ received about the documentary, only four expressed anger, with twenty-six commending it, four requesting information on the IGRM and six callers requesting the time the programme was aired.[124] One viewer, Margaret Kegley, felt the need to write to O'Shannon personally to applaud him and the homosexuals who appeared on the show:

> May I say I was impressed by your handling of such an explosive and unpopular subject. Being a viewer of BBC I was not too unaware, but certainly I gained a measure of respect for the men who talked and who admitted they were homosexual. I feel you may have let yourself in for a lot of flak but on the plus side, it is a social problem that must be faced squarely, not only by homosexuals, but by all the population, particularly parents.[125]

Kegley herself appears to have somewhat changed her opinion of homosexuals following the documentary. Acknowledging her own misgivings prior to the documentary and the bravery of O'Shannon in tackling this 'explosive subject', Kegley recognised that the homosexuals in the documentary could be respected and the topic itself was one that needed greater discussion within Irish society.

The extent to which Kegley was not alone in finding the programme informative was evident in a number of letters sent to the *Sunday Independent* in response to a negative review by Peter Cleary on the programme. Just as Cleary had condemned the *Last House* interview in July 1975, he similarly lambasted the *Tuesday Report* documentary, writing that 'there was damn-all about the corrupting effect homosexuality can have in a community. If RTÉ had any sense of balance they might have had someone to recall that it has had an appalling history in creating its own pagan atmosphere of decadence.'[126] Cleary's review was in stark contrast to Val Mulkerns in the *Evening Press*, who described the documentary as 'probably one of the finest pieces of TV reporting that will come our way in 1977'.[127] This was a view shared by those who sent letters specifically to condemn Cleary's review. The number of letters sent in response to Cleary's comments saw the *Sunday Independent* devote a half page to the letters under the title 'Cleary's comments drew readers' fire'.[128] One such letter was from Anne Dempsey, who dismissed Cleary's assertion that many viewers would have switched the programme off, telling how 'as someone who knew very little heretofore about the subject, I did not switch off, but rather took the opportunity to gain a little insight and understanding into the problems of a much-misunderstood minority. I am sure I speak for many when I thank R.T.E. for a worthwhile, balanced and long-overdue report.' Hilary Boyle shared Dempsey's views, writing that Cleary's 'critique of Cathal O'Shannon's dignified and sympathetic programme about homosexuality made me very sad indeed. Why should Mr. Cleary be so sure he is better than other people. Does he really not realise that to be born a homosexual is no more the fault of that person than to be born with red hair.'[129]

Interestingly, whereas *Last House* was found to have broken Section 4 of the code of Public Affairs Broadcasting practice, a complaint submitted to the Broadcasting Complaints Commission by Maire Breathnach about *Tuesday Report* was not upheld on this occasion. In its ruling, the Broadcasting Complaints Commission accepted RTÉ's statement that the 'programme was in the main a report of the position of homosexuals in Irish society and that they attempted to examine a human problem with understanding and factual explanation of an existing situation'.[130] This was a significant turn of events in the space of just two years. Therefore, as we have seen, by 1977 the IGRM had succeeded in bringing greater attention to the issue of homosexuality within the Irish media than was the case before its establishment. While some did not welcome this, clearly others did welcome the opportunity to learn more about homosexuality.

Gay movement seeks rights

While the IGRM worked to reinvent the image of homosexuals, they recognised that as a small organisation they could not bring about the type of reform they wanted alone; they would also need the support of influential stakeholders in Irish society. As we have seen from the 1975 interview and the 1977 documentary, the IGRM had secured support from some individuals and organisations inside and outside Ireland. One organisation that did not appear in both programmes, however, but had been one of the first organisations to come out in support of gay rights in Ireland, was the Union of Students of Ireland (USI). In January 1974 the USI had held its annual general conference in Wexford, at which a motion calling on the USI 'to fight against gay oppression as expressed in legislation and social attitudes' was proposed.[131] Prior to this motion going forward, the USI had received a discussion document on homosexuality from one of its working groups, while Peter Bradley had presented a report on the 1973 Coleraine conference in which he argued that the USI should make a public statement in support of gay rights.[132] Bradley's views were supported in the discussion document, which described the legal situation facing homosexuals in Ireland as 'barbaric'. Citing the situation in England and Wales, the document stated that 'the only rational conclusion that any reasonable person can reach is that homosexuals should enjoy the same recognition and sexual freedom as do all other members of our society. To deny this basic right to homosexuals is to perpetuate centuries of intolerance, bigotry and injustice'.[133] These arguments proved persuasive and the aforementioned motion was adopted by USI delegates.[134]

The USI, then representing almost 47,000 students, became one of the strongest allies of the gay rights movement in Ireland, often providing the IGRM with the opportunity to engage with the student population on the issue of gay rights through their annual conferences, events on campus and the different student presses throughout Ireland. In many respects, Irish universities became battlegrounds in the gay rights campaign and sites where the efforts to change mindsets about homosexuality in Ireland took place – this, of course, was not an Irish phenomenon. On the contrary, internationally students and university campuses were at the centre of many battles, not just those restricted to sexuality.[135]

In 1976 the Dublin University Sociological Society in TCD organised a symposium on homosexuality, at which David Norris told those in attendance that 'discrimination against homosexuals in Ireland was exactly similar to that practised in other countries against Jews, Catholics and Negroes'.[136] One year later, Edmund Lynch was invited to address a USI conference on human sexuality at QUB in November 1977. In his letter to the IGRM inviting them to participate, Peter Davies, Deputy USI president, explained that the conference was being organised to 'discuss the whole question of attitudes to sexuality generally, and homosexuality in particular'.[137] At a time when there were few other organisations willing to engage with the IGRM, the USI's support was encouraging and helped shift the campaign outside the confines of the IGRM. This could also be seen in student presses, where sympathetic articles on homosexuality began to appear. In January 1975, for example, *Trinity News* published an in-depth interview with David Norris on the IGRM. While this article does not appear to have generated any controversy, this was not the case for Maynooth University's student magazine, *Educational Matters*, in March 1976. According to a report in the *Irish Press*, Maynooth University's 'college secretarial service had been pressurised into not releasing copies of the magazine because it contained an article by the secretary of the Irish Gay Rights Movement, Mr. David Norris'.[138] Instead, the authorities planned to release that issue of the magazine excluding the article. The student union president, Peter Finnegan, told the *Irish Press* that they would be protesting the decision, which was not acceptable to the union.[139] This protest would appear to have been successful, as Norris' article later appeared in the September 1976 issue.

The USI and the wider student movement were the exception rather than the norm, forcing the IGRM to work hard to garner support from others. Among the sectors that the IGRM had viewed as crucial to the gay rights campaign in the Republic of Ireland were the different religious denominations. In January 1975, the *Catholic Standard* reported that, following their attendance at an International Gay Rights Congress in Edinburgh in December 1974, which had explored the relationship between homosexuality and Christianity, David Norris and Sean Connolly had sent a 'highly critical' letter to the different churches in Ireland. The letter argued that 'the cruellest oppressive forces against homosexuality could be traced to sources in Christian moral teaching'.[140] While the *Catholic Standard* noted that IGRM had asked the bishops for a response to the letter, it thought it 'extremely unlikely that any will consider the time ripe for any comment on this area of law reform'.[141] In relation to the response of the hierarchy of the Roman Catholic Church, this was an accurate statement. However, the Church of Ireland Archbishop of Dublin, Alan Buchanan, did reply, telling Norris and Connolly that 'I believe we are unwilling to shelve the problems that you set before us.'[142]

The Church of Ireland was more disposed to engage with the IGRM. Not only did they request the IGRM to send as much information as possible on homosexuality but the IGRM was also invited to give a talk to a sub-committee of the Board for Social Responsibility of the Church of Ireland.[143] Later, in 1975, the IGRM was asked to send a representative to a meeting of the Social Services Committee, which was to discuss the possibility of recommending that the Board for Social Responsibility take up this issue through the organising of a seminar on homosexuality.[144] This meeting subsequently supported the organisation of such a seminar in February 1976.

In advance of the February 1976 seminar, invitations were sent to all bishops of the Church of Ireland whose dioceses fell within the twenty-six counties and to the corresponding authorities in the Presbyterian and Methodist Churches.[145] Those who turned up included bishops, social workers, a district court justice and Frank Cluskey, then a Labour Party TD and member of the government.[146] The IGRM was represented by David Norris, Theresa Blanche, James Malone, Sean Connolly, Noel Clarke, Martin Barnes and Edmund Lynch. According to the *IGRM Newsletter*, David Norris gave an address to delegates before the seminar broke into small discussion groups, with each group having an IGRM member as a leader. The IGRM report on the seminar noted that there were some 'very interesting questions', with many clergymen displaying 'considerable awareness of the true homosexual capacity for living and loving'. In what was a sign of the relationship that the IGRM had built up with some Church of Ireland clergymen, a number of them (sixteen) returned with the IGRM members to the Phoenix Club for a 'small sherry reception'. The IGRM described the meeting as 'the first really valuable exchange of ideas with such an influential body – the first of many we hope'.[147]

Just how significant this engagement was with the Church of Ireland was evident two months later, when Archbishop Buchanan, speaking at the Church of Ireland General Synod, called for reform of the laws criminalising sexual activity between men. In his address, Buchanan urged churchmen 'to be more ready to listen to medical advice on the nature of homosexuality', stressing that homosexuals 'have this tendency from birth, or soon after birth. They cannot be responsible for these tendencies any more than the rest of us for the heterosexual instincts we inherit … There is a general uneasiness among ourselves and Social Responsibility about the laws against homosexuality which we feel need examination.'[148] This was a highly momentous intervention, with *The Irish Times* describing Buchanan's speech as 'influential'.[149]

If the Church of Ireland was willing to support law reform, the hierarchy of the Roman Catholic Church was not. From the beginning it was clear that the hierarchy was unwilling to engage with the IGRM on the issue. In and around the same time the Church of Ireland was preparing to meet with the IGRM, the Bishop of Ardagh and Clonmacnoise, Cathal Daly, repeated his support for the Vatican's recent statement, *Persona Humana*, which had condemned premarital sex, masturbation and homosexuality.[150] This led David Norris to write to the *Catholic Standard* imploring the Roman Catholic Church 'not to use this already discredited document to justify interference with the political expression of the individual human rights of Irish citizens, catholic and non-Catholic alike'.[151] On one of the rare occasions when the IGRM did receive a response, the diocesan secretary to the Archdiocese of Armagh, Cardinal Conway, informed them that in regard to 'the moral teaching of the Catholic Church on homosexuality, the Cardinal can only refer you to Section 8 of the recent authoritative statement by the Holy See. With reference to the law of the State on this matter, this is essentially a matter for the civil legislators and their judgement as to its relevance to the common good'.[152] In many respects, the Roman Catholic Church's attitude to the issue of homosexuality and the decriminalisation of sexual activity between men resembled that of the Irish government and political parties more generally.

As we have seen, Dr Noel Browne was rare amongst Irish politicians in speaking out in support of gay rights. From as early as April 1975 Browne had raised the issue in Leinster House, asking the then Attorney General, Declan Costello, *Fine Gael* TD, if he would consider asking the Law Reform Commission to examine the 'inhuman' laws relating to sexual activity between men in the Republic of Ireland.[153] This was not a request the Attorney General took up. In the same year that Browne raised the issue in Leinster House, the IGRM had sought to put pressure on the Irish government during an EEC summit in Dublin in March 1975. In an attempt to undermine the government, the IGRM sent a letter to EEC leaders calling on them to support their demands for rights, describing the present legal situation in Ireland as 'vicious'.[154] Interestingly, one month later Infor-Homosexualite, a gay organisation in Belgium, wrote to the Irish embassy in Brussels condemning the criminalisation of sexual activity between men, insisting that 'it seems abnormal that such a law should remain in force'.[155] Such interventions from international gay rights organisations would be a regular feature in the years ahead. In September 1976, for example, André Baudry, founder of the French homophile review, *Arcadie*, wrote to the Irish Ambassador to France to enquire about the legal situation relating to homosexuality in Ireland.[156]

In the absence of any public or private support coming from the government for reform of the 1861 and 1885 laws, the IGRM drafted a Bill in January 1977, which, if passed, would have allowed sexual activity between consenting men over 18 years of age. Supporters of the Bill included Senators Noel Browne, Augustine Martin and Ruairí Quinn.[157] Speaking to the *Irish Press* about the prospects of the proposed Bill, Quinn expressed his doubt over whether or not the Bill would even get a first reading in light of the fact that they couldn't get the Family Law Bill through'.[158] It would seem that just as Quinn had predicted, the Bill did not get a first reading, as there is no record of such a Bill being proposed that year. Dr Browne made another attempt to get the government to act in December 1977, asking the newly appointed Minister for Justice, Gerry Collins (*Fianna Fáil* TD), if he had any intention of amending the laws. Replying, Collins told Browne that 'I am honestly convinced that I have other priorities which must be dealt with before I get to this particular one', leading Browne to quip that 'the Minister is lucky he is not homosexual then, presumably'.[159] It would be another sixteen years before an Irish Minister for Justice 'dealt' with the issue.

A palace coup

While the efforts to generate support from the Roman Catholic Church and politicians bore little fruit, problems of a different nature were brewing within the leadership of the IGRM. On 7 January 1977, David Norris sent a letter to the IGRM National Executive deriding what he described as the 'very severe difficulties I encounter in attempting to fulfil my role as Chairman given the present attitude of the general secretary Sean Connolly'.[160] According to Norris, he had been subjected to personal affronts from Connolly and 'valuable energies were being wasted at all levels of the organisation in fighting off personality based attacks and futile point scoring exercises'. In particular, Norris signalled out seven issues of concern: 'personality cult', 'illegal meetings', 'usurping of authority by insult and innuendo', 'refusal to act as secretary' and 'general abusiveness to members of the Movement'.[161]

The deterioration in the relationship between Norris and Connolly became evident in March 1977, when Connolly submitted his letter of resignation.[162] While Connolly had stated his intention to resign effective from 4 April 1977, Bernard Keogh proposed at a meeting on 13 March that his resignation should be taken as effective from the date the letter was written.[163] Keogh's proposal was seconded by Phil Carson and approved by six votes to four. Those who voted with Keogh and Carson included Norris, Michael Bergin, Theresa Blanche and Martin Barnes. Those against were Clement Clancy, James Malone, Noel Clarke and Connolly himself. It was evident from that March meeting that cliques of a sort had developed behind Norris and Connolly. Those who supported Connolly reacted by sending a notice to IGRM members of their intention to hold an extraordinary general meeting on 6 April to deal with what they described as a 'crisis' within the IGRM.[164]

Initially, the tension had been confined to the IGRM National Executive, but by April it had filtered out to the general membership. For some a complete overhaul of personalities was now needed to rescue the IGRM. In manifestos for election to the new IGRM National Executive in May, the discontent with the outgoing National Executive was evident. Numerous candidates' manifestos spoke of a 'lack of momentum', 'lack of enthusiasm', 'lack of proper leadership', and the desire for an 'end to the present divisiveness'.[165] One candidate, Tony O'Connell, noted that he felt 'of late the committee has lost much of its original momentum and it will require a radical change of personnel to bring the movement back on course'.[166]

According to *Gay News*, following the May annual general meeting, 'Tony O'Connell took over from David Norris as Chairman of the IGRM in a palace coup'.[167] There can be no doubt that Norris believed that some within the IGRM had conspired to oust him from his position within the IGRM. His disappointment and annoyance with how these events had unfolded were obvious in a letter he sent to Frank Ryan, then General Secretary of the IGRM, six months after the election refusing to take up the position of Chairman of the IGRM legal sub-committee. While thanking the IGRM National Executive for offering him the position, Norris declined on the basis that:

> You will further recall that the first action of the newly elected committee was a contest for the post of chairman, in which I did not receive the vote of one single committee member, new or old, could only be described as a massive vote of no confidence in my leadership and of absolute confidence in the abilities of Mr. O'Connell and the new executive members. I note with a certain wry satisfaction that some of those voices loudest in denouncing both my personality and my policies have suffered a diminuendo since taking over certain sections of the work I was engaged in at the time of the Connolly-inspired Coup.[168]

The events of May 1977 would leave a bitter trail and resulted in some IGRM members walking away, including Norris and Lynch.

Not long after Norris and Lynch had left the IGRM, however, they came together with Bernard Keogh to establish the Campaign for Homosexual Law Reform (CHLR). The CHLR, unlike the IGRM, had the sole objective of reforming the 1861 and 1885 laws and secured support from prominent individuals in Irish society such as: Kadar Asmal, a senior law lecturer at TCD and founding member of the Irish Council for Civil Liberties; Prof. Mary McAleese, then Reid Chair of Criminal Law, Criminology and Penology at TCD (future President of Ireland); Catherine McGuinness, then a Barrister and later an Irish Senator and Supreme Court Justice; Hugh Leonard, an Irish dramatist; and Victor Bewley, owner of Bewley's café and Travellers' rights activist.[169] With the support of the CHLR, and represented by Senior Counsel Garret Cooney and Junior Counsels Paul Carney and Mary Robinson, Norris lodged plenary summons in the Irish High Court in November 1977 seeking a declaration that the 1861 and 1885 laws were inconsistent with the Irish constitution and interfered with his right to respect for private life.[170] The legal battle to decriminalise sexual activity between men had begun in earnest.

While the CHLR turned its attention to the 1861 and 1885 laws, things went from bad to worse within the IGRM. Tony O'Connell, Norris' successor as IGRM chairman, lasted only eight months in his position before resigning along with John Ryan and Desmond Duffy.[171] Then, in 1978, the IGRM lost its lease at Parnell Square. Without a premises, the IGRM was no longer able to organise events, bringing the curtains down on the organisation as it was then. There can be no doubt that the fallout between Norris and Connolly had a detrimental impact on the IGRM and left a trail of bitterness and antagonism between the different personalities involved for many years. However, despite the collapse of the IGRM in 1978, it had achieved a lot in four years. It had helped break the silence surrounding homosexuality in the Republic of Ireland and demonstrated the extent to which there were a number of individuals who were committed to challenging the status quo with regard to homosexuality. More importantly it had acted as a voice for Irish homosexuals and provided a space where they could meet and socialise. In doing so, it provided hope for a better future to come.

2

Social Life as Resistance in 1980s Dublin

In July 1984, *The Irish Times* journalist Maurice Haugh described Fownes Street in Temple Bar as the 'Gay Paree' of Dublin. Haugh's article had explored the reasons behind the revival of Temple Bar and had included the Hirschfeld Centre, a gay community centre established by the National Gay Federation (NGF) in 1979, as one of the reasons why Temple Bar had taken on a new lease of life.[1] Haugh's reference to a 'Gay Paree' in mid-1980s Ireland is insightful, particularly the positive contribution that he perceived the gay community to have had on a once derelict area of Dublin's inner centre. Incidentally, Haugh's article coincided with another article that same year that not only alluded to a greater awareness and visibility of a gay community in the Republic of Ireland but also the existence of an emerging pink economy. Niall O'Dowd and Mary Kavanagh's article in *Success* claimed that Dublin had become the focus of 'social activity for an increasing number of well-heeled homosexuals'.[2] They went on to list the different venues and locations targeting Ireland's gay community, asserting that 'while products, shops, or businesses geared exclusively to the gay market may be a bit thin on the ground in Ireland at the moment there is no doubt that the influence and spending power of the gay community has had considerable reverberations throughout society'.[3]

Within the context of 1980s Ireland these articles are revealing. That one of Ireland's leading mainstream publications and leading business magazines both acknowledged the existence of a gay scene/gay community demonstrates the greater awareness of both amongst the non-gay community. It would appear that the gay subculture of the 1970s had to some degree made way for a more visible gay scene in the 1980s. The emergence of a more visible gay community and awareness of a gay scene in the 1980s, however, was not inevitable. Looking back at this period, Ailbhe Smyth, a long-time feminist and LGBT activist, recalled that:

> the 1980s were such bad times in Ireland that a lot of the movement activity – whether it was the women's movement or whether it was lesbian or gay or whether it was socialist – tended to be very much in abeyance and very much less visible. I remember from my own involvement in movements that they tended to be off the public agenda. It was just so difficult to be overtly involved in social movement politics or to be involved in direct action.[4]

There can be no doubt that the 1980s had its setbacks for progressive groups in the Republic of Ireland, epitomised by passage of the 8th Amendment to the Irish constitution, which placed a constitutional ban on abortion, and the defeat of the 1986 Divorce Referendum, but it was also a time when gay and lesbian individuals became more visible. The aforementioned articles are evidence that despite the context of 1980s Ireland, a gay community and gay scene had become more visible. Therefore, the question remains, how is it that a more visible gay community and gay scene had developed during this period? To explain this, we need to move beyond an exclusive focus on so-called political actions and begin to consider the impact of 'social activities' and 'social spaces' in raising the profile of gay and lesbian individuals and Ireland's burgeoning gay scene.

The NGF described the Hirschfeld Centre as a social centre that facilitated the organisation of a number of events (discos, befriending groups, cinema, youth groups, women-only meetings). While the Hirschfeld Centre was a successful social centre, it was more than simply a space for social events. Symbolically, it was also a centre of resistance and the events therein cannot simply be described or dismissed as social. In fact, there is a strong political element to them.[5] For many Irish gay and lesbian individuals, the public sphere generally was not a place that tolerated or welcomed them. This could also be applied to the homes of many gay and lesbian individuals, which could often be places where they were subjected to verbal and physical abuse once their sexuality became known. However, within spaces like the Hirschfeld Centre, gay and lesbian individuals could find a more welcoming environment (not always). This more welcoming environment allowed gay and lesbian individuals to become more confident in their sexuality. Therefore, if we accept the feminist mantra that the personal is political, then, in this regard, these centres could be considered to have had a radical political dimension, particularly in fostering a sense of a gay community and greater acceptance in one's sexuality. Moreover, the willingness of thousands of Irish gay and lesbian individuals to cross the threshold of the Hirschfeld Centre must be acknowledged as a form of resistance; this very action was a challenge to the status quo in the Republic of Ireland. In taking the decision to visit spaces like the Hirschfeld Centre, telephoning a gay switchboard, attending a gay disco, participating in a gay youth group or participating in discussion groups on homosexuality, gay and lesbian individuals sent a clear message that they rejected society's disdain for homosexuality and were going to embrace their sexuality. This was an act of insubordination and facilitated a considerable challenge to the status quo.

What emerged in 1980s Ireland, therefore, was a willingness by many gay and lesbian individuals to accept their sexuality, to be more public with their sexuality, more willing to frequent openly gay venues and more willing to speak out about their sexuality, which, in turn, raised the profile of gay and lesbian individuals in the Republic of Ireland. Consequently, this greater awareness also resulted in some businesses beginning to recognise the spending power of Ireland's gay community. Therefore, while the 1980s in Ireland may be characterised as a reactionary decade, it was also a period in which gay and lesbian individuals became more confident and willing to publicly embrace their sexuality. As Ciaran McKinney recalls: 'I certainly am aware of people talking about the recession and stuff in the 80s. I honestly just partied the whole time and the gay scene was extraordinarily vibrant.'[6] If Ailbhe Smyth believed that overt political action was less visible and in abeyance, which I do not necessarily agree with, then the gay scene and its political and social ramifications certainly were not, as we will now discover.

'"Gay" group opens new headquarters'

In 1979 *The Irish Times* and *Irish Press* both carried articles on the opening of the Hirschfeld Centre, a new three-storey gay community centre, at 10 Fownes Street, Temple Bar, Dublin.⁷ Named after Magnus Hirschfeld, the pioneering German sexologist and homophile reform activist, it opened on St Patrick's Day 1979 and became the headquarters for the newly formed National Gay Federation (NGF). The NGF had been established by David Norris, Edmund Lynch and Bernard Keogh earlier that year. Explaining his decision behind naming the Hirschfeld Centre after Magnus Hirschfeld, Norris stated that it was part of an attempt to recover Hirschfeld's memory and to reawaken the world to him.⁸ In a conversation with Tonie Walsh in 2021 on the same topic, he stressed how there was a conscious decision taken in the naming of the Hirschfeld Centre and the disco inside it – the disco was named Flikkers, Dutch for faggots – to pay homage to the efforts of individuals in Germany and the Netherlands, particularly their role in advancing civil rights for gay and lesbian individuals prior to the Stonewall riots. Walsh maintains that this was a deliberate attempt to remind Irish gay and lesbian individuals that they were part of a 'wider European socio-cultural and political discourse' and 'to patch Irish LGBT people into our mainland European heritage … to remind people that there was life in Europe before the Nazis so comprehensively obliterated any evidence of our lives.'⁹

Speaking to the *Irish Press* about the Hirschfeld Centre, Norris expressed the hope that it would become a 'first class comfortable venue where all homosexual people could feel welcome and fully accepted.'¹⁰ Its opening marked a considerable turnaround in fortunes for Dublin's gay community following the collapse of the IGRM's Phoenix Club in 1978 and it quickly developed a reputation for being a home from home for Ireland's gay community in the 1980s. For Bill Hughes it 'was a place where you could just be your complete self and just let it all hang out.'¹¹

Like the IGRM, the NGF saw the Hirschfeld Centre as a means to provide a space for social activities for the gay community while simultaneously helping fund the NGF's political activities. The NGF operated under the motto that 'gay rights are not extravagant demands, gay rights are simply human rights'. They worked:

(a) To achieve for gay men and women full equal rights with their heterosexual counterparts.
(b) To campaign for the removal of all discriminatory sanctions against homosexual behaviour.
(c) To promote, by education and example, greater understanding of homosexuality by society in general, and by medical, legal and religious institutions in particular.
(d) To seek from educational authorities the implementation, in programmes of education in sex and personal relationships, of the presentation of factual, non-biased information relating to the nature and incidence of homosexuality.

(e) To provide counselling and befriending facilities for the gay community.
(f) To offer help and information to persons contacting NGF for assistance.
(g) To place professional and other qualified advice, assistance and information, particularly relating to medical, legal and religious matters, at the disposal of the gay community.
(h) To manage premises for the benefit of NGF members and the gay community generally.
(i) To provide social events and amenities for members of NGF.
(j) To encourage the growth of a spirit of community among gay women and men in all parts of Ireland.
(k) To provide, wherever this is found possible, social services and amenities for the gay community, generally and for NGF members in particular.
(l) To work for the establishment of NGF Groups in provincial centres.
(m) To work for the elimination of sexism in the gay community and in society in general.[12]

In an interview with *Gay News* in 1979, an unnamed NGF representative insisted that the NGF was only set up 'when it was clear that IGRM had folded completely. They were evicted from their premises and there was no progress being made at all for gay rights. We felt something had to be done ... We are building up again after the disasters of the last two years of IGRM ...'[13] This was not a sentiment shared by some former IGRM members, who disputed the assertion that the IGRM had folded. Clement Clancy, for example, dismissed this claim, telling *Gay News* that the 'IGRM is still on the map. We are giving it the kiss of life.'[14]

In the same year that the NGF was established, Clement Clancy, Sean Connolly, Pat Mahoney-Rysh, Aidan Lacey and John Ryan had regrouped and began organising discos under the name of the Irish Gay Rights Movement, at Bellamy's nightclub on St. Stephen's Green, Dublin.[15] This decision was described by the NGF as a 'blatant attempt to split the community'.[16] While it was not until March 1980 that the IGRM opened its own venue at 18 North Lotts, Bachelor's Walk, Dublin (named the Phoenix Club) it was evident that the leaders of both organisations did not welcome the other's existence. A *Gay News* article on the IGRM's (re)emergence reported that it would 'open old wounds in Ireland'.[17]

From as early as October 1979 the vitriol between both groups was evident, with *Gay News* reporting that the NGF 'blamed a rival gay group for continual harassment and attempted sabotage of the work of the capital's six-month old gay centre'.[18] The IGRM strongly denied this accusation and responded with its own claim that the NGF was behind repeated raids of their discos by Dublin's drug squad.[19] In January 1980, the NGF accused the IGRM of stirring up 'civil war in the gay community' by launching legal actions against the NGF.[20] The IGRM had initiated legal proceedings over what they claimed was the NGF's unlawful position of property belonging to the IGRM.[21] This formed part of the dispute over which organisation was the rightful heir to the IGRM (1974–1978), with both organisations claiming they were the legitimate heir. While publicly the IGRM and NGF claimed they wanted to resolve their differences, even holding two meetings to discuss the situation, there does not appear to have been a genuine attempt to put their differences aside. They continued to be at odds with each other until the IGRM's lease at North Lotts finished towards the end of 1982, bringing the curtain down on the Phoenix Club and the Dublin-based IGRM.

'A centre for counsel and friendship'

Despite the tension between the IGRM and the NGF, Chris Kirk, a journalist with *Gay News*, remarked that the 'best thing about the split is that it means there are two centres, two discos, for uninvolved Dubliners to go to, instead of one'.[22] Both the Phoenix Club and the Hirschfeld Centre were open seven days a week and members could avail of a range of different activities: discos four nights a week (including women-only discos); the Hirschfeld Biograph (a 55-seater cinema in the Hirschfeld Centre); a theatre group in the Phoenix Club; befriending groups, Parents Enquiry; a youth group; discussion groups; outdoor activities; and a café and welfare service in the Hirschfeld Centre. There now also existed two separate telephone befriending services: Tel-A-Friend, which was housed in the Hirschfeld Centre, and the Irish Gay Switchboard, which operated out of the Phoenix Club. The Hirschfeld Centre also became home to Ireland's first gay magazine *Identity* (1981–1984), later replaced by *OUT* (1984–1988) and *Gay Community News* (1988–), which continues today as Ireland's leading LGBTQ+ magazine.[23]

The Hirschfeld Centre also had an international profile, as it housed the International Secretariat for the International Gay Association (IGA) from 1979–1982. David Norris was one of a number of Irish individuals who had helped found the IGA in Coventry, England, in 1978. Together with Edmund Lynch, Norris pushed for the IGA Secretariat to be based in Dublin, arguing that if it was based in Amsterdam the 'world in general would say "So what? Sure that's what you'd expect. But opening the first HQ of an international gay organisation in holy Catholic Ireland would really create waves.'[24] Norris and Lynch won the day and the Hirschfeld Centre became home to the IGA Secretariat, placing the NGF at the centre of international communications on gay rights, while also bringing it into contact with gay rights organisations throughout the world.[25]

The IGRM and NGF did not shy away from promoting their centres as gay centres. On the contrary, they sought to advertise as widely as possible in *In Dublin* and *Hot Press*. In other words, these were not clandestine venues, but very much publicly advertised gay centres. In one such advertisement in *In Dublin*, the IGRM promoted their disco as the 'BEST GAY DISCO IN TOWN'.[26] The willingness to not hide away from publicising the centres as gay centres was a strong public statement of intent to resist the legal and socio-cultural climate and to forge visible spaces for Ireland's gay community. The Hirschfeld Centre, in particular, generated a high profile. As noted previously, its opening was covered by two of Ireland's mainstream nationals. One year later, *In Dublin* and *Hot Press* both featured articles on the centre, with journalist Lynn Geldof encouraging her readers to 'check it out'.[27] Even RTÉ took notice of the Hirschfeld Centre. In November 1981, *Ireland's Eye* produced a short piece on the Hirschfeld Centre and the activities of the NGF. Sensing a more visible gay community now emerging in the Republic of Ireland, reporter Brian Black sought to understand this, asking Eamon Somers, President of the NGF Council, 'why is it the image of gay people seems to have taken on a profile?'[28] Responding to this question, Eamon Somers expressed the view that it was:

> because of places like this. The centre has established itself, because the NGF has made its profile public, has come out in many ways to the public, made itself known to the media, made itself known to other people, has established a social centre, a community centre here in Dublin. So, it's possible for gay people to come in and relate to themselves, discover their own personalities, discover their own sexuality and then go back out to the world that bit more confident and that bit more aware of what they are and consequently communicate to other people that they are gay. This raises their own profile and encourages other people to do likewise.[29]

The visibility of the Hirschfeld Centre was just one reason that a more visible gay community was emerging at that time. Within the Hirschfeld Centre there were a range of activities that were also factoring into this greater visibility, which in turn, as Eamon Somers noted, encouraged more and more gay and lesbian individuals to become confident in their sexuality and to be more open about it with others. Two of the most popular activities within the Hirschfeld Centre were Flikkers and the Hirschfeld Biograph. Flikkers (the Dutch word for faggots) was the disco organised within the Hirschfeld Centre four nights a week. A look at the numbers who visited Flikkers in the first half of the 1980s reveals just how popular it was. Between December 1980 and November 1984 (excluding 16 weeks when no figures were given) there were roughly 119,148 entries to Flikkers, an average of 2,480 entries each month.[30] Saturdays alone often attracted between 250 to 350 people. It was through the revenue generated by Flikkers that the NGF was able to run the centre and numerous other activities, eventually acquiring sufficient funds to purchase the building in 1982. Even outside the gay community Flikkers was recognised as one of the liveliest and musically up-to-date discos in town. This, Maurice Haugh argued, owed much to the NGF's ability to import records directly from London and play them months before they hit the radio charts in Ireland.[31]

The Hirschfeld Biograph similarly generated a lot of respect both inside and outside the Hirschfeld Centre. In the course of its six-and-a-half-year history the Biograph screened 137 films, including the Irish premiere of *The Times of Harvey Milk*, *We Were One Man* and *Victor Victoria*.[32] Johnny McEvoy, who ran the Hirschfeld Biograph, explained that it came about because there was a desire to ensure that 'all gay persons, regardless of age, could attend without having the feeling of being left out of things or being in a cruisy atmosphere they felt uncomfortable with'.[33] McEvoy had a lot of connections within the film industry that he called upon to the benefit of the Hirschfeld Biograph. In 1980 he succeeded in making the Hirschfeld Biograph an honorary member of the Federation of Irish Film Societies, helping to save it over £500 in annual affiliation fees. Later, in 1984, thanks to his connections in the British Film Institute, McEvoy invited Terence Davies to speak at the Hirschfeld Biograph on his acclaimed trilogy of films: *Children* (1976), *Madonna and Child* (1980) and *Death and Transfiguration* (1983).[34] Of all the films that were screened at the Hirschfeld Biograph, Davies' generated the most positive reviews and attention outside the Hirschfeld Centre. Writing in *The Irish Times*, Ray Comiskey stated that the 'Hirschfeld Biograph club members will have an opportunity to see a marvellous piece of film ...', while *In Dublin* was so impressed with the production that they selected it as their recommended event for readers that week.[35]

Although not every film shown at the Hirschfeld Biograph generated the same level of attention that Davies' films did, it was nevertheless important that the Hirschfeld Biograph was acknowledged in mainstream publications. The nonchalant references to it give the impression that these reviewers simply viewed the Hirschfeld Biograph as a cinema, not a gay cinema to be feared or avoided, but rather one which screened high quality films. In reporting on the films screened at the Hirschfeld Biograph, these publications helped to promote gay-themed films in the Republic of Ireland. Moreover, the Hirschfeld Biograph served as an alternative activity for gay and lesbian individuals who wanted something outside of a disco. For Ciaran Coleman, who remembered attending the Hirschfeld Biograph in the 1980s, it opened up a whole new world for him:

> For me, the Hirschfeld Biograph was one of the wonderful things about the Hirschfeld Centre, you know, to see movies and documentaries about, you know – at the time, we had no internet, you know, so it was like seeing things about places far away, about the gay community, and really, I suppose you know, San Francisco and the whole Harvey Milk thing really informed the gay community on, you know, about rights and what we should do et cetera ... So, yeah, Harvey Milk, Hirschfeld Centre, that whole thing was – really was part of my – it was part of, I suppose, my own personal liberation movement for myself ...[36]

There can be no doubt that these activities were extremely popular amongst NGF members. However, the NGF also recognised that these activities were primarily frequented by those who were, for the most part, relatively comfortable in their sexuality or were at least coping better than others. Many Irish gay and lesbian individuals were not coping well and there was a realisation that something needed to be done to help them. This was particularly the case with those under 18 who were prohibited from joining the NGF. Outside of telephoning the Samaritans or Tel-A-Friend, there were few outlets for young Irish gay and lesbian individuals. Trying to help those of 18 and younger caused some headache for the NGF, but there were some like Bernard Keogh who believed that the NGF had a moral obligation to try to help younger individuals. Keogh was aware that providing a space for gay youths could result in the NGF coming in for heavy criticism from conservative forces who would argue that they were out to corrupt the youth of Ireland and convert them to homosexuality.[37] The gay adolescent was seen by some, Keogh wrote, as 'living proof in the public's eye that gay people are out to recruit the young and that they succeed in doing so'.[38]

Despite the obvious pitfalls, Keogh, with the support of Chris Heaume of the London Gay Teenage Group, sought to convince the NGF Administrative Council not to turn its back on those under 18.[39] Drawing on the experience of international gay youth groups like the London Gay Teenage Group and Gay and Young in New York, Keogh produced a fifty-five page report on the merits of setting up a youth group.[40] The report covered topics such as 'adolescent breakdown', 'it's only a phase, isn't it?' and 'the claim of recruitment'. Keogh's report argued that a 'youth group would provide the young person with a validation not usually available to him in the wider society ... [and] provide an environment where these young people could relate to each other in a relaxed supportive atmosphere ...'.[41] In many respects, Keogh's report was as much a blueprint for how the NGF could respond to criticism from opponents as it was a case for the establishment of a gay youth group. But in the context of this period, Keogh's report was exactly the type of reassurance that the NGF needed. In late 1979 a majority of the NGF Administrative Council voted to support the establishment of an NGF youth group; however, it implemented strict rules to safeguard not only the youths attending the Hirschfeld Centre, but also the NGF's reputation.[42] During the youth group's meetings every Sunday from 3p.m.–6p.m., access was restricted to those under 21. With the exception of Keogh, who became the liaison officer for the NGF youth group, every other member of the NGF was prohibited from using the centre during those times.[43]

The NGF youth group's main objective was to foster a spirit of mutual validation among its members and to provide facilities for young gay and lesbian individuals to meet socially in a peer group environment.[44] Within two years, it had successfully affiliated to *Comhairle Le Leas Óige* (Dublin Youth Service), which awarded them a £200 grant.[45] This grant, however, was strongly condemned by some high-profile individuals who felt the money should not have been awarded to a gay group. The *Irish Independent* reported that Tom Holt, a member of the Dublin Vocational Education Committee, of which *Comhairle Le Leas Óige* was a sub-committee, condemned the grant on the basis that:

> The money should be used properly and especially for children taking part in manly games. Mr. Holt warned that by approving grants to these types of groups, the VEC was failing in its big responsibility in the forming of the character of young people. By giving financial support to groups like this we are not helping to form characters but to deform them.[46]

Holt was supported by Larry McMahon, a *Fine Gael* TD, who argued that gay and lesbian individuals were 'misguided and sick people and the money should be spent putting them back on the right road'.[47] Despite these protestations the director of *Comhairle Le Leas Óige*, Michael McGee, defended the NGF youth group receiving the grant and they continued to be an affiliated member until 1986 when, for reasons unknown, *Comhairle Le Leas Óige* refused to re-register the group.[48]

The NGF youth group sought to involve itself in the efforts to change negative attitudes like those expressed by Holt and McMahon. One of the means it sought to do so was through its Open Days held on the last Sunday of every month. The Open Day offered the NGF youth group the opportunity to invite family, friends and outside organisations to the Hirschfeld Centre to discuss issues related to homosexuality. At one Open Day a discussion took place on 'counselling' with representatives of the Samaritans, Hope, Contact, TAF and the National Youth Council of Ireland all invited to participate.[49] Derek Moloney, who was a member of the NGF youth group in the 1980s, remembers another discussion took place on what it takes to be a parent, recalling that 'we had this fantastic session on what does it take to be a parent because if some parents were wonderful about it and some parents weren't so wonderful about it, you'd tend to have judgements, and we had to go through a thought process of how a parent learns being a parent, and a person learns their sexuality'.[50]

The impact one's sexuality could have on their relationship with their parents was a key concern for many gay and lesbian individuals in the Republic of Ireland, with many fearing their parents would disown them if they disclosed their sexuality. This reality was evident in an interview Philip, an NGF youth group member, gave to *The Irish Times* in 1980. During the course of that interview, Philip was referred to as the 'gay with parents', a nod to the fact that many individuals were disowned by their parents once they disclosed their sexuality.[51] On a visit to Dublin in June 1980, Rose Robertson (Parents Enquiry) explained that 'after isolation and the suffering of coming to terms with their homosexuality ... the biggest problem for children is fear of their parents' reaction'.[52] Easing the pressure of coming out to one's parents was something Philip revealed was a priority for the NGF youth group, telling *The Irish Times* that they hoped to establish a Parents Enquiry Group in the Republic of Ireland. With the support of Rose Robertson and the NGF, the NGF youth group played a central role in establishment of an Irish branch of Parents Enquiry in 1982.

Phil Moore, a founding member of Parents Enquiry, recalled how they 'spoke in schools, we spoke at universities, we spoke at meetings. We talked our heads off to papers and, you know, all over the country ... People would come to me and I'd meet them, and we'd talk and chat, usually in a pub or coffee, Bewley's or some place. And they would tell their stories.'[53] One of the first media interviews Moore gave was to the *Evening Herald* in November 1983, during which she recalled how when her son revealed he was gay, she and her husband first felt like they were 'going to drown in a huge wave of misery', not realising beforehand how 'many horrible myths and prejudices' they had about gay and lesbian individuals.[54] However, after talking with their son, they realised 'just what was important. We love our son. He hasn't changed. He's happy. So why shouldn't we accept it?' Addressing parents specifically in the interview, Moore offered the following advice should their son or daughter disclose that they are gay:

> Well if you are lucky and your child approaches you and says I'm gay I hope you will realise that what he/she is asking is – Will you still love me even though I'm gay? I'm sure for most parents that will be true. And please accept what they tell you. If they say they are gay, they are as sure as anyone can be of their preferred sexual orientation.[55]

Walt Kilroy, whose mother Patricia Kilroy was an active member of Parents Enquiry, recalled how Parents Enquiry did a fantastic job in spreading the message of love and acceptance and 'what matters isn't whether your son or daughter is gay, it's are they going to be happy, are they going to live a good and fulfilled life? And they did terrific work in reaching parts of Irish society that you couldn't reach by marching on the streets, although they marched on the streets as well.'[56]

Parents Enquiry became a core group of the NGF's Welfare and Counselling Service set-up in June 1983. This service formed part of the NGF's efforts to provide a comprehensive service to gay and lesbian individuals in the Republic of Ireland.[57] This reflected the absence of such services specifically for gay and lesbian individuals within the broader society. The NGF was fortunate that some of its members were trained professionals who helped run the Welfare and Counselling Service, which provided advice on issues such as: social welfare and health services; housing and flat problems; legal and medical problems; as well as personal issues such as relationship difficulties, self-acceptance, loneliness, anxiety, fear and alcoholism. Carl Berkeley, a counsellor, took over the responsibility of running the service with the support of two other professionals: a social worker specialising in dealing with the difficulties of coming out to spouses, parents and other family members, and Freddie Smyth, a counsellor specialising in problems with alcoholism.

Alcoholism in particular was highlighted as a problem for many Irish lesbians. At the first International Lesbian conference in Amsterdam in December 1980, members of Liberation for Irish Lesbians (LIL) highlighted two issues in particular that were of concern for Irish lesbians: custody of their children; and alcoholism.[58] The latter issue was later discussed at the Second National Gay Conference held at Trinity College Dublin in June 1982, where a workshop on gays and alcoholism was held. Those in attendance felt that the facilitates for dealing with alcoholism in Ireland were heterosexually orientated and something needed to be done to help gay and lesbian individuals. Following this workshop, a Gay Alcoholics Anonymous Group was established, contactable through TAF.[59]

One of the objectives of the Second National Gay Conference had been to explore the relationship between lesbian women and gay men and how they could best work together. Joint workshops were organised between women and men to discuss, amongst others, the issue of sexism. While there had been optimism before the conference, a women's report revealed considerable disappointment afterwards, noting that 'apart from a minority of gay men who had made some effort to tackle their own sexism, the bulk were either aggressively defensive, or blissfully unaware of their own oppressive role in a patriarchal society'.[60] Since the foundation of the IGRM in 1974, the gay rights movement had been dominated by gay men, with the membership of the IGRM and NGF overwhelmingly male. The fact that the issue of sexism and the relationship between lesbian women and gay men had been discussed at the Second National Gay Conference owed much to the efforts of Liberation for Irish Lesbians.

While the IGRM crumbled due to infighting, some lesbian women, many of whom had been involved with the IGRM, came together seeking a means of furthering a greater awareness and understanding of lesbian sexuality in the Republic of Ireland. One of the defining moments for Irish lesbians in the 1970s had been the organisation of Ireland's first women's conference on lesbianism at TCD in May 1978. Later that year a meeting took place at the Resources Centre in Ratgar, at which Joni Crone (aka Joni Sheerin), Liz Noonan, Ruth Jacobs, Mary Dorcey, Majella, Mary, Carol and Phil (a lesbian mother with five children) all attended. It was decided at this meeting that it was now time to work for the liberation of Irish lesbians.[61] Thus, Liberation for Irish Lesbians (LIL) was born in 1978.[62]

'Lesbians, Ireland's sexual exiles'

In 1979, *GPU News* reported Sheerin as stating that 'Liberation for Irish lesbians is a political sounding name and it represents our highest aspiration. It sounds as if we'd be out on the streets tomorrow. We're not quite ready for that yet – but the day will come. Now we have something to build from and co-operation with men for the first time ever. That's a great step forward.'[63] LIL's optimism was evident in Sheerin's comment, but so too was the pragmatism. LIL was all too aware of the difficulties lesbian women had to overcome in a society that did not even acknowledge lesbian women existed. For this very reason the foundation of a specific lesbian group was important. By naming the new group Liberation for Irish Lesbians, LIL drew attention to the fact that Irish and lesbian were not mutually exclusive.

Following the establishment of the NGF in 1979, David Norris invited LIL to affiliate to the NGF, which LIL accepted. This was a pragmatic decision on LIL's part. By affiliating to the NGF, LIL could remain an independent organisation while availing of the space and services within the Hirschfeld Centre. Moreover, this invitation permitted LIL to nominate members to the NGF Administrative Council in the hope that it would give LIL greater autonomy and influence within the organisation and the running of the Hirschfeld Centre.[64] LIL's first priority, therefore, was to try to create a welcoming space for lesbian women within the Hirschfeld Centre, then an overwhelmingly male-dominated venue. Of the 1,027 members registered with the NGF in 1980, 983 were men and only 44 were women.[65] In fact, there were no women NGF members outside Dublin.

LIL sought to create a 'forum for discussion of women's issues and lesbians' gay political ideas, [while also seeking to offer a] social environment where lesbians can meet and simply be themselves'.[66] Working along similar lines to their male counterparts, LIL sought to reach out to lonely and isolated lesbian women, while also seeking to provide a space for them to socialise. Their first success was obtaining the use of the Hirschfeld Centre for women-only socials every Wednesday night from 8p.m.–10p.m. They also secured the use of TAF every Wednesday for women only, later renaming that service Lesbian Line. While the number of women contacting TAF was smaller than the number of gay men, with only sixteen women contacting the service from 1981 to 1982 compared to 261 men for the same period, LIL gradually built up awareness of the service amongst women in Ireland.[67] By 1984, *The Irish Times* reported that an average of fifteen calls a night were made to the Lesbian Line.[68] Those who volunteered with the Lesbian Line recalled that women rang to talk about 'the women they love ... depression and suicide attempts. They talk about parents, husbands, children and work. They want to know about being lesbian – are we happy? Is it possible? Is there anyone else like them?'[69]

While LIL was able to arrange these activities within the Hirschfeld Centre, a problem they faced was getting women to attend. Although some did, many others did not. Sheerin put this down to: 'Firstly, the sheer size of the place is off-putting to a newcomer. Secondly, the presence of hundreds of men at a weekend disco and only the odd woman here and there, again is not very encouraging to women members or guests.'[70] This reality led LIL to also organise events outside the Hirschfeld Centre. In March 1980, for example, they began organising a women's social at the Parliament Inn, on Parliament Street, every Friday and Saturday. Within just a few months, forty members had registered with LIL for the women's disco with expectations high that by August 1980 this number would reach seventy.[71] The opening of a new women's only disco meant that women now had more choice than in previous years, with women-only discos organised at the Parliament Inn, Hirschfeld Centre and the Phoenix Club. In 1981, LIL moved from the Parliament Inn to J. J. Smyth's on Aungier Street, which became a popular space for women throughout the 1980s. According to Pauline O'Donnell, J. J.'s was 'like a home for gay women for about fifteen years', recalling that:

> what was really wonderful at those discos on a Saturday night in J.J.'s, was women coming together, we'd all join a big circle, and the most popular song, I suppose at the time in the early years was Cris Williamson's, 'Song of the Soul'... So, there was a great feeling of belonging to a community.[72]

This was a view shared by Gráinne Healy, who remembered J. J.'s as a 'place that you could be yourself'. Healy also recalled how after J. J.'s the women would head to house parties that usually went on until the following Sunday evening, describing these as 'good times'.[73] Both Healy and O'Donnell's reflections on J. J.'s highlight the significance of LIL organising events outside male-dominated venues and their role in fostering a lesbian community in the Republic of Ireland.

During Healy's aforementioned interview in 2013, she recalled one particular moment in the 1980s which was 'wow' for her, that of watching Joni Crone being interviewed by Gay Byrne on RTÉ's *The Late Late Show* in February 1980.[74] Healy described how she was 'stuck to the sofa, watching it with all my family and thinking, my God, that she's so brave.'[75] In appearing on *The Late Late Show*, Crone sought to raise the visibility of lesbian women in Irish society, while at the same time trying to challenge the ignorance surrounding lesbian sexuality. The extent of the task Crone had set for herself was summed up by an audience member who, on seeing Crone, remarked that 'she doesn't look like a lesbian'.[76]

Similar to her counterparts in 1975 and 1977, Crone confidently discussed the difficulties of coming to the stage where she could come out publicly and speak positively about her sexuality. She declared to Byrne that 'I'm gay and I'm proud, I'm not abnormal, I'm not sick, I'm not perverted, I'm happy, I'm a human being like anybody else, I just happen to have a different sexual orientation than you.'[77] Rather than seeing her sexuality as a problem, Crone highlighted that she had found love, caring friends, support from her family and was enjoying success in her career, even as an out lesbian. Her sexuality, she maintained, was only one facet of her life. She was happy with it and it was for society to change, not her. Crone's confidence and acceptance of her sexuality had taken a long time, revealing that she had gone through 'ten years of pain, confusion, ignorance about what I am, so have my family, so have my friends and I know an enormous amount of women who are going through the same thing ... I thought I was the only one in the world'.[78]

The public reaction to Crone's appearance was mixed. One caller commended her, stating that 'if every heterosexual was as sincere and honest as that lady, the world would be a much happier place.'[79] Another stated that 'she came across as a very nice person and will surely help many people of both sexes'. Others, however, lambasted RTÉ, with one caller complaining that Byrne 'had a prostitute on last week and he insults us further by bringing on a lesbian'.[80] *The Irish Times* also reported that a member of Parents and Friends of the Mentally Handicapped had sent a letter to RTÉ condemning the interview.[81] The League of Decency viewed Crone's interview as 'the latest RTÉ attack on Catholic morality'.[82] Leslie Quelch, president of the League of Decency, feared that the show had 'pushed lesbianism as being normal' and could have 'a bad effect on girls and young women'.[83] During her interview, Crone had explained that one of her intentions in appearing on the show was to dispel the ignorance surrounding homosexuality. It would seem that she had succeeded to some degree in trying to normalise it, so much so that it raised concerns within the League of Decency.

Perhaps, however, the biggest impact of Crone's interview was on lesbian women who watched it and felt a weight lifted off their shoulders knowing that they were not alone. As we have seen already, Healy remembered the positive impact Crone's interview had on her, while Majella Breen noted how her appearance encouraged 'quite a few women to ring up our TAF service with enquiries'.[84] One of those women was Máire Ní Bheagliach, who remembered that 'Joni's coming out on *The Late Late Show* had a more dramatic effect and as a result of this I contacted the NGF, read some literature and met my first lesbians, who surprised me by being very ordinary! Life would never be the same again.'[85]

Crone's appearance on *The Late Late Show* coincided with a period in which some lesbian women were willing to be more public about their sexuality. Only a few months after Crone's interview, TCD hosted the first lesbian conference in Ireland in June 1980. The naming of this conference as a lesbian conference was significant. In contrast to the 1978 conference at TCD, which was titled a 'women's conference on lesbianism', the 1980 conference was specifically advertised as a lesbian conference. Crone explained that the reason the 1978 conference was called a women's conference on lesbianism was because 'we realised that if we called the event a "lesbian conference" most of the organising collective would be unable to attend because walking through the door would be a public statement ... Our compromise solution was to call the weekend a Women's Conference on Lesbianism. This meant that women of every sexual persuasion were free to attend.'[86] From the outset then, the organisers of the 1980 conference clearly believed that more women would be willing to attend a conference specifically advertised as a lesbian conference.

The 1980 lesbian conference focused on five main issues: coming out, sexuality, relationships, isolation and lesbian mothers.[87] The issue of lesbian mothers in particular appeared to be a concern for Irish lesbian women. As noted previously, it had been raised as an issue at the first International Lesbian conference in Amsterdam. According to Mary (LIL):

in Ireland and England there had been a number of cases over the past few years where divorced women have wanted to retain custody of their own children. Usually, in these countries women are awarded custody of their children, because women usually have responsibility for children. But if a woman is a lesbian, the usual procedure is suddenly reversed. Then it is considered better for the children if the father is given custody.[88]

The reality of this injustice was revealed in *Out for Ourselves* by Máire Ní Bheagliach, who revealed that she 'couldn't apply for custody of the children because of the homophobia of the legal profession when it suits it. Having tried the law and failed the only thing for me to do now is to brazen it out and expose them as much as possible.'[89] Later, in 1982, Action of Lesbian Mothers was set up at the Second National Gay Conference 'to enable lesbian mothers to get together to talk and to act as a pressure group for change in custody procedures and to support individual women, if they wish'.[90] Mary Kinnane stated that Action for Lesbian Mothers is 'a women's group who see the area of lesbians with children as sadly neglected.'[91]

The year 1982 was an eventful year for lesbian women in the Republic of Ireland. In October a second lesbian conference took place at the Dublin Women's Centre, at which eighty-two women registered and over 140 later attended a late-night disco in Newman's House.[92] Crucially, this conference generated media attention. One of the organisers, Annie Dillon (LIL), was interviewed for RTÉ's *Women Today* and for an hour-long Radio Leinster segment on 'lesbianism and gay politics', while the *Sunday World* featured an article on what it was like being a lesbian in Ireland or, as they described them, 'Ireland's sexual exiles'.[93] The *Sunday World* article featured an interview with three LIL members (Liz, Mary and Claire), who were only in a position to reveal their first names for fear of outing themselves and losing their jobs. Liz called on readers 'to understand and accept lesbianism for what it is – a lifestyle, not a perverted sexual preference'. In a poignant conclusion to the article all three explained that all they were asking for was 'acceptance and the right to choose our own lifestyle in society. The three of us are from rural areas and our parents don't know that we are lesbian. We hope that in years to come lesbians will be able to come out totally and say that they are lesbian without fear of losing parental respect and endangering their jobs'.[94]

That same year had also seen Liz Noonan, a founding member of LIL, run as an independent lesbian feminist candidate in the Dublin South East constituency in the February general election. Although Noonan was not elected, her 309 votes saw her receive the highest number of first preference votes of any other independent candidate who ran in that constituency. This was impressive considering that Noonan's manifesto was radical within the context of the period. Her election posters proudly declared that she was a 'lesbian feminist' who was campaigning for divorce, abortion, women's centres, contraception and the end of violence against women. In a short feature on Noonan's campaign, the *Sunday Independent* described her as 'one of the more colourful and outspoken candidates . . . [who] made an issue of her sexuality in this election . . .'[95] According to Liz's election agent, Ruth Jacobs (another founding member of LIL and Ruth's partner), despite the radical nature of her manifesto 'the reaction to Liz both on the doorstep and in the street has been very positive indeed. We met with no harm or abuse whatsoever.'[96]

Like Crone, Liz Noonan and Ruth Jacobs were unafraid to speak publicly about their sexuality. In an interview two years later with Caroline Walsh for *The Irish Times*, Noonan and Jacobs spoke openly about their relationship, becoming, to my knowledge, the first lesbian couple to declare their relationship publicly in the Republic of Ireland (*The Irish Times* included a picture of Jacobs and Noonan together).[97] Jacobs proudly declared that 'making love with another woman is very beautiful. As a lesbian I don't measure lovemaking by orgasms. It doesn't have a beginning or an end. It's kind of a communication that is there between us and it's there as much in a look or a touch of the hand as in giving each other sexual pleasure.'[98] The openness with which Noonan and Jacobs discussed their sexuality and relationship was not something Irish society would have been accustomed to, particularly when it related to two women. Nevertheless, theirs was a positive story that no doubt was welcomed by Irish lesbian women.

In the space of a few short years, therefore, LIL had helped raise the profile of lesbian women in the Republic of Ireland. However, this had not been without its difficulties. Inside the Hirschfeld Centre, LIL and the NGF did not always see eye to eye. In September 1979, for example, the minutes of an NGF Administrative Council meeting reveal that Bernard Keogh was asked to send a letter to Joni seeking reasons as to 'why the women should hold on to Wednesday nights?' and to inform them that on special occasions such as Halloween, national holidays, etc., 'the Wednesday night will become flexible'.[99] This attitude to the women-only nights later led Majella Breen to tell Chris Kirk that within the Hirschfeld Centre 'women in her group can't feel that it's as much "our place as the men do"'.[100]

LIL were not afraid to defend what they believed was their right to a women's-only space within the Hirschfeld Centre. Following three occasions in 1981 when the women's night social had been cancelled, LIL sent a strongly worded letter to the NGF Administrative Council setting out their grievances. These incidents, LIL claimed, had undermined the credibility of the women's group in the eyes of both new and old members.[101] To rectify this they called for certain safeguards to be implemented, which included that the 'administrative council does not sanction alternative activities on Women's Night without prior consultation with, and agreement from the representatives of the Women's Group.' These safeguards were agreed to by the NGF Administrative Council, who would now give at least one month's notice to LIL of any proposed alternative event on Women's Night.[102]

While the NGF was willing to cede to LIL's requests in 1981, they were not as willing to cede to others. In July 1982, Joni Crone and Majella Breen proposed that the NGF should affiliate to the Women's Right to Choose Campaign (WRTCC).[103] Breen, speaking in favour of the motion, argued that the 'campaign concerned itself with the basic right of the individual to control over [their] own body, the campaign was quite directly associated to gay liberation in that many lesbians were mothers of children and the issue affected them dearly'.[104] Although the NGF council supported the motion at this meeting, it never followed through with its support. In fact, the proposal set in motion a heated debate within the wider NGF, culminating one year later in the reversal of this decision – much to the resentment of some LIL members.

The arguments for and against affiliation boiled down to whether or not a woman's right to choose was a gay rights issue and whether or not affiliation would benefit the NGF. Whereas Crone and Breen were adamant that a woman's right to choose was a gay rights issue, for Bernard Keogh affiliation to the WRTCC:

> would be enormously damaging both for NGF and for gay rights, that we should never again enjoy the same credibility within the media as commentators on gay affairs that the public's willingness to give a fair hearing to the gay rights cause will be dismissed – in short – that we will have thrown away advantages in these areas that we have earned only through long years of hard, patient work.[105]

Keogh was clearly of the belief that affiliating to the WRTCC would jeopardise the NGF's 'credibility' and weaken their position as commentators on gay issues, a view he was not alone in sharing. This followed the logic that abortion was extremely divisive in the Republic of Ireland, which it was. Within the NGF, no other issue proved as controversial, with some members even threatening to withdraw their membership if the NGF affiliated. Such was the predicament that the NGF Administrative Council had found themselves in, that they had decided to ballot members on whether or not it should affiliate to the WRTCC. Of the 400 ballot papers sent out at the beginning of 1983, 110 were returned, with 58 voting in favour and 52 voting against.[106] Despite a slim majority in favour, the NGF Administrative Council opted not to affiliate to the WRTCC.[107] No reason was given as to why the NGF opted against affiliation. Clearly, however, arguments put forward by Bernard Keogh and others proved more persuasive than those put forward by proponents of affiliation such as Crone and Breen.

Crone later wrote that 'this betrayal of lesbian and heterosexual women who had campaigned previously for gay male law reform resulted in lesbians leaving the NGF. And it was the last time that many of us chose to work in any official capacity in solidarity with gay men.'[108] While there was disappointment within LIL over this decision, it must be noted that LIL and the NGF did work well together on many other activities, in particular the organisation of Ireland's first gay pride week celebrations.

'70 faggots and dykes all bedecked with pink carnations'

The debate within the NGF over affiliating to the WRTCC took place during a one-year period in which the vulnerability of Ireland's gay community was most apparent. The period between 1982 and 1983 saw the brutal killing of two gay men, Charles Self (killed in his home) and Declan Flynn (beaten to death in Fairview Park), in January and September 1982 respectively. The subsequent police inquiry into the killing of Self saw almost 1,500 gay men interviewed, with the police turning up at many individuals' homes and workplaces, thereby outing some to work colleagues, friends and family.[109] Such was the anger amongst some within the gay community that they formed a Gay Defence Committee and picketed the Pearse Street Garda Station in Dublin city centre. This group, comprising amongst others Cathal Kerrigan, Melissa Murray, Maura Molloy, Mick Quinlan, Clodagh Boyd, Bill Foley and Christopher Robson, later established the Dublin Gay Collective (DGC) in June 1982, describing itself as a 'mixed collective of progressive gay people with a definite activist orientation'.[110]

The DGC was critical of the IGRM and NGF, describing both organisations as having 'a very real fear of being political because it might draw unfavourable attention from the gardaí and the media'.[111] The distrust felt by some towards the police was heightened in April 1982, when *The Irish Times* reported that Jack Marrinan, general secretary of the Garda Representative Association, declared that 'the values of society had taken a plunge in recent years with people like homosexuals and pro-abortionists demanding rights ...', thereby creating, according to Marrinan, an atmosphere in which 'crime thrives'.[112] Worse, however, was when those responsible for killing Declan Flynn (no one has been brought to justice for the killing of Charles Self) were only found guilty of manslaughter and controversially given suspended five-year sentences in March 1983. This verdict was handed down despite the five youths having admitted that they were 'part of a team to get rid of queers from Fairview Park'.[113]

The killing of Declan Flynn and the subsequent verdict is widely accepted as a watershed moment in Irish queer history and the primary impetus for the first major gay rights protest march held in March 1983, and later the organisation of a pride protest march in June that same year. There can be no doubt that Flynn's killing, and the verdict, were major factors in the organisation of these marches, but it must also be acknowledged that the June 1983 gay pride protest march was not the first time gay pride had been celebrated in the Republic of Ireland. In fact, since 1979 the NGF and LIL had been organising week-long gay pride celebrations, yet they have been overlooked because a parade/march did not take place. However, these gay pride celebrations also contributed to paving the way for a more public manifestation of gay pride in June 1983. In many respects, they were precursors to the June 1983 gay pride protest march.

On 25 June 1979, the *Irish Press* reported that 'on Thursday next, Dublin citizens will find a number of their fellow-citizens sporting triangles. If in their curiosity they ask the meaning of this symbol they will be told that it celebrates "Gay Pride Week", that is, that it asserts an acceptance of and even pride in being homosexual.'[114] The Republic of Ireland's first gay pride week celebration took place from the 25 June to 1 July 1979 in the Hirschfeld Centre and included a political forum at the Hirschfeld Centre with Michael Keating (*Fine Gael*), Niall Andrews (*Fianna Fáil*), Ruairí Quinn (Labour Party) and Noel Browne; a leafletting campaign at the top of Grafton Street; a fancy dress ball at Flikkers; a women's night; a public picnic in the Phoenix Park; and a pub zap. Announcing their week-long celebration, the NGF and LIL called on those members who could afford to, i.e., those who would not lose their job or their home, to wear a pink triangle or pink carnation, visible international symbols of gay pride. They also encouraged those who felt ready to use gay pride week as an opportunity to come out to their family, friends and work colleagues.[115]

Between 1979 and 1982, the NGF/LIL's gay pride week celebrations varied, with events ranging from a Gala Night, an outing to Glendalough, art exhibitions, jumble sales, poetry readings, film nights, folk music sessions, a fundraiser for David Norris' legal battle, discos, and leafleting on Dublin streets.[116] During 1981 gay pride week, for example, *The Irish Times* reported that the NGF unveiled a pink triangle outside the

Hirschfeld Centre as a tribute to all those who died during the Holocaust.[117] Two events, however, that were regular features of the week-long gay pride celebrations were the public picnics and pub zaps. The picnics, which took place on the last day of the gay pride week, were an opportunity to bring gay pride into the open, with many individuals sporting pride badges, pink triangles or pink carnations. Tonie Walsh, writing about the 1980 gay pride picnic at Merrion Square, remarked that 'if one could only visualise seventy faggots and dykes all bedecked with pink carnations and triangles squatting on the grass in the middle of a public park! The sun shone down in all its glory on beaming happy faces and everyone, I think, enjoyed themselves immensely.'[118]

The pub zap, on the other hand, was more provocative, involving gay and lesbian individuals wearing a pink carnation or pride badge and going into as many bars as possible to see how long it would take before they were asked to leave. The NGF explained that 'in a pub zap gays seem to lose by winning. That is we may force people to think about the gay issue but suffer rejection as a result. In that sense, these annual booze-ups are ideally named: ZAP.'[119] One individual who spoke to *Gay News* after being ejected from Tobin's bar during the 1979 pub zap stated that the pub 'seems to be used by people who would faint at the sight of a gay badge. The place is a haven for closet cases who seem upset whenever anyone comes out. It was only to be expected, I suppose. They haven't seen the last of us yet. It's about time a touch of gay pride crept into a bar like this.'[120] During the 1982 pub zap individuals were refused service in five out of the eight pubs that they visited.[121]

Although no gay pride parade took place between 1979 and 1982, these week-long celebrations did, as we have seen, generate media attention. From as early as June 1979, *The Irish Times*, *Evening Herald*, *Irish Independent*, *In Dublin* and *Hot Press* had all covered or advertised the gay pride week celebrations. Some publications even sought to provide readers with an insight into the concept and origins of gay pride. In 1981, for example, *The Irish Times* published an article by Carl Berkeley on gay pride, in which he explained that:

> Gay Pride is a reaction to the many years of Gay Shame, that most gay people have experienced ... We do not ask for special treatment, we only ask for our rights – rights which most people do not have to ask for, such as the right to work in whatever job we please, the right to live with the person we choose to live with and the right to play our full part in society.[122]

By 1982, therefore, gay pride had entered Irish public consciousness to some degree; it was in 1983, however, that it took on an even higher consciousness. As noted previously, the March 1983 verdict on the Declan Flynn killing generated anger within Ireland's gay community. Recalling this verdict in 2019, Marina Forrestal remembered how she was 'so upset and I was raging, I was raging at what could happen to us ... There was no consequences to even the murder of one of us.'[123] Such was the rage and anger within the gay community, that it was decided to hold a protest march on 19 March 1983. The Dublin Gay Collective, who led the efforts to organise a march, were joined by the NGF, LIL, the Cork Gay Collective and Parents Enquiry as well as the Union of Students in Ireland, People's Democracy, Socialist Worker's Movement,

Sinn Féin, the Irish Republican Socialist Party, Democratic Socialists and the Rape Crisis Centre.

The march began from Liberty Hall and ended in Fairview Park. Along the way, marchers carried banners that declared: 'Gays are Human', 'Gays have the right to Life' and 'Stop Violence against Gays and Women'.[124] The number of individuals reported to have marched was 400, but the organisers claimed a figure closer to 1,000. Even if the 400 figure is to be accepted, this still represents a significant turn-out for the first mass demonstration on gay rights. The march itself was headline news in many of Ireland's mainstream publications, including the *Sunday World*, *Evening Herald*, *Sunday Independent*, *Sunday Press* and *The Irish Times*, while *Gay News* also covered it.[125] Speaking to marchers in Fairview Park, Cathal Kerrigan declared that the 'violence we had marched against was not restricted to one park for gays anymore than it was restricted to a few dark streets for women. Sexual violence was everywhere, an everyday occurrence which this patriarchal capitalist society had not only managed to accommodate but deliberately tolerate as a form of social control.'[126] The march, Kerrigan continued, was not an isolated event, but rather it was only the start of a new campaign for lesbian and gay rights.[127] The organisers of the Fairview March had also sought to highlight the violence faced by women, reflecting the feminist and anti-patriarchal outlook of many members of the DGC. The DGC, NGF, LIL and the Cork Gay Collective were then actively involved with the Anti-Amendment Campaign (AAC), which fought to prevent a constitutional ban on abortion. The Hirschfeld Centre was used on a number of occasions to hold fundraisers for the AAC and many of those who marched to Fairview Park were affiliated to the AAC and sought to lend their support to the gay community in return.

The Fairview Park Protest March was a symbolic moment for Ireland's gay community and provided many with the confidence to take to the streets to challenge and confront the treatment of gay and lesbian individuals. Patrick O'Byrne explained how he wasn't really someone who marched 'but the one time I did go on a march with a lot of people was when Declan Flynn was murdered in Fairview Park. And it was very important then to be seen publicly to be outraged at what happened there, and the way the murderer/murderers basically got off scot-free. So, that was one of the times that I did.'[128]

The Fairview Park Protest March also provided the momentum and confidence to organise a gay pride protest march on 25 June 1983; the first of its kind in Ireland since the 27 June 1974 SLM gay pride demonstration outside the British Embassy in Dublin and the Department of Justice. In an announcement in *The Irish Times* preceding the protest march, Noel Walsh, a member of the NGF's parade steering committee (LIL and DGC were also part of the steering committee), explained that the march was being organised to 'celebrate this pride in our identity, but also to protest at the lack of humanity and equality shown to lesbians and gay men'.[129] From the outset, then, organisers sought to highlight that this was a protest, rather than simply a celebratory parade. The marchers assembled at St Stephen's Green, where the march began at 3p.m, stopping at important landmarks such as the General Post Office, before culminating at The Garden Remembrance.[130] One of those marchers was Tonie Walsh, who later recalled the significance of the 1983 gay pride protest march:

> I will never ever forget, to the day I die, that feeling, 200 of us, walking down through newly pedestrianised Grafton Street from the Fusiliers Arch through Grafton Street and then that wonderful moment when you're walking Westmoreland Street, and the vista opens up, and you get that great expanse of the river, and then you're into O'Connell Street, and there was this just – I mean, even now when I think about, I just get a lump in my throat and I just – there's this great sense of fierce acclamation and that you've arrived somehow as you are walking into Dublin's main elegant thoroughfare. And there we were, this raggle-taggle bunch from Belfast, Cork and Dublin, only a few months after the horror of the Declan Flynn murder and the protest march ... We came across a stand that had been set up for the National Children's Day parade that was going to be held the next day. And, of course, everybody, being opportunistic lesbians and gay men, decided to take over the stand outside the GPO. We put up some banners and everything else and then we made our speeches ... I remember we stopped the traffic, and the police were there, and the police were on tenterhooks about how to deal with us because it was the first time there had ever been a big public pride event.[131]

It is evident from Walsh's reflection that even after thirty years the emotion and sense of pride he felt marching with 200 other gay and lesbian individuals still remains. It is also clear just how significant Walsh viewed this event, an event which for him, signified that gay and lesbian individuals had 'arrived somehow' and were claiming their space on the major streets of Dublin's city centre. The 1983 gay pride protest march was a defiant statement after the sentences handed down in the Declan Flynn killing. Interestingly, however, this gay pride protest march does not appear to have been reported in any of Ireland's mainstream nationals.

The Dublin gay pride parades, however, were short-lived. While two more took place in 1984 and 1985, with smaller numbers, there would not be another thereafter until 1992. This coincided with efforts to respond to the emerging AIDS epidemic in the Republic of Ireland, which became particularly prominent from 1985 onwards. With an Irish government unwilling to recognise the severity of the developing AIDS situation, the efforts to counteract its spread and devastating impact fell squarely on the shoulders of Ireland's gay community. The year 1985, in many respects, was a mixed year for the NGF and LIL. One of the high points was the NGF youth group's successful staging of the 2nd International Gay Youth Congress in July 1985, only made possible after the European Youth Foundation awarded the NGF youth group FF66,000 to hold the congress. Attempts to secure funding from similar organisations in the Republic of Ireland were unsuccessful. The congress saw over fifty delegates from the Netherlands, Denmark, Norway, Great Britain and the USA descend upon the Hirschfeld Centre to discuss issues such as: 'Problems of Gay Youth Groups', 'Sex and Sexuality', 'AIDS and Gay Health', and 'Gay Youth Internationally'.[132] Tonie Walsh, then NGF president, described the Congress as one of the most memorable events in the six-year history of the Hirschfeld Centre.[133]

However, 1985 was also the year that LIL disbanded. Since 1983 LIL had been dwindling as an organisation, with many involved becoming fatigued and few newcomers coming on board. LIL's 1984 report revealed that 'no major developments of a positive nature can be reported ... The collective which was shrinking at that stage has been further depleted, those who still remain are finding it increasingly difficult to even run the regular Thursday night disco at the Hirschfeld.'[134] LIL was last listed as an organisation in the June/July 1985 issue of *OUT*. Thereafter, the priority for lesbian women was maintaining the Lesbian Line, which they did successfully.

Gay paree of Dublin

Nicole E. Roberts has argued that as visibility of gay and lesbian individuals and their demands increased in San Francisco, so too did the voices of those opposed to homosexuality.[135] In the Republic of Ireland, the situation was similar. As we have seen already, organisations such as Parents and Friends of the Mentally Handicapped and The League of Decency had condemned Joni Crone's appearance on *The Late Late Show*, while Jack Marrinan had blamed the increase in crime on the demand for gay rights. Others who spoke out during this period did so in the belief that the gay rights movement was a threat to the family and young people. In his address to the Christian Family Movement on the importance of the family, the Bishop of Ferns, Brendan Comiskey, went so far as to label homosexuality as an enemy of the family. Along with abortion, contraception and divorce, Comiskey argued that 'another enemy would be the efforts to equate the family with other so-called social units, such as homosexual marriages and relationships'.[136] All these issues, Comiskey maintained, were examples of the 'Christian family under attack'.[137]

Comiskey was not alone in viewing homosexuality as a threat. Earlier that year, *Our Family*, which described itself as a publication dedicated to the traditional family, printed one of the most virulent attacks on gay and lesbian individuals and the gay rights movement in the Republic of Ireland. Taking advantage of the AIDS epidemic, *Our Family* labelled AIDS as 'the gay plague' and condemned the greater demand in Ireland for gay rights, something that it maintained received a warm reception within the Irish media. Citing statistics from the USA, *Our Family* argued that the average homosexual had 500 partners, with 30% having almost 1,000, making homosexuals a threat to the very fabric of society. This demand for new partners, it argued, could only be met through the 'seduction or the rape of the young'.[138]

Credence was lent to *Our Family*'s utterances by the hierarchy of the Roman Catholic Church in 1985 with the publication of *Love is for Life*, which highlighted the unease amongst the hierarchy about the growing strength of the gay rights movement. Effectively, *Love is for Life* was a guide for Irish Catholics on the do's and don'ts concerning sex and the family. Drawing attention to what they considered the 'vigorous campaign in recent years to vindicate the rights of the homosexual community', the Bishops insisted that 'this campaign often claims for homosexual acts complete social, legal and moral parity with heterosexual acts. Such a campaign damages the homosexual community. It encourages others whose sexuality is not exclusively or irreversibly homosexual, to indulge in homosexual acts and habits.'[139] *Love is for Life* further maintained that 'objectively homosexual acts are intrinsically and gravely immoral.'[140]

The then Bishop of Galway, Eamonn Casey, called for the incorporation of the document into the Irish school curriculum. Ironically, this was the same Bishop Casey who was later discovered to have had a sexual relationship with Annie Murphy, an American woman, with whom he fathered a child.[141] The NGF retorted by labelling *Love is for Life* as 'an audacious and hypocritical document'.[142] While the rhetoric of the hierarchy of the Irish Roman Catholic Church remained critical of homosexual relationships, there were some positive developments for gay and lesbian Christians in Ireland one year later when *OUT* advertised the existence of two groups for Irish gay and lesbian Christians: Reach and The Julian Fellowship (for Gay Christian Women), both of which were based in Dublin.

While the more vocal criticism of gay rights and homosexuality was not welcomed, it was clear that gay and lesbian individuals had made their presence known to such a degree that opponents felt compelled to speak out against their demands and greater visibility. Just how much more visible they were was evident when *In Dublin* produced a special issue on 'the "Gay" generation' in 1985. Rhona McSweeney, in her introduction to the issue, remarked that 'Dublin's "gay" population, formerly invisible, have now begun to reflect the times that are in it and adopt a higher profile in the life of the city'.[143] *In Dublin* was certainly more in tune with the gay rights movement and gay scene than most others, having introduced a 'Gay' section as early as October 1983 that gave readers a list of the places that may be of interest to gay and lesbian individuals.[144] However, others were also becoming more aware of Ireland's gay community, particularly its perceived spending power. *In Dublin*'s '"Gay" generation' issue, for example, noted that Easons (Ireland's largest book retailer and distributor) and Book Upstairs had introduced gay sections in their bookstores. Book Upstairs, in fact, had been one of the first businesses to reach out to the gay community, entering into an arrangement with the NGF in 1981 to provide a mail order book service for gay people throughout the Republic of Ireland.[145] The agreement saw Book Upstairs agree to publish and update a list of titles of relevance and interest to gay people, which the NGF then distributed to its members. By the late 1980s, Book Upstairs and Easons were joined by other bookstores in Ireland, such as Well Read Books on Crow Street and Waterstones on Dawson Street, in stocking and distributing gay material.[146]

Within the magazines published by the NGF, namely *Identity* (1981–1984), *OUT* (1984–1988) and *Gay Community News* (1988–), it is evident that businesses were now increasingly more interested in advertising to the gay community. *OUT*, in fact, was distributed throughout Ireland by Eason's, again reflecting what can only be described as Eason's realisation that there was a demand for such a magazine. Whereas in the late 1970s the IGRM and NGF had to reach out to magazines such as *In Dublin* and *Hot Press* to promote their existence, by the mid-1980s gay and non-gay businesses, both inside and outside Ireland, ranging from restaurants, bars, guesthouses, music stores, bookshops, fashion outlets, travel agencies, nightclubs, theatres, condom companies and two saunas were now using Irish gay publications to advertise their business. In fact, the existence of two saunas (Incognito and the Gym) publicly advertising in a gay magazine highlights the growing business interest in the spending power of Ireland's gay community in the 1980s. Both often used images of topless men in their advertisements to entice readers.

In 1985 *OUT* had a circulation of 1,890 in Ireland, while 610 were exported to the United Kingdom, North America and Europe, areas with large Irish communities. Within a year, this had increased to 3,500 with an estimated readership figure of 7,000. The geographical spread of the personal advertisements confirms that those who were looking to meet individuals in counties in Ireland were confident that others in that county would see their advertisement; therefore, confirming that *OUT* was accessible in the overwhelming majority of counties in Ireland. These personal advertisements are quite interesting in their own right, revealing the considerable degree to which men throughout Ireland were looking to live out some of their sexual fantasies. In many respects, they provide a glimpse into a cohort of individuals who were willing to defy the socio-cultural and legal context of the period to engage in what many would have deemed non-normative sexual activities. One individual, for example, sent in an advertisement looking to meet 'young skinheads (18–24yrs), Dublin area into spanking and watersports'. Another expressed his desire for 'moustached and bearded men especially rugby players, firemen, army guys and men in uniform. I also have a fetish for "boots".'[147] While it's impossible to know if either of these individuals found someone, their advertisements are evidence of individuals in Ireland seeking sexual pleasure through the personal advertisement section of *OUT*. Such stories are noticeably absent in Irish historiography but could provide an opportunity to further explore stories of pleasure and the joys of sex in twentieth-century Ireland.

Returning, however, to the circulation and readership figures for *OUT*, it's clear that the NGF sought to use these figures to their advantage. In 1986, for example, Edmund Lynch sent a letter to businesses in which he noted that 'you may also be interested to learn that our sales on the British market have increased considerably with recent issues. I hope that the enclosed articles will convince you of the viability of directing advertising towards what has been called the "Pink Economy"'.[148] Lynch's letter also drew attention to the 1984 *Success* article, stating that since that article had been published the number of gay pubs, clubs and venues in the Republic of Ireland had increased significantly.

While 'significantly' is exaggerating the increase, there certainly was an expansion in clubs/pubs targeting Ireland's gay community by the mid-1980s. One such venue was SIDES, 26 Dame Lane, Dublin, which opened in 1986. Speaking about its opening, John Nolan explained that he felt 'there was a gap which needed to be filled, an opening for an international gay club. In a way, SIDES is a positive demonstration that the gay scene has come of age.'[149] One year later, Hooray Henry's, at Powerscourt Townhouse, Dublin, joined SIDES as another gay venue. Hooray Henry's became the first fully seven-nights-a-week licensed gay nightclub in the Republic of Ireland.[150] Another venue that emerged during this period was the George Bar, on South George's St, which remains one of the most popular and recognisable gay bars in Ireland today. While a 'consumer revolution' is a step too far, there certainly was a much more pronounced gay scene by the mid-1980s and more willingness from some businesses to now openly target Ireland's gay community. The willingness of these businesses to do so also suggests that they did not believe there would be a negative impact for their business if they advertised in a gay magazine.

It was not, however, all positive for Dublin's gay scene. One major disappointment was that the Hirschfeld Centre did not survive the 1980s. In October 1987 it was destroyed by a fire (many suspected started deliberately), bringing an end to Ireland's oldest gay community centre. While a small part of the Hirschfeld Centre re-opened in March 1989, from this point on the NGF and the Hirschfeld Centre were effectively a changed organisation and centre. In a letter sent to members updating them on the changes, the NGF stated that it would be dropping its role of trying to run a gay community centre. From now on the organisation would concentrate its attention on the publication of *Gay Community News*, updating of the Gay/Lesbian Archive and helping other gay organisations like the newly established Gay and Lesbian Equality Network (GLEN – established in 1988) to lobby for legal reforms.[151]

The Hirschfeld Centre, however, left a considerable legacy, particularly its contribution to generating a greater awareness of and confidence amongst Ireland's gay community. Remarkably its contribution was even acknowledged in the Irish parliament. Brian O'Shea, a Labour Party Senator, was one of many who voiced support for granting National Lottery funding to rebuild the Hirschfeld Centre in *Seanad Éireann* in 1988, stating that 'the Hirschfeld Centre serviced a real need in our national life. It provided a dignified and sympathetic atmosphere for a minority group. It took on board the pain not alone of the homosexual community but also provided a caring service for the traumas suffered by the families of homosexual people.'[152] Many individuals who visited the Hirschfeld Centre have similarly noted its impact in fostering a sense of community. Gerard Lawlor, for example, described the Hirschfeld Centre as:

> the best thing that happened in Ireland to the gay scene because suddenly we had a place to go to that was organised for us and where you could attend – you could go to discos, you could go in during the week and have coffee. It was a great place. What most of us of course enjoyed was the discos on the Friday and Saturday nights, at the weekends. They were excellent. And there was just a wonderful friendly atmosphere and a great place for gay people to go to.[153]

Lawlor's continued reference to *us*, rather than *I*, suggests a greater awareness of being part of something collective during that time. Spaces like the Hirschfeld Centre allowed individuals to live out a gay or lesbian lifestyle at a time when few such options existed. It provided a space where many Irish gays and lesbians could become more comfortable with their sexuality, while also allowing them to foster friendships and relationships. But the Hirschfeld Centre would not have survived were it not for the thousands of Irish gay and lesbian individuals who made a conscious decision to cross its threshold. In choosing to embrace their sexuality and subsequently speaking out against their oppression, they challenged the status quo and together brought a hitherto invisible gay community much more out into the open in the 1980s. In writing the history of such movements we must be careful to not only measure success by political gain. To do so obscures the other gains that can and do take place, which, while not meeting the traditional characteristics of political action, can have political and social ramifications. It was a radical act to open a gay community centre when sexual activity between men was criminal and it was a radical act for gay men and lesbian women to enter these centres. These acts were a form of resistance and they contributed to undermining the status quo and raising the visibility of Ireland's gay community.

3

1980s Provincial Activism: Cork and Galway

In June 1988, the *Galway Advertiser* reported on the inaugural Peader O'Donnell Achievement Awards ceremony in Galway. The award was conceived by the Peader O'Donnell Centre (a centre for the unemployed) as an opportunity to recognise those who helped 'to improve the community we all share in'.[1] Praising the award, Bridie O'Flaherty, Deputy Mayor of Galway, stated that it provided an opportunity to give people the recognition they deserved. The list of recipients comprised a mixed group of organisations such as: the Mervue Adult Education Group; the Women's Drop-In Centre; and the Galway Music Workshop, Artspace. Amongst the 1988 winners, however, one group stood out: the Galway Lesbian and Gay Collective.

That the Galway Lesbian and Gay Collective was the recipient of a Peader O'Donnell Achievement Award, the first time such a prize was awarded to a gay and lesbian group in Ireland, is noteworthy. As highlighted previously, this was a period in which laws criminalising sexual activity between men still existed and were being enforced (see Chapter 1). Moreover, the fact that the award was granted to a gay and lesbian group in Galway, a provincial region, makes this even more remarkable. This is not a period or region one might expect a gay and lesbian group to be acknowledged as having contributed to the improvement of Irish society. Only four years earlier, Galway County Council had written to RTÉ asking them not to broadcast a programme dealing with the issue of gay rights in the Republic of Ireland.[2] Yet, within the space of four years the Deputy Mayor of Galway was now participating in an awards ceremony that acknowledged the positive contribution of a gay and lesbian group.

Historically, provincial regions have been characterised as 'backward' and reliant on urban areas to guide them towards gay liberation. The majority of international queer history remains overwhelmingly focused on major urban areas. One is left with the distinct impression that it is only in these urban regions that important events occur, movements emerge, and ideas and strategies devised and diffused to non-metropole areas. Some scholars, however, have challenged this simple notion of diffusion being a one-way system and provincial regions as being overwhelmingly 'backward'.[3] Larry Knopp and Michael Brown, for example, argue that:

> it appears that resistance happens everywhere, and that the tight-knit and intimate personal networks that characterise smaller communities and, incidentally, closets – can create, at times, opportunities for, rather than constraints on, fairly radical forms of resistance, whereas in large metropolitan environments (and other spaces

where 'outness' is common) such goals can as easily be compromised as enhanced by the presence and pursuit of (relatively) abundant material resources and status.[4]

Notwithstanding the importance of urban areas in the history of gay rights activism, the predominate focus on them has hindered our broader understanding of the history of gay rights activism. This is especially the case for the Republic of Ireland. While Dublin may well have been the epicentre of gay rights activism, and the IGRM and NGF the supposed embodiment of the Irish gay rights movement, it is also the case that gay and lesbian individuals outside of Dublin were not passive agents in this campaign. Instead, they too were active agents through the establishment of their own groups, own events and own support base.

Rather than being an exception, Galway was just one region where efforts took place to forge a space for gay and lesbian individuals in 1980s Ireland. As noted in Chapter 1, efforts had also emerged in Cork in the late 1970s. Despite greater restrictions in these regions due to smaller populations, lack of infrastructure and resources, less anonymity and what was perceived as a more conservative attitude towards issues surrounding sex and sexuality, Galway and Cork are two examples of regions outside Dublin where gay and lesbian individuals were able to organise and provide a means for individuals to become part of a gay community. If we are to fully contextualise the history of gay and lesbian activism in the Republic of Ireland, we must look beyond the Dublin-based IGRM and NGF, and beyond Dublin more broadly. Exploring the efforts taking place in Cork and Galway provides one such opportunity.

NGF and IGRM: national organisations?

County Cork, commonly referred to as the 'rebel county', is situated in the south of Ireland along the Celtic Sea bordering Tipperary, Kerry, Waterford and Limerick, in the province of Munster. It is the largest county in terms of land area, and with a population of 402,465 in 1981, was the second most populated county in the Republic of Ireland.[5] Galway, on the other hand, is situated on the mid-western coast of Ireland in the province of Connacht. According to the 1981 census the total population of Galway was 172,018, with the majority of those (114,018) residing in small towns and villages. This made Galway the third most populated county in the Republic of Ireland. However, to put the populations of Cork and Galway into context it is worth noting that the entire province of Connacht, which comprises five counties (Mayo, Roscommon, Sligo, Leitrim, Galway), had a population of just 424,410 in 1981, while Munster, which has six counties (Clare, Limerick, Tipperary, Kerry, Cork, Waterford), had a population of 998,315. In contrast, Dublin alone had a population of 1,003,164.[6] Therefore, while Cork and Galway may well have been the second and third most populated counties in the Republic of Ireland, their overall population paled in comparison with that of Dublin.

While gay and lesbian individuals in Dublin could take comfort in the knowledge that there were two exclusively gay venues to choose from, the majority of gay and lesbian individuals outside of Dublin did not have this luxury. The struggles of living in provincial Ireland are evident in a letter sent to the NGF from one young Galway man in 1979:

> I am an 18-year-old student and I am homosexual. My problem is that I have not yet met a similar student with the same quality. I was glad to read your letter in the Sunday World. Perhaps you could put me in touch with a 'gay' of same age or younger and we could discuss our problem. It would be ideal if I could meet one in Galway or nearer. I am sure you have many contacts. Please write to me as soon as possible. My parents or friends are not aware of my problem, so please keep this in the strictest privacy.[7]

Unfortunately for this individual, far from having 'many contacts', Bernard Keogh replied that the NGF did 'not have any contacts in the West. If you are unlikely to be visiting Dublin in the near future, perhaps you would be interested in meeting a priest counsellor living in Galway who is personally known to me and who I have no hesitation in recommending?'[8] It is not known whether this individual accepted Keogh's offer, but it must have come as a disappointment to him to learn that the only option available outside of travelling to Dublin was talking to a priest. It's also worth noting how this individual wrote the word gay in his letter. While he did not place homosexual within quotation marks, he did use them for 'gay'. This most likely reflects how this individual would have seen gay written at that time, as many of the mainstream publications often placed gay within quotation marks.

Both the IGRM and NGF described themselves as 'national' organisations and yet, while the IGRM did see branches emerge outside Dublin, the NGF did not. This was not helped by the fact that only a minority of the NGF's membership came from outside Leinster. A breakdown of the 1980 NGF membership reveals that those living in Connacht, Ulster (referring to Donegal only) and Munster only accounted for 6.8% of the NGF's total membership (70 out of 1,027 members).[9] It is only natural to assume, then, that without individuals from these regions becoming actively involved with the NGF, the task of expanding outside Dublin was complicated. However, there were those who felt that the NGF had not done enough to expand the organisation beyond Dublin. Denis O'Neill, for example, wrote to the NGF Administrative Council in 1982 criticising them over this very issue, asking 'is it not about time that we got off our backsides and did something about this situation?'[10]

There can be no doubt that it was a difficult task to establish a branch outside Dublin (resources/individuals to run the branch/financial costs etc.), however, there was another issue at play that influenced how the NGF approached this particular issue. In fact, it would appear that the NGF Administrative Council made the conscious decision to refrain from these efforts as a direct result of its relationship with the IGRM. A May 1982 NGF document marked 'strictly confidential' notes that 'although the NGF constitution makes explicit provision for the establishment of NGF local groups and lays down guidelines as to how these would operate, the NGF Administrative Council has deliberately refrained from embarking upon a deliberate plan of action in this area'.[11] The document explained that the NGF adopted these 'self-imposed restrictions' because of a 'sensitivity to the situation arising from past divisions in the gay community'. In particular, it revealed that the NGF took this decision to avoid placing itself in 'direct competition with IGRM which had a clear policy of colonialization'.[12] What this demonstrates is the extent to which the antagonism between both groups had a direct impact on provincial gay and lesbian individuals and the objectives of the NGF.

In his aforementioned letter, Denis O'Neill noted, perhaps to the disdain of the NGF Administrative Council, that 'the provisional IGRM also claim to be the National organisation, and to many people, gay and straight alike, have proved it.'[13] While there is a question mark over the extent to which the IGRM 'proved it', it did succeed in establishing branches in a number of counties. Although there is scant primary material available, we can say with certainty that local branches emerged in Limerick, Galway, Waterford and Kilkenny. According to local media, the Limerick IGRM in 1981 and Kilkenny IGRM in 1982 claimed to have membership figures of 150 and 300 respectively.[14] These numbers cannot be verified and seem quite high, but both the Kilkenny IGRM and Limerick IGRM did succeed in getting their organisations promoted within their respective provincial papers: the *Kilkenny People* and *Limerick Echo*. The *Kilkenny People* even published the number of the Kilkenny IGRM's Gay Switchboard, which operated Sundays from 7p.m.–10p.m, while Brian Looney in the *Limerick Echo* took the establishment of the Limerick IGRM as an opportunity to explore the situation facing gay and lesbian individuals in the Republic of Ireland, telling readers that 'Perhaps it is time that we recognised that there are homosexuals in our midst, and that they are humans too.'[15] Similarly, the Galway IGRM (1981–1982) was successful in getting provincial publications such as the *Galway Advertiser* and *Mayo News* to advertise their existence.

The IGRM's biggest success outside of Dublin, as we have seen, was in Cork, where the Cork IGRM opened its own premises, the Phoenix Centre, at 4 MacCurtain Street in 1977. Whereas the Dublin IGRM crumbled due to infighting in 1978, the Cork IGRM managed to avoid a similar situation and in the second half of 1980 it reopened the Phoenix Centre following renovations. The refurbished centre led Cork IGRM secretary, Stephen Quillinan, to claim that they now had one 'of the finest gay centres in these islands outside of commercial hands'.[16] Eric Presland, writing in *Capital Gay*, was similarly impressed, describing it as:

> being on a more modest scale than Dublin's Hirschfeld Centre. An anonymous door next to a garage in MacCurtain Street leads up a steep staircase to a first floor disco with room for 40 or so dancers; there's a candle lit alcove off the disco floor with sofas to sit and chat, plus the coffee bar ... [It has] a caring friendly concern, which is a positive quality of small town gay life which many larger more anonymous places lose.[17]

Helen Slattery recalled that 'you didn't walk in [to the Phoenix Centre]. You came to a steel door that you banged on. Somebody slid a thing across, and they said: "Do you know where you are?", You'd go, "I do, I do, no problem". Then they would unbolt the door and you'd go up the stairs ...'.[18] This safety mechanism reflected the climate of the period and the requirement of such venues to have precautions in place. During his visit to the centre in 1983, Presland remarked on the cautiousness with which Pat O'Mahony-Rysh had opened the door of the Phoenix Centre. O'Mahony-Rysh explained his actions on the basis that the Phoenix Centre 'had half a dozen troublemakers tonight. The *Sunday World* (an Irish gutter paper) ran a gay story today and we had a few weirdos around. It always happens.'[19] The Cork IGRM's ability to rent its own venue was crucial in ensuring that it had greater freedom and independence. In particular, the ability to generate its own revenue reduced its reliance on the Dublin IGRM.

Following the Phoenix Centre's renovation, the Cork IGRM ramped up its efforts to promote the organisation with a number of advertisements on local radios and in local journals. For example, Suirside Radio in Waterford and *Gay News* were used to advertise the Cork IGRM, while over seventy ads appeared on Radio City Cork, along with a six-month advertising contract with the *Cork Review* in 1981.[20] These efforts ensured that the advertisement campaign reached a broad cohort of individuals, not just those in Cork. Speaking at the February 1981 IGRM annual general meeting at the Cork Phoenix Centre, the first of its kind to take place outside of Dublin, Pat O'Mahony-Rysh delighted in the Cork IGRM's growth, telling delegates that:

> our membership in Munster, not only in Cork, but also in Limerick, Waterford and the adjoining counties has grown at a steady rate. Who could have thought 16 months ago that Cork alone would have achieved a membership of 198 persons, that Limerick would have such a fast-growing group with its own post office box and that Waterford would have broadcast six radio interviews, a regular advertising campaign and their own post office box.[21]

O'Mahony-Rysh's reflection on the growth of the Cork IGRM provides an interesting contrast with the movements in Cork and Dublin. Although Cork was the second most populated county after Dublin, the numbers and sheer size of the scene were considerably different. While 198 members was considered significant for the Cork IGRM, in Dublin this represented an average night at Flikkers.

The Cork IGRM not only succeeded in increasing its membership, but also increased its activities/services, which now included a youth group, the headquarters of the International Gay Association for religious affairs, video nights, discos three nights a week, a theatre group and the Munster Gay Switchboard, which acted as an information and counselling service for gay men and lesbian women.[22] Initially, contact with the Munster Gay Switchboard was made through the postal service before a telephone line was installed in April 1981. The Cork IGRM had struggled to get a telephone line installed and even had to write to the Minister for Post and Telegraphs to try and speed up the process.[23] Following the installation of the telephone line the demand for the service increased substantially, so much so that it began operating six days a week by 1982 (up from once a week in 1981). This was all the more impressive considering that efforts to have the Munster Gay Switchboard advertised in the *Cork Examiner* and *Evening Echo* were unsuccessful, reportedly due to what the advertising department of both papers stated was the 'unacceptable' nature of the advertisement.[24] Bizarrely, within a year of the telephone line being installed, the Cork IGRM reported that the

Department of Posts and Telegraphs had severed their telephone line for no known reason. According to *Out Front*, the line was only reinstated in September 1982 after the local police informed the Department of Posts and Telegraphs that the helpline might help to solve a gay-related murder in the area.[25] This was not the last time that the Cork IGRM encountered difficulties with state officials. In April 1985, *The Irish Times* reported that the Cork IGRM had alleged that for the last six years letters addressed to the 'MacCurtain Street office of the movement in Cork have been opened at the nearby Brian Boru Post Office'.[26]

While the Cork IGRM enjoyed success in providing a space for gay and lesbian individuals in Cork and Munster, at the same time its relationship with the Dublin IGRM began to deteriorate. During the February 1981 IGRM annual general meeting, criticism was expressed at the 'lack of communication between the Dublin-based national executive and the provinces'.[27] The meeting subsequently passed a motion calling for a 'national council distinct from the national executive [to] be set up to co-ordinate the work of the regional convenors and to give them a chance to get together on a regular basis to discuss mutual co-operation and problems'.[28] In essence, this was an attempt to spread the decision making within the IGRM outside of the Dublin-based IGRM and to give regional branches a greater say. This decision was also influenced by a desire, particularly within the Cork IGRM, for the Dublin IGRM and the NGF to put their differences aside, something the Cork IGRM did not believe their Dublin counterparts were prioritising.[29]

Within one year of the aforementioned proposal, Stephen Quillinan sent a letter to Eamon Somers, then NGF President, that highlighted the considerable breakdown in the relationship between the Cork IGRM and the Dublin IGRM. Quillinan informed Eamon Somers that as of March 1982 the Cork IGRM was a 'fully independent body within the IGRM answerable to no other committee ... [and] does not recognise the existence of any "National Executive" of the IGRM and in this instance we would specifically refer to the Dublin-based committee of IGRM which has arrogated this title to itself'. The reason behind the Cork IGRM's decision, Quillinan revealed, was the 'demands of the membership nationwide for devolution of powers to the regions and open democratic participation of the members in the direction of IGRM'.[30] *Gay News* also reported that this decision had been influenced by a feeling within the Cork IGRM that 'we [Cork IGRM and Dublin IGRM] just don't see things the same way. We want a united stand on what's happening here at the moment – the Kincora incident, the Charles Self murder, and the Dublin IGRM has not been co-operative, they've just dug their heels in ... We're sick of it ...'.[31]

The Cork IGRM was clearly disillusioned with the Dublin IGRM and the direction they felt it was taking the wider organisation in. What direction the Cork IGRM wanted to travel in, however, was not explicitly stated but one area that was clearly of concern to the Cork IGRM was that of bringing about unity between the IGRM and NGF. Quillinan expressed the view that 'obduracy of a certain section of the IGRM (mainly located in Dublin), who, despite the overwhelming desire of the rank and file membership of IGRM, have consistently and scandalously obstructed the process of reconciliation'. As a result, the Cork IGRM stated that it would remain an independent organisation until a new national council of the IGRM was established that 'reflected the wishes of the provinces by having an equal number of elected council members from each region – each region to elect them'.³² This never materialised. As noted in Chapter 2, the Dublin IGRM disbanded in late 1982, leaving the Cork IGRM to carry the banner of the IGRM for the next four years. During that period, it continued to provide an important social space for gay and lesbian individuals in Cork as well as running the Munster Gay Switchboard, before disbanding in 1986. Looking back at the Cork IGRM's legacy, Cathal Kerrigan credits it with transforming 'gay life in Cork'.³³

'In Dublin they just saw us as provincial lunatics'

The acrimonious relationship between the Dublin IGRM and NGF reached beyond the individuals involved in these organisations and beyond Dublin – it had a direct impact on provincial gay and lesbian individuals. As a result, it undermined their claims in the eyes of some to be 'national organisations'. The climate the split generated led some individuals to try to forge a new form of gay politics; one that did not involve either taking the title of the IGRM or the NGF. This did not mean that they did not want to work with either organisation, quite the contrary, but rather that they would form independently and seek to have an input into the direction of gay rights activism in the Republic of Ireland, which, until the early 1980s, was overwhelmingly centralised in Dublin.

One such group was the Cork Gay Collective (CGC), which emerged in 1980. For much of its history the CGC comprised only a handful of members, mainly gay men, among them the founding members: Arthur Leahy, Laurie Steele, Kieran Rose and Cathal Kerrigan. With the exception of Steele, who was Australian, the others were from Cork. At that time, Rose worked in a Cork local authority, while Kerrigan was studying at University College Cork, where he led successful efforts to establish a gay society. Leahy and Steele had only recently returned from London, where they had been actively involved in the squatting movement and setting up of co-operatives, lessons from which they would apply to their activism in Cork. Both were also in a relationship and had gone public about it in February 1980 on RTÉ's *Week In*, becoming the first openly gay couple to appear on Irish television.

Leahy and Steele's interview with Áine O'Connor focused on what life was like as a gay couple and provided a poignant insight into the turmoil and difficulties two individuals experienced as they tried to maintain a gay relationship in an unaccommodating Ireland.³⁴ During the course of the interview, Arthur and Laurie spoke about the challenges they faced as a gay couple, telling O'Connor that 'society does not accommodate gay couples, you don't see other gay couples'.³⁵ In the context of this period, Laurie and Arthur's appearance as a gay couple was important in sending a clear message that gay couples existed in the Republic of Ireland. By disclosing that their relationship was five years old, they challenged the assumption that gay men in particular were typically promiscuous. Both men's public acknowledgment of their status as a gay couple resisted the 'official' view that heterosexual relationships were the only possible acceptable form of intimate relationship in Irish society, something that led Barbara McKeon to write that 'the two men, who live in Cork, were quite courageous within the context of our society's hostility towards non-conformity. Long relationships between two 'gays' are unusual, but as suggested by one of the two, this is because they are not reinforced by society's acceptance of such relationships.'[36]

Steele and Leahy's appearance on *Week In* broke new ground in Ireland's gay rights campaign and highlighted the role being played by individuals outside of Dublin, of which the CGC became central players. Those involved with the CGC characterised themselves as either left-wing, socialist or socialist republican. When asked in 2016 why he did not join the Cork IGRM, Kieran Rose explained that:

> I would have a socialist background, socialist commitment, maybe that's one of the reasons I didn't get involved in the Cork IGRM because they were fairly mainstream, or whatever. It wouldn't have interested me that much. I think they were more interested in discos and stuff. Which is grand. I don't know how, but I met Arthur Leahy and Laurie Steele, who had just come back from London, and they were classic gay left activists, housing co-operatives, squats, etc. So, we kind of met up socially and we started talking ... We were youngish, leftie.[37]

According to Kerrigan, the CGC wanted a 'revolution, a revolution for everyone, not just gays'. This, he remembered, led some 'Cork people basically [to see] us as off the wall, unrealistic, loony lefties. In Dublin, they just saw us as provincial lunatics.'[38] In many respects, the CGC's professed commitment to fighting for the liberation of all oppressed groups, not just gay and lesbian individuals, resembled the rhetoric and vision of the Gay Liberation Front. This can be seen in the CGC's manifesto published in January 1981.

The CGC manifesto explained that as an 'internationalist' group they declared 'their solidarity with our sisters and brothers everywhere who suffer oppression because of their sexual orientation and we make this solidarity part of our practical work'. While recognising the importance of legal reform, the CGC insisted that this was 'merely' the 'beginning' and that society's view of sexuality and the structures reflecting that view must be altered. To achieve this, they encouraged gay people to have a positive view of their sexuality, to live fully and to challenge society's control by coming out in the family, work, church and social life. The manifesto further declared that the CGC would fight for an 'end to job discrimination, equal access to accommodation, for freedom from harassment and for equal right to express feelings'.[39] While the aforementioned objectives did not differ to those of the IGRM and NGF, it was the CGC's commitment to the following that separated them from the NGF and the IGRM:

> We are convinced that this struggle cannot take place in isolation and that gay liberation involves the freeing of all oppressed groups. Therefore, we work towards forging links with other movements for social progress. In particular, we emphasise our solidarity with the women's movement, recognising that our shared oppression derives from the abuse of sexuality as a tool of exploitation which necessitated strict gender stereotyping and the denial of sexual fulfilment.[40]

In contrast, David Norris, speaking one year later at the NGF's annual general meeting, defended the NGF as a 'single-issue organisation':

> Let me say here I am absolutely committed to the continuation of NGF as a one issue organisation. I say this with wisdom and hindsight ... I will oppose any move to sacrifice political achievement on the altar of a self-indulgent ideological purity. There is to my mind no practical justification for the opening up of a second front on issues other than those directly affecting gay people because they are gay. In other worlds [sic] a public commitment to active support of other organisations in other areas however laudable such as abortion, contraception, prisoners' rights, national unity, capital punishment or the like could in my judgement be a serious tactical error on our part.[41]

While the CGC had a different vision to that of the IGRM and NGF, it was in fact the division between the latter two groups that had also influenced the CGC's emergence. The CGC was critical of the IGRM and NGF for maintaining a split; a split they contended had a 'destructive influence on the energy of people inside and outside those movements'.[42] More than any other group the CGC sought to bring about reconciliation between the IGRM and the NGF. In an effort to begin this process, the CGC organised a meeting at the Glencree Reconciliation Centre (Wicklow) in November 1980 at which '*all* concerned gay groups and individuals, could together assess and evaluate the effectiveness of their efforts in the past and develop new ideas and relationships for the future ...'.[43] This one-day meeting saw representatives from the CGC, Cork IGRM, Dublin IGRM and NGF attend and resulted in the adoption of the following motions:

1. That this meeting calls upon all gay activists and organisations to support the convening and organisation of a national conference for gay activists to be initiated by the Cork Gay Collective.
2. That this meeting calls on the gay organisations to recognise that towns outside Dublin cannot support a divided gay community and to actively promote unified gay communities in such towns.
3. That negotiations between the national groups should be continued. That the independent groups remain in touch with both national organisations. That all organisations and groups commit themselves to the eventual foundation of a joint committee or council of gay organisations and groups.[44]

Ironically, within two weeks of this meeting on reconciliation, the Cork IGRM sent a letter to the CGC (the CGC had been holding their meetings at the Phoenix Centre), notifying them that:

> it is directed that all future gatherings of individuals on these premises must constitute an integral part of the Organisation and be seen to be working for the good of the Gay Community at large, within the framework and ideals of the IGRM. In taking this decision, we are fully cognisant of those individuals working

under the title "Cork Gay Collective" and we wish them well in whatever other premises they choose to meet at from this date.⁴⁵

The CGC were effectively given an ultimatum: either they joined the Cork IGRM, or they find a separate venue to hold their meetings. The CGC choose the latter option. Remarkably the Cork IGRM's letter did not result in any significant fallout between the CGC and Cork IGRM. In fact, one signatory of the aforementioned letter, Pat O'Mahony-Rysh, joined with fellow Cork IGRM member Oliver Cogan, along with Majella Breen (LIL) and CGC members Cathal Kerrigan and Arthur Leahy, to form a steering committee to organise the first National Gay Conference in Cork in May 1981, as called for at Glencree.

The conference, titled 'Gays in the Eighties: Which Way Forward', took place from 15–17 May at Connolly Hall, the headquarters of the trade union movement in Cork. Although billed as a national conference, it resembled more an international conference with over 200 delegates (roughly 150 men 50 women) attending from Dublin, Cork, Galway, Limerick, Northern Ireland, Great Britain and North America. The organisations represented included: the NGF; LIL; Dublin IGRM; CGC; NIGRA; Galway Gay Collective; Dignity New York; the Scottish Homosexual Rights Group; London Friend/Gays and Housing U.K.; Gay Teachers and Gay Left Collectives U.K.; Gay Christian Movement (England); National Council for Civil Liberties (England); the Campaign for Homosexual Equality.⁴⁶

Over the weekend, delegates took part in a number of workshops, plenary sessions and social activities, with over eighteen different topics discussed, ranging from 'gay identity' to 'gays and religion', 'structures for development', 'gays in the media' and 'gays in isolation'. Following these workshops over fifty different motions were passed, the majority of which concerned 'Gays and the Law' and 'Gays and Trade Unions', while others called on the Irish Medical Association and Irish Medical Union to declare publicly that 'a homosexual orientation is not a medical or psychiatric illness/disorder' and that 'enquiries be made into whether aversion therapy is taking place in any part of Ireland ...'. Earlier that year, Bernard Keogh (NGF) had written to the then Minister for Health, Dr Michael Woods, requesting to know 'all the techniques used in Irish mental health institutions in attempts to alter a man or woman's homosexual orientation'. Keogh also enquired about the use of electro convulsion therapy within Irish institutions, telling the Minister that 'in the course of our casework over the years we have been made aware that numbers of homosexual men are admitted as patients to mental health institutions for "treatment" of their homosexual orientation.'⁴⁷ Although this never became a high-profile issue of the gay rights campaign in the Republic of Ireland, it certainly was a concern. In years to come, however, it may well make the headlines if evidence does emerge that such treatments were practised in the Republic of Ireland. This may take a while as access to this type of material is currently not possible due to the personal and sensitive nature of the records. I was not able to uncover whether the Minister responded to Keogh's letter.

Along with the workshops, the conference also provided an opportunity for those who attended to socialise and have fun. Discos were organised at the Phoenix Centre, while Connolly Hall hosted book stalls, exhibitions and screenings of *Word is Out* and

Comedy in Six Unnatural Acts. According to the conference report, a Gala dance held at Connolly Hall was the highlight of the entire weekend as 'the words gay and straight almost lost their meaning in the light of such genuine community feeling. For us this dance was as politically important as the rest of the Conference and it certainly was a night to remember for anyone who had attended.'[48]

The importance of the first National Gay Conference was reflected in the widespread media attention it generated in the *Cork Examiner, Sunday Tribune, Irish Press, Irish Independent* and *The Irish Times*. For those who participated it was a milestone moment in the history of gay rights activism in the Republic of Ireland. Tom McClean (NGF) went so far as to say that:

> The Cork Conference will, I feel, become to the gay rights movement in Ireland what Stonewall is to the gay liberation movement worldwide. It was not so much the discussions at the workshops or the strategy for the future which we talked about, but rather the spirit of unity and the recognition of diversity of view and approach which marks the threshold which we have crossed. The Cork Conference is already the symbol of the unity of the gay movement in Ireland.[49]

Despite McClean's optimism, however, a more united gay movement in the Republic of Ireland did not emerge, but the conference nonetheless succeeded in providing a welcome opportunity for activists outside Dublin to have an input into the direction of gay rights activism in the country. Moreover, the National Gay Conference resulted in two more National Gay Conferences being organised in Dublin in 1982 and Belfast in 1983, which allowed for further reflections on the gay rights movement in Ireland.

The willingness of the Cork IGRM and Cork CGC to work together, however, was further evident when together they organised the first gay pride week celebrations in Cork in June 1981.[50] It is more accurate to call that year's gay pride celebration the Munster gay pride, as the activities were not confined solely to Cork. The events included leafletting on the streets of Cork and Waterford, sponsored advertising campaigns on local radio in both counties on behalf of the Munster Gay Switchboard, and the circulation of a petition on gay rights in Cork city. Kieran Rose explained that the leaflet campaign formed part of their efforts to increase 'public awareness' and to gain 'wider support for our just demands'.[51] The leaflet declared that 'gay rights are human rights', while informing readers that 'Ireland is the only European country which still legislates against gays.'[52] The high point of the gay pride week celebrations was the erection of a giant pink triangle by members of the Cork and Waterford IGRM at the top of the Comeragh Mountains 'to symbolise the unity of gay people in Munster in our fight for civil rights'.[53] This latter event was not welcomed by a member of the public, Margaret Rossiter, who, after reading about it in *The Irish Times*, sent a letter condemning the action as an 'act of extraordinary insensitivity, especially coming from people who ask for sensitivity in the acceptance and understanding of their own sexual predilections'.[54] Rossiter revealed that she did not understand the point behind the erection of the pink triangle and called on those involved to remove their 'ugly piece of vandalism'.[55] While Rossiter might not have welcomed the actions of the Cork and Waterford IGRM, it was evident by her letter that the organisers of the Munster gay pride celebrations had achieved their goal, to some degree at least, of generating public awareness and discussion. Symbolically, the 1981 Munster gay pride celebrations were a significant moment for gay rights activism in provincial Ireland. Outside of Cork, however, other provincial activists were also seeking to bring about change.

'The peculiar circumstances of organising people in the West of Ireland'

As noted from those who attended the 1981 National Gay Conference, the CGC was not the only 'collective' present; there was also the Galway Gay Collective (GGC). The GGC was established in 1980 and while it similarly adopted 'collective' in its title it differed from the CGC and was a distinct group in its own right. Whereas the CGC had a clearly defined vision expressed through its manifesto, the GGC's primary reason for coming together was, according to one of its founding members, Marese Walsh, because 'we were just lonely, we just wanted to meet others'.[56] The GGC primarily sought to reach out to homosexuals who had spent the majority of their lives in the 'closet' and to try to help end their isolation.[57] It was, as Walsh explained, very much a social group. Walsh, together with fellow Galwegian John Porter who had returned from a spell living in London, was among the driving forces behind the GGC in its formative years.

As noted previously in this chapter, a branch of the IGRM also existed in Galway, but rather than working together, the relationship between both groups, at times, often mirrored that of the NGF and Dublin IGRM. Walsh put this down to the fact that the GGC was more aligned with the NGF (NGF often sent donations to the GGC), while the Galway IGRM was aligned with the IGRM. This, she believed, explained why she was not welcome at Galway IGRM meetings.[58] According to a letter Walsh sent to Bernard Keogh in 1981, the GGC was 'asked to suspend our activities, such as discos and close the box no. to give IGRM a break'.[59] Walsh was of the view that this was an attempt by the 'Dublin [IGRM] to 'curb our autonomy'.[60] Unlike Dublin, Galway was undoubtedly too small for two independent groups competing against each other.

With just Walsh and Porter actively involved with the GGC, they were not in a position to acquire a premises and, instead, both had to organise from their homes, a situation that was far from ideal. Both Walsh and Porter sought to keep their involvement with the GGC secret from those with whom they lived. At certain times of the year, Walsh lived with her family and this had implications for her involvement with the GGC. In the summer of 1980, for example, she asked Bernard Keogh only to send letters of small things to her home address and large parcels like copies of *In Touch* (NGF's newsletter) to another address because her 'sister is incurably nosey'.[61] It was common for the NGF to send Walsh material, which if opened, would have revealed her interest in the topic of homosexuality and gay rights.[62] Walsh's efforts to prevent such material going unnoticed were not always successful. On one occasion her sister went through her letters and found a GGC notice, leading Walsh to say that she was asked to type-up the notice for work, so as to avoid admitting she was involved with the group.[63] Similarly, in letters sent by John Porter he requested that replies be marked private for fear of people finding out his involvement with such a group.[64]

The GGC and the Galway IGRM were fortunate in that they did not struggle with advertising their organisations in the local press. The *Galway Advertiser* and *Mayo News*, for example, accepted advertisements from the GGC and Galway IGRM. This contrasted with the experiences of the Cork IGRM, which had encountered problems advertising the Munster Gay Switchboard. However, it is worth noting the extent to which these advertisements were more clandestine than those of the IGRM or NGF. Whereas the NGF and IGRM publicly stated their location and list of events, neither the GGC nor the Galway IGRM did. Instead, they sought to retain some form of anonymity in their advertisements. The advertisements only contained the minimum amount of information the GGC and Galway IGRM could provide. Rather than announcing the location of events, the advertisements simply noted that a social group existed for 'gay women and men' in Galway and those wanting to get in touch could contact the P.O. box address for more information. The primary objective of these advertisements was to inform people of the existence of the group and to give them their contact address in the hope that individuals would then write to them. Therefore, the ability to acquire a P.O. box number in these regions took on even greater significance. The reasons for this are best summed up by Bernard Keogh in a letter congratulating the GGC on securing a P.O. box number, where he delighted in Porter's 'excellent work in securing a post office box in Galway; this will prove of tremendous benefit to gay people writing to us from the West as we can now refer them directly to the local organisers in Galway where they can begin to make friends'.[65]

Despite the obstacles they faced, the GGC and Galway IGRM succeeded in providing an outlet for gay and lesbian individuals to socialise in Galway.[66] The first event organised by the GGC was a cheese/wine party in April 1980 at the Lenaboy Arms Hotel in Salthill. Incidentally, this took place on the same night of the Eurovision Song Contest, which apparently facilitated 'much merry making and shedding of inhibitions'.[67] The GGC was delighted with how their first event went, writing in *In Touch* that:

> Wine and wit flowed in an atmosphere of warmth and conviviality till about 12:30 when, feeling gayer than usual we all took for a constitutional along the sea-front. Arms around one another and behaving outrageously camp, we marched towards the beach – the ultra-straight nightlife of Salthill got quite a shock... Everybody had great fun and the social was, we feel a very successful venture.[68]

These social events also took the form of occasional dinner evenings or weekly meetings at the Tavern Bar in the city centre as a means of keeping up the morale of those who were hoping for a better social alternative. Walsh, however, remembers the difficulty of getting individuals to attend their events, noting that on one occasion she organised a dinner, but nobody turned up.[69] Encouraging gay and lesbian individuals to become actively involved was a constant struggle for the GGC, which at times was frustrating. In a letter to Bernard Keogh concerning a visit by the NGF to Galway, Porter summed up his frustration by stating that 'with respect to you organising a group to visit here, I think myself because of the enclosed nature of Galway, nothing will bring the gays to their senses. I'll be doing all I can for the present. It's not as easy as one might think when individuals think of themselves only.'[70] Walsh believed this was a result of many being too afraid to join a gay group.[71] This, she claimed, was 'too much like a commitment, or too much like saying "I am gay"', something she described as the 'peculiar circumstances of organising people in the West of Ireland'.[72] Discos organised by the GGC and Galway IGRM, however, do appear to have been more popular. At the first disco organised by the GGC at the Lenaboy Arms Hotel in October 1981, over thirty people turned up, while the first disco organised by the Galway IGRM at the Rockland's Hotel in Salthill in January 1982 attracted roughly eighty people from areas as far away as Cork and Waterford.[73] The success of these discos, which were held roughly every three weeks, led Sean Rabbitte (Galway IGRM) to declare that 'change of a type was beginning to happen'.[74]

In planning their events the GGC was cognisant that they could not choose any venue or openly publicise the events as ones organised by a gay group. Walsh, for example, recalls that when she first booked the Lenaboy Arms Hotel she informed the manager that they were a social club rather than a gay collective.[75] The locations and degree of privacy a venue could provide was also important. Quite often the venues chosen were hotels or guesthouses, which allowed for greater privacy through the booking of private rooms. The Lenaboy Arms Hotel located close to the city centre was considered ideal and according to Walsh it was favourable to those attending because it was 'not too big and everybody is relaxed and friendly'.[76] However, in 1981 she expressed her concerns over the proposed location of a disco organised by the Galway IGRM, stating that 'it is quite near a cop shop and we know the boys in blue [police] drink there. For this reason the women won't come there'.[77]

The need to ensure privacy was reflected in how the events were organised and promoted. A look at the way the meetings took place reveals that there was a considerable degree of secrecy involved and one could not simply come upon a meeting by chance. In other words, if one turned up to a location of a GGC meeting they would not necessarily know that it was a meeting of gay and lesbian individuals. In Galway, the location of an event was never publicly advertised. Instead, those who contacted would be given information; for example, that in the Tavern Bar, the group would be at a particular end of the bar counter from a specific time.[78] Symbols were also used as a means of recognising GGC organisers. In the case of a GGC outing to Connemara in 1983, which involved meeting at the Lyons Tower in Eyre Square, organisers informed those wishing to attend that they would be recognised by a flower (pink carnation) in their lapels.[79] The other means by which the GGC promoted their events was through the NGF, who, on being informed of a GGC event, would promote it to callers who contacted TAF from a surrounding area.[80]

Whether or not the venues chosen were aware of the fact that these events were being organised by gay organisations is debatable. As noted previously, Walsh disguised the true nature of the first GGC meeting; however, there does seem to be evidence to suggest that some locations were aware of the character of the events being held on their premises and simply tried to keep things as low-key as possible. For example, in a letter to Bernard Keogh notifying him about an upcoming GGC disco, Porter requested that the NGF inform any individuals they know who might be interested in attending but to be discreet because 'the manager wishes no publicity or advertising'.[81]

In the space of two years the GGC and Galway IGRM had created an outlet for gay and lesbian individuals to meet under challenging circumstances. However, just when it seemed things were improving for Galway's gay community, a situation emerged in October 1982 that turned these efforts upside down. For reasons unknown the Lenaboy Arms Hotel, Rockland's Hotel and the Tavern Bar no longer facilitated the organisation of GGC and Galway IGRM events, and the Tavern Bar apparently no longer welcomed the custom of gay and lesbian individuals. According to Porter 'thirty homosexuals' were refused sandwiches and coffee both day and night at the Tavern Bar, something he maintained was the result of 'one of the bar staff [who] helped this process along'.[82] In the same letter, Porter mentioned 'other circumstances' for the ending of the discos at the Lenaboy Arms Hotel, stating there was 'an atmosphere of uncertainty around, we cannot say for sure if IGRM were unwelcome, the same applied to the collective'.[83] No other explanations were given, but this situation was described by Sean Rabbitte as a 'boot in the bollocks'.[84]

Whatever the reasons for the abrupt ending of these events, it demonstrated the fragility of provincial activism outside Dublin and the reliance of activists on third party venues to host their events. Without their own venue or the ability to find another one, provincial activists had a difficult task in organising events. The barring from the Tavern Bar and inability to host discos at Rockland's Hotel and Lenaboy Arms Hotel resulted in an absence of events for gay and lesbian individuals in the West of Ireland for almost one year as the GGC sought out new venues and means of hosting events. Therefore, while the GGC and Galway IGRM had succeeded in organising discos/meetings since 1980, by the end of 1982 they had been abruptly brought to an end, and with them an end to the Galway IGRM later that year.

'Lesbians are everywhere'

The situation facing the GGC and Galway IGRM in late 1982 epitomised the difficulty of organising in provincial Ireland without a venue. They were not, however, alone. Arthur Leahy, recalling the challenges of organising in Cork in the 1980s compared to Dublin, explained that 'because all these groups didn't have the viability to exist on their own in Cork, which they did in Dublin ... there was a need for people, a real value in people coming together and sharing basic facilities'.[85] It was this reality that led the CGC to join up with other groups in Cork and to open the Quay Co-Op on Sullivan's Quay in May 1982. The Quay Co-Op was a pragmatic decision by those involved who recognised that alone such an endeavour could not have been achieved. It was not, however, straightforward – it required fundraising and the voluntary labour of many to transform the old building into the Quay Co-Op. Groups such as Women Against Violence Against Women, Friends of the Earth, Campaign for Nuclear Disarmament and Alliance for Safety and Health all formed part of the Quay Co-Op along with the CGC. The wide cross-section of groups within the Quay Co-Op led Eric Presland to describe it as 'the centre of alternative and radical activity'.[86] It was this very reputation that resulted in the Quay Co-Op being raided by the *Gardaí Síochana* on occasion. In 1984, for example, *The Irish Times* reported that the Gardaí raided the centre under

Section 30 of the Offences Against the State Act due to what the *Evening Echo* reported was the belief that the Quay Co-Op was being 'used as a haunt by subversives and as a base where information on garda Special Branch operations is collected'.[87] Donal Sheehan (CGC), however, disputed this, stating that the 'questions asked and the documents seized had no possible reference to offences under that Act or to crime of any form whatever.'[88]

The Quay Co-Op provided a comprehensive space for a women's centre, a café, a nursery, space for exhibitions, a general office and a bookshop that stocked a number of gay publications including *Identity*, *OUT*, *Gay Star*, *Gay Scotland* and *Body Politic*.[89] In 1984, the bookshop began a confidential lesbian/gay mail order service, akin to the one the NGF offered in conjunction with Book Upstairs.[90] The structure of the Quay Co-Op reflected the anti-patriarchal and anti-hierarchical outlook of the groups organising within the Quay Co-Op. In particular, it aimed to 'ensure that women, as the single largest minority grouping in society, continue to have their special needs recognised and catered for within the Co-Operative structure'.[91] To ensure this, the Co-Op's Committee was divided equally between three men and three women.

The Women's Place in the Quay Co-Op in particular proved to be an empowering space for lesbian women.[92] According to the Women's Place Definitions and Directives:

> Women in the Co-Op have taken a separate space for ourselves and other women to use and to develop our own identity, to work on women's issues from a feminist perspective, and for those of us who are lesbian, to take space for ourselves to work on lesbian politics, and provide a supportive atmosphere and environment for our sexuality to emerge.[93]

It was within the Women's Place that the Cork Lesbian Group (CLG) emerged in November 1983 with the objective of 'getting together to combat isolation and provide support' for lesbian women in Cork and Munster.[94] Helen Slattery explained that the CLG was set up simply 'to meet like-minded women and to talk about what it was like to come out in the country. To talk to someone else who was out, because the majority weren't. We were the only ones who we knew who were gay. There weren't many lesbians.'[95] Meeting Thursdays at 8p.m. at the Quay Co-Op, the CLG offered an opportunity for lesbian women to meet informally.[96] The *Munster Women's Newsletter* reported that those who attended were a mixture of 'those that had known they were lesbians for a long time and those that were attempting the first step of discovering their sexuality. And others still who did not consider themselves lesbian but wished to discuss their sexuality in an open and inhibiting atmosphere.'[97] Deirdre Walsh (CLG), who returned to Ireland in 1982 after moving to Berlin to 'come out', remembers conversations focused on life as a lesbian, recalling that 'a lot of it was about coming out stories, and stuff like that. Just living the lesbian life, some people being more out than others, some being very paranoid about their identity being known to others.'[98]

Through these meetings the CLG was able to provide a space for lesbian women in Cork and Munster, but also to generate a small income. The Women's Place report noted that the CLG brought in a weekly income of £2.20 (approximately €6 today) by January 1984.[99] As a means of raising more money the CLG helped organise a Cork

Women's Fun Weekend in April 1984. According to Joan McCarthy (CLG), who helped organise the first Fun Weekend, the weekend was also an opportunity to have:

> a bit of a rest from politics. So we created this event. Funnily enough it has lasted longer than any of our political groups. It was again to do with lesbian identity. Really it started out as a women's weekend that was inclusive of all women because it was coming from a feminist place. But over the years it evolved primarily into a lesbian event ... Our main event wasn't women only because we were afraid that there wouldn't be anybody there. So it was a mixed event so a lot of our gay supporters or political activist friends came along to it.[100]

The first Cork Women's Fun Weekend took place at the Quay Co-Op from the 13–15 April 1984. The activities organised included a disco, cabaret performance, women's films, discussions and workshops. Louise Walsh remembers the first Fun Weekend as being a:

> huge event for the Cork women to organise, but they pulled it off. Women travelled from all parts of the country. Like a lot of women in Cork I found the idea of going to a cabaret of all women performers, having days of women's films, discussions, workshops and card games totally mind-blowing. I identified as heterosexual at the time, but as I watched all these women dancing together, celebrating and flirting in this wonderful atmosphere I knew something quite important and powerful had happened. A strong open lesbian community had rooted itself in Cork...[101]

The feeling that this weekend offered lesbian women an opportunity to be amongst other lesbians in a non-judgemental environment was shared by Mary Flanagan, who travelled from Galway to the Cork Women's Fun Weekend in 1985. Flanagan's reflections on the weekend echo those of Walsh's:

> My first outing where I saw lesbians kissing was in a wild and wonderful weekend down in Cork, it happens every year, and I remember going down there with a straight friend of mine because this other woman encouraged us to go and we went on the Friday night and there was a disco and at the disco they were dancing. My God, I couldn't believe it, it was like being in heaven and the next morning, I remember the Office Bar down in Cork, on the Sunday morning, there was a gathering around half twelve, and that was just tremendous. I can still feel it. You go in and all these lovely women are inside, nothing but women and the craic was great and there was intimacy, you know, and I just remember coming out to my friends at that stage and that's 1985, I think it was, so that was my first kind of lovely feeling...[102]

Although Flanagan was speaking twenty-eight years later, it is evident her first Fun Weekend was still vivid in her mind, particularly the positive impact it had on her; a sense, as she said, of being in 'heaven'.

From 1984 onwards the popularity of the Cork Women's Fun Weekend grew, with women even travelling from Great Britain and Europe to attend. Whereas in 1984 the events were confined to the Quay Co-Op, by 1988, while still being hosted in the Quay Co-Op, the organisers were able to host events in venues such as Moore's Hotel and the Windsor Hotel. Securing Moore's Hotel appears to have been a huge morale boost for organisers, who in previous years had struggled to obtain a venue outside the Quay Co-Op. Helen Slattery fondly remembers Moore's Hotel and the struggles of securing a location:

> Basically, what we did was we went to every different hotel in Cork. We could do it for a year, then they would go, oh lesbians, no ye can't have it next year so. Until we landed in Moore's Hotel. That was great. They fucking loved us. They fucking loved us because we drank all-round the place and we had no trouble, we basically leased ourselves. We had our own bouncers, no need for them for paying out for money for anything. We had our own bouncers and, basically, we were a sound bunch of people who spent loads of money at the bar.[103]

The argument could be made that Moore's Hotel recognised the value of the 'pink pound' and it was not alone. Just as a gay consumer culture had begun to emerge in Dublin in the late 1980s, it would seem that there were signs of its emergence in 1980s Cork. This was further reflected in the fact that the 1988 Cork Women's Fun Weekend had secured sponsorship from Murphy's Brewery and Loafer's Pub, which had become a popular bar for the Cork lesbian and gay community since 1983.[104] In fact, one of the highlights of the entire Cork Women's Fun Weekend took place at Loafer's Pub: the quiz. According to Deirdre Walsh the quiz 'was just hilarious. All different teams. We had a golden Barbie painted pink and that was what you would win. Loafers closed down for it. It was just exclusively us. All squashed into it. It would be a singsong for the rest of the night then. It was good fun.'[105] Since the first Cork Women's Fun Weekend in 1984, it has become a staple event not only for Cork's lesbian community but Ireland's wider lesbian community. Orla Egan maintains that the event 'helped to forge and foster relationships between women from Cork and elsewhere, Belfast, Galway, Dublin, London etc. I remember literally busloads of women travelling down from Belfast to attend the Cork Women's Fun Weekend in the 1980s.'[106]

The Quay Co-Op was central in providing a supportive base from which the CLG could organise and create a space for lesbian women. This was also helped by the fact that both the CLG and the CGC enjoyed a good relationship, often working together to improve the situation for Cork's gay community. In 1984, for example, Joan McCarthy, Kieran Rose and Arthur Leahy participated in an educational talk organised by the Churchfield Women's Group at the Combat Poverty Resource Project in Cork City. The Churchfield Women's Group subsequently wrote a positive report on the event, stating that the talk was 'a great eye-opener for us and helped us get more understanding of their side of things. Because of the way Joan and Arthur and Kieran told us about themselves as people, and how they grew up and gradually realised they were gay, we began to change our minds about many things.'[107] That same year the CGC, CLG and the Cork IGRM had come together to launch the Cork Lesbian and Gay Community Project with the objective of securing a new premises for the gay community in Cork, the establishment of a befriending service for 'rural homosexuals' and new mid-week socials.[108]

The Cork Lesbian and Gay Community Project came about due to changing circumstances in Cork, particularly within the Cork IGRM and CGC. During his visit to the Phoenix Club in 1983, Eric Presland reported that the numbers attending the Phoenix Club had been declining. By the end of 1983 the discos in the Phoenix Club had been reduced to Saturday and Sundays only, but according to Presland Saturday was the only 'day worth writing about'.[109] The declining disco numbers added further pressure on the Cork IGRM, which was already struggling to attract volunteers to help run the organisation and the Munster Gay Switchboard. According to Presland, there were only five members actively involved with the Cork IGRM in late 1983.[110] But the Cork IGRM was not alone; the CGC was also re-evaluating its priorities. In 1984 it announced that:

> There is a general agreement that we should look more to our own needs and that local work should be our priority. We feel that we have tended to ignore the local situation and that if it is not growing strong it is not good for ourselves and also it does not make much sense to be concentrating on national issues. There is also a feeling that we should be more analytical before we take on new work, i.e. questions like 'what do we hope to achieve? Is this feasible given our energies and resources? We tend to be isolated from many of the gay men in the city ...[111]

Prior to this, the CGC had been actively involved in a number of other campaigns, in particular the Anti-Amendment Campaign and efforts to stop the introduction of the 1983 Criminal Justice Bill that granted new powers to the gardai to arrest, detain and interrogate people.[112] As a small group, however, this took its toll on the CGC.

While acquiring a new premises for Cork's gay community proved too ambitious, two important developments did come from the Cork Lesbian and Gay Community Project: the Cork Lesbian Line; and Gay Information Cork. Launched in January 1985, the Cork Lesbian Line and Gay Information Cork focused on providing positive information on lesbian and gay life as well as engaging outside agencies such as the health service, welfare, libraries and educational groups to ensure they had good information for gay and lesbian individuals.[113] The launch of both services coincided with the ending of the Munster Gay Switchboard that same year.

Helen Slattery recalled that their 'training was quite good, very comprehensive because we went to London Lesbian Line'.[114] Along with the telephone service, the Cork Lesbian Line also organised befriending meetings with those who contacted the line. However, there were strict procedures around meeting up with callers, with Deirdre Walsh stating one rule in particular that had to be adhered to was 'you couldn't sleep with the person you were befriending'.[115] This, Helen Slattery explained, was because 'you were talking about someone who was very vulnerable. So you were a little step better along the way because you were out for a little bit longer. So you would always meet in twos, because a lot of the time the person could end up having a crush on the first lesbian they met, which also happened.'[116] These befriending meetings often took place in Loafer's Bar, which had allowed women to meet in one of the rooms every Thursday, becoming affectionally known as lesbian night in Loafers.[117]

With any service of this nature, advertising was crucial. In Cork this proved challenging as both lines met resistance from the *Cork Examiner* and *Evening Echo*. In a June 1985 letter to the editor of the *Evening Echo*, Kieran Rose (Gay Information Cork) and Paula Keenan (Cork Lesbian Line) noted that while initially Gay Information Cork had been advertised for five weeks, when they tried to renew this advertisement the *Evening Echo* reportedly refused on the basis that the advertisement submitted to them 'was illegal under the present law in Ireland and as such we can do nothing about the publication of your notice'.[118] With the Cork Lesbian Line the situation was slightly different. While the *Cork Examiner* had accepted £4.50 from the Cork Lesbian Line to advertise the service, no advertisement appeared.[119] When contacted by the Cork Lesbian Line, the *Cork Examiner* reportedly informed them that the paper 'objected to the word lesbian and would not print an advertisement with that word in it'.[120] Not to be deterred, Gay Information Cork and Cork Lesbian Line engaged in a sticker campaign throughout Cork to promote the services. Helen Slattery recalled how they would do a 'blitz of the city and put stickers on telephone boxes, women's toilets, pubs'.[121] One of the stickers boldly stated that 'Lesbians are Everywhere'.[122]

While the Cork Lesbian Line's primary objective was to provide a service for lesbian women to make contact with other lesbian women, it also helped foster a greater sense of community amongst those running the different Lesbian Lines throughout Ireland, both north and south of the border. In November 1988, in what the *Women's Space Newsletter* described as a very special date in the history of the Lesbian Lines in Ireland, an exchange took place in Galway between Lesbian Lines from Cork, Galway, Belfast and Derry. This exchange had been made possible by a grant the CLG received under the Women's Links project of the Co-Operation North Exchange Programme and facilitated workshops on counselling/befriending, difficulty in recruiting new members, how to maintain distance from new befriendees on the social scene and alcohol.[123] A follow-up exchange took place the following year in Belfast, after which point the Cork Lesbian Line and Belfast Line were declared joint first prize winners in the Women's Link section for 1989.[124] Orla Egan maintains that these Lesbian Line exchanges:

> wove a very strong network between us all for the continuation of skills, information and fund raising. It is only because the exchange took place that we were enabled to begin to do many of these things. As isolated groups we have neither information, skills or money to get much of the work needed to be done, done. As a larger national network, all things are possible.[125]

By the close of the decade then, lesbian women in Cork had succeeded in creating a space for lesbian women to meet and socialise and in the process created a more visible and open lesbian community in Cork.

Galway march for international gay pride day

One individual who participated in the Cork Women's Fun Weekends and benefitted from engagement with the Cork Lesbian Line and Belfast Lesbian Line was Nuala Ward, who had moved to Galway from Athlone in 1986. On arrival in Galway, Ward made contact with Marese Walsh through the GGC's P.O. box number, which Walsh had kept running throughout the mid-1980s.[126] In the period between late 1982 and 1986, the GGC had sought to continue organising events, but this had proved challenging, as events were sporadic, with the odd camping trip to Connemara, boat trips along the Corrib River, weekend cycling trips and the occasional social.[127] One noteworthy development in Galway during this period, however, was the short-lived establishment of a Student Gay-line, similar to TAF, under the auspices of the Students Union at University College Galway (UCG) in November 1984.[128]

Like other universities in Ireland, UCG had seen attempts to establish a gay society come and go throughout the 1980s. According to the *Connacht Sentinel* a UCG gay society had sought official recognition from college authorities in 1981 but were denied by five votes to three.[129] Three years later the *Connacht Sentinel* again referenced the existence of a gay society at UCG, reporting that for the first time in the history of the college a gay society had secured a stall at Societies Day.[130] The Student Gay-line was advertised through the *Galway Advertiser* and *OUT*, and operated Thursdays from 7.30pm–8.30pm.[131] According to the Deputy President of the Students Union, Garbhan Downey, securing advertising space within UCG proved difficult because 'Galway is a very conservative university still very much in the dark ages'.[132] It is therefore hardly surprising that the UCG gay society and the Gay-line ceased operation sometime between May and June 1985.

Therefore, when Ward moved to Galway in 1986 the only activity, she recalled, was Marese Walsh responding to letters sent to the GGC P.O. box number. It was at that moment that Walsh, due to personal reasons, asked Ward to take over the P.O. box number, which Ward subsequently did.[133] After attending one of the Cork Women's Fun Weekends and witnessing the work of the Cork Lesbian Line, Ward sought to establish something similar in Galway. Together with five other women, Ward travelled to Belfast and Cork to be trained on how to run a telephone support service in 1987.[134] The problem for Ward, however, was finding a space to run such a helpline. Ward recalled that 'the minute Lesbian and Gay was mentioned the doors were closed to us'. It was only after Ward contacted Marie Crawley and Deidre Forthroll of the UCG Students Union that a space was offered to them in 1988 to run what became known as the Galway Gay and Lesbian Line. At the same time, the GGC's P.O. box number continued to be advertised and Ward recalls that they also began to organise workshops 'on all kinds of issues' in the Peader O'Donnell Centre, leading to them becoming recipients of a Peader O'Donnell Achievement Award in 1988.[135] Within two years, such was the 'volume of calls from LGBT people' that the Galway Gay and Lesbian Line was divided into the Galway Gay Line for gay men every Wednesday and the Galway Lesbian Line for lesbian women every Thursday.

Ward recalls that it was towards the late 1980s that she also began to think about organising a gay pride parade in Galway, but the lack of support from others to do so hindered such plans. However, she recollected that in 1990 two of her straight friends agreed to march with her if she wanted to organise a gay pride parade in Galway. Recalling that conversation with Jane Talbot and Natalie Sebald, Ward remembers that she said '"I'd love to have a parade" and they were like, "sure why don't you?". I said, "no-one will march with me" and they said, "we'll march with ya" . . . I was like, "okay", I was crying, "this is fantastic"'.[136] With the support of her friends, Ward set about planning the first gay pride parade in the West of Ireland. One of the first things she did was to hand in a letter to the police station in Mill Street informing them of a gay pride parade taking place, which she said received a muted response, something she took to mean that they would not object to the parade.[137] Soon after she appeared on Galway Bay FM to advertise the parade, while she also featured in an article in the *Galway Advertiser* to promote the event and to encourage individuals to take part.[138]

In the lead up to the parade day on 30 June, Ward, Talbot and Sebald made a banner that read 'Galway Gay Pride' and a giant pink carnation. The incorporation of the pink carnation into the parade was not only a recognition of it being an international gay pride symbol but to also honour 'Marese [Walsh] and what she had done with the P.O. box number'. According to Ward, Walsh told her:

> in the 1970s/1980s around Pride time, Walsh would put a pink carnation in her lapel and walk up and down Shop Street just to see, because apparently that was a symbol back then that you were gay if you wore it. It was a secret way of meeting up but Marese said that all that she ever got from people that knew her was: 'Hiya loveen were you at a wedding?'[139]

Ward later described the four days prior to the parade as the most 'terrifying and most exciting time', not knowing if anyone else would turn up. To her relief, however, others did turn up. On the day, there was a total of fifteen individuals, including two American gay men, the only gay men to march that year, three lesbians and ten heterosexuals. The parade took off from Eyre Square, down Shop Street, Galway's busiest thoroughfare, before finishing at the Spanish Arch.[140] Bob Pritchard, one of the three lesbian women to march, recalled how there 'wasn't any hassle, no eggs, no tomatoes. All your fears, you had beforehand were like, wow that went down quite well. It was a positive experience. The first parade was very much ground-breaking. To me, it proved we could do it and there was a need for it.'[141] This was a feeling shared by Ward, who remembered her relief after the parade:

> I don't think I ever felt so many different emotions, so intense. Then not sleeping because I was so excited, but also I was quite scared there would be some violence, but my gut feeling told me there wouldn't be, but I was still worried there might be. People were looking, some people hadn't a clue what it was because the banner just said Galway Gay Pride. Some people clapped, which was like wow. It was a bit surreal. I kept asking myself did we really do that? It was great.[142]

The 1990 Galway gay parade was all the more significant because since 1985 no public gay pride parade had taken place in Ireland. It was not until 1992 that Dublin activists once more took to the streets celebrating gay pride. Today Galway has the longest continuous running gay pride parade in Ireland.

In contrast to the events taking place in Dublin in the 1980s, the efforts in Galway and Cork have been overlooked in the wider scheme of milestone moments in the history of gay rights activism in the Republic of Ireland. While Galway and Cork may not have reached the same heights or visibility as those in Dublin, their efforts were not inconsequential. The resistance and activism taking place in Cork and Galway was significant. Firstly, their efforts created a space for gay and lesbian individuals to meet others and to come to accept their sexuality in these regions. Had it not been for the efforts of local gay and lesbian individuals in Cork and Galway we can say with certainty that the situation for gay and lesbian individuals there would have been much worse in the 1980s. As noted in Bernard Keogh's response to an individual who wrote to the NGF in 1979, outside of visiting Dublin his only option was a sympathetic priest counsellor. These groups provided considerable hope to isolated gay and lesbian individuals in these regions during a particularly challenging decade. Finally, these efforts demonstrated clearly that provincial gay and lesbian individuals were not passive agents in the history of gay rights activism in the Republic of Ireland; rather they were active agents in the efforts to bring about change for Ireland's gay and lesbian citizens.

4

Gay Rights are not Extravagant Demands

On 24 June 1980, David Norris' court case, which sought a declaration that Sections 61 and 62 of the Offences against the Person Act 1861 and Section 11 of the Criminal Law (Amendment) Act 1885 were inconsistent with the Irish Constitution under Article 50, began before Justice McWilliams at the High Court.[1] Mary Robinson, representing Norris, also argued that the state had no business in the field of private morality and therefore no right to legislate for the private sexual conduct of consenting adults.[2] Norris had the support of a number of high profile and well-respected international witnesses, including: Professor John P. Spiegel, former president of the American Psychiatric Association; Professor Donald West, consultant psychiatrist and professor of clinical criminology at Cambridge University; Rev Dr Michael MacGreil, lecturer in sociology at Maynooth University; Dr Ivor Browne, professor of psychiatry at University College Dublin; Fr Joseph O'Leary; and Rose Robertson. In contrast, the Irish government called no witnesses. R. J. O'Hanlon, representing the Attorney General, defended the laws on the basis that 'sexual relations outside marriage constituted a violation of bodily integrity, and homosexual intercourse did so in a particularly grave manner as being against the order of nature and a perversion of the biological functions of the sexual organs'.[3] He further maintained that all the legislation strongly reflected:

> the Christian and Judaeo-Christian belief in the sanctity of the human body and the profanation of the body by indulgence in sexual activities outside of marriage. The law in Ireland had continued to reflect adherence to this Christian teaching down to the present time ... the welfare of society required that the State shall intervene by its law to curb the grosser breaches of morality ...[4]

In his ruling delivered in October 1980, Justice McWilliams, while accepting much of what Norris and his witnesses had argued, nevertheless declared that the laws were not unconstitutional because:

> it is reasonably clear that current Christian morality in this country does not approve of buggery, or of any sexual activity between persons of the same sex ... Having regard to the observations of Mr. Justice Walsh in the McGee case, this morality must be associated with the morality generally advocated by the Christian Churches in the country. Considering the matter in that manner and having regard

to the fact that marriage was recognised and guaranteed by the Constitution and that homosexual relationships were not ... the statutes relating to buggery did not offend against the Constitution.[5]

Following this ruling Norris appealed to the Supreme Court, which upheld the lower court's judgment in a 3:2 majority decision on 22 April 1983. Chief Justice O'Higgins in the majority stated that:

> on the ground of the Christian nature of our State and on the grounds that the deliberate practice of homosexuality is morally wrong, that it is damaging to the health both of individuals and the public, and finally, that it is potentially harmful to the institution of marriage, I can find no inconsistency with the Constitution in the laws which make such conduct criminal.[6]

The Supreme Court ruling now meant that Norris had exhausted all legal avenues in the Republic of Ireland and just as Jeffrey Dudgeon had done in Northern Ireland, Norris turned to the European Court of Human Rights for redress.

There can be no doubt that the defeats in the Irish courts were a bitter blow for the gay rights movement in the Republic of Ireland and bolstered those who sought to maintain the status quo. While acknowledging that Norris' losses in 1980 and 1983 were setbacks, these defeats have, however, come to dominate the narrative of the Irish gay rights movement in the 1980s. As a result, the courtroom is seen as the epicentre of Ireland's gay rights campaign during this decade, to the exclusion of the other sites of gay rights activism. In fact, this decade also saw advances for the gay rights movement in the Republic of Ireland, not just setbacks. In particular, this period witnessed a number of influential non-gay organisations coming out in support of the gay rights movement and increased pressure on the Irish government and political parties to protect gay and lesbian individuals. In looking at this period, therefore, we need to broaden our focus beyond the courtroom and to explore the other sites of gay rights activism. With this in mind, this chapter concentrates on the efforts of the gay rights movement to forge alliances with non-gay organisations, particularly the Trade Union Movement and Irish Council for Civil Liberties, as well as efforts within Irish universities and the attempts to increase pressure on the Irish government to support gay rights.

'The gay society would be an embarrassment to the college'

In seeking to forge alliances with other organisations, activists argued that gay and lesbian individuals were among the largest unrecognised oppressed minority groupings in Ireland.[7] Presenting gay and lesbian individuals as a social minority (rather than as unconnected individuals) allowed activists to argue that they were being denied basic human rights. Although the gay rights movement called for 'Gay Rights', it actively denied that these rights were somehow special rights to privilege a minority grouping. Instead, they argued that gay rights were human rights. It was this assertion that gay rights were human rights that led Hubert Mannion (University College Dublin Students' Union) to write into the *Irish Press* in July 1982 condemning two articles by Reverend Professor Denis O'Callaghan on homosexuality. Mannion argued that 'gay people are the last minority which can be attacked and victimised with impunity. It says a great deal about the Catholic Church, which received its emancipation in 1828, that in 1982 it is doing all in its power to prevent a minority in the community from being granted even the most basic of human rights, i.e. the right to love'.[8] Mannion's efforts to challenge O'Callaghan's article was representative of the strong support the student movement in Ireland had given to the gay rights organisations.

As noted in Chapter 1, the Union of Students in Ireland (USI) had been one of the first non-gay organisations to come out in support of gay rights, providing the IGRM with the opportunity to engage with the student body on the issue of gay rights in the 1970s. One of the high points of this support was the USI's organisation of a conference on gay rights at TCD in 1979, at which Mary McAleese, David Norris, Edmund Lynch, Bernard Keogh and representatives from the USI and the Samaritans all participated.[9] Into the 1980s, the USI stepped up its support for gay rights. In its 1981 Welfare Policy booklet, for example, the USI called on student officers throughout Ireland to 'launch an immediate campaign on gay rights in cooperation with gay organisations to create a "positive gay consciousness"'.[10]

While the student movement was willing to campaign for gay rights, its efforts on campus were not welcomed by everyone, particularly university authorities. This was evident at University College Cork (UCC) in 1980. During the 1980/81 academic year, UCC's students' union (Cathal Kerrigan was a member at that time) published its Welfare Handbook, which included for the first time a section on homosexuality and contact details for the different gay rights organisations in Ireland. Along with dismissing the stereotype that homosexuals were child molesters, the handbook also declared that 'homosexuality is not a problem – it doesn't do you any harm and can be lots of fun'.[11] It was this positive statement on homosexuality that generated unease amongst college authorities, elected officials and some parents. According to the *Evening Echo*, parents feared that 'their student sons and daughters are being indoctrinated and brainwashed by influences beyond their control, on issues which they feel has nothing to do with student life ...'.[12] One mother who spoke to the paper criticised the handbook for assuming that 'all first year students are lacking in moral responsibilities and are going to be totally promiscuous from the time they enter college, getting their kicks from homosexual activities, sex and drugs'.[13] The UCC Governing Body received complaints from the Mayor of Waterford, a UCC professor, and the UCC Student Health Officer, who warned that the material on homosexuality was 'potentially very harmful'.[14] Such was the 'adverse publicity' the handbook generated that the UCC Governing Body established a sub-committee to investigate the relationship between the UCC students' union and university authorities.[15]

Before this sub-committee presented its findings, however, the UCC Governing Body decided that 'in future any publication intended for distribution by the students' union and that contains material in the areas of Health, Medical Care and Morality shall be submitted for consultation to the Student Health Officer and College Chaplains prior to its circulation to the student body'.[16] The recommendations that emerged from the sub-committee similarly sought to curtail the actions of the students' union, presenting the UCC Governing Body with a 'framework for a regulated students' union that would encourage it to show "concern for the good relationship between the College and the community at large"'.[17]

The fallout from the 1980/81 UCC students' union Welfare Handbook is representative of wider tensions that existed between university authorities and student bodies over the issue of gay rights. In fact, university campuses became battlegrounds in the gay rights campaign, as students sought to advance the rights of gay and lesbian students to claim a visible presence on university campuses through the establishment of gay societies. This was something that brought them into direct conflict with many university authorities in the Republic of Ireland. In the same year that the UCC students' union found itself embroiled in controversy over its Welfare Handbook, the USI had circulated a briefing document to student bodies throughout Ireland on how to go about establishing a gay society.[18] Along with a sample article on homosexuality that could be printed in the student press, the document contained the contact details of the NGF and IGRM, an encouragement to students to support the legal fund for Norris' court case, and instructions on the practicalities of setting up a gay society.[19]

Since the mid-1970s gay societies already existed at TCD and University College Dublin (UCD), while in the early 1980s gay societies came and went at UCC, UCG and Maynooth University.[20] The majority of Irish university authorities, however, were not inclined to grant official recognition to gay societies. Between June 1977 and November 1983, for example, the UCD gay society was denied recognition on four separate occasions.[21] Each time no explanation was given as to why recognition was denied. UCD Academic Council minutes only noted that there was 'a short discussion on the UCD Gay Society' and the 'Academic Council decided not to grant recognition to the proposed society'.[22]

In UCC the gay society had been subjected to the same treatment. UCC's gay society had been established following a debate in November 1980 on the motion that 'this house would support the establishment of a gay society in UCC'.[23] According to the *Cork Examiner*, over 350 students attended and voted overwhelmingly to support the formation of a gay society. Two months later, in January 1981, the UCC gay society was officially launched with the objective of promoting 'the social, political, and legal wellbeing of gay people in UCC and in society at large'.[24] That same month, the society sought official recognition from university authorities, but this was denied by the UCC Joint Board without any explanation. The *Sunday Tribune* reported that this decision led to some societies within the college passing 'motions of censure on the joint board ...'[25] This was a trend that continued for much of the 1980s. When Maynooth University's gay society, which had 176 registered students, sought recognition in 1988, it too was denied recognition. *OUT* reported that the decision was a result of the Joint Board fearing that 'the Gay Society would be an embarrassment to the College' and there would be a 'real danger that Maynooth would become the subject of barrack-room jokes among the press'.[26] The rare exception to this trend had been TCD's gay society, which had been formally recognised during the 1982/83 academic year.[27]

The refusal of university authorities to grant official recognition presented many obstacles for gay societies. Not only did it deny them the opportunity to book rooms within the university, but it also deprived them of funding to run the society.[28] More profound, perhaps, was the fact that each refusal sent a clear message to gay and lesbian students that university authorities were not willing to support their right to a space on campus. According to UCD's *Bulletin*, the UCD gay society was refused advertising space at the UCD notice board, which 'supposedly offers free space to students and staff'.[29] In March 1981 the *Irish Press* reported that problems between the UCC gay society and university authorities had escalated after the university barred the society from 'having any meetings on the campus as they are not an official college society – even in the students' union offices'.[30] Both incidents demonstrated the active attempts of UCC and UCD authorities to thwart the efforts of gay societies.

Following the refusal to recognise UCD's gay society in November 1983, Tomas Campbell (UCD gay society) announced that the 'GaySoc is tired of politely asking to be recognised, only to face the indignity of repeated rejection'.[31] While clearly dejected, UCD's gay society began a long campaign to mobilise the support of student bodies and outside organisations to put pressure on the university authorities to grant official recognition. While it was not until 1988 that the UCD gay society again sought official recognition, it was clear that in the interim years they had mobilised support inside and outside UCD. Unlike their efforts in 1983, in 1988 the UCD gay society presented a petition with 1,730 signatures in support of recognition, while the UCD registrar noted that letters of support had been received from UCD professors, Young *Fine Gael*, the USI, the UCD students' union and UCD Chaplains.[32] In their letter the UCD's students' union argued that by refusing recognition in light of the gay society's contribution to college life, the governing body was 'practising blatant discrimination'.[33] Although the UCD Academic Council again refused recognition, the margin between those in favour and those against was only four votes.[34] Moreover, whereas in previous years there had been no discussion on the constitution of the UCD gay society – it had simply been dismissed – at this March 1988 meeting, the society's constitution was discussed, with one professor noting that it would require amendments of a drafting nature.[35] That same month, *Hot Press* printed a detailed article on the efforts of gay societies to gain recognition, writing that 'contrary to their popular image as centres of enlightenment and free expression, many of the country's third level colleges house unsympathetic and sometimes deeply hostile attitudes towards gays in their midst'.[36]

At the time of UCD gay society's fifth attempt to gain official recognition, efforts had also re-emerged in UCC. UCC's gay society had regrouped in 1987, following a number of dormant years. Encouraged by David Norris' success at the ECHR in 1988, they sought official recognition. The renewed efforts of UCC's gay society included: the circulation of fliers in the college library, common room and restaurants; participating in the Law Society's Legal Rights Awareness Week; and circulating a petition. In early 1989 they also wrote to each UCC club and society requesting that they support their campaign, noting that 'now is the time, especially in the light of the Norris decision to upgrade our position to that of other societies in college...'[37] In one letter of support, the Sociological Society's secretary contended that:

> the denial of recognition is a vicious oppression on those who need most the energy of university debate. We recall the previous decisions of UCD and Maynooth as

petty attempts to climb to a Catholic censorship. As students we deplore any forms of censorship ... Gays have the right to form their own, even if it is un-traditional, opinions and desires based in their autonomy and intelligence.[38]

In the lead up to the UCC Joint Board and Academic Council meetings to vote on recognition in March 1989, the gay society organised a gay and lesbian awareness week to highlight the need for the society. The week's events included videos in the UCC common room, a public meeting and a poster campaign. The UCC Joint Board and Academic Council were also presented with a number of letters from other societies expressing their support for the gay society, including a letter from a Garrett Barden, a UCC professor, who sought to defuse the argument, in light of the Norris verdict, that it would be illegal to grant official recognition to the society.[39]

In a surprising move, the UCC Joint Board and UCC Academic Council voted four to two and twenty-seven to seven respectively in favour of granting official recognition.[40] One month later, the UCC Governing Body, by thirteen votes to seven, approved the recommendation of the UCC Academic Council.[41] The decision was headline news in the *Cork Examiner*, which noted that UCC 'yesterday became the first constituent college of the National University of Ireland to officially recognise a lesbian or gay college group ...'.[42] Speaking to the *Cork Examiner* after securing official recognition, Josephine O'Halloran (UCC gay society) stated that:

People recognise the psychological injury to lesbian and gay students caused by treating us as if we did not exist. Lesbian and gay students must have the right to meet; to discuss issues that affect us, and to seek improvements in the way we are treated in College ... We are often told how conservative and intolerant Irish people are on issues like this. The experience of this campaign suggests that, whatever fears and prejudices may have been instilled into us, Irish people are fundamentally tolerant and respectful of individual rights when they are faced with real people rather than abstractions.[43]

The UCC gay society's success provided hope to other gay societies in Ireland, none more so than UCD's. Akin to the actions of those in UCC, the UCD gay society sought to take advantage of the Norris verdict, issuing a press release expressing their hope that in light of the Norris verdict the UCD university authorities would grant official recognition. They also continued to circulate petitions and organise awareness weeks, which included a cuddle-in protest outside the UCD administration building. According to *Gay Community News*, the awareness week was a considerable success as a high volume of 'straight students' offered to do a 'stint giving out awareness leaflets or staffing the petition table', while students also 'happily bought and wore pink triangle badges that had been specially printed for the week. The stock of 500 was sold out by Wednesday afternoon'.[44]

When the UCD Academic Council met in March 1990 to vote on official recognition, over 2,000 individuals had signed the petition, while letters of support had been received from eighteen organisations, including the Irish Council for Civil Liberties (ICCL) and Irish Congress of Trade Unions (ICTU). Letters of support were also sent from Senators David Norris, Brendan Ryan, Shane Ross, John Murphy and Proinsias de Rossa, TD.[45] During the Academic Council meeting the registrar noted the 'substantial volume of correspondence, together with the petition', as well as the decision at UCC, while also stating that the society's constitution 'appeared to be in order' and 'that the provisions therein did not contravene the law'.[46] While a minority of professors did object to recognising the gay society, even writing a letter that warned 'students could become emotionally kidnapped through encounters with an organised homosexual movement', the UCD Academic Council and Governing Body voted to recognise the gay society.[47]

Symbolically the decisions of both the UCC and UCD governing authorities were important in sending a clear message that gay and lesbian students had a right to claim a space on university campuses and that this space was now being recognised by their respective university authorities. Speaking to the *Sunday Tribune*, Lance Pettit (UCD gay society) proclaimed that the decision was a sign that there was 'a growing tolerance amongst young people towards homosexuality'.[48]

'The right not to lose our job or promotion because of our sexual orientation'

The strong support the UCD gay society received from the ICCL and the ICTU is rooted in the early 1980s, when gay and lesbian activists lobbied both organisations to support gay rights. As noted in Chapter 1, the Campaign for Homosexual Law Reform (CHLR) had the support of Kadar Asmal, a TCD lecturer and founding member of the ICCL in 1976. As an organisation fast becoming an influential voice in the sphere of human rights in Ireland, the NGF, in particular David Norris, sought to forge an alliance with the ICCL. During the course of the ICCL's annual general meeting on 9 June 1980, Norris, who had written to the ICCL one month earlier requesting that a workshop on gay rights be facilitated, proposed a motion asking the ICCL to urge the Irish government to repeal the 1861 and 1885 laws 'thus sparing Ireland the humiliation of being found guilty of violations of human rights …'.[49] This motion was supported by the ICCL delegates.

The ICCL became a strong supporter of the gay rights movement, establishing a Gay Rights Committee in 1981 chaired by Fintan O'Toole, an ICCL executive member and then a journalist with *In Dublin* (later a prominent columnist with *The Irish Times*).[50] In explaining its decision to establish a special committee on gay rights, the ICCL noted that gay and lesbian individuals were 'one of the most harassed and the most discriminated against' in Irish society.[51] At the first meeting of the ICCL Gay Rights Committee in October 1981, which included NGF members Tom McClean, Joni Sheerin (Crone), Edmund Lynch, Bernard Keogh and Eamon Somers, an ambitious programme was agreed. The ICCL Gay Rights Committee's main priorities would be: Employment, Housing, Taxation, Inheritance, Financial support for dependent partners, parental rights and custody, religious attitudes, sex education, privacy, compulsory medical treatment and age of consent.[52]

The ICCL did not shy away from speaking out publicly against the ill-treatment of gay and lesbian individuals. As noted previously, the police investigation into the killing of Charles Self had caused concern within the gay community and this concern was shared by the ICCL. In a letter to the Minister for Justice and the Commissioner of an Garda Síochána, the ICCL expressed its alarm at the treatment of persons interviewed by the police in connection with the Charles Self murder investigation, noting that 'any statement by the Garda Siochana calculated to reveal a person's sexual orientation to that person's family or employer, or any exploitation of information gained during the current investigation would constitute a gross violation of the right to domestic privacy'.[53] Later that year, the ICCL issued a statement condemning the banning of *Gay News* by the Censorship Board. According to the *Irish Press*, the Censorship Board had banned *Gay News* in August 1982 on the grounds that it was 'indecent and obscene and relates of the crimes of buggery'.[54] This decision, the ICCL argued, highlighted yet again the 'level of repression confronting the gay community'.[55] It called upon the Irish government to repeal the 'obnoxious nineteenth century laws against homosexual acts', insisting that without these 'discredited and anachronistic laws the Censorship Board would have little grounds to defend their ban'.[56]

The banning of *Gay News*, the brutal killing of Charles Self (and the subsequent Garda investigation), the killing of Declan Flynn and the Kincora Boys' Home scandal were just some of the events in 1982 that reinforced the vulnerability of gay and lesbian individuals in Ireland. A less high-profile incident that year, but no doubt an example of many other such cases in Ireland during this period, was the dismissal of a member of an Garda Síochána over suspicions of 'alleged involvement in homosexual activity'.[57] This story only came to light in 2019 after the individual went public with their story and documents released by the Garda Commissioner, Drew Harris, confirmed that they had been fired because of their sexual orientation.[58]

While there are no available official records documenting individuals being dismissed from their employment because of their sexual orientation during this period, anecdotally there are accounts of such incidents. In *Out for Ourselves*, for example, one individual recounted the impact the attitude towards homosexuality had on their career after coming out to colleagues:

> In short, I was isolated at work. My work suffered as a result . . . This situation lasted for about six months at which time I was expecting to have a nervous breakdown. It was at this time that I had my final interview with my manager. He assured me that I didn't have a future with the company. That my 'sort of person' didn't fit in. He offered a fairly large financial settlement and asked that I resign. I was discouraged from talking to my shop steward or supervisor.[59]

One year after the publication of *Out for Ourselves*, the *Sunday Independent* reported that a woman had been fired from her job in the public service when her superiors discovered she was a lesbian, even warning her that she 'mustn't fight the sacking'.[60] If either individual had sought to fight their dismissal, it is highly unlikely they would have been successful. Most likely, they would have suffered a similar fate to that of Eileen Flynn. While Flynn was not a lesbian, she had been dismissed as a teacher for failing to adhere to the social norms of the period – Flynn was in a relationship with a separated man whom she had a child with, something her employers deemed a sackable offence in 1982. Flynn subsequently took a court case against her employers arguing that her dismissal was unlawful, but Justice Declan Costello ruled in 1985 that the employers had not breached any laws, on the basis that he did not:

> think that the respondents over-emphasise the power of example on the lives of the pupils in the school and they were entitled to conclude that the appellant's conduct was capable of damaging their efforts to foster in their pupils norms of behaviour and religious tenets which the schools had been established to promote.[61]

In an interview with *In Dublin* that same year, one lesbian schoolteacher stated that 'there is no way she can come out in work because her school is run by Roman Catholic clergy. Since the Eileen Flynn case, there is absolutely no chance of a Gay Teachers' Alliance.'[62] At that time the two relevant employment laws – the Unfair Dismissals Act 1977 and the Employment Equality Act 1977 – did not include protection on the grounds of sexual orientation. In reality, outside the gay rights movement sexual orientation was not a term that was widely used in Ireland. It was this lack of protection for gay and lesbian workers that had motivated gay rights activists to turn to the trade union movement in 1980.

In Ireland the overwhelming majority of trade unions were affiliated to the ICTU. In the 1980s, it represented over half a million workers and had considerable sway over the Irish government, which often sought the organisation's views on issues related to workers' rights. Securing support from such an influential body would be invaluable to the gay rights movement's efforts to introduce protective legislation for gay and lesbian workers. Moreover, as an organisation representing a considerable percentage of the Irish population, it would greatly help the process of engaging with the wider Irish society on the issue of gay rights.

At the NGF's first annual general meeting in 1980, Ian Dunn, a member of the Scottish Homosexual Rights Group (SHRG) spoke about the importance of the labour movement in advancing gay rights. Dunn's speech took place within the context of a campaign the SHRG was engaged with in Scotland to have John Sanders reinstated in his job. Sanders had been dismissed from the Scottish National Camps Association in August 1979 over claims that he 'indulged in homosexuality', actions considered totally unsuitable by the Camps Association for someone working with school children and teenagers'.[63] To prevent further cases similar to that of John Sanders, Dunn emphasised 'the importance of working with the Labour Movement and the need for cooperation with trade unions as steps towards changing the discriminatory laws ...'.[64]

Following that annual general meeting, the NGF sent a questionnaire to twenty-eight trade unions who fell under the terms of the Unfair Dismissals Act 1977. The questionnaire sought to garner the level of support for the introduction of legislation outlawing discrimination against gay and lesbian workers.[65] Of the twenty-eight unions contacted, ten returned the questionnaire, with six of those having completed it. While the majority chose not to reply, the NGF was nonetheless encouraged by the response.[66] Of the six that completed the questionnaire, five stated that in principle they would support the amendment of the Unfair Dismissals Act 1977 to include sexual orientation. The Irish Federation of University Teachers (IFUT) was the only union to mark 'uncertain' to that question.[67]

The IFUT's 'uncertain' response was surprising, considering that at that stage it was the only union in the Republic of Ireland to have actually considered the issue and voted in favour of outlawing discrimination based on sexual orientation. This had followed a motion proposed by Kadar Asmal and David Norris (both members of the 1,000-strong IFUT) at the IFUT's annual general meeting in November 1980.[68] Asmal's motion pledged the IFUT to support attempts to decriminalise sexual activity between consenting male adults in private and to resist any attempts to discriminate against its membership in their employment on the basis of their sexual orientation.[69] While IFUT delegates supported this motion by a two-to-one majority, in April 1981 the IFUT executive council overturned this decision by thirteen votes to eight. The council explained its decision on the basis that the November 1980 vote had not been 'truly representative of the IFUT members' views', leading the NGF to label the decision a coup de grâce.[70]

While the IFUT executive council's decision ended hopes of a motion going forward to the ICTU's annual general congress in July 1981, the issue of gay rights was not absent from that year's ICTU meeting. Along with Kieran Rose (CGC) writing to the ICTU seeking permission to hold a fringe meeting on the theme of 'gays at work' during the congress, the National Gay Conference Organising Committee (NGCOC) also sent a letter to the ICTU condemning the actions of the IFUT.[71] The NGCOC argued that 'the defence of any worker under attack is the first priority for trade unionists. It was upon this foundation that Connolly and Larkin built the Labour Movement in Ireland ... As gay workers we are demanding the basic democratic rights taken for granted by others: the right not to lose our job or promotion because of our sexual orientation.'[72] Members of the CGC also picketed outside Cork City Hall (the venue of the ICTU meeting) carrying a placard that stated 'Gay Rights Workers Rights', while also handing out leaflets to delegates as they entered.

The CGC became centrally involved in trade union activism in Ireland. In fact, it had been decided at the National Gay Conference in May 1981 that the CGC would act as the information centre for all individuals working on the issue of gay rights at work. Kieran Rose, in particular, spearheaded the efforts to get the Irish trade union movement behind gay rights. Rose was a member of the Local Government and Public Services Union (LGPSU), which at the time represented over 17,000 members nationally. As we have seen, the LGPSU was one of only five trade unions to respond positively to the NGF questionnaire, supporting the amendment of the Unfair Dismissals Act 1977 to include sexual orientation. However, as Harold O'Sullivan (LGPSU General Secretary) noted in his response: 'The Information supplied is intended to be factual in character and not to convey any statement of policy by this Union for the reason that the views of our membership were not obtained in the compilation of the replies to your questionnaire ...'[73] In other words, such a proposition would have to be put to and passed by the LGPSU membership before a policy in favour of gay rights could be adopted. O'Sullivan, however, ended his letter on a positive note, telling the NGF that he believed the 'Union would in fairness support the elimination of criminality in the case of male homosexuals bearing in mind that criminality does not appear to apply in the case of female homosexual practices'.[74]

The first real test of O'Sullivan's reading of the LGPSU memberships' views on this issue occurred in March 1982 at a general meeting of the Cork branch of the LGPSU. At this meeting, Rose, together with Tricia Treacy (an LGPSU member who worked with Rose in the Cork County Council) proposed the following motion:

> This Union calls on the Irish Congress of Trade Unions to work for (1) Repeal of those laws criminalising consenting homosexual acts between men (i.e. section 51 and 52 of the Offences Against the Person Act 1861 and section 2 of the Criminal Law Amendment Act 1885) (2) Amendment of the Unfair Dismissals Act 1977, the employment Equality Act 1977 and the legislation dealing with the employment of civil servants, the armed forces and the Gardaí to prevent discrimination on the basis of sexual orientation.[75]

In his address to Cork LGPSU members, Rose sought to appeal to the long tradition of worker solidarity within the trade union movement, i.e., an injury to one is an injury to all. This tradition, Rose argued, should be applied to the rights of gay and lesbian workers because 'solidarity among workers is the basis of our strength and of the considerable social progress that has been achieved since the Movement was founded'.[76] Rose presented the issue as one of human rights, whereby gay and lesbian workers were a minority group who were being denied their basic human rights. The motion, Rose maintained, simply calls for:

> civil and human rights for a minority that represents 5% to 10% of the population; that is the lesbians and gay men of Ireland ... Besides the threat of imprisonment, gay people experience the same range of discrimination, stigmatisation and prejudice as other minorities. Living as a gay person in Ireland is in many ways like being black in Alabama ... The right to work and to a fair deal at work are basic workers' rights which everyone is entitled to whether black or white, male or female, gay or heterosexual.[77]

Rather than presenting the demands of gay and lesbian workers as something unique to this group, Rose situated the rights of gay/lesbian workers within the realm of basic workers' rights; rights that the trade union movement admittedly strived to uphold.

Rose's speech had the desired effect, with delegates voting in favour of the motion, thereby paving the way for it to go before the LGPSU's annual conference in Tralee in May 1982. According to the *Cork Examiner*, the motion led to a twenty-minute contentious debate with one Limerick branch member, Tom Henn, describing the motion as nauseating, declaring that 'if Cork have problems with homosexuality then let them go away and solve them quietly without publicity'.[78] Henn's comments were reportedly described by one unnamed delegate as 'bigoted rubbish', while Tom Bogue, LGPSU president, urged the conference to adopt the motion, telling them that 'we have a repressed minority. They are repressed by laws and attitudes which are widely held throughout the community'. Despite Mr Henn's strong protestation, only 6 delegates out of 360 present voted against the motion. The LGPSU's support was a strong demonstration of solidarity with gay and lesbian workers during a challenging period. The adoption of the motion took place only a month after Jack Marrinan's comments at the Garda Representative Association meeting in April and against the background of the Kincora Boys' Home scandal, both of which were referenced by Cork LGPSU member, John Murphy, during his speech in support of the motion.[79]

As the LGPSU was voting on supporting gay and lesbian workers, the IFUT membership succeeded in overturning the IFUT executive council's decision of April 1981. As a result, Bernard McCartan, IFUT president, proposed motion 106 at the ICTU's annual congress in Belfast in July 1982. The motion, 'Job Discrimination on Sexual Grounds', moved that the 'conference supports the decriminalisation of homosexual behaviour between consenting male adults in private and as a consequence of such support urges affiliated Unions to resist any attempt to discriminate against their members in their employment'.[80] Prior to the vote on the motion, the CGC distributed a leaflet calling on delegates to support motion 106 because 'the rights to work and to be protected from personal prejudice of employers are basic trade union demands and apply whether the worker is black or white, male or female, heterosexual or homosexual, atheist or believer.'[81]

In his address to delegates, McCartan informed them that despite the Wolfenden Report, the 1967 Sexual Offences Act, and the recent Council of Europe declaration that favoured the decriminalisation of sexual activity between men, the Republic of Ireland still maintained what he labelled 'Victorian laws' criminalising sexual activity between men.[82] He also sought to dismiss the notion that in the absence of any reported cases of discrimination against gay and lesbian workers, there was no need for protective legislation. On the contrary, McCartan insisted that the absence of reported cases was a direct result of gay and lesbian workers being too fearful to report discrimination for the very reason that there was no redress for them under current employment legislation. Reinforcing his point that such discrimination did take place, he highlighted the John Sanders case in Scotland, noting that despite no complaints being made against him, Sanders had been dismissed simply because he was gay. McCartan proclaimed that 'one's attitudes and one's activities away from the workplace should have no bearing whatsoever on employment'.[83]

McCartan's speech proved persuasive, with the ICTU's 1982 Annual Report noting that motion 106 was carried.[84] Arthur Leahy and Kieran Rose later described the passing of motion 106 as a significant development for the Irish gay rights movement because it was the first time that such a 'widely representative and influential body has come out in favour of gay rights'.[85] That the ICTU came out in support of gay rights when it did is noteworthy when one considers that countries with a much longer tradition of gay rights activism, such as the United States of America and England, did not generate such support until 1983 and 1985 respectively.[86]

After the passage of motion 106 the challenge for gay rights activists was to ensure that the issue did not become side-lined within the trade union movement. In its report on the Second National Gay Conference, the organising committee, while recognising the significance of the ICTU's decision, noted that 'this would be only the first, large step on the road [and] it will be necessary to make this resolution work in practice. It was said that this would require the passing of resolutions at section, branch and national level by more individual unions.'[87] Some unions, however, did begin to look into the issue following the ICTU conference. The Electricity Supply Board Officers Association (ESBOA), for example, charged Bernard Keogh with examining the question of gay rights within their union. According to a letter sent to Tonie Walsh, the ESBOA was to begin a promotional campaign to bring greater awareness and understanding within the union on the issues affecting gay workers and hoped that the NGF could provide any information they considered suitable for such a campaign.[88] Within a year of this letter, the ESBOA produced an information leaflet on gay rights. Along with providing the contact details for the NGF, LIL, TAF, DGC, CGC and the GGC, the leaflet provided an overview of the situation facing gay and lesbian individuals in Ireland, telling members to be 'supportive of gay friends, relatives and work colleagues' and to 'support legal reforms to secure equal treatment under the law'.[89]

At that time, however, the ESBOA was only one of a handful of unions engaging with the issue of gay rights, and this caused some concern amongst gay activists that the issue was not progressing at a speed they would have liked. This sentiment was expressed by Kieran Rose in a letter to the ICTU in 1984 in which, along with requesting permission to organise a workshop at the forthcoming ICTU conference in Waterford, he stated that 'there has been little practical progress made and we feel that now is the time for the Trade Union Movement to renew its support for Lesbian and Gay workers'.[90]

Rose's request for a workshop was granted and it was organised under the title 'Discrimination against Lesbian and Gay Workers'. Roughly twenty individuals attended, including Phil Flynn, general secretary of the LGPSU. Those who spoke at the workshop included Inez McCormack (National Union of Public Employees), Mickey Duffy (Northern Ireland Public Service Alliance), Padraigín Ní Mhurchú (Irish Women Workers Union), and John Lindsay (England-based Gay Rights at Work). Kieran Rose and Joe Lynch, representing the CGC, spoke on the current state of affairs for Irish gay and lesbian individuals. The extent to which the Kincora Boys' Home scandal was still a topical issue in 1984 was evidenced by McCormack and Duffy focusing their attention on the scandal and its implications not just for gay workers but also heterosexual workers. Duffy contended that as a result of the Kincora scandal, positive vetting had been introduced for social care jobs, something McCormack maintained was a threat to all workers.[91] She revealed that one social worker, who was not gay but shared a flat with a gay man, was suspended for eight months. This, Rose argued, demonstrated the extent to which 'threats to lesbian/gay workers are dangerous for all workers and vice versa ...'. Ní Mhurchú, in her contribution, painted a more depressing picture, telling attendees that she would 'not encourage lesbian trade unionists to come out. I know of three lesbians forced out of work by their colleagues'.[92] While she accepted that the ICTU had recommended that sexual orientation be included in employment legislation, she believed that progress for lesbian/gay workers would depend on advances made by women.

Just how important advances for women would be for gay and lesbian workers was evident a few months later with the publication of the ICTU's Women's Charter. The

Women's Charter coincided with the end of the United Nations Decade for Women and set out nineteen principles that trade unions were asked to act upon to improve the situation for women workers in Ireland. Crucially for gay and lesbian workers the Charter made explicit reference to sexual orientation, stating that the ICTU 'recognises and demands the right of everyone, irrespective of race, ethnic origin, creed, political opinion, age, sex, marital status or sexual orientation to have the means to pursue their economic independence and to full participation in the social, cultural and political life of the community in conditions of freedom, dignity and equal opportunity'.[93]

Prior to the publication of the Women's Charter, Phil Flynn (LGPSU), who had attended the CGC's 1984 workshop on 'Discrimination against Lesbian and Gay Workers' had sought to move the issue of gay rights forward within the trade union movement. In a May 1985 letter to Donal Nevin (ICTU General Secretary), Flynn requested that the ICTU sponsor a seminar/workshop on the problems facing gay people in employment. Flynn's request was approved by the ICTU Executive Council and in November 1985 the ICTU sponsored its first half-day workshop on 'Discrimination in Employment in Relation to Sexual Orientation'.[94] The workshop addressed three main issues: 'The role of legal change in tackling this form of discrimination', 'the role of lesbian and gay workers in fighting discrimination' and 'the role of Trade Unions'. Those who addressed delegates included: Prof Fr Michael MacGreil (Maynooth University Sociology Lecturer), Kieran Rose (CGC & LGPSU), Marie Mulholland (National Union of Public Employees) and Laurence Plumley (Northern Ireland Public Service Alliance).[95] Although the summary report of the conference noted that the seminar 'uncovered a lot of prejudice and discrimination' within the unions, delegates agreed to a number of recommendations, notably:

- Education and training programmes should deal with the issue of anti-lesbian/gay prejudice and discrimination.
- Information material should be prepared for the general membership, shop stewards.
- Drawing up of Guidelines for Negotiators on discrimination in employment in relation to sexual orientation.[96]

At a meeting at the LGPSU head office in Dublin in May 1986, Joan McCarthy, Mick Quinlan, Kieran Rose, Marie Quiery, Christopher Robson, Cathal Kerrigan and Imelda (surname unknown) met to consider how to proceed following the ICTU seminar in November 1985. It was decided at this meeting that a new group – Lesbian and Gay Rights at Work (LGRW) – was to be established. Others who were actively involved with LGRW included Donal Sheehan and Brenda Harvey. Collectively, these individuals were members of the LGPSU, Federated Workers Union of Ireland (FWUI), IDATU, and Union of Professional and Technical Civil Servants (UPTCS). LGRW worked to get a charter for the rights of lesbian and gay workers from the ICTU, act as an information exchange for those working on the issue and raise the issue of workers' rights and trade unions within the lesbian/gay community.[97] Later that same year, Donal Nevin wrote to John Mitchell to inform him that the ICTU had agreed to a number of actions in relation to discrimination in employment due to sexual orientation, notably:

- the motion adopted by the 1982 Conference should be re-circulated to Unions.
- that the Health Education Bureau be requested to arrange a joint ICTU/HEB seminar on AIDS as a workplace issue.
- That the Congress Trade Union Education and Training programme should cover the issue of discrimination on the basis of sexual orientation.
- That guidelines to assist trade union negotiators should be prepared.[98]

Mitchell had been lobbying Nevin throughout June and July 1986 to get the ICTU to consider the recommendations adopted at the November 1985 seminar.[99]

Gay and lesbian workers did not have to wait long before the aforementioned action points became a reality. In June 1987, in what was a significant moment in the history of gay and lesbian activism in Ireland, the ICTU published *Lesbian and Gay Rights in the Workplace: Guidelines for Negotiators*. This historic document made clear that the rights of gay and lesbian workers were an integral part of the trade union movement and laid out a series of important measures that unions affiliated to the ICTU should adopt to ensure that gay and lesbian workers would be protected:

- Negotiate equality agreements with employers which specifically refer to discrimination on grounds of sexuality.
- Communicate union policy throughout the Union pointing out that discrimination will not be tolerated and that the Union will treat such discrimination as a serious workplace issue.
- Cover the issue of discrimination on grounds of sexuality on union education and training course.
- Where equality clauses already exist in union agreements, it is recommended that these be amended to include discrimination on grounds of sexuality.[100]

On the heels of these recommendations, the UPTCS, FWUI and LGPSU all passed resolutions affirming their commitment to implementing the 1987 ICTU guidelines.[101] The UPTCS successfully used these guidelines to protect gay and lesbian workers in the Irish civil service. Following negotiations led by UPTCS members Christopher Robson and Tom Lacey, the Department of Finance issued a circular on 'Civil Service Policy on AIDS' in June 1988, which, amongst other issues, prohibited discrimination on the basis of sexual orientation. The circular also set out that officers who were 'HIV positive or who suffer from AIDS' would be retained in their jobs as long as they could perform their duties.[102] This contrasted sharply with the British government's introduction of Section 28 of the Local Government Act that same year. Therefore, in the space of seven years, gay and lesbian activists had succeeded in generating support from the trade union movement for gay rights as well as the adoption of policies protecting gay and lesbian workers. Crucially, as we will now see, the ICTU did not shy away from lobbying the Irish government on this issue.

'Bringing Irish law into line with civilised European opinion'

The Department of Finance's 1988 circular on AIDS was a historic document in its own right. This was the first time that an Irish government had introduced a positive directive that sought to provide some form of protection for individuals being discriminated against based on their sexual orientation within the civil service. Since the foundation of the IGRM in 1974, successive governments and political parties more generally had tended to avoid the issue of gay rights and decriminalisation. This was not a priority for any of the main political parties (*Fianna Fáil, Fine Gael* and the Labour Party). Throughout the 1980s there had been little inclination that any form of positive change would be introduced by the government to protect gay and lesbian individuals. On the contrary, successive governments had been, after all, steadfastly defending the 1861 and 1885 laws. The government's unwillingness to amend the laws was not for want of trying by gay rights activists and it is worth exploring their rhetoric and efforts in trying to shift attitudes on this issue within government.

In the personal papers of Noel Browne there is a letter sent to him from David Norris in July 1978, containing a circular, which was to be sent to all members of the Irish parliament and which Norris sought Browne's opinion on. While it has not been possible to find a response to Norris' letter, comments by Browne in Leinster House in October 1978 clearly demonstrate that he approved of the contents and approach. In Norris' letter he argued that 'Ireland remains the only sovereign state in Europe to have avoided the reform of these laws ...'[103] In noting that there would be an attempt in the near future to change these laws, the letter insisted that 'our European partners will watch with interest the debate on this question which touches civil rights issues on which Ireland has a long and involved record'.[104] In a strikingly similar line of argument during questions to the then Taoiseach, Jack Lynch (*Fianna Fáil*), on whether or not homosexuality would be included in the terms of reference for the Law Reform Commission, Browne argued that 'is it not a fact on the issues referred that the laws of our country in relation to these subjects compared to those of western Europe are both illiberal and unjust. In these circumstances, if we are to become full partners in Europe, should we not now make some attempt as a matter of urgency to bring our laws into line with western usage in this regard?'[105] Lynch, however, was not moved and did not recommend that homosexuality be included as part of the remit of the Law Reform Commission.

We have seen previously in this chapter that gay and lesbian activists spoke about gay rights in terms of human rights, arguing that gay and lesbian individuals were an oppressed minority grouping. This was a rhetoric that the Student Movement, ICCL and the Trade Union Movement supported. Gay rights activists worked hard to promote their message that what they were asking for was simply 'fundamental human rights'. Linked with this focus on human rights was the argument that these laws were unjust. In fact, activists used quite powerful language in condemning the treatment of gay and lesbian individuals in the Republic of Ireland. In numerous documents issued by the IGRM, NGF and CGC, the situation regarding homosexuality in the Republic of Ireland was frequently described as barbaric, uncivilised, repressive, medieval and antiquated. In one such example from an NGF 1980 Gay Pride booklet, the NGF declared that 'the homosexual minority in Ireland has long been a repressed and oppressed minority ... frightened to live their lifestyle in a country with a barbarous official attitude towards it ... Ireland is the only remaining sovereign state in western Europe which criminalises male homosexuality. The laws are uncivilised.'[106]

Within the aforementioned quote from the NGF's 1980 gay pride booklet, Norris' 1978 letter, and Browne's comments in Leinster House, however, is another key tenet of the gay rights movement's rhetoric: that of the Republic of Ireland being the only remaining sovereign state in western Europe that criminalises sexual activity between men. Irish gay rights activists and their international counterparts used Ireland's membership of the EEC to criticise the maintenance of the 1861 and 1885 laws. They persistently contrasted the situation of gay and lesbian individuals in the Republic of Ireland with their counterparts in Europe, presenting the Republic of Ireland as 'out of step' with the direction in which modern Europe was travelling. While Europe symbolised modernity, progressiveness and tolerance, the Republic of Ireland was presented as antiquated, backward and intolerant. In one NGF press release following Scotland's decision to decriminalise sexual activity between men in 1980, the NGF maintained that by calling for gay rights in the Republic of Ireland, they were simply fulfilling their 'patriotic duty to make this last effort to prevent further humiliation of our country in the light of European public opinion'.[107] That same statement declared that 'Ireland's voice will carry greater weight in the councils of international diplomacy when her politicians take the lead in putting an end to a form of discrimination that has been judged by the European Court at Strasbourg to be a denial of fundamental human rights'.[108] The argument, therefore, was that the emancipation of Ireland's gay community would send a message to the world that Ireland did not condone the repressive and barbaric treatment of its gay and lesbian citizens. Put simply, creating a more tolerant environment for gay and lesbian individuals would present the Republic of Ireland in a more positive international light. This was an argument that international gay organisations got behind and did not shy away from making to Irish officials.

In the September 1980 issue of the *IGA Newsletter*, the NGF requested that IGA members put pressure on the Irish government to amend the laws.[109] Files from the Department of Foreign Affairs show that following Norris' defeat in the Irish High Court in 1980, the Federation of Working Groups Homophily (FWGH), a Belgian organisation, sent a letter complaining about Ireland's maintenance of the 1861 and 1885 laws. Jackie Boekyns, FWGH president, wrote that 'from our own daily experiences in Belgium in the field of homosexuality we cannot understand such a condemnation in a European nation. At a time when in so many countries homosexual men and women can live openly their preference, we are taken aback on the out of date philosophy hidden behind this recent sentence'.[110] This was a view shared by Kevin C. Griffin from the Canadian organisation, Society for Political Action for Gay People. In his letter to Ireland's ambassador to Canada, Sean P. Kennan, Griffin described Ireland as being 'out of step with recent developments in Europe and North America', imploring him to 'make known to your government the opposition to these laws by the gay citizens of Vancouver' on the basis that their maintenance was a 'retrograde step in the worldwide struggle for human rights'.[111]

Others sought to warn Irish officials of the damage these laws and the wider treatment of gay and lesbian individuals would have on the country's international reputation. This was particularly noticeable following the banning of *Gay News* in 1982. As we have seen previously, this decision was strongly condemned by the ICCL, but it was also condemned outside Ireland. Sam Staggs, editor-in-chief of the USA-based gay magazine, *MANDATE*, wrote to Noel Dorr, Ireland's Permanent Representative to the United Nations, seeking his aid 'in ending a human rights violation in your country'.[112] Making specific reference to the banning of *Gay News*, Staggs complained that 'such persecution of a minority group cannot enhance the image of Ireland abroad; on the contrary, it makes one look upon your country (erroneously, perhaps, but not without some foundation) as backward'. Staggs even hinted that there could be economic consequences for Ireland, warning that 'gay and non-gay persons in the United States and throughout the world will be watching events in Ireland, and many will exercise economic and travel boycotts against your country if the cruel treatment of gays continues. I myself have cancelled plans to visit Ireland in January 1983 pending resolution of this urgent problem.'[113]

It is not known if Staggs did eventually travel to Ireland, but he was not alone in condemning the banning of *Gay News*. Ian Christie, international secretary of the SHRG, shared Stagg's concerns. On this occasion Christie directed his letter to the Director of the Office of Censorship of Publications, urging him to 'reflect on the international implications of your decision, creating as it does the impression that Éire is among the most intolerant and obscurantist countries in the world'.[114] In fact, Christie revealed that the SHRG viewed it as 'both strange and sad that Eire [sic] is exercising such a censorship, a policy which would be enthusiastically supported by the Rev Ian Paisley in North Ireland and President Bresnev [sic] in the Soviet Union'.[115] Paisley was a protestant evangelical minister, a co-founder of the Free Presbyterian Church of Ulster and leader of the Democratic Unionist Party in Northern Ireland. He spearheaded the 'Save Ulster from Sodomy' campaign of the late 1970s, which opposed the 'social and legal acceptance of homosexuality as "normal" in Northern Ireland'.[116]

Interestingly, Christie's reference to the Soviet Union was not the first time a direct comparison had been made between Ireland and the Soviet Union. Four years earlier, David Norris and Bernard Keogh had similarly compared Ireland to the Soviet Union. In a letter to the *Irish Press* in July 1978, Norris stated that:

> let us remember that even in Ireland, we are not always the Snow-White champions of individual liberty and freedom of conscience that we like to present ourselves as being, particularly when the issues involved disturb our personal complacency. Let us bear in mind, for example, that Ireland alone of the European countries shares with Russia an outdated legal code under which adult male homosexuals can be subjected to police harassment and jail for conduct of their private lives.[117]

This comparison was later made by Liz Doran in an interview she conducted with Kieran Rose in 1983. Beginning her article, Doran remarked that:

> To the ordinary straight people of Ireland, there are few similarities between Communist Russia and our beloved republican democracy ... Yet despite the sacred regard by the Irish for 'freedom' and 'civil rights' there are many citizens who believe they may as well be living in the U.S.S.R. as here. Thirty-year-old Kieran Rose feels this way.[118]

It was clear from Doran's article that the rhetoric of the gay rights movement was gaining traction. This approach formed part of an attempt to highlight the hypocrisy of successive Irish governments and politicians who were quick to condemn breaches of human rights outside of Irish shores yet maintain the status quo with regard to the treatment of its gay and lesbian individuals.

While the government persisted in maintaining the status quo, the Republic of Ireland did find itself drifting further away from its European peers in the 1980s, often finding itself signalled out for its unwillingness to shift direction. In May 1980, for example, the Dutch Liberal Party and the Christian Democrats succeeded in having a motion passed in the Dutch parliament condemning the legal situation in the Republic of Ireland, even calling on the Irish government to amend the laws. In defending their decision to interfere with internal Irish politics both parties explained that 'now there are such close links between the countries in the EEC, it feels it can state that the legislation is no longer in line with general norms'.[119] This intervention incensed Noel Davern, *Fianna Fáil* TD and MEP, who insisted that the Dutch parliament had 'nothing better to do than pass resolutions on homosexuality in Ireland'.[120] Davern's annoyance was shared by Michael Keating, *Fine Gael* TD and spokesman on Human Rights and Law Reform, who declared unequivocally that 'no outside attempts to force Ireland to change its values would succeed'.[121]

While Davern's objections to the Dutch motion may not have taken many by surprise, Keating's condemnation may well have, considering that only one year earlier *Fine Gael* had passed its own motion supporting reform of the 1861 and 1885 laws. During its April 1979 *Ard Fheis* (national conference), Roy Dooney, then Young *Fine Gael* national chair, proposed that *Fine Gael* should support 'the repeal of the oppressive legislation against homosexuals in this country'.[122] In proposing the motion, Dooney adopted similar language to that of gay rights activists, emphasising the degree to which Ireland's 'medieval' laws did not align with those of its European counterparts.[123] To the welcome of gay rights organisations, this motion was carried, making *Fine Gael* the first major political party in the Republic of Ireland to endorse the decriminalisation of sexual activity between men. However, as Keating's criticism of the 1980 Dutch motion demonstrated, *Fine Gael* had clearly moved away from this position within just one year.

The difficulty for the Irish government was that not only were some criticising its maintenance of the 1861 and 1885 laws, but efforts were also being made to enhance the rights of gay and lesbian citizens in Europe. This could be seen in October 1981 with the passage of Recommendation 924 and Resolution 756 in the Parliamentary Assembly of the Council of Europe.[124] Both focused broadly on ending discrimination against homosexuals in areas such as employment, custody cases, ending conversion therapy and the removal by the World Health Organisation of homosexuality from its international classification of diseases. Particularly problematic for the Republic of Ireland was Recommendation 924's call on governments to abolish laws that criminalised homosexual acts between consenting adults.

According to files within the National Archives, recommendation 924 caused some headache for the Irish government, with one handwritten note from J. Liddy (Legal Division – Department of Foreign Affairs) suggesting that 'pending the Supreme Court decision in the Norris case it will be difficult for Ireland to take any clear-cut position on the recommendation as a whole, and the permanent representative may wish to consider ways of playing for time.'[125] The state clearly recognised that it was in an awkward position, but successfully played for time on the matter. The NGF did, however, use Recommendation 924 to request a meeting with the then Minister of State for Law Reform, Dick Spring (Labour Party), in the hope of convincing him 'to bring Ireland into line with the developing situation'.[126] This was a request Spring agreed to in November 1981, but the meeting did not result in any policy shift.

Within four months of the passage of Recommendation 924 and Resolution 756, a general election was held in the Republic of Ireland, which the Munster (Cork) IGRM took as an opportunity to gauge support for gay rights within the different political parties. This was the first time such a survey was conducted and provided an insight into the extent to which gay rights organisations had been able to make any progress on the issue of gay rights within Irish political parties.[127] The responses, however, were mixed. Smaller left-wing parties such as *Sinn Fein* The Workers Party, *Sein Fein* (Provisional) and the Connolly Youth Movement/Communist Party of Ireland all replied that they would support the decriminalisation of sexual activity between men and the extension of legislation to protect individuals against being dismissed from employment because of their sexual orientation.[128] Of the three main political parties, however, only the Labour Party responded that it favoured the decriminalisation of sexual activity between men and the extension of legislation to protect gay and lesbian workers. *Fianna Fáil*, on the other hand, side-stepped giving a direct response to the 1982 survey, replying that they regarded 'these proposals as being sub-judice in view of ongoing case of David Norris v. Attorney General ... When we get back to power however we are reviewing – as already stated – the criminal code and updating it with particular reference to 19th Century laws'. What changes they had in mind is difficult to know, but *Fianna Fáil* subsequently supported the holding of a referendum to introduce a constitutional ban on abortion in 1983. *Fine Gael*, in a sign of just how far they had moved from their 1979 *Ard Fheis* position, refused to answer the survey, informing the Munster (Cork) IGRM that 'no statement would be issued on any of the three points ...'.[129]

Both *Fine Gael* and *Fianna Fáil* were comfortable in distancing themselves from recommendations to protect gay and lesbian individuals on the European stage. During a vote in the European Parliament in March 1984 on a proposal to outlaw discrimination against homosexuals in the workplace, *Fine Gael* MEPs abstained reportedly 'on the grounds that the issue was one for individual member states', while *Fianna Fáil* MEPs voted against the proposal.[130] Brendan Halligan, Labour Party MEP, was the only Irish MEP to vote in favour, telling the parliament that this issue 'was not likely in the foreseeable future to be discussed in the Dáil and the European Parliament was the only parliamentary forum open to an Irish politician to debate this issue in public'.[131]

The March 1984 vote in the European Parliament had followed a report presented by Dr Vera Squarcialupi (Italian MEP) on behalf of the Committee on Social Affairs and Employment; a report that signalled out the Republic of Ireland as the only member state that criminalised sexual activity between men.[132] The primary focus of the report was on sexual discrimination in the workplace, and during the course of her research

Squarcialupi had contacted the Munster (Cork) IGRM seeking information on the situation in the Republic of Ireland. On the heels of this request, Stephen Quillinan wrote to the Minister for Labour asking if his department condoned the practice of job applicants being refused employment solely on the grounds of their sexual orientation or being dismissed from employment on these grounds.[133] In response to Quillinan's letter, Freda Nolan, private secretary to the Minister for Labour, replied that:

> The position as regards recruitment to the Civil Service is that sexual orientation is not a factor in the recruitment process. Neither are Civil Servants dismissed on such grounds ... The Minister is concerned about all forms of discrimination in employment and is anxious to take whatever steps are necessary to protect individuals from such discrimination. However, in the absence of strong evidence to the contrary there would not appear to be a case for introducing legislation to combat discrimination based on sexual orientation at this point in time. There are therefore, no immediate proposals to amend the law in this area.[134]

While Nolan focused on the absence of reported cases of such discrimination as the reason no legislation had been considered on this issue in her official response to Quillinan, documents from the Department of Labour show that, when preparing their response, officials also expressed the belief that such a law outlawing discrimination against individuals based on their sexual orientation may not have public support. One briefing document noted that 'the main force of public opinion is not sympathetic towards homosexuality. I feel that there are no signs that society is ready to change this attitude. It is difficult to imagine parents accepting that a known homosexual should be allowed to take charge of a class of young boys on the grounds that it would be unlawful to object.'[135]

The difficulty for gay rights activists was that in the absence of official cases of this nature, it was difficult to counteract the Department of Labour's contention that there was no evidence of such discrimination taking place. Although they lacked evidence from within Ireland, Irish gay activists, with the support of the ICTU, continued to pressure the Irish government to amend the employment legislation. In its 1985 annual report, the ICTU noted that it had forwarded a number of recommendations on amendments to the Unfair Dismissals Act 1977 to the Minister for Labour, Ruairí Quinn, among them the inclusion of sexual orientation.[136]

During the second half of 1986, a period when the government was reviewing employment legislation, there was a concerted effort by LGRW to lobby the Department of Labour for an amendment to the Unfair Dismissals Act 1977 and the Employment Equality Act 1977. Letters were sent to the Minister for Labour from: John Mitchell (IDATU), LGRW, TAF, ICTU and the Employment Equality Authority (EEA), a state body established under the Employment Equality Act 1977.[137] The EEA had come out in support of amending the Unfair Dismissals Act 1977 and the Employment Equality Act 1977 earlier that year, following a meeting between Sylvia Meehan (EEA chairwoman) and Kieran Rose and Maura Molloy, representing the LGRW.[138]

LGRW were conscious that previous attempts to have the law amended had been dismissed due to lack of any evidence. While in 1986 there were still no reported domestic cases, LGRW decided to draw on international cases in its efforts to demonstrate that such discrimination did occur. In its letter dated 22 September 1986, requesting that the Minister include sexual orientation in the legislation, LGRW included a document that listed numerous cases from Great Britain to demonstrate that discrimination did actually occur, including the John Sanders case.[139] Other evidence attached included the 1984 European Parliament working document on sexual discrimination and the 1982 ICTU policy in support of amending the 1977 legislation.[140]

The extent to which these efforts were having an impact was evidenced by the Minister for Labour writing to the Attorney General seeking his opinion on whether or not the laws could be amended with the current 1861 and 1885 laws still being in existence.[141] Quinn also wrote to the EEA seeking a detailed explanation as to why it was recommending the amendment of the legislation, while department officials reached out to the ICTU and Federated Union of Employers (FUE) to seek their views on the matter. Of those who were contacted, the FUE was the only organisation to respond that it would be 'opposed to any revision of the legislation' to include sexual orientation. John Dunne, FUE director, argued that 'there is no information available to suggest or verify that discrimination of any form exists as a result of the sexual orientation of any employee or prospective employee'.[142]

In contrast, Patricia O'Donovan, ICTU legislation and equality officer, who at that stage was actively involved in developing the ICTU's *Guidelines for Negotiators*, reiterated the ICTU's strong support for the amendment of the legislation, citing the motion adopted at the 1982 ICTU's annual congress and the 1985 Women's Charter.[143] Sylvia Meehan was also equally supportive in her response to Quinn. While Meehan acknowledged that there had been no reported cases in Ireland, she noted that representations by 'certain trade unionists' had been made to the agency 'that such discrimination takes place in the employment sphere'.[144] Meehan argued that the lack of 'documented cases does not mean that discrimination does not take place' and that cases would emerge 'if redress was provided'. Just as LGRW had done, Meehan cited cases from Britain as evidence that such discrimination did occur, including, for example: a copy of the British Labour Campaign for Lesbian and Gay Rights publication, *Legislation for Lesbian and Gay Rights: A Manifesto*; a section from *Out for Ourselves* discussing discrimination in the workplace due to sexual orientation; and the aforementioned Recommendation 924, Resolution 756 and the Squarcialupi report.[145]

Just when it appeared that there might be progress in this particular area, the *Fine Gael*-Labour Party coalition collapsed in January 1987. In a survey conducted by *OUT* during the general election on party support for gay rights, *Fianna Fáil* and *Fine Gael* replied that they had no plans to legislate for the decriminalisation of sexual activity between men. The Labour Party replied that this 'has never been debated by the Annual Conference, which is the supreme policy-making body of the party'.[146] This contrasted sharply with the response to the Munster (Cork) IGRM's survey in 1982. The Labour Party spokesperson did, however, state that they believed most of the party would support this, although there was no official policy.[147] Once more, it was the smaller parties who were willing to publicly declare their support for decriminalisation. These included *Sinn Féin* and the Workers' Party.

While the gay rights movement did not succeed in generating enough support from the political class in the 1980s, they nevertheless had made significant progress with other influential organisations during this decade. As we shall see in Chapter 6, these organisations continued to lend their support to gay rights in the Republic of Ireland and played a significant role in the introduction of progressive legislation in 1993. What is also clear from this chapter is the extent to which there were a number of different sites where gay rights activism took place throughout the country in the 1980s, not just in the courtroom. Moreover, the arguments adopted were not just legalistic ones focused on the constitutionality or otherwise of the laws, but rather, activists sought to focus on human rights, Ireland's international reputation and Ireland's place in Europe in their efforts to change the narrative on the 1861 and 1885 laws. The 1980s did see setbacks for the gay rights movement, but as we have also seen in this chapter, they also saw a number of significant advances – advances that paved the way for subsequent changes in the early 1990s.

5

Ireland was Ill-Equipped to deal with the AIDS Epidemic

In March 1987, *The Irish Times* reported on the establishment of a nineteen-member National Task Force on AIDS, set-up following an Irish Catholic Bishops' conference held that same month. With an initial budget of £20,000, the Task Force's main objective was to provide education and information on AIDS to priests, seminarians, community and church workers and schools within the 'context of a programme for a positive Christian living'.[1] Bishop Cassidy explained that the message would be not to abuse sex or drugs and that the 'best vaccine for this virus is virtue'; this message would form the cornerstone of the Roman Catholic Church's response to AIDS in the Republic of Ireland.[2]

The responsibility of leading this Task Force fell to Rev Paul Lavelle, who took up the role of pastoral care co-ordinator.[3] Lavelle was joined by district judge Gillian Hussey, who acted as chairperson, and seventeen other individuals representing a myriad of professions such as doctors working in the area of sexual health, a drug addiction counsellor, a journalist, and representatives from the Irish Haemophiliac Society, Mountjoy Prison, the National Catholic Marriage Advisory Council, the Religious Teachers' Association and the Department of Health.[4] Also present on the Task Force were representatives from a small group known as Gay Health Action (GHA).

GHA had been set up in 1985 as an umbrella group for the different Irish gay and lesbian organisations to respond to AIDS. To some observers the inclusion of GHA, which had been promoting the use of condoms and safer sex in their efforts to combat AIDS, may have been contradictory to the stated objectives of the Task Force, i.e., to respond to AIDS within a 'programme for a positive Christian living'. GHA had repeatedly dismissed moral concerns around the promotion of condoms and explicit information, arguing instead that AIDS was a medical issue that could affect everyone, irrespective of their religion. Ciaran McKinney, the GHA representative on the AIDS Task Force, however, was under no illusion that he or GHA would be able to change the Church's position on the use of condoms. Instead, GHA's objective in participating on the Task Force was not to try 'to get the Church to change its mind on condoms, but to see what areas the Church could get involved as a caring service . . .'.[5]

GHA's inclusion could be passed off as the Task Force recognising that the gay community (particularly gay men) were one of the so-called 'high-risk groups' most affected by AIDS. While that certainly was true, it is also the case that GHA's inclusion reflected the reality that by 1987 it had developed a reputation as one of the leading expert groups on AIDS in Ireland. Not only had it pioneered public AIDS education campaigns in the country, but it had also pioneered services for those affected by HIV and AIDS. At a time when the Irish government was sluggish in its response to AIDS, GHA demonstrated remarkable leadership in getting as much information out to the Irish public as possible. The expertise of GHA was acknowledged by Rev Lavelle, who the *Irish Independent* reported had stated that 'homosexuals are more up to date in their knowledge of support for AIDS victims'.[6]

While the approach of GHA and the Roman Catholic Church to combat AIDS remained decidedly different throughout the 1980s, the inclusion of GHA in the Task Force is representative of just how crucial a role GHA had come to play in responding to AIDS in the Republic of Ireland. It is no exaggeration to state that GHA was arguably one of the most important AIDS organisations – and gay organisations – set up in 1980s Ireland. Like their international counterparts, Ireland's gay community led the fight against AIDS from the beginning. In doing so, GHA not only provided the wider Irish public with vital information on AIDS, at a time when few other sources were readily available, but they also shielded the gay community from being scapegoated for AIDS. While AIDS was certainly linked to homosexuality in the Irish media, the early and effective response of GHA led many to pay tribute and acknowledge their efforts. It is the efforts of GHA, in particular its public AIDS education campaigns, that this chapter focuses on.

'Hear no Sex, See no Sex, Speak no Sex'

Writing in 1987, four years after the first two AIDS cases were confirmed in Ireland, Dr Derek Freedman, one of Ireland's leading specialists in sexual health, concluded that Ireland was 'ill-equipped to deal with the AIDS epidemic'.[7] There are a number of reasons that this was the case, but all of which are bound up in a society ill at ease with any public discussion on sex or sexual health. The Irish state, as noted in earlier chapters, sought to impose strict sexual norms on its citizens. This conservative attitude was very much reflected in Irish laws. For example, the Family Planning Bill 1979 (later amended in 1985) ensured that contraceptives were not easily accessible. The 1985 amendments allowed individuals eighteen and over to purchase condoms, but only from chemists, doctors' surgeries, health boards, family planning clinics and hospitals.[8] Shops and vending machines were not permitted to sell condoms under this amendment and, to complicate matters, doctors and chemists could refuse to sell condoms on moral grounds. Despite the Act not granting wholesale access to condoms, many TDs strongly opposed the liberalisation of the law on contraceptives. The then *Fine Gael*/Labour Party government only succeeded in passing the amendments with a majority of three votes.[9]

Other legislation complicated AIDS related-matters further. In particular, the Indecent Advertisement Act of 1889, later amended in 1929 under the Censorship of Publications Act, made it an offence to print material advertising or referring to 'any disease affecting the generative organs of either sex, or to any complaint or infirmity arising from or relating to sexual intercourse ...'.[10] It effectively made it illegal to print material in public spaces that offered information on AIDS or any other sexually transmitted diseases (STDs). The restrictions of this Act became evident to the Minister for Health in 1983, when his department encountered problems after it sought to place notices in public toilets informing the public where they could receive treatment for STDs in Ireland. This was prohibited under the 1929 Act and resulted in the Minister having to explore other means of advertising these services.[11]

Although GHA and the government later circumvented this legislation, its existence nevertheless gives an insight into the socio-cultural and legal climate of this period, particularly in relation to STDs, which were not a matter for public discourse. Ironically, if the Minister had succeeded in getting the notices published in public toilets, the list of clinics would not have been extensive. In fact, the facilities to treat STDs in the Republic of Ireland were so lamentable, that Dr Freedman was led to 'liken [them] to a cattle market'.[12] Along with three clinics in Dublin (the Mater hospital, Sir Patrick Dun's hospital, Dr Steevens' hospital), there were only two other such services outside Dublin: St Finbarr's hospital in Cork and a clinic in Galway that could be contacted through a confidential phone line.[13] The inadequate facilities were further compounded by a poor system of reporting cases. In 1983 the Minister for Health revealed that there were roughly 2,000 STDs reported each year. However, this was believed to be only a fraction of the actual numbers, as a considerable majority of individuals decided to visit local doctors for treatment, who, the Minister remarked, were often reluctant to report confirmed cases due to the intimate nature of STDs.[14]

It is also worth emphasising the almost complete lack of sex education within the Irish educational sphere, which further added to the unease and embarrassment around discussing sex and sexual health.[15] The attitude to sex education in the Republic of Ireland was best summed up in one letter to *The Irish Times* in 1985, when the writer stated that 'ignorance was the main deterrent long ago when sex education consisted of hear no sex, see no sex, speak no sex'.[16] At that time the Irish Roman Catholic Church held considerable sway over educational matters, with the vast majority of schools coming under the patronage of the Irish Roman Catholic Church. As a result, it allowed the clergy to flex their muscles to prevent anything they deemed not in-keeping with the religious ethos of the school from entering the classroom. The issue of secular sex education entering classrooms was something the hierarchy of the church was very wary of. Dr McNamara, Archbishop of Dublin, for example, warned in January 1985 that a sex education programme introduced 'in a value free context or in the context of values other than Christian ones, would only have the effect of making children more vulnerable to these evils. The all too predictable consequence of an incursion by the State into the field of sex education would be a marked decline in the standards of sexual morality among the young'.[17]

Combined, the aforementioned attitudes and laws complicated efforts to respond to AIDS in the Republic of Ireland and placed extra restrictions, burdens and pressure on those seeking to provide information to the wider public. Therefore, it would be an understatement to say that the Republic of Ireland was ill-prepared to confront AIDS when it arrived.

'Gay disease hits children'

Archbishop McNamara's aforementioned comments appeared at a time when AIDS was becoming a more topical news issue within the mainstream Irish media. While the first reported references to AIDS appeared in 1982, by early 1985 it had become more topical as the number of cases slowly began to increase – there were four confirmed AIDS cases (three homosexuals, one haemophiliac) in the Republic of Ireland in January 1985, up two since the first two cases were confirmed in 1983. Much like their international counterparts, the mainstream Irish media did not shy away from sensationalising some of their articles, many of which characterised it as a 'gay disease'. Articles appeared with headlines such as 'Gay disease hits children', 'Killer disease is here', 'AIDS may be widespread' and 'Death lurks in blood bank'.[18] Within these articles journalists often referred to AIDS as the 'gay disease', 'gay cancer' or 'gay plague' because, according to one *Irish Times* journalist, it was 'commonest among male homosexuals' as it 'chose victims who for the most part had known a high level of sexual activity: as many as a thousand partners or more'.[19]

Noticeably absent from these articles was information on how one developed AIDS or where to find further information. Moreover, its presentation as a 'gay disease' only added to the ignorance then surrounding the syndrome and the reality that anyone, irrespective of their sexual orientation, could be affected. This is hardly surprising when the Irish government appeared more like observers rather than those responsible for addressing the matter of AIDS. When asked in June 1983 about the steps the government had taken to deal with AIDS, the Minister for Health, Barry Desmond, responded that his department had 'asked each director of community care and medical health officer to investigate whether any cases of the disease had occurred in their areas'.[20] This led the *Irish Independent* to remark that such a request would be particularly difficult in a country where 'only a fraction of sexually transmitted diseases are reported to the authorities'.[21] Interestingly, Elgy Gillespie, in an article in *The Irish Times*, reported that 'unsurprisingly the illness has caused fear and panic in the gay community of the United States, and now over here, where the National Gay Federation devoted the whole of a recent issue of their house magazine to explaining the illness'.[22] While the NGF did devote an issue of *NGF News* to AIDS in January/February 1983, the tone of the issue was a far cry from one of panic. Unlike the vast majority of the mainstream media, which sensationalised AIDS, the Irish gay community adopted a more measured approach in its coverage of the disease. The coverage sought to reassure readers that AIDS was not a 'gay disease' and that there were steps they could take to reduce the risk of contracting the virus.

At the time the NGF published its special issue on AIDS, there had been no reported AIDS cases in the Republic of Ireland, but Christopher Robson nevertheless encouraged readers to prepare themselves for its possible arrival. Robson, later a founding member of GHA, provided an overview of the symptoms of AIDS, as well as the judgemental treatment many of those living with AIDS were subjected to, while at the same time condemning the media coverage of AIDS. It was Robson's contention that while there were no cases of AIDS in the Republic of Ireland, 'it will require a shift in attitudes more than anything: an abandoning of the idea (shared by most of us) that other gays are just people in pubs or faces on the scene. Gays are our brothers and sisters, and should expect and receive from the community the support that traditionally comes from the family'.[23] Sensing the detrimental effects that the sensationalised media coverage could pose for the gay community, Robson warned that 'we should not accept the category gay cancer or allow any such categorisation'.[24]

A similar tone was expressed in an article published by the Cork Gay Collective in *Quare Times* in Spring 1984. Donal Sheehan, who became an active member of the Cork branch of GHA, lambasted the presentation of AIDS as a 'gay disease', arguing that 'the myth of A.I.D.S travels faster than the disease itself'.[25] Sheehan sought to dismiss the view of AIDS as a 'gay plague', while also taking aim at the poor state of the facilities for treating STDs, something he feared would only worsen the situation. While Sheehan did not shy away from acknowledging the seriousness of AIDS, noting that many had died, he also argued that while 'it is a frightening disease ... a disease is ... a disease – to be treated, prevented and, if possible, cured. A.I.D.S. is turning into something more than just a disease, like cancer it is becoming a metaphor'.[26]

Whereas Robson and Sheehan's article sought to dismiss the myth of AIDS as a 'gay disease' and to provide information on what it really was, a number of other articles on AIDS appeared throughout 1984 in *NGF News*, which sought to provide the latest up-to-date information on AIDS. These articles formed part of what the NGF labelled its Gay Health Care Report. In one such article Edmund Lynch reported on a 1984 International Gay Association AIDS conference held in Amsterdam. Lynch, much like Robson, reminded readers that there was 'no need to panic' and encouraged them to have regular check-ups if they were sexually active. 'Regular Sex = Regular Check-Ups', Lynch declared.[27] It would seem from Lynch's article that TAF had also become involved in disseminating information at this stage, particularly providing callers with the details of where they could receive advice/treatment for STDs. Two other AIDS articles that same year introduced the concept of safer sex to Ireland's gay community. In what would be a reoccurring motif of the Irish gay community's rhetoric on AIDS, Walt Kilroy stressed that steps could be taken to reduce the risks associated with sexual activity, which did not mean celibacy. Kilroy's article encouraged readers to reduce their number of different sexual partners, to avoid the exchange of bodily fluids ('cumming inside your partner'), and particularly to avoid what he labelled 'high-risk sexual practices' such as fist-fucking, anal sex and rimming. However, he reassured readers that kissing, cuddling, massaging and mutual masturbation had a very low risk of transmission, while condoms would also help.[28]

Robson, Sheehan, Lynch and Kilroy were in the position to disseminate information on AIDS at a relatively early stage in the Republic of Ireland, due to the connections that Irish gay and lesbian organisations had built up with their international counterparts over the years. In their aforementioned articles, for example, both Robson and Sheehan quoted directly from the *Body Politic*. Along with the *Body Politic*, the *New York Native*, as well as material from the AIDS Foundation in San Francisco and the Minnesota AIDS project, was often reproduced in *OUT* throughout the 1980s. The International Gay Association was also useful in disseminating information to gay organisations. As we shall see, these connections were crucial to GHA's efforts.

'If you decide to fuck, using a condom will significantly reduce your risk'

With the increased media coverage of AIDS, in January 1985 a meeting was arranged at the Hirschfeld Centre to discuss the developing AIDS situation in Ireland.[29] Those represented included the CGC, DGC, Gay Information Line (Cork), Cork IGRM, NGF, TAF and Trinity College Dublin's gay society. The primary impetus for calling the meeting was the increased media coverage of AIDS and its possible impact on the gay community, something the aforementioned organisations believed required a co-ordinated response. Along with the unease about the media coverage, concern was also raised about the state of Ireland's facilities to treat STDs. At a follow-up meeting in February at TCD with representatives from the Dublin Lesbian and Gay Men's Collective, CGC, NGF, TCD gay society and the Cork IGRM, it was decided that there was a need to focus on two specific areas: the media coverage of AIDS; and canvassing for the improvement of the current STD clinic services in Ireland.[30] It was agreed at this meeting that members from the aforementioned groups would now work under the umbrella of a new organisation, which became known as Gay Health Action (GHA).

GHA was primarily comprised of a small cohort of individuals based in Dublin and Cork, most notably Mick Quinlan, Christopher Robson, Arthur Leahy, Ciaran McKinney, Cathal Kerrigan, Bill Foley, Donal Sheehan, Brenda Harvey and Ray Gaston. These individuals formed the core group of GHA, but the minutes of GHA meetings also show that others participated, although only first names were given, yet these names do reveal that more women were also involved with GHA. These minutes also reveal that there was interaction and co-operation with groups from Northern Ireland, such as Cara-Friend Derry, Magee Gay Liberation Society, Cara-Friend Belfast and the National Union of Public Employees (NUPE), as well as the Northern Ireland Gay Rights Association.[31]

Based at the Hirschfeld Centre and the Quay Co-Op, GHA got to work quickly. Early on it set about establishing contact with international AIDS organisations such as the Terrence Higgins Trust (THT), the European AIDS Foundation, the New York Gay Men's Health Crisis and the Shanti Project. Despite the lack of finances, GHA members often travelled abroad to meet with these organisations or to participate in international AIDS conferences. At one GHA meeting in February 1986 there was a report on 'Mick's travel last December', which included trips to London for a THT conference, Belgium, the Netherlands and Germany.[32] The THT in particular became an important ally to the GHA, providing both information and funding to them to carry out its work.

While the February 1985 meeting identified two key areas of priority – the media coverage of AIDS and the poor state of STD facilities in Ireland – GHA quickly found itself leading the efforts to instigate a public AIDS education campaign. These education campaigns, which centred around leaflets, cards, booklets and posters, ensured that explicit information on the means of transmission and steps individuals could take to reduce their risk of contracting the virus entered the mainstream discourse in Ireland. GHA was steadfast in its determination to challenge the characterisation of AIDS as a 'gay disease' and that sex confined to marriage or celibacy were the only means of combatting its spread. Instead, GHA focused on the best means of preventing the spread of AIDS, which they believed could be realistically achieved through a public education campaign promoting safer sex habits. This, they were keen to emphasise, did not have to mean less sex. Rather than blaming casual sex as the root problem of AIDS, GHA instead focused its attention on altering unsafe sex practices. It was this reality that drove GHA's explicit campaign of safer sex, of which the condom and explicit information played central roles.

Within only a few months of its establishment, GHA produced the Republic of Ireland's first AIDS information leaflet in May 1985. It is keenly evident that one of the primary concerns GHA wanted to confront in this leaflet was the myth that AIDS was a 'gay disease' and that it could be contracted through everyday social interactions. They also wanted to promote the steps individuals could take to avoid contracting the virus. At the same time, they sought to use the contents of the leaflet as a means to shield the gay community from unwarranted attacks on foot of AIDS' frequent presentation as a 'gay disease'. In 1985 a backlash against the gay community was not an exaggerated fear as there were certain segments of Irish society who did see AIDS as an opportunity to attack the gay community. In 1985 a group referring to itself as the National Socialist Party distributed a leaflet in Dublin listing the steps it believed needed to be implemented to combat the spread of AIDS. The leaflet, titled 'Smash AIDS Blitzkrieg', blamed AIDS on the 'Gay – AIDS spreaders and the junkies' and proposed the enforcement of the law criminalising sexual activity between men, with a minimum of ten years, as well as the burning down of 'suspect discos, gay bars, clubs etc'.[33] While Christopher Robson reported the leaflet to the police for incitement to crime, the police informed him that 'they didn't think they had a case under existing legislation'.[34]

The AIDS information leaflet, therefore, formed part of GHA's efforts to combat misinformation while also providing information on how to avoid contracting the virus. The leaflet was targeted at gay men and sought to address the main concerns and questions surrounding AIDS: 'How do you get AIDS?'; 'What is the treatment?'; 'Is AIDS in Ireland?'; 'Why do only some people with the virus get AIDS?'. GHA did not claim to have definitive answers to all these questions but sought to dismiss the many known falsehoods about the syndrome. The leaflet emphasised at the beginning that AIDS 'is not a homosexual disease, a gay plague, a moral problem, or a punishment from God', rather it was something like Hepatitis B albeit more severe, and could affect any Irish individual irrespective of their sexuality.[35] They advised readers that it could not be contracted through social kissing, by touching, shared bathrooms or from drinking from another person's glass.

The second noticeable objective of the leaflet was to introduce and promote safer sex practices. These safer sex recommendations included: sex with fewer partners; having sex with men who have few other sexual partners; avoiding anal sex (except with a regular partner); not receiving other men's semen into one's body; avoiding rimming. By Irish standards this was explicit language, yet surprisingly, the leaflet was not censored by the Irish authorities. Interestingly, however, this leaflet was rather cautious about promoting the use of condoms, insisting that while condoms may help, 'do not rely on them for protection'.[36] This may well have been a result of the fact that the GHA had received a small grant from the Health Education Bureau (HEB) and some restraints on the promotion of condoms may have been necessary for its publication. I note this because within the Irish gay press, condoms along with water-based lubricants had been strongly advised and encouraged since 1984. However, it is difficult to ascertain whether or not the HEB did review the contents. While the *Sunday Independent* reported a GHA member as stating that the leaflet was submitted to the HEB, which did not seek or make any changes, that same article also revealed that the HEB refused to confirm or deny that it had vetted the contents of the leaflet.

The reaction to GHA's AIDS information leaflet was mixed. Those who condemned the leaflet did so for one main reason: the leaflet did not condemn homosexuality. Instead, they argued the leaflet encouraged it. In turn, this resulted in further controversy when it was revealed that GHA had received a small grant (£790) from the HEB to cover the cost of printing the leaflet. This grant, however, did not cover the full cost of printing the 16,000 leaflets, with GHA having to make up the rest of the cost themselves. Both the *Sunday Independent* and *Irish Independent* reported that some hospitals and doctors did not want to use the leaflet because it did not advise against homosexual activity, which they felt would have 'the effect of spreading the disease'.[37] One doctor who spoke to the *Sunday Independent* reportedly claimed that 'certain homosexual activity helps spread AIDS and any leaflet paid for by the Department of Health funds should have made that clear, instead of doing the opposite'.[38]

Others reacted more positively to the leaflet, believing GHA's approach was helpful. This was the view of the Northern Ireland Family Planning Association (NIFPA), which contacted GHA requesting copies of its leaflets. Alison Wightman, NIFPA Regional Administrator, described them as 'wonderful [with] really good language, positive approach, clear information, [and] great lay-out'.[39] Recognising the financial constraints on the GHA, Wightman also enclosed a donation. NIFPA was just one of many organisations that contacted GHA requesting its leaflets throughout 1985. Although geared primarily towards gay men, GHA noted that the leaflet had been requested by 'public libraries, social welfare offices, doctors, prison welfare offices, and people working with IV drug users'.[40] The demand for the leaflets resulted in GHA having to reprint a further 15,000 in early 1986; this time, however, without any funding from the HEB.

Following the controversy over the HEB grant to GHA, the GHA did not receive any further grants from the Department of Health, thereby placing pressure on GHA to self-fund.[41] Fortunately for the GHA, support was forthcoming from organisations inside and outside Ireland. The GHA had received a donation from the THT to assist with the production of its first AIDS Information leaflet. This early support from international organisations like the THT was crucial to the development of GHA's campaigns. In August 1985, for example, GHA organised a conference on AIDS at TCD, at which John Fitzpatrick of the THT took part in a question and answer session and provided a lot of 'valuable information' to GHA.[42] Around that same time, the NGF had received a letter from Dr Glen Margo, San Francisco Office of Health Promotion and Education, and Dr John Dupree, Director of Education for the East Bay AIDS Project in Berkeley and Oakland, offering their time to the Irish gay community. In their letter they offered to give a two-day workshop on training and developing educational programs around AIDS, along with programs designed to train volunteer counsellors to help people living with AIDS.[43] The NGF readily agreed. The importance GHA attached to Margo and Dupree's workshop was evident in a letter it sent to the Director of TAF, which informed him that TAF volunteers would have to attend the entire sixteen hours of the workshop with no option to drop in and out, and they would be expected to attend even if it 'mean[t] giving up a day's work/holiday'.[44]

Along with the information delivered on AIDS education programmes and providing counselling to people living with AIDS, both doctors donated copies of videos that covered all aspects of dealing with AIDS and running support groups. These videos, which were not available in Ireland, facilitated the NGF/GHA in running AIDS information evenings at the Hirschfeld Centre every second Monday.[45] Along with these bi-weekly sessions, the videos also provided a solid basis for GHA to provide training sessions to TAF volunteers and later to non-gay organisations.[46] Dupree's and Margo's workshop could not have come at a better time for TAF in particular. Whereas the TAF report for 1984 to April 1985 showed no calls related to AIDS, the following year's report showed that 127 calls were AIDS-related.[47]

Perhaps, however, one of the most important developments to come from Margo's and Dupree's workshop was the foundation of Cairde in September 1985. Cairde, the Irish for friends, was modelled on the San Francisco-based Buddies and became a sub-group of GHA dedicated to providing a confidential help service to people living with AIDS.[48] It was the first support group of its kind in the Republic of Ireland and was run entirely by volunteers operating from the Hirschfeld Centre. For those looking for non-judgemental support, Cairde was a lifeline. One individual who chronicled his experience of living with AIDS in *Magill* recalled how it was through Cairde he received the contact details for sympathetic doctors in Ireland, something a friend who also had AIDS struggled to find.[49] As well as being a support service for individuals and their families affected by AIDS, Cairde actively involved itself in providing information to the wider public through workshops, discussion groups, question and answer sessions and providing training to any organisation wanting to train individuals to work with people affected by AIDS. The demand for a service like Cairde quickly became evident and in 1986 it announced that 'due to the lack of information and organisation by the Department of Health, we have decided not to limit ourselves to the gay section of the community and are available to support anyone who is affected from whatever section of society'.[50] For the remainder of the 1980s, Cairde was the leading support group for individuals affected by AIDS in the Republic of Ireland.

There can be no doubt that due to the lack of information emanating from the Department of Health, extra pressure was placed on GHA. The minutes of a February 1986 GHA meeting noted that the:

> office has become very busy with requests for info and educationals. The main changes over the past few months have been the change to the I.V. Drug users as the main risk group and demands been made on GHA to meet information needs in this case ... It has become clear that we need to look closely at the structure and funding if we are to respond effectively to the growing demands being made on us.[51]

The increased pressure on GHA had two consequences: firstly, it resulted in GHA shifting the focus of its information campaign away from an exclusive concentration on gay men; secondly, to GHA reaching out to other groups in Ireland to form an alliance to share the efforts of combatting AIDS.

At the aforementioned February 1986 GHA meeting, it was noted that GHA had sent letters to other voluntary organisations working with so-called high-risk groups in Ireland seeking a meeting to discuss sharing expertise, resources and the possibility of working more closely on AIDS-related matters. Those who were contacted included the Ana Liffey Project (which provided services to people who used drugs) and the Irish Haemophiliac Society, both of whom responded positively to GHA's request. The result of these meetings was the establishment of the AIDS Action Alliance (AAA) in March 1986. AAA became a co-ordinating group for those working on AIDS as well as a pressure group focused on lobbying the government to provide adequate resources to meet the demands of responding to AIDS. Within the space of two years, AAA had helped establish branches in Cork and Galway; set up an AIDS Helpline (AIDS Helpline Dublin), thereby reducing the pressure on GHA; and published a newsletter, *AIDS Action News*. During that same period those affiliated with the AAA had increased substantially to include, amongst others, Women and AIDS, Body Positive (a support group for those diagnosed HIV positive), the Irish Association of Social Workers, Irish Distributive and Administrative Trade Union, Irish Family Planning Association, Local Government and Public Services Union, Union of Students in Ireland and Union of Professional and Technical Civil Servants.[52] Many of the unions included members actively involved with GHA such as Kieran Rose, Donal Sheehan and Christopher Robson.

The establishment of AIDS Helpline Dublin marked an important development in the campaign to combat AIDS in the Republic of Ireland. Prior to its establishment, GHA and TAF had shared the burden of responding to calls for information. The *Irish Examiner*, for example, reporting on the plans to establish AIDS Helpline Dublin in March 1987, informed readers that, in the meantime, information on AIDS was available from GHA and TAF.[53] That these were the only two helplines mentioned in 1987 speaks volumes about the government's response to AIDS. In fact, announcing the establishment of AIDS Helpline Dublin, the *Evening Herald* described it as 'the first community-based service not connected to the Gay Health Action committee'.[54] This comment reinforced the extent to which up to this point, GHA had shouldered the burden of developing a response to AIDS and providing services for those affected. While AIDS Helpline Dublin was independent of GHA, GHA nevertheless helped with its establishment through the creation of the AAA. Moreover, those volunteering with the new helpline were trained by TAF and Cairde volunteers.

The establishment of the AAA came at a time when GHA was under considerable pressure to meet the growing demand for information, not just from within the gay community, but also from other cohorts of society and the media. As the only organisation that had taken the lead in issuing a public AIDS information leaflet, many sectors of Irish society had turned to them for information. On the heels of this growing demand, GHA realised that more information needed to be produced, but that this material needed to include information of relevance to other demographics rather than just for gay men. This shift was evident with the publication of its Play Safe Card and AIDS Information Booklet, published in February and December 1986 respectively.

The GHA also printed 15,000 revised versions of its AIDS Information leaflet in 1986 to meet this growing demand.

Within the Play Safe Card and the revised AIDS Information leaflet, there are subtle differences compared to the 1985 AIDS information leaflet that reveal the extent to which GHA sought to expand its focus beyond just gay men. For example, the Play Safe Card, which divided certain activities into safe, possibly risky and very risky, made reference to other sexual activities such as vaginal intercourse with a condom, which it characterised as possibly risky, along with cunnilingus, while vaginal intercourse without a condom and I.V. drug users sharing needles fell into the category of very risky. Also included amongst very risky activities were swallowing semen, watersports in the mouth or on broken skin, sharing dildos, toys and rimming. The safe activities remained the same as those listed in the 1985 leaflet. Moreover, whereas GHA noted in its 1985 AIDS Information leaflet that 'all gay men should follow the safer sex guidelines', the 1986 revised leaflet replaced that with 'anyone in an at-risk group should follow the safe-sex guidelines'.[55] Similarly, when discussing donating blood, the 1985 AIDS Information leaflet advised gay men against doing so, while the 1986 leaflet now encouraged all those in the risk groups to avoid donating. Therefore, there had been a shift from a primary focus on gay men to a much broader audience, which included women, heterosexuals, I.V. drug users and haemophiliacs.

The changes between the 1985 and 1986 leaflet also reflected a greater understanding about AIDS. While in 1985 GHA stated it was 'relatively easy to catch the virus by full sexual contact', by 1986 they now described it as 'difficult to contract: it can only be transmitted by full sexual intercourse, or by contact with infected blood or blood products'. This evolving understanding of AIDS was also reflected under the section on 'what should you do if a partner develops AIDS or is tested positive'. While both leaflets encouraged readers not to panic, the 1986 advice was much more direct than that of 1985. In 1985, the advice was simply 'don't panic, your risk is small' and 'consult a doctor at a STD clinic'. In contrast, the 1986 leaflet, while again repeating 'don't panic', warned that 'you may be more at risk ... Since it seems that repeated exposure to the virus increases the risk to health, it would be wise to follow the safe sex guidelines. The virus can also be passed to an unborn child by either the Father or Mother ... People at risk should therefore ensure reliable contraception'.[56] It is clear from the reference to father and mother that the use of the word 'partner' in the 1986 document was different to that of its use in 1985. In 1985 there was no mention of fathers or mothers and it generally seemed to apply to gay male partners.

What had not changed in GHA's approach, however, was its commitment to the promotion of safer sex practices. This unapologetic strategy of disseminating explicit information in the Republic of Ireland was repeated in the GHA's *AIDS Information Booklet* published in December 1986. In a sign of the GHA's growing stature at that time, the booklet's launch was covered by RTÉ. The media attention GHA was able to generate was extremely important, as the subsequent reporting of GHA events and their messaging helped to spread their guidance to a wider audience. Christopher Robson, speaking to RTÉ, explained that the reason the booklet was being published was because the situation had become extremely serious and GHA decided to publish this booklet to 'ensure that it doesn't go on to become appallingly serious'.[57] One month prior to the booklet's launch, the Minister for Health had announced that there were now 12 confirmed AIDS cases in the Republic of Ireland, of which 7 had died, and 502 individuals had tested HIV positive.[58]

The *AIDS Information Booklet* was part of an information pack geared at health care workers, social service workers, politicians and journalists, who it was hoped would distribute accurate information to the public.[59] The pack contained the National Union of Journalists' guidelines on the reporting of AIDS; *Medical Answers About AIDS* (published by Gay Men's Health Crisis in New York); and the GHA's own produced *AIDS Information Booklet*. The *AIDS Information Booklet* provided an overview of the AIDS situation internationally and in Ireland, advice on infection control procedures, and information on the means of transmission. GHA informed readers that:

> the only ways it can be passed are: blood to blood, either by transfusion, or by sharing intravenous needles while taking drugs, by semen in any sexual act where semen is passed from one body to another, in any sexual act which involves the exchange of vaginal fluids or menstrual blood; from mother to foetus or from an infected woman to her nursing child through breastmilk.[60]

Repeating the advice given in its Play Safe Card, the booklet warned that 'safe sex guidelines must also be followed, of course, by anybody, gay or straight . . . no intercourse without a condom; any blood to blood contact must be avoided'.[61]

While the booklet's primary objective was to disseminate information on AIDS, GHA also used it as an opportunity to condemn the lack of support it and others had received from the government. At the launch of the booklet, GHA warned that without resources being put in place and increased funding, there would be an average of one new case of AIDS each week in Ireland for the next two years. To combat this, GHA called for an accurate and detailed public education programme, arguing that moral considerations and embarrassment about sexual matters had to be overcome in order to actively prevent the spread of AIDS. What was needed, GHA further contended, was advertisements in the press giving detailed information on risk prevention, advertisements on radio and TV and posters – particularly in areas where I.V. drug use was most common.

The booklet's launch attracted considerable media attention. Along with RTÉ's coverage, *The Irish Times*, *Irish Independent*, *Evening Herald* and *Irish Examiner* all covered the launch. Crucially, these articles printed criticism and advice aired by GHA. According to the *Irish Independent*, GHA reportedly accused the Catholic Hierarchy of performing 'moral gymnastics' over the use of condoms.[62] Speaking on behalf of GHA, Donal Sheehan insisted that 'the use of condoms was a key factor in combatting the disease and remarked that AIDS was not selective about religion – whether Catholic or Protestant'.[63] Sheehan was supported in his views by Joan Brady writing in the *Evening Herald*. Like GHA, Brady condemned the hierarchy's approach to the use of condoms, insisting that they 'must be a part of the fight against AIDS. Anything else is suicidal'.[64] Brady at the same time praised GHA's booklet as comprehensive and one that manages to emphasise the seriousness of the problem, something 'of course the Government should have started . . . two years ago'.[65] The *AIDS Information Booklet* and the attention it generated heightened the GHA's reputation as one of the leading organisations working to educate the public on AIDS in the Republic of Ireland.

'This work is not the concern of 10 or so people, it is the concern of you all'

By the end of 1986 GHA had published: two AIDS Information Leaflets; a Play Safe Card; a leaflet on the HTLV-3 test; an *AIDS Information Booklet*; set up Cairde; led the establishment of AAA; and responded to hundreds of telephone queries from individuals and the media. *The Irish Times* estimated that by June 1986 GHA had produced almost 77,000 information leaflets on AIDS.[66] All these publications, for the most part, GHA had completed without any statutory funding. Notwithstanding the demand from different sectors on GHA to provide information, GHA at the same time had to find ways to fund these information campaigns, which added further pressure on them. In their *AIDS Information Booklet*, GHA warned that 'we cannot hope to continue this work adequately without the financial support of public health authorities'.[67]

With the exception of the HEB grant in 1985, GHA did not receive any other funding from the Department of Health for its campaigns throughout the 1980s.[68] Had it not been for the existence of an organised gay community, particularly around the Hirschfeld Centre and the Quay Co-Op, the funds for such information campaigns would not have materialised. Not only did both centres provide an office and meeting space for GHA, but they also facilitated fundraising events. For the most part, discos provided the means by which GHA was able to fund its activities, but even getting these fundraisers advertised presented a challenge.

In the lead-up to the publication of its *AIDS Information Booklet* in December 1986, GHA had sought to publicise a number of fundraising events to help cover the cost of printing, which was estimated at £2,500 (roughly €6,000 in today's currency). However, these efforts soon made the headlines when the *RTÉ Guide* refused to accept an advertisement from GHA. The advertisement comprised a notice about two discos, a Christmas bop and a raffle under the title of 'Aid to Fight AIDS', but it was deemed unacceptable to the *RTÉ Guide* because theirs was a 'family magazine'. According to the *Irish Press*, the *RTÉ Guide*, while in sympathy with what was being done to combat AIDS, nevertheless concluded that it would be 'difficult to justify to our readers the idea of taking an ad from a movement that a lot of them would find offensive'.[69] The problem, therefore, was not with GHA's activities as such, but rather the fact that GHA was a gay organisation. GHA did, however, manage to promote its fundraising events through *In Dublin* and *Hot Press*.

Coincidently, five months later RTÉ found itself covering one of GHA's fundraising efforts on Dublin's Grafton Street.[70] As part of International AIDS Day in April 1987, the GHA organised Ireland's first International AIDS Weekend and used the opportunity to raise funds for their efforts. The weekend began with collections in local gay bars and a fundraiser at the Hirschfeld Centre. That same night, *OUT* arranged for Fr Bernárd Lynch, an Irish priest living in New York who was actively involved in caring for those living with AIDS, to appear on *The Late Late Show* to talk about the Church, homosexuality and AIDS.[71] The main focus of the weekend was a street collection on Grafton Street, which raised over £1,000, before the weekend events concluded with a forum at the Hirschfeld Centre with Fr Lynch, hosted by David Norris.

On occasion the source of funding generated criticism from within the gay community. While the majority of GHA donations came from fundraisers organised at the Hirschfeld Centre, the Quay Co-Op, Sides, street collections and international organisations, establishments such as the Gym also made donations. The Gym, along with Incognito, was one of two popular saunas in Dublin. However, when it was discovered by members of the Northern Ireland Gay Rights Association (NIGRA) that the Gym had donated to GHA, they sent a letter strongly condemning GHA for accepting financial support from the Gym. In a stinging rebuke of the Gym, Incognito and GHA, NIGRA insisted that GHA 'return this blood money', labelling its acceptance as 'utterly shameful'.[72] Describing the Gym as a 'licensed brothel' run by 'greedy capitalists' who 'care not a whit for the welfare of the gay community', NIGRA called on GHA to 'actively campaign for the immediate closure of these health hazards'.[73] Whereas in the USA, particularly in San Francisco and New York, public officials had called for the closure of such establishments, no such demand, that I am aware of, was made by public officials in the Republic of Ireland.[74] Instead, this demand came from within the gay community itself, through NIGRA. Whether or not GHA returned the donation is not known. GHA did, however, contact the Gym and Incognito to ascertain what precautions, if any, they had implemented. While Incognito stated that they supplied condoms, the Gym revealed that they would not do so because of legal reasons, but that customers could bring their own.[75] They did, however, note that they provided clients with GHA's play safe card.

Funding was just one of a number of challenges GHA faced. While GHA's workload expanded considerably, the numbers volunteering with GHA did not. On numerous occasions GHA raised the lack of volunteers not only as a problem, but also a considerable disappointment. In one such example, Michael Bergin, then general secretary of the NGF, condemned the lack of volunteers offering assistance to GHA, insisting that:

> The response to the initial work carried on by GHA has been nothing short of dismal. This work is not the concern of 10 or so people, it is the concern of you all ... A major programme of work is now underway by GHA and my primary aim at the moment is to request more and more of you to come forward and help with the work of GHA.[76]

This plea appears to have fallen on deaf ears. Rather than improving, the situation worsened in 1986. During the course of a GHA meeting in February 1986 it was noted that 'new people are not becoming active in GHA'.[77] Even more worrying was the announcement by members of the Cork GHA branch that 'numbers active in Cork have dropped and in the future, it seems unlikely that there will be a growing level of activity'.[78] Writing later in *OUT*, a despondent Ciaran McKinney remarked that:

> For the last few weeks I've been looking at Capital Gay and reading about all the pubs and clubs raising money for the Terrence Higgins Trust. As a worker for GHA I feel a bit envious and puzzled. What are they doing right that we're not? ... One of the problems we in GHA experience is isolation. We rarely receive feedback from the gay community and we need it.[79]

While GHA desperately sought more volunteers, their efforts nevertheless had not gone unnoticed, with media outlets often encouraging readers to contact GHA if they were looking for information about AIDS. As early as 1986, positive media reports had appeared about GHA. In the *Evening Herald*, for example, GHA was described as the organisation 'to the forefront in providing information about AIDS'.[80] Later that year *The Irish Times* reported that the Deputy Chief medical officer of the Department of Health had praised the gay community in Ireland for 'acting responsibly in the face of the AIDS threat'.[81] This was a view shared by Young *Fine Gael*, who issued a statement in March 1987 insisting that 'until now, Gay Health Action have been the only group dealing responsibly with the issue'.[82] It was not just media outlets that had praised GHA; those who were directly affected by AIDS had also recognised their actions. One mother speaking to the *Irish Press* about her son, who contracted HIV through using drugs, later developing AIDS, singled out the gay community in particular for praise, insisting that 'the gay men were great. They've been fantastic to us, very helpful'.[83]

GHA was also credited with having helped reduce the number of HIV cases amongst homosexuals in the Republic of Ireland. In contrast with other European countries and particularly North America, the reported percentage of HIV cases in 1980s Ireland was highest not amongst homosexuals, but rather amongst intravenous drug users. Mark Hennessy reported in January 1987 that because GHA had managed to publish 'under severe financial pressure ... a number of well-researched and presented leaflets', the number of new HIV cases amongst gay men was dropping.[84] Quoting Dr Jack Cantillon, who worked at the STD Clinic in the Victoria Hospital in Cork, Hennessy revealed that in 1985, 13% of homosexuals coming for testing had the virus. Now, in 1987, just 6% of those coming forward had it. This was a view shared by Dr Derek Freedman, who accredited the decline to the early intervention by GHA. Freedman stated that:

> Gay Health Action on its own initiative and with little or no funding set about informing people, organising lectures, producing leaflets, providing a telephone helpline service and set up an HIVab+ counselling group. This occurred years before anybody else saw the need ... They have been rewarded with an apparent low HIVab+ rate and a reduction in the rate of AIDS cases in this group since 1985.[85]

While GHA and the gay community came in for praise, the same could not be said for the Irish government. Helena Mulkerns, writing in *Hot Press* in February 1987, described the actions of the Department of Health and HEB as tardy, while at the same time telling readers that 'there is however one organisation which has been working actively against the prevalent ignorance regarding AIDS in this country – the Gay

Health Action group ... Since GHA were the first group to provide information on the subject they have been consulted and contacted by a variety of groups and individuals such as prisons, doctors, psychologists, drug users, students and hospitals.'[86] The extent of the Irish government's appreciation of the threat AIDS posed and its seriousness about combatting it became evident with the release of state files in 2015 at the National Archives of Ireland. These files show that the government explored the possibility of using AIDS in its defence at the ECHR as justification for maintaining the laws that criminalised sexual activity between men.[87] Ironically, there was a belief within certain sections of the government that the laws criminalising sexual activity between men actually hindered the fight against AIDS. Barry Desmond, Minister for Health, set this out quite clearly in a letter to then Attorney General, John Rogers, in May 1985:

> In the interim the developed countries are depending on valid reporting of cases, health education and counselling of groups at risk such as the 'Gay Community' and Drug Addicts. It is arguable that our laws relevant to homosexuality are a constraint on both of these measures. Certainly reputable medical experts working in the control of this disease would take this view. I would find difficulty in identifying a reputable expert at international level who would see our present laws on homosexuality as working in the interest of the Public Health. Indeed, any attempt to make a case for our present laws based on this premise could I believe have a rebound effect.[88]

Despite the above information, and the Minister for Health stating in October 1985 'that every effort would be made to control its [AIDS] growth in Ireland', the Irish government failed to amend those laws.[89] It would not be until 1987 that a public AIDS education campaign was instigated and not until 1993 that the laws criminalising sexual activity between men were amended. The government also persisted in ignoring GHA requests for support. In a February 1986 letter to the Minister for Health, GHA lambasted the government's response, decrying that 'the entire responsibility of public education and training on AIDS in Ireland has landed on our shoulders: to put it bluntly, we are doing your department's job'.[90]

'Stay with one faithful partner, and remain faithful to that partner'

When the Irish government eventually involved itself in a public AIDS education campaign, its early efforts sought to appease the Irish Roman Catholic Church. While the government wanted to give the impression that it was taking AIDS seriously, its lacklustre response belied this reality. The earliest attempt by a state-sponsored body to provide some level of information on AIDS outside the medical profession did not materialise until July 1986 with the publication of a leaflet by the HEB on AIDS. This leaflet was distributed at health boards throughout the country; a move which limited its impact, particularly in reaching those most at risk.[91] However, the publication of this booklet immediately raised controversy after reports the HEB decided to leave out explicit information on unsafe sex practices over fears that such information would have resulted in some health boards refusing to distribute the booklet. According to *The Irish Times*, the original text warned 'of the dangers of anal sex and oral sex', while also emphasising 'the vulnerability to AIDS of all partners, male and female, of promiscuous homosexual or bisexual men'.[92] In contrast, the reportedly amended text warned against unsafe forms of sex, with no specific guidelines on what they might be. Dermot Hayes contended that guidelines on safer sex had been omitted because they might be offensive and because certain homosexual practices were illegal.[93] The director of the HEB, Dr Harry Crawley, disputed *The Irish Times*' assertion that the booklet had been amended. Dr Crawley explained that no amendments could have taken place because 'it was never intended that the booklet would include information recommending specific forms of sexual behaviour and no such text was ever compiled by the bureau'.[94]

The refusal to endorse an explicit public education campaign that focused on safer sex practices persisted, even with the launch of the government's so-called 'major public information' campaign in May 1987. When the government announced its intention in late 1986 to instigate a major AIDS public health campaign through television, advertisements and leaflets, the focus was on informing the 'Irish people of the facts and dangers they face from AIDS'.[95] Although the objective was to launch this major public information campaign in January 1987, the collapse of the government led to its postponement until May 1987. The *Fine Gael*/Labour coalition was subsequently replaced by a *Fianna Fáil* government, with Rory O'Hanlon, who had strongly opposed the liberalisation on the sale of condoms in 1985, becoming Ireland's new Minister for Health. On the day (1 May 1987) that the government launched its public AIDS education campaign, the number of AIDS cases had reached 19 and 581 individuals had tested positive for HIV. A total of 11 individuals had died from AIDS-related illnesses.[96]

At the launch of the government's AIDS education campaign, Minister O'Hanlon summed up the government's entire approach to AIDS when he stated that 'it cannot be too strongly stressed that to avoid AIDS, the most effective way of all is to stay with one faithful partner and remain faithful to that partner'.[97] This viewpoint was almost identical to that of the hierarchy of the Irish Roman Catholic Church, which had issued a statement on 12 January 1987 setting out its views on how to deal with AIDS. At the centre of the church's message, much like the government, was the promotion of chastity and fidelity. In the eyes of the church these were the only morally acceptable ways of preventing the spread of AIDS. First and foremost, the statement noted that the church would be a place of understanding and tolerance for people living with AIDS, who would be treated with compassion and care, maintaining that 'the Christian community must be a sign of Christ's love, especially for the marginalised and the suffering'.[98] If the church was willing to be compassionate with those who had developed AIDS, they were not sympathetic with the campaign to promote safer sex or condoms. The statement was unequivocal in its condemnation of both, highlighting what the Bishops perceived as the dangers posed by the abuse of sex, insisting that 'the only reliable safe guard against contracting the virus by sexual means is through faithfulness to one's partner in marriage and through self-denial and self-restraint outside of marriage. It is vital that this be made crystal clear'. To promote any other message, particularly the use of condoms, would, it argued, 'give further encouragement to permissiveness and this in itself would contribute to a further spread of the disease'.[99] The church's rhetoric, much like that of the government, presented sex in general (outside marriage/either safer sex or unsafe sex practices) as the main cause of AIDS.

Returning to the government's public AIDS education campaign then, we can see the extent to which the government's approach aligned with that of the Roman Catholic Church. Along with an AIDS Information Booklet distributed to doctors and health boards, the government also published an 'AIDS: the facts' leaflet – which appeared in Irish newspapers – and a TV commercial. The 'AIDS: the facts' leaflet left readers under no illusions that it was 'CASUAL SEX [that] SPREADS AIDS' rather than unsafe sex practices. The leaflet, in fact, did not even mention safer sex practices. The four ways listed as to 'how is AIDS caught' were:

- receiving AIDS-infected blood in countries without adequate screening services;
- from infected mother to unborn baby;
- sharing injection needles with an infected person;
- intimate sexual contact with an infected person.

Nowhere in the public advertisement was 'intimate sexual contact' elaborated on, nor was any greater clarity given as to what constituted intimate sexual contact. It is in this instance, then, that one can appreciate why GHA's campaigns were often characterised as explicit and comprehensive and why the governments came to be branded as vague and moralistic. In listing the four ways 'how to avoid AIDS', the campaign encouraged staying with one faithful partner, remaining faithful to that partner, avoiding sharing needles or equipment and, if in doubt, asking a doctor about the use of condoms.[100] No mention was made of safer sex practices, while the effectiveness of the condom was at best vague. Readers were told to contact their doctor to enquire about the use of condoms.

The tone of the government's campaign was grounded in moralistic overtones and this was reinforced in the TV commercial, which warned that 'sleeping around is a gamble' and that 'casual sex spreads'.[101] The commercial was also equally vague on what kind of sexual activity it referred to, simply stating that 'one act of intercourse may give AIDS and lead to death'.[102] Although reference was made to condoms giving some protection, the steps individuals could take to reduce the risk of transmission during intercourse were ignored in the commercial.

Within the government's *AIDS Information Booklet*, the means of 'how to avoid AIDS' were the same as those in the 'AIDS: the facts' leaflet. Interestingly, this booklet did introduce 'safer sex' advice, but the information supplied was again extremely vague. Readers who had reason to believe their partner was living with AIDS were informed that 'strong condoms with a water-based lubricant offer you increased protection', while oral and anal sex were stated as increasing the risk of 'spreading the AIDS risk virus'.[103] The main focus of the booklet's 'safer sex' advice centred on telling readers that the most effective method was to stay with one faithful partner and remain faithful to that partner; if they wanted to avoid the risk completely, they should abstain from sex altogether.

When the government announced its intention to launch a public AIDS education campaign back in late 1986, GHA was sceptical of its approach, issuing a statement shortly afterwards telling of their 'concern at the promiscuity is out message being promoted by some officials ... If the focus of the campaign is on telling us that the entire population must confine themselves to a lifetime sexual partner, it is bound to fail.'[104] They later denounced the campaign, particularly its reluctance to encourage the use of condoms or to promote safer sex practices, describing the campaign as 'simplistic, ineffective, moralising and concerned more with reinforcing traditional moral values than with combatting the spread of AIDS'.[105]

The criticism of the government's campaign, however, was not limited to GHA. Other sectors of Irish society also criticised the government's efforts, while simultaneously praising the efforts of the gay community. In *Liberty News*, the journal of the Irish Transport and General Workers' Union, the government's campaign was reported to have:

> suffered in two respects – it has missed its target in the sense that the principal campaign of marital fidelity is one which is irrelevant to the known high-risk groups in this country, intravenous drug abusers, haemophiliacs and homosexuals. Secondly, even in dealing with the risk of transmission among heterosexuals the campaign has confused public health with public morality in underplaying the role of condoms in preventing the spread of the disease.[106]

In contrast, *Liberty News* characterised the gay community as 'perhaps the best informed and most aware of the AIDS problem, but this has been achieved in spite of, rather than because of, the efforts of Government'.[107] Similarly, Nuala O'Faolain criticised the government's campaign in *The Irish Times*, which she felt was 'short on street credibility' and ignored 'aspects of the real world' in fighting AIDS.[108] However, she signalled out the gay community for considerable praise, insisting that 'they, alone in Ireland, took responsibility for themselves. Their continuing campaign should have been Government funded, if only because it is gay communities which offer the only example of people actually changing their sexual behaviour in each other's interests'.[109]

In the intervening period between the Catholic Bishops' January 1987 statement and the launch of the government's public AIDS education campaign in May 1987, GHA had continued its own campaign with the launch of a 'Condom Card' in April 1987. The condom card, of which 20,000 were printed and distributed amongst the gay scene, family planning clinics and student unions, was effectively a guide on how to use condoms. In the absence of such information being disseminated in other public AIDS education campaigns, the condom card was important in giving plain simple instructions on how to use condoms properly. Such was the novelty of this card at the time, that *The Irish Times* described it as 'Ireland's first explicit AIDS education guide'.[110] In robust language, GHA's condom card declared that 'fucking without a condom represents the highest risk for contracting the AIDS virus ... If you decide to fuck, using a condom will significantly reduce your risk; it is not an absolute safeguard, but it is greatly safer than unprotected sex'.[111] Central to the condom card was a guide on the do's and don'ts of using condoms, emphasising that they were only effective if used properly. Readers were given detailed instructions on how to properly put a condom on, how to remove them, what lubricant to use, what not to do with them, and where to get them.[112]

The increased focus on condoms in the first half of 1987 resulted in considerable, often heated, discussion. Bernie Ni Fhlatharta and Cathy Halloran, writing in the *Connacht Sentinel* following two RTÉ programmes – *Borderline* and *The Late Late Show* – which had discussed the use of condoms, remarked that 'it wouldn't be all that surprising if half the nation were using condoms on their fingers after watching some of the RTÉ programmes that dealt with AIDS where the displays of the rubber protection were a dime a dozen'.[113] In one segment of *The Late Late Show*, Gay Byrne, referring to the condom as the 'dreaded object', asked his panel, which comprised Fr Paul Lavelle, Dr Harry Crawley, Dr Derek Freedman and journalist Ann Marie Hourihane, if he were to show a video on how to use a condom, would he be 'pursuing the condom mentality'.[114] Responding to Byrne, Dr Freedman stated that he thought it was 'perfectly acceptable to show people how to use a harmless piece of rubber, it's not going to bite you'.[115] One audience member, however, objected, telling Byrne that 'he wouldn't want his eighteen-year old daughter to see 'these things'.[116] Incidentally, a *Sunday World* poll published in February 1987 had revealed that 51% of respondents believed that condoms should be promoted in the AIDS education campaigns. Only 24% responded that they should not.[117]

GHA followed up its condom card with what would be its last public AIDS education publication, the 'Joys of Sex' poster, in 1988. The turquoise poster with images of bare-chested men doubled down on GHA's message of safer sex and the use of condoms, while also reassuring gay men that sex did not have to be a thing of the past because of AIDS, rather reminding them that once safer sex practices were adopted, 'sex can be safe'. In many respects, the 'Joys of Sex' poster was one of the raunchiest GHA publications and was quite brazen in its encouragement of men engaging in a myriad of sexual activities, bearing in mind that such activities were still a criminal offence in the Republic of Ireland. While the poster's primary objective was to reinforce safer sex practices, it could also, to some degree, have been described as a Karma Sutra manual for Ireland's gay community. In fact, the poster was quite upfront in acknowledging that it sought to impart new ideas onto Ireland's gay community, stating that 'our bodies are amazing things and we can give and receive sensual and sexual pleasures in countless ways. We hope we've given you some new ideas, or perhaps new angles on old ideas.'[118]

Sex was very much discussed in a positive manner throughout the Joys of Sex poster and readers were encouraged to discuss sex openly with their sexual partners. Under its safe category, GHA provided a range of activities that could be enjoyed safely, such as exploring each other's bodies, to which they suggested 'kissing him all over' or finding other erotic zones such as 'thighs, balls, neck, back, nipples'. Massaging, role play, fantasy, mutual masturbation, fucking or being fucked between the legs, bondage, spanking, sexual toys and dressing up were also characterised as safe. Oral sex, finger fucking and anal intercourse with a condom fell under the low-risk category, while anal intercourse fucking, being fucked without a condom by an infected person and rimming were characterised as high risk.[119]

The explicit nature of the Joys of Sex poster and its encouragement to gay men to engage in safe sexual activity do not appear to have generated condemnation. In fact, in the same year that GHA published its Joys of Sex poster, Monica Barnes, *Fine Gael* TD and the chair of the *Oireachtas* Joint Committee on Women's Rights, called on the Department of Health to hire a member of the gay community to 'help develop a realistic programme to combat AIDS', noting that 'after all, they had taken the time to study the problem'.[120] The Minister for Health did not take up this advice, nor was he willing to explain why he continued to refuse funding to GHA. In questions to the Minister for Health on the government's response to AIDS, Michael D. Higgins, Labour Party TD, asked 'why groups working with the gay community were refused assistance – I am referring to the Gay Health Action group'.[121] Responding, the Minister stated that 'I am sure that in the booklet we produced reference was made to the Gay Health Action Group as one of those groups that persons who felt they might need assistance in combatting or avoiding AIDS could approach for information'.[122] No answer was given as to why financial assistance was denied to GHA.

The government persisted in its defence of its approach. Speaking in 1989, Minister O'Hanlon insisted his plan was working and that people would continue to be told that the best way to avoid being infected was to have sex with only their marriage partner and to remain monogamous. He added that 'my own view is that to talk about condoms as the only dimension of AIDS prevention is trivialising the problem. There are a whole lot of strategies which are necessary before you use condoms.'[123] Statistics for 1989 showed that 886 people had tested HIV positive and 113 were living with AIDS in the Republic of Ireland. Since 1984, 54 had died from AIDS-related illnesses.[124] While the Minister for Health believed his campaign was working, GHA did not, declaring that the:

> message for the Department of Health is simple: take seriously the question of HIV AIDS among gay and bi-sexual men ... Our statistics show clearly for the first time, the extent of the spread of the HIV among gay and bi-sexual men in Ireland, approximately 1,600 people ... For years, we have asked for a national campaign that provides explicit specific information for those gays and bisexuals whom we cannot reach ... It's about time the Government took some responsibility for the health and welfare of their gay and bisexual citizens.'[125]

One of GHA's biggest obstacles at that stage was trying to convince the government that they needed to also focus their efforts on the gay community, not just IV drug users. GHA lambasted the fact that 'the media and the Department of Health stress that in Ireland AIDS is almost entirely a problem that affects IV drug users. It isn't; it's a problem that affects gay and bi-sexual men at least as much as IV drug users and their sexual partners. The national priorities, national campaigns and funding must reflect that fact'.[126] In comparison to other western societies, IV drug users, rather than homosexuals, accounted for the highest percentage of HIV cases in the Republic of Ireland; as much as 60% of HIV cases in 1988 were among IV drug users.[127]

Ironically, the praise GHA had received for its efforts resulted in the gay community being overlooked as a group which needed to be targeted in any government campaign. GHA wrote that 'for too long politicians and officials have been saying the gay community has done a wonderful job and now there is no longer a serious risk'.[128]

Clearly, GHA believed that their good work was used as a justification by the government for not supporting/funding their efforts or for prioritising the gay community. The fact that the government continually denied funding to GHA would suggest that GHA had every reason to believe that the government was content to leave the responsibility of educating the gay community on HIV and AIDS solely to GHA.

The above results were garnered from a survey GHA conducted between July and October 1988; a survey the Department of Health refused to fund.[129] Over 600 surveys were distributed throughout gay bars/clubs/discos, saunas and TAF, of which 265 were returned. While the results did reveal that the incidence of HIV amongst the gay community was most likely higher than official results showed (9% in GHA survey compared to 5% in figures provided by the Department of Health), there was cause for optimism amongst GHA. The survey revealed that 80% of respondents had reported adopting safer sex practices and that there was a high level of knowledge of the risks involved, i.e., 95% correctly answered that anal sex without a condom was very risky. Moreover, the results showed that GHA's campaigns were more effective than those of the government, with 80% of respondents describing the information provided by GHA to have been very useful, in comparison to only 38% who found the government's campaign useful.[130] In many respects, these results affirmed the approach adopted by GHA since its inception in 1985.

'The heterosexual community owe a debt to the homosexual community'

At the end of an article in *AIDS Action News* in 1989, GHA noted that 'the government must also, at last give proper funding to GHA to continue our own work. We are a small group and frankly we are both exhausted and broke'.[131] This was a plea that the government once more ignored. As a result, in July 1990 GHA announced 'with sadness' that it had 'decided to disband'.[132] Explaining the reasons behind this decision, GHA noted that:

> Most of us have been with GHA from the start, in January 1985, and we now, as individuals wish to work in different ways, or in different areas, or to step back for a while ... GHA had perhaps become too specifically associated with a small group of people and instead of being the focus for a new phase of work, was in danger of being a barrier to it.[133]

This announcement brought to an end one of the most important gay organisations set up in Ireland. Although GHA disbanded in 1990 it left behind an impressive legacy, which had helped generate a newfound respect and appreciation for members of Ireland's gay community. Speaking in *Seanad Éireann* in December 1990, Senator Shane Ross commented that 'the heterosexual community owe a debt to the homosexual community in that the gay community, especially in Ireland, took the initiative on the AIDS problem ... The gay community tackled this problem responsibly, and presumably, protected many in that community and many heterosexuals from the

AIDS virus'.[134] For a country that maintained laws criminalising sexual activity between men, AIDS, initially considered a 'gay disease', could well have resulted in considerable public apathy and institutional clampdown on gay individuals and gay venues. On the whole, this did not happen, due to the efforts of GHA, which had been at the fore in responding to AIDS in the Republic of Ireland. In its attempt to protect the gay community from vilification for AIDS, while also providing much needed information on AIDS, GHA ensured that the progresses gay activists had made in the 1980s did not result in the sudden submersion of this community once AIDS cases were reported in Ireland. Rather, gay activists became even more public as they took the lead in the public education campaigns. This was a contributory factor in changing the negative perceptions of gay and lesbian individuals as irresponsible and deviant. Instead, the actions of GHA helped generate an image of a gay community that acted respectably and responsibly. Their ability to do so, despite the considerable constraints they faced, only furthered an appreciation of what GHA had done during this period.

6

Gay Rights: It's Time

On 23 June 1993, Máire Geoghegan-Quinn, then Minister for Justice, introduced the Criminal Law (Sexual Offences) Bill 1993 to *Dáil Éireann*, which decriminalised sexual activity between men in the Republic of Ireland.[1] From now on there would be an equal age of consent (17) for both heterosexual and homosexual relations, something the Republic of Ireland's closest neighbours, England and Wales, had not legislated for in 1967, nor Northern Ireland in 1982. In introducing the Bill, Geoghegan-Quinn explained that:

> while it is the case that the main sections of the Bill arise against a background of the European Court decision in the Norris case, it would be a pity to use that judgement as the sole pretext for the action we are now taking so as to avoid facing up to the issues themselves. What we are concerned with fundamentally in this Bill is a necessary development of human rights.[2]

Rather than taking shelter behind the ECHR judgement for political expediency, Geoghegan-Quinn presented the Bill as a necessary development in the area of human rights. Geoghegan-Quinn was correct; the Bill she introduced could not have been accredited solely to the ECHR judgement. The 1988 decision in the Norris case did not stipulate the type of law reform that the Irish government would have to introduce; it simply stated that the laws in question were in breach of Article 8 of the European Convention on Human Rights. In other words, Geoghegan-Quinn and her cabinet colleagues could have introduced a more restrictive law, one akin to that introduced in England and Wales in 1967, but they chose not to – why was this? Moreover, the ECHR judgement does not help to explain why the Unfair Dismissals Act 1977 was also amended that year to include sexual orientation.

For an answer to these questions, we must look to the actions of gay and lesbian activists in the period following the 1988 ECHR judgement, particularly how they successfully lobbied the government to introduce not only an equal age of consent for homosexual and heterosexual activity, but also legislation protecting gay and lesbian workers. Gay and lesbian activists were meticulous in how they went about lobbying the Irish government to support progressive legislation. What we see in 1993, therefore, is the extent to which gay and lesbian activists had succeeded in getting both Ministers to buy into the rhetoric of the gay rights movement, a rhetoric that was grounded in a belief that gay rights are human rights.

The changes introduced in 1993 were not inevitable and at times it appeared that the Irish government was going to ignore the ECHR judgement. However, gay and lesbian activists ensured that continuous pressure was maintained on the Irish government, while at the same time working to build up a broad coalition of supporters. When the Irish government eventually decided to amend the laws, there was overwhelming support to introduce progressive legislation. It is to these actions that this chapter now turns in an attempt to contextualise the introduction of progressive legislation in 1993 and to assess the extent to which gay and lesbian activists had succeeded in renegotiating popular attitudes to homosexuality, both institutionally and socio-culturally.

'We must divide the opposition and isolate the bigots'

When the ECHR ruled in favour of David Norris on 26 October 1988, it marked a watershed moment in Irish queer history. Norris had taken his case to the ECHR following his defeat at the Irish High Court and Supreme Court in 1980 and 1983 respectively. There he argued that the laws were in breach of Article 8 (right to respect for private and family life) of the European Convention on Human Rights. The European Commission of Human Rights had previously declared Norris' case admissible on 12 March 1987, finding that the case was indistinguishable from that of Jeffrey Dudgeon's.[3] The Irish government disputed the Commission's findings, however, arguing that Norris could not claim to be a victim and that 'although a Catholic society, Ireland should not be seen as intolerant. Nor should it be assumed that, in the sphere of judicial review, orthodox Catholic teaching is a touchstone when considering the curtailment of liberty.'[4] The ECHR, however, dismissed the government's defence and in an 8 to 6 ruling found that Ireland's laws breached Article 8 of the convention. The Republic of Ireland was now required to change the law or face the possible suspension from the Council of Europe.

In anticipation of a judgement in the Norris case, the NGF, the Lesbian Discussion Group, GHA, TAF, CGC and the ICCL met on 17 September 1988 to prepare a united response. In promoting the meeting, the organisers stressed that 'this is one battle we cannot lose. More than anything else we win or lose, this will set the limits for the progress lesbians and gay men can make in Ireland.'[5] While many believed that the stakes were high for the gay community, there was also a strong sense of determination, confidence and optimism amongst those in attendance. Whereas the original law reform bill drafted by the IGRM in 1977 would have introduced a higher age of consent (18) for sexual activity between men compared with heterosexuals, in 1988 gay and lesbian activists would now only accept an equal age of consent. Speaking at the seminar, Tom Cooney (ICCL) argued that what 'is needed is legislation based on the principle of equality ... The ICCL believes gays and lesbians should not accept less than this.' It was this emphasis on *equality* that subsequently became the central tenet of the law reform campaign, hence the decision to include the word in the title of the new organisation that emerged following this meeting: the Gay and Lesbian Equality Network (GLEN).

To achieve equality GLEN demanded the introduction of a law ensuring that same-sex sexual activity would not be subjected to any restrictions that did not apply equally to other forms of sexual behaviour. It also demanded the recognition of same-sex relationships, protection in employment, removing sexual orientation of the parent as a factor in child custody cases, the right to have public displays of affection, the right to promote positive images of lesbian and gay lifestyles and protection against physical assault. In particular, activists were determined to avoid the introduction of a law akin to the more restrictive one introduced in England and Wales in 1967. To avoid this and to bring about equality, Kieran Rose argued that they needed to:

> win over the doubtful ... listen to what they are saying and answer their questions. Mistakes were made in this regard during the Divorce Referendum debate. We must divide the opposition and isolate the bigots. As we are a small grouping we have to get others to do some of the work. We must involve other organisations, get good advice and recognise that there is a role for everyone.[6]

Rose and GLEN were clearly trying to learn from previous (unsuccessful) campaigns that had sought to bring about legislative change, such as the Divorce Referendum in 1986, which had seen efforts to legalise divorce in the Republic of Ireland defeated.

GLEN divided its campaign into two areas. The first area focused on identifying the key decision makers on the relevant issues. Crucial to this was ensuring that lawmakers did not reach an early consensus on reform before GLEN was able to publish their views. The second area focused on the development of a broad-based public debate on the issues in which GLEN could effectively mobilise their own constituency and influence other people to support or at best not oppose their demands. A central feature of this approach was ensuring that the campaign was not 'too gay orientated'.[7] GLEN's strategy focused on securing as much support from non-gay organisations, who were then encouraged to become actively involved in promoting law reform, thereby demonstrating the wide cross-section of support behind GLEN's campaign. Christopher Robson, writing a number of years after decriminalisation in 1993, stated that 'our programmes had to be clear, well argued, highly specific and above all, be seen to demand no special privileges. An effective way to present demands is to get others to argue them on your behalf'.[8]

At the September 1988 meeting, plans of actions were drawn up. The ICTU, for example, was tasked with lobbying the Minister for Justice to include sexual orientation in the Unfair Dismissals Act 1977, while the Irish Family Planning Association and USI were to lobby the National Youth Council of Ireland to come out in support of decriminalisation of sexual activity between men. Politicians of all political parties were also to be lobbied, while efforts were to be made to encourage members of the domestic and international gay community to lobby politicians both inside and outside Ireland. The media in particular was prioritised as a means of promoting GLEN's message among a wider public. Articles and features were to be written promoting positive images, while sympathetic journalists were to be identified, contacted and encouraged to promote law reform.

Although GLEN had limited resources, it was meticulous in both the planning and implementation of its strategy. While its primary objective was to ensure equality for gay and lesbian citizens, its public strategy was to present their demands in as reassuring and non-threatening a manner as possible. In other words, while the enacting of their demands would have signalled a tremendous positive change in the lives of gay and lesbian citizens in the Republic of Ireland, GLEN sought to downplay any fears that these changes would be a threat to the fabric of Irish society. By focusing on a message of equality, GLEN prioritised ensuring that gay rights were not characterised or dismissed as special rights, but rather basic human rights currently denied to a minority group. As Christopher Robson later noted, 'we knew vaguely what we were doing when we gave a name to the organisation, but it turned out to be absolutely crucially important because it contains the word equality ... It was a very strong rock on which to stand the word EQUALITY.'[9]

'I was taught that the Irish hate oppression'

As noted in previous chapters, Irish gay and lesbian organisations had succeeded in garnering support from a number of influential organisations, namely the Irish Congress of Trade Unions (ICTU), Irish Council for Civil Liberties (ICCL), Union of Students in Ireland (USI), the Employment Equality Authority (EEA) and even the Church of Ireland. Following Norris' victory these organisations welcomed the verdict, with the ICCL declaring that the 'court had unequivocally endorsed the view that the legal emancipation of lesbians and gay men is an inviolable human rights obligation which the Government is bound to take seriously'.[10] Just how seriously the Irish government would take this decision was uncertain at that early stage. Speaking in *Dáil Éireann*, the *Tánaiste* and Minister for Foreign Affairs, Brian Lenihan, was coy on what the government's plan of action would be, simply stating that 'the Government would be examining the decision on homosexual rights by "this very important court" so as to decide on a course of action'.[11] With the exception of the Labour Party and the Workers Party, both of whom welcomed the decision, the other political parties remained silent on the ECHR judgement.

Within a month of Norris' victory, an opportunity arose within Leinster House to test the extent to which attitudes within the political class had changed on foot of the ECHR judgement. In 1987 the Irish gay rights movement enjoyed a considerable step forward with the election of David Norris to *Seanad Éireann* for the TCD panel. Norris' election ensured that Ireland's gay community now had a strong voice within Leinster House. On 30 November 1988, Norris got the opportunity to use his position as a newly elected Senator to promote gay rights following the introduction of the Prohibition of Incitement to Racial, Religious or National Hatred Bill, by the Minister for Justice, Gerry Collins.

In introducing the Bill, Collins prefaced it with a statement on its importance in the sphere of human rights, noting that one of the main reasons the government was introducing the Bill was to enable Ireland to 'ratify the United Nations Covenant on Civil and Political Rights'.[12] Collins went on to explain how the horrors of the Second World War had led to the development of the concept of an international law of human rights, resulting in amongst others the Universal Declaration of Human Rights and the

European Convention on Human Rights. To some, the irony of Collins championing human rights and referencing the ECHR just one month after the Norris judgement did not go unnoticed. Collins, after all, was the same Minister for Justice who, when asked in 1977 if he had any intention of amending the laws on homosexuality, declared that 'I am honestly convinced I have other priorities which must be dealt with before I get to this particular one'.[13] Norris did not shy away from telling Collins that 'ten years is quite a long time and I am sure that we will have the emergence of a very mature and balanced view at this point'.[14] Norris had risen to move an amendment to the Bill, which, if adopted, would have seen sexual orientation and membership of the travelling community added to the terms of the Bill. Only a handful of Senators (Nuala Fennell, Brendan Ryan, Katherine Bulbulia, John Robb, Joe O'Toole, Shane Ross), however, supported Norris' call for sexual orientation to be included. In advance of the Bill's debate in *Dáil Éireann*, the NGF had sought to lobby politicians to support the inclusion of sexual orientation; however, when the Bill came up for debate only the Labour Party and the Workers' Party proposed amending the Bill to include sexual orientation.[15] Just as he had succeeded in voting down the inclusion of sexual orientation in *Seanad Éireann*, Collins similarly succeeded in having it voted down in *Dáil Eireann*, stating that while the 'case for inclusion of the travellers has been made, and accepted, the case for sexual orientation has not'.[16]

Before Collins' Bill passed all stages and became law, a snap General Election was called in June 1989, halting his efforts. Sensing an opportunity to raise their profile and to promote, as they said, a chance to 'set the agenda for any legislative regulations the Dáil will introduce', GLEN ran three candidates in that year's General Election: Don Donnelly (Dublin North Central); Pastor Michael Foley (Dublin South Central); Tonie Walsh (Dublin South East). GLEN's manifesto called for a number of legislative changes to protect Irish gay and lesbian individuals, including:

- anti-discrimination legislation in housing, employment and access to employment;
- ending discrimination in custody rights and in the rights of access to children, particularly for lesbian mothers but also gay fathers;
- introduction of a single age of sexual consent for everyone;
- the introduction of comprehensive sexual education for all schools which includes non-judgemental education on sexual diversity.[17]

While none of GLEN's candidates came close to being elected, their campaign, which secured a combined total of 1,517 votes, helped to raise GLEN's profile. Prior to polling day, *The Irish Times* had covered GLEN's campaign launch and manifesto.[18]

Although the subsequent programme for government agreed between *Fianna Fáil* and the Progressive Democrats made no reference to introducing legislation to comply with the ECHR judgement, the new government did bring some unexpected but welcome developments for Ireland's gay community. Firstly, during the course of the 1989 general election the Council for the Status of Women (CSW) sought support for a ten-point charter for women's rights, which included a 'second commission on the status of women to be established to advise on programmes and to review progress since publication of the report of the First Commission in 1972'.[19] Following the general election a nineteen-member commission comprised of sixteen women and three men was appointed by *Taoiseach* Charles Haughey. Crucially for Ireland's gay community, a Lesbian Support Group had been affiliated to the CSW for a number of years and together with the Cork Lesbian Line and Lesbian Line Dublin, Joni Crone and Ann-Louise Gilligan became actively involved in advocating for Ireland's gay community within the Second Commission, submitting numerous written and oral submissions as well as organising a workshop on homophobia.[20] As we shall see later on, these efforts were successful in influencing the Commission's recommendations to government.

Secondly, Charles Haughey appointed Ray Burke as Minister for Justice, taking over this portfolio from Gerry Collins. In what would be a remarkable U-turn by *Fianna Fáil*, Burke announced in November 1989 that he would accept the amendments to include sexual orientation in the Prohibition of Incitement to Hatred Bill. In explaining his decision to do so, Burke argued that 'sympathy alone is of very little benefit to homosexuals when they are being verbally attacked and abused. An opportunity has now arisen to be more than just sympathetic, and I am happy to be able to avail of this opportunity to give the protection afforded by the Bill to homosexuals.'[21] Burke received considerable praise from many within Leinster House and the gay community, with *Gay Community News* describing it as a historic decision. Speaking in *Seanad Éireann*, Senator Norris remarked that it:

> indicates that we have matured as a people and as a Government. Particularly in the context of the next few months it is very important that these kinds of amendments be made during a period when we will be assuming the Presidency of the European Community. This is a valuable indicator of the fact that we are an equal intellectual and moral partner with the other countries in the European Community.[22]

As we have seen in Chapters 1 and 4, the Republic of Ireland's position in Europe was used to put pressure on the Irish government to amend the laws. This strategy also became a focal point of GLEN's campaign. Early on GLEN sought to mobilise support for their campaign from international gay and lesbian organisations. In July 1989 Cathal Kerrigan (GLEN) travelled to the International Lesbian and Gay Association's (ILGA) annual conference in Vienna to encourage members to support the efforts in the Republic of Ireland. In a subsequent letter to David Norris, Kerrigan noted that he had requested members to write to *Taoiseach* Charles Haughey and other members of the government supporting law reform and to publicise the issue in their own countries.[23] In his lobbying efforts, Kerrigan sought to present the issue of law reform as an issue affecting gay and lesbian individuals throughout Europe, not just within the Republic of Ireland, insisting that 'a defeat in Ireland would be a set-back for lesbians and gay men internationally and particularly in the E.E.C. as moves are being made to harmonise social legislation with the creation of the Single European Market in 1992'.[24]

ILGA members were encouraged to send letters that GLEN had drafted for them to the *Taoiseach* and other government members. GLEN was conscious of the timing of their letter writing campaigns, choosing moments that would optimise their potential impact. In a December 1989 letter encouraging ILGA members to write to the *Taoiseach*, Kieran Rose maintained that because the Republic of Ireland was taking over the presidency of the EEC Council of Ministers in January 1990, 'our government is more sensitive than ever to European pressure'.[25] These letters often sought to commend the government for progressive changes it had introduced, while at the same time continuing to highlight how out-of-step the Republic of Ireland was with the rest of Europe. In the letter Rose attached for ILGA members in December 1989, it began by praising the Irish government for its decision to include sexual orientation in the Prohibition of Incitement to Hatred Act 1989, and encouraged the *Taoiseach* to 'continue his principled policy by responding to the European Court of Human Rights decision of October 1988 on the basis of equality between heterosexuals and homosexuals, as was recommended by your Law Reform Commission'.[26] It then went on to highlight, once more, continental Europe's more tolerant attitude towards gay and lesbian individuals, urging the *Taoiseach* to 'introduce anti-discrimination legislation (to include lesbians and gay men) as other European countries such as Denmark, Netherlands, France and Sweden have already done'. The letter concluded by asking the 'leader of a country with a traditional concern for justice … to dismantle this barrier of prejudice. Such an action would be in the spirit of the times and would be widely welcomed by Europeans especially when Ireland is undertaking the Presidency of the Council of Minister of the European Communities'.[27]

Rose noted in his December 1989 letter to ILGA that GLEN had 'been getting great international support and letters from abroad are replied to by An *Taoiseach* and by the Minister for Justice'.[28] One such letter from New Yorker Philip Bockman (he also cc'd the Gay and Lesbian Alliance Against Defamation and *New York Native*) to the *Taoiseach* called on him to enact legislation following the ECHR judgement, stating that 'some of my ancestors came from Ireland, and I was taught that the Irish hate oppression. Bring your tradition to bear on the lives of gay people in your country'.[29] In an almost identical letter from Arthur Leonard (New York Law School), he expressed his surprise that Ireland was determined to resist the ECHR ruling, insisting that 'lesbian and gay citizens of Ireland deserve better from a country founded on opposition to oppression and religious bigotry'.[30]

Linked with this focus on the Republic of Ireland's position in Europe was GLEN's efforts to contrast the treatment of gay and lesbian individuals in other predominantly Catholic European countries with the situation in the Republic of Ireland. Whereas gay and lesbian activists had condemned the rhetoric of the Roman Catholic Church in the 1980s and the Christian nature of the Irish constitution had been used by both the High Court and Supreme Court as justification for the constitutionality of the 1861 and 1885 laws, GLEN strategically embraced Catholic Ireland in an attempt to reassure Irish society about law reform. After numerous attempts to table a discussion on the 1988 ECHR judgement in *Seanad Éireann*, David Norris succeeded on 12 December 1990. In the course of numerous statements supporting law reform, including from the Minister for Justice, Ray Burke, Norris highlighted how:

> France reformed its law with a common age of consent of 15 in 1791 and Catholic Spain in 1822 with a common age of consent of 12. Portugal has a common age of consent of 16 since 1852 … Poland, good Catholic Poland, an ideal analogue to the State of Ireland, has an age of consent of 15 since 1932.[31]

Spain, now 'Catholic Spain' and Poland, 'good Catholic Poland', were examples Catholic Ireland should be following. Although they had decriminalised sexual activity between men and introduced an equal age of consent, the intended message was that the moral fibre of both nations had not suffered. Cathal Kerrigan remembered going to a meeting with then *Fine Gael* leader, John Bruton, in 1990 when this very point was made, recalling that GLEN 'presented ILGA documentation about how it has been legal in Poland and Spain, these Catholic countries and there has been no problem for years'.[32] This was a reoccurring theme in both interactions with politicians and newspaper articles. One article by Christopher Robson for *The Irish Times* raised this exact point. Robson noted that 'in all of the traditional Catholic countries of Europe in Italy, France, Poland, Spain, Belgium and Portugal homosexuality is legal and the ages of consent are the same for all their citizens. There is no suggestion that these laws be changed. Not from politicians. Not from the church.'[33] In making these comparisons GLEN sought to emphasise the extent to which the introduction of an equal age of consent would align the Republic of Ireland closely with other Catholic countries in Europe. Moreover, they emphasised that their proposed age of consent of 17 years would be one of the highest in Europe. Put simply, this was a conservative amendment to the Irish law, rather than a radical one. The extent to which this argument was getting across was reflected in an article in *The Irish Times* where Nuala O'Faolain quipped that despite an equal age of consent of 15 years, Poland had nevertheless managed to produce a Pope.[34]

'Not too gay orientated'

As highlighted in GLEN's drafted letters for ILGA, reference was made to recommendations from 'your Law Reform Commission'. These recommendations would, more than any other event following Norris' victory in 1988, prove vital in GLEN's campaign. The Law Reform Commission had been set up in October 1975 to examine areas of Irish law that might need reform. Since that time the issue of homosexuality had not factored in the Commission's work; however, in the course of the new Commission's investigations into the laws on sexual offences, particularly the law relating to rape and the sexual abuse of children, the Commission noted that:

> it became obvious at an early stage that no sensible proposals for the reform of the substantive criminal law in the area of child sexual abuse could be formulated unless it was prepared to undertake an examination of the entire law relating to what might be broadly described as consensual sexual activity. That in turn led the Commission to examine the present state of the law as to consensual homosexual offences in the light of the decisions of the Supreme Court and the European Court of Human Rights in *Norris*.[35]

The Commission's decision provided GLEN with an opportunity to make their case for law reform to them. Together with GHA, the NGF and the ICCL, GLEN made a number of written submissions encouraging the introduction of an equal age of consent for sexual activity between men.[36] Later, in October 1989, the Commission invited oral submissions from GLEN and the NGF, with Don Donnelly and Kieran Rose representing GLEN and John Bergin representing the NGF. In the Commission's subsequent recommendations, which can only be described as one of the most effective propaganda tools for GLEN, the Commission declared that the same legal regime *should* obtain for consensual homosexual activity as for heterosexual and that *no* case had been established for providing that the age of consent should be any different.[37] GLEN used this decision to strengthen their case for equal law reform, writing to *The Irish Times* that the Commission:

> in its findings showed an enlightened and humane understanding of our need for equality and of the need for legal reform which would bring us in line with our EC counterparts. That an objective legal commission would concur both with the ICCL report and also with our own demands is the cleared indication of the urgent need for action and for real reform.[38]

The Law Reform Commission's recommendations complimented GLEN's strategy of getting others to make the case for law reform on behalf of Ireland's gay community. While the Law Reform Commission did not lobby the government to implement its recommendations on behalf of the gay community, their recommendations nevertheless facilitated GLEN in arguing that what they were calling for was recommended by a state-sponsored body, i.e., it was not just the gay community who were recommending these changes. These recommendations, however, were just one of two important interventions that year from a so-called non-gay organisation. Prior to the Law Reform Commission publishing its recommendations in September 1990, the ICCL had launched *Equality Now for Lesbians and Gay Men* in March that same year. This publication was the culmination of two years' work on the part of the ICCL's working group on Lesbian and Gay Rights, which included Ursula Barry, Tom Cooney, Aideen McCabe, Christopher Robson and Kieran Rose. *Equality Now* was a comprehensive sixty-page report setting out the justification and merits for law reform and was sent to every member of the *Oireachtas*.[39]

The ICCL prefaced *Equality Now* by stating that the 'time is therefore surely ripe for a contribution to the debate by an independent, broad-based civil liberties organisation such as the ICCL'.[40] This opening statement sought to lend credibility to the publication as one based on an objective approach to the subject by a non-gay organisation. David Norris had emphasised this exact point at the book's launch, insisting that it represented the work of a 'non-gay organisation'.[41] At the beginning of *Equality Now*, the ICCL reiterated its strong commitment to law reform, declaring that:

> ICCL firmly holds that lesbians and gay men have an inviolable human right to equality of treatment. Unequivocally, we claim that homosexuality is a normal variation in the range of diverse human sexualities. Unconditionally, we say that the law relating to homosexual behaviour should be placed on the same basis as the law relating to heterosexual behaviour.[42]

Effectively the report sought to reassure readers why this change should be embraced and not feared. The first half of the report focused on dismissing a number of myths surrounding homosexuality such as: 'homosexual people prey on vulnerable people'; 'decriminalised homosexuality would cause a decline in heterosexual marriage'; 'gay men are inherently sexually promiscuous and are incapable of maintaining stable, loving relationships'. The ICCL used international reports to further dismiss the belief that an individual could be seduced into being gay or lesbian. Citing the Dutch 1968 Speijer committee report, the ICCL noted that of the seventeen experts who gave evidence to that committee, sixteen 'rejected the assumption that a 16-year-old person can be transformed into a lesbian or gay man through seduction'.[43] Coupled with this, they presented evidence from two expert committees in Denmark and Switzerland that concluded sexual orientation was settled before the age of fourteen and a recommendation from the Royal College of Psychiatrists in Britain advising that the 'age of consent for homosexuals and heterosexuals be fixed at 16.'[44] This was one year younger than the age of consent GLEN was advocating.

Not only should law reform and a common age of consent not be feared, but *Equality Now* actually argued that it should be embraced for its positive benefits for society. To make this point, the ICCL cited a Geis, Garrett and Wilson survey of gay men, district attorneys and police in seven states in the USA that had decriminalised sexual activity between men. According to the ICCL, the survey suggested that not only was there no evidence that decriminalisation had been socially disruptive, but the police actually felt that it 'enabled them to devote more time and resources to real crime'.[45] Moreover, based on a 1985 study by Fr Sinclair and Dr Ross on a comparison between gay men in two Australian states, Victoria before decriminalisation and South Australia eight years after decriminalisation, the ICCL noted that 'decriminalisation did not include an increase in what were alleged to be negative aspects of homosexual activity, such as public solicitation of partners or sexually transmissible disease'. In fact, they emphasised that the study showed that the incidence 'of sexually transmissible diseases was higher in Victoria, a fact attributable to the pressure the criminal law put on gay men to find anonymous sexual partners in public spaces'.[46] In making these points, the ICCL sought to win over the doubtful by taking their concerns on board and presenting evidence to counter them.

The ICCL was just one organisation that was willing to get actively involved in GLEN's campaign. The ICTU was also involved through lobbying the Minister for Justice, expressing 'its concern at the inordinate delay in dealing with this matter which affects the quality of life of thousands of Irish citizens. This delay also shows little regard for the status of the European Convention on Human Rights and the commitment of the Irish government to abide by its provisions.'[47] A similar letter was sent to the Minister for Justice from the Director of the National Youth Council of Ireland, in which they unequivocally called on the Minister to end the 'present anomalous situation which discriminates against young homosexuals and which contravenes the European Convention on Human Rights. We would now request, Minister, that you introduce a gay law reform bill that would implement the law reform commission proposals that there be an equal age of consent for both heterosexuals and homosexuals'.[48]

Pressure to include sexual orientation in the Unfair Dismissals Act 1977 was also put on the government during this period. In its January 1991 *Programme for Economic and Social Progress*, the government had committed to amend the Act but did not stipulate what type of amendments they would introduce. As we have seen in Chapter 4, the ICTU and EEA had publicly called on the government to amend the Act to include sexual orientation. *The Irish Times* reported in September 1991 that the EEA had again recommended to the government that discrimination on the grounds of sexual orientation should be included in the amendments to the Unfair Dismissals Act.[49] While this in itself was noteworthy, perhaps a more significant development was the fact that the report also noted that the EEA had received twenty complaints from individuals who stated they had been sacked because their employers discovered they were not heterosexual.[50] The government's defence of maintaining that no cases had been reported would now be difficult to sustain, because the EEA had now reported cases of such discrimination. Phil Flynn, general secretary of the trade union IMPACT (Irish Municipal, Public and Civil Trade Union), further supported this view in his letter to the Minister for Labour. In urging the Minister to include sexual orientation, Flynn contended that 'while such cases are difficult to establish, we are satisfied that an already vulnerable group in our society are made even more vulnerable by the absence of such a provision'.[51]

The extent to which GLEN was succeeding in getting broad-based support behind its campaign was publicly visible in October 1991 with the launch of 'Campaign for Equality', a coalition of groups representing travellers, people with disabilities, those living with HIV and AIDS and lesbians and gay men. At the launch of the campaign at the European Commission offices in Dublin were members of the Dublin Travellers Education and Development Group, Forum of People with Disabilities, the Labour Party, the Workers Party, the Green Party, the Council for the Status of Women, ICTU, Young *Fine Gael* and the EEA.[52] There can be no doubt that the location chosen for the campaign's launch was symbolic, particularly as GLEN was continually trying to shift the law in the direction of European standards.

The Campaign for Equality allowed GLEN to reinforce the wide cross-section of individuals and organisations now supporting law reform. GLEN described the campaign as 'a simple mechanism for the public declaration of support for our main aims'.[53] Speaking at the campaign's launch, Monica Barnes, *Fine Gael* TD, and chairperson of the *Oireachtas* Committee on Women's Affairs, stated that they would continue to remind the Minister for Justice to keep law reform on the agenda, noting that they had 'already written to the Minister for Labour supporting amending legislation to include sexual orientation under the terms of the Employment Equality Act and Unfair Dismissals Act'.[54] The Campaign for Equality, therefore, was a symbol of the support behind GLEN's campaign. However, those who were adamantly against GLEN's campaign were also making their voices heard.

'The Homosexual Challenge'

GLEN did not have it all their own way. Opponents also succeeded in airing their concerns about any form of law reform. But who were these opponents? As we have seen in previous chapters, the Irish Roman Catholic Church did not support amending the 1861 and 1885 laws, a stance they did not deviate from. However, while it did not welcome the amending of the law in 1993, the hierarchy of the Irish Roman Catholic Church was, for the most part, relatively silent in the public debates leading up to law reform, focusing its attention instead on condemning contraception, divorce and abortion; all subjects which were topical in the Republic of Ireland during this period. The main opposition to law reform came from a small but influential group, Family Solidarity (a lay Christian organisation). Following Norris' victory in 1988, Family Solidarity had condemned the decision because 'in the midst of an AIDS epidemic, any measure which would increase the practice of homosexuality was to be deplored'.[55]

Family Solidarity's strategy was to stir up Irish nationalism, claiming that an outside court had forced this decision on the Republic of Ireland, but also to play on the fear of AIDS, laying the blame for its prevalence on homosexuality. Like GLEN, Family Solidarity sought to lobby Irish politicians and to use the media to get their message out. In the same year that the ICCL published *Equality Now*, Family Solidarity published its own booklet on the subject, *The Homosexual Challenge: Analysis and Response*, which it also sent to Irish politicians. Whereas *Equality Now* had sought to reassure Irish society about the benefits of law reform, *The Homosexual Challenge* sought to instil a sense of fear about *any* reform of the law. In the opening section of the book, Family Solidarity described homosexuality as something which was acquired or learned, not inborn.[56] Homosexuals, they maintained, were more promiscuous than heterosexuals and 'do not engage in a sexual life in the context of a lifelong relationship with one other person ... [thereby making them] the perfect vehicle for spreading the disease [AIDS]'.[57] To amend the laws in any form they argued would 'be understood by some members of the public, especially young people as approval for the Acts ... and have great public consequences for education, health and the general good of society'.[58]

A central feature of *The Homosexual Challenge* was to criticise the rhetorical progress Family Solidarity believed the gay rights movement had achieved, particularly what it described as the linguistic changes whose acceptance in Irish society 'at face value have already gone halfway to accepting the ideology which informed them'.[59] Family Solidarity took exception to the wider use of the word 'gay', insisting that 'those who out of politeness or fashion start to use it are taking on board its approving content, whether they know it or not'.[60] They further maintained that the wider acceptance of the language promoted by gay rights organisations had closed off other interpretations of homosexuality, particularly the 'once accepted vocabulary' used to describe homosexuality, such as: immoral, contrary to the law, unnatural, indecent, abnormal. Rather than being abusive terms, Family Solidarity argued that they were 'polite and academic'.[61] This rhetorical shift now unfairly presented those who condemned homosexuality as unkind or unloving. In the midst of an AIDS epidemic, they contended that:

> when homosexual behaviour is discussed in the context of AIDS, and is framed in the context of *compassion*, it is very difficult to say that such behaviour is wrong without appearing hard and unloving. Thus, since the advent of AIDS, discussions involving homosexual matters have often been presented so as to make one feel guilty for questioning homosexual practices – as if doing so were tantamount to refusing sympathy toward those who suffer.

Family Solidarity warned that just as the gay rights movement had re-defined the terms used to describe homosexuality, they were also intent on re-defining the definition of the family to include 'male-male, female-female, temporary or permanent, exclusive or non-exclusive forms'.[62] The implication being that the continued acceptance of the gay rights movement's rhetoric only facilitated the re-definition of the family in the Republic of Ireland. While Family Solidarity did not welcome the rhetorical advances of the gay rights movement, their emphasis on this particular issue clearly demonstrated the extent to which the gay rights movement had succeeded to some degree in changing how Irish society discussed gay rights and homosexuality, so much so that it caused concern within Family Solidarity.

Just as GLEN had used the mainstream media to promote its views, so too did Family Solidarity. In an article in *The Irish Times*, Dr Joseph McCarroll (Family Solidarity) challenged Irish society to confront the ideology of homosexuals, maintaining that although homosexuals should be respected as persons their 'ideology' should not, noting that 'one is not showing real respect for an alcoholic by agreeing with his denial that he has a problem. In the same way, for those who regard homosexuality as a disorder, real respect and compassion demands that we challenge the homosexual ideology.'[63] Rather than being the enemy of homosexuals, Family Solidarity sought to present itself as an ally of the homosexual, who they were trying to help overcome this 'disorder/problem' for the betterment of the individual and society at large. For this reason, McCarroll argued that the 'laws against them [homosexuals] should be retained for their socially valuable educative function. They send an effective social signal, especially to the young, that society regards these types of behaviour as unacceptable.'[64]

While we have seen in Chapter 5 that the Irish government opted against using AIDS as justification for the maintenance of the laws, Family Solidarity chose to embrace this argument. McCarroll, referencing the ECHR, which permits a government to pass laws interfering with the privacy of an individual when it is necessary to protect health or morals, insisted that 'sodomy and such acts pose a significant danger to health. They put those who practise them at high risk of contracting the fatal AIDS disease. The need to protect health, then provides a compelling and sufficient reason for maintaining the present laws against these acts.'[65] McCarroll further argued that the government should derogate from the ECHR decision because the Strasbourg Court could not overrule the Irish Constitution as interpreted by the Irish Supreme Court.

What is noteworthy about Family Solidarity's campaign is the extent to which their efforts provoked some to challenge and condemn its rhetoric, and not just from within the gay community. When *The Homosexual Challenge* was published it was met with harsh criticism from GLEN and the NGF, who described it as ridiculous and very dangerous, as well as from Waterford councillor Gary O'Halloran and Young *Fine Gael*.[66] Young *Fine Gael*'s statement described the document as a witch hunt demonstrating a total lack of compassion, understanding and tolerance on the part of Family Solidarity. The statement insisted that the 'claim by the booklet that homosexuals engendered a pool of infection and disease is typical of the type of misinformed claims and statements used by this organisation in this and other publications'.[67] During a meeting of the Waterford County Council, Councillor O'Halloran justified speaking out on the issue because he did not want 'his silence to be interpreted as tacit support for the Family Solidarity documents'.[68] He described the document as the 'worst kind of bigotry by people who may also be religious maniacs ...' and even described Family Solidarity as part of an international fascist movement.[69] Both Councillor O'Halloran and Young *Fine Gael* called on the Director of Public Prosecutions to charge Family Solidarity under the Incitement to Hatred Act.

'The law on homosexuality in the Republic is a bad and stupid law'

While Family Solidarity focused on trying to secure support for the maintenance of the laws, GLEN focused on keeping the issue of law reform on the agenda of the Irish government. Ever since the 1988 ECHR judgement, Irish governments had studiously avoided the introduction of legislation to comply with the ECHR ruling, despite a commitment in December 1990 from the Minister for Justice, Ray Burke, that legislation would be introduced to change the laws within a year. By 1992, however, in the absence of any evidence that a Bill would be introduced, GLEN's patience reached its limit and in April of that year it lodged an official complaint with the ECHR against Ireland for its failure to amend the 1861 and 1885 laws.[70] That same month Ruairí Quinn (Labour Party TD) and Eamon Gilmore (Workers' Party TD) asked the Minister for Labour, Brian Crown, if, based on the advice of the EEA, sexual orientation would be included in the Unfair Dismissals Act.[71] While Cowen responded that consideration was being given to the matter, he refused to confirm that sexual orientation would be included.

The expediency of amending the laws was not just being promoted by GLEN and its allies by that stage. In April 1992 the National AIDS Strategy Committee, established by former Minister for Health, Mary O'Rourke, issued a number of recommendations on how best to respond to the AIDS epidemic in the Republic of Ireland. One of those recommendations included 'that consideration of decriminalisation of homosexual acts between male adults should be given priority'.[72] This now marked the second occasion in which a state sponsored body/committee had come out in support of decriminalisation, in this case viewing it as a 'priority'. The timing of the National AIDS Strategy Committee's report was particularly opportune, as within a month of its publication, the Irish government was called upon by the Council of Europe to explain its failure to amend the laws. At the May meeting, Liam Rigney, Ireland's ambassador to the Council of Europe, announced that the government now intended to bring forward legislation to decriminalise sexual activity between men before the end of the year.[73] The optimism this announcement generated, however, was short-lived. During questions on the legislation on homosexuality in *Dáil Éireann* on 3 June *Taoiseach* Albert Reynolds, while acknowledging that Ambassador Rigney was 'quite in order in what he said', nevertheless stated that the government had changed its priorities since then. As a result, Reynolds declared that legislation to amend the 1861 and 1885 laws would not be proceeded with in 1992 and, in fact, such moves to amend the laws were down the line in terms of the government's priorities.[74] Reynolds repeated this in September 1992, however, by stating the amendment of the 1861 and 1885 laws had now reached the 'bottom of the list of priorities'.[75] This led Fintan O'Toole to take aim at Reynolds, writing that:

> we know already that the law on homosexuality in the Republic is a bad and stupid law which helps to bring the criminal justice system into disrepute ... If he [Reynolds] believes that it should be repealed but finds that he and his ministers don't have the time or the courage or the commitment to do so, then he should simply announce that his government will not obstruct a Private Member's Bill from the opposition parties which puts into effect the European court ruling ...[76]

The frustration evident in O'Toole's article was also apparent in GLEN's response to Reynolds' comments. After four years of broken promises and inaction, GLEN wrote to the Human Rights Directorate of the Council of Europe suggesting that the fitting response from the Council of Europe would be a statement that should Ireland not introduce legislation within three months, it should be suspended from the Council.[77] GLEN followed this letter up with a protest outside Leinster House on 28 October 1992, exactly four years since the ECHR had ruled in favour of Norris. Standing beside a giant pink paper cake with the words 'Happy Birthday Norris' and four large candles, Kieran Rose stated that 'there's an incredible disappointment and cynicism in the gay and lesbian community ... The Government is neglecting to fulfil its international human rights obligations.'[78] Rose was joined by Chris Robson, Mick Quinlan, Suzy Byrne and Senator Norris, along with Roger Garland (Green Party), Emmet Stagg (Labour Party), Democratic Left members Pat McCarten, Eric Byrne and Proinsias De Rossa, Sylvia Meehan (EEA) and Eileen Walsh of the Dublin Lesbian Line.

Within days of GLEN's protest outside Leinster House, two important developments occurred. Firstly, on 5 November Reynolds was forced into calling a General Election following the collapse of his coalition government with the Progressive Democrats. Secondly, five days later the Council of Europe gave Ireland six months to comply with the 1988 ECHR judgement.[79] While GLEN had run three candidates in the previous general election, on this occasion it did not, deciding instead to focus on lobbying the political parties. At a press conference under the umbrella of the Campaign for Equality, GLEN, together with the EEA, Dublin Travellers' Education Development and Support Group, Women's Coalition, Dublin AIDS Alliance and the Forum of People with Disabilities, called on all political parties to support the enactment of full anti-discrimination legislation and amending of existing labour legislation specifically to protect people under the separate categories of ethnic identity, sexual orientation, disability and health status. The growth in support for the Campaign for Equality was evident at that press conference. Whereas the initial launch saw only a handful of groups and individuals commit their support to the campaign, this number had now grown to thirty-seven organisations, ranging from the Waterford Women's Federation to Focus Point, the Rape Crisis Centre and Divorce Action Group.[80] The signatories also included a respectable number of TDs, Senators and MEPs, including Pat Cox, Mary Banotti, Proinsias De Rossa, Ruairí Quinn, Des Geraghty and Brendan Ryan.

The General Election results, which would be a turning point in GLEN's campaign, saw *Fianna Fáil* suffer its worst electoral result since 1927, while the Labour Party enjoyed its best result ever. Crucially for GLEN, the Labour Party's manifesto had included a commitment to the 'implementation of the Norris judgement'.[81] As no party had received an overall majority, a series of government formation talks got underway in December 1992. In an effort to influence a programme for government, GLEN and the ICCL submitted proposals that called for legislation to be introduced amending the 1861 and 1885 laws by May 1993 and for the inclusion of sexual orientation in the Unfair Dismissals Act.[82]

GLEN's efforts received a massive boost two weeks later, when President Mary Robinson invited representatives from gay and lesbian groups throughout Ireland to a reception at *Áras an Uachtaráin* (President's residency). Robinson's invitation was described by Uinsionn Mac Dubhghaill as 'an affirmation of the gay and lesbian community in Ireland'.[83] Remembering the event in 2016, at which thirty-four representatives of gay and lesbian groups from Dublin, Belfast, Derry, Cork, Limerick and Galway attended, Robinson stated that 'it was something that I really felt was important to do. I'd been reaching out to various groups; this was an important group to do it.'[84] In his address to President Robinson, Kieran Rose declared that 'by welcoming an often excluded and stigmatised community into the symbolic home of all Irish people, you are creating a powerful image which will work to heal the wounds of prejudice. On this bright day for our community, we can remember those who did not survive the wounds of prejudice'.[85] Just how fitting Rose's comments were was apparent in a letter the *Evening Herald* received after the event. The unnamed author revealed that 'all my life I have felt an outsider in my own country. But now our President is making me feel that this is a place where, at last, I can be proudly at home. While we have an immense distance to travel to attain justice and equality for gay and lesbian people, the President's gesture is at least proof that the journey is beginning.'[86] *The Irish Times* journalist Mary Holland summed up the event by writing:

> What was left unsaid although the message came through clear as a bell was that now perhaps, after this a new government will be shamed into changing the laws on homosexuality ... Re-reading the shameful catalogue of excuses and prevarications it seems that successive governments have seen no real need to change the laws at all, let alone to do so as a matter of urgency ... Not for the first time, our President effortlessly and generously subversive of entrenched prejudice has given a signal that cannot be ignored.[87]

Outside of Ireland, Cathal Kerrigan, who had moved to Amsterdam in early 1992, sought to maintain the strong support of the ILGA by travelling to its European regional conference in Brussels in December 1992. Not only did Kerrigan succeed in persuading the ILGA to send a delegation to the Irish embassy to present a letter of complaint, but the ILGA also agreed to issue a press release to the Irish media in Brussels.[88] The letter, which had the support of 115 delegates from 25 countries and was also sent to the director of the Human Rights Directorate of the Council of Europe, declared 'that should the required legislation not be introduced within three months, then Ireland should be suspended from the Council and remain suspended until the Court's decision has been implemented'.[89] *The Irish Times* noted that the ILGA had highlighted the huge discrepancies between EC countries over gay rights, with 'Denmark, which has an anti-discrimination law, [being] the most progressive with Ireland the least'.[90]

The ILGA's support for GLEN's campaign, and the media attention it generated, rounded off a period in which the issue of gay rights had attained considerable media and political attention in the Republic of Ireland towards the end of 1992. As a new year began, however, the issue of gay rights continued to be topical and ensured the political class could not avoid the issue. In many respects, there was a certain degree of momentum building behind GLEN's campaign. Five days into the start of the new year, this momentum continued, with the *Evening Herald* reporting that Dublin City councillors had agreed a motion in the name of Progressive Democrats councillor Liz O'Donnell and Claire Wheeler of the Green Party, calling on the Minister for Justice to bring forward legislation decriminalising sexual acts between men.[91] A week later, following a number of weeks of negotiations, both *Fianna Fáil* and the Labour Party devised a programme for government, which included a commitment to bring the country's law into conformity with the European Convention on Human Rights and to introduce legislation outlawing discrimination on the grounds of sexual orientation.[92] The two Ministers that became central to GLEN's campaign were Máire Geoghegan-Quinn, the newly appointed Minister for Justice and Mary O'Rourke, Minister for State at the Department of Enterprise and Employment.

Within days of Geoghegan-Quinn's appointment, Christopher Robson sent her a letter setting out GLEN's hopes for law reform. Robson's letter brought together all of GLEN's arguments since 1988, emphasising that the Law Reform Commission had recommended an equal age of consent for heterosexual and homosexual activity and that by accepting the Commission's recommendations it would 'bring Ireland fully into line with modern European standards where, for example, all Catholic countries have equal ages of consent, usually slightly less than 17 years'.[93] Robson's letter was just one of many that were sent to members of the new government after they took office. The Irish Queer Archive holds copies of letters sent to the *Taoiseach*, *Tánaiste* and on occasion the President of Ireland from the ILGA and gay rights organisations in Spain, Germany, Sweden, Great Britain and the USA. Some of these organisations, such as *Die Andere Welt*, the Swedish Federation for Gay and Lesbian Rights and *Landsforeningen for Lesbik og Homofil Frigjøring-Bergen* did not limit their letter writing campaigns to Irish politicians. For example, Tobias Wikström of the Swedish Federation for Gay and Lesbian Rights wrote to the Irish ambassador in Sweden, Paul Dempsey, calling on him to convey its views on the 'absolute necessity of gay law reform in Ireland'.[94] Meanwhile, the *Landsforeningen for Lesbik* sent copies to the Norwegian Foreign Minister and Norwegian ambassador to the Council of Europe notifying them of the situation in the Republic of Ireland.[95] *Die Andere Welt*, on the other hand, focused its attention on the German Foreign Minister and twenty members of the European Parliament.[96] All of these letters sent between January and May 1993 were almost identical in content, demonstrating the extent to which GLEN's efforts to get the support of international gay and lesbian organisations was highly successful, but also the extent to which international organisations clearly viewed the issue of law reform in the Republic of Ireland as important.

The formation of a new government coincided with the Second Commission on the Status of Women presenting its recommendations to the government, in what would prove to be another important intervention by a state-sponsored body. In their report, the Commission noted that it had been represented to them that:

> Lesbians are dismissed from jobs, lose custody of children, are evicted from housing, are rejected by their families, are beaten up and harassed, are ejected from political, religious or other social groups and are barred from public places in Ireland – all for revealing their sexual orientation, or having been identified as lesbian ... Sexual orientation is not included as a category for protection in the Employment Equality Act or Unfair Dismissals Acts.[97]

The Commission described this situation as repugnant and produced a number of recommendations that called for: legislation to decriminalise sexual activity between men, the inclusion of sexual orientation in the Unfair Dismissals Act, the inclusion of a module on homophobia in the proposed sex and relationship education course in second level schools, and that lesbian groups be made eligible for funding from the Department of Social Welfare's scheme of grants for local women's groups involved in development.[98] These recommendations proved influential and timely. An example of just how influential this report was can be seen in a letter GLEN received in February 1993 from the Department of Equality and Law Reform. In this letter, Brian Fitzpatrick requested GLEN to provide its thoughts on amending legislation in relation to employment equality, noting the government's desire to 'respond as soon as possible to the considered recommendations of the Second Commission on the Status of Women'.[99]

That a government department was now reaching out to GLEN in itself was significant; this had not been the case in previous years. This request suggests that GLEN (and by definition the wider gay community in the Republic of Ireland) had achieved a certain degree of legitimacy in the eyes of state officials. Moreover, it is worth noting that while GLEN was primarily a male-dominated organisation, had it not been for the work of lesbian groups throughout Ireland, who involved themselves in the Council for the Status of Women, it is highly unlikely that this state-sponsored body would have come out in support of law reform when it did. The behind-the-scenes efforts of lesbian groups was influential in bringing the Council for the Status of Women to the point where they were willing to produce progressive recommendations in favour of gay and lesbian individuals. These recommendations further added to the ever-increasing pressure on the government to amend legislation.

In a 2015 interview Máire Geoghegan-Quinn remembered the discussions within her department on the issue of law reform, recalling that:

> On the legislation I was going down through it and almost at the bottom was the de-criminalisation of homosexuality. And I kinda' thought to myself like what on the list is the most difficult to do and by far that was going to be the most difficult, politically. And I said, at the table, when did David Norris take this case? And they said when and I said that's X number of years ago and you know it's coming up to a time when he probably will go back to the courts and I don't think that Ireland

should be shamed again for not doing the right thing. So, I said, I feel that we should push that up the list and bring it up to the top. And I think a few people around the table kind of said, not maybe directly, but kind of hinted that this could be a difficult political hot potato to handle.[100]

According to Geoghegan-Quinn, she also met with a delegation from GLEN during this period. In particular, Geoghegan-Quinn singled out the role of Phil Moore, a founding member of Parents Enquiry. Recalling in great detail an event from almost twenty-two years before, Geoghegan-Quinn remembered how Moore discussed her own son's coming out experience and her acceptance of it, telling Geoghegan-Quinn: 'What am I going to say to him now? I don't like what I am hearing, it goes against everything I believe in. But I love the man, and I'm going to continue to love and support him ... You tell me that he is a criminal.' Geoghegan-Quinn described this as the 'most profound statement that had happened during that conversation and it really affected me. Afterwards, when I came back to the Department, I said we have to do something and that was the catalyst really, that caused the change'.[101]

While Geoghegan-Quinn and the Department of Justice mulled over amending the 1861 and 1885 laws, Minister O'Rourke and the Department of Enterprise and Employment moved swiftly to amend the Unfair Dismissals Act 1977. On 10 March 1993, O'Rourke announced a series of amendments to the Act, among them the inclusion of sexual orientation. With this amendment it would now be illegal to dismiss someone from their employment on the basis of sexual orientation. O'Rourke announced that the bill is 'about people, about workers' rights and the creation of a proper business environment.'[102] Focusing specifically on the issue of sexual orientation, O'Rourke told Senators that 'I am pleased to have included it in this Bill and I hope the House will welcome it.'[103] As it transpired, its inclusion was warmly welcomed from all sides. What is perhaps most interesting is the extent to which the addition of sexual orientation to the Act did not factor in the debates and complaints over amendments to the Act. Rather the exclusion of the travelling community was at the centre of the criticism. In terms of socio-cultural attitudes with regard to sexual orientation or homosexuality, this suggested a markedly positive shift since, unlike the process of amending the 1861 and 1885 laws, the amendment of the Unfair Dismissals Act 1977 had not been a requirement of any judicial ruling, but rather the direct result of lobbying on the part of gay and lesbian activists and their allies. The amendments were passed on 24 June 1993 in *Dáil Éireann* and in *Seanad Éireann* on 7 July 1993 with cross-party support.

While the inclusion of sexual orientation in the Unfair Dismissals Act 1977 does not appear to have caused any political headache for O'Rourke, Geoghegan-Quinn did not have it as easy. In the aforementioned interview, she remembered how difficult an issue it was for her within *Fianna Fáil*, with some threatening to bring down the government over this issue because they believed this was not an issue on which *Fianna Fáil* should lead.[104] In a draft memo on the possible types of amendments that might be introduced, it was clear that Geoghegan-Quinn was also fearful of alienating opponents and proponents of law reform. According to *The Irish Times*, Geoghegan-Quinn had produced a memorandum for the government in April 1993 that included the two options her department had devised to comply with the ECHR judgement.[105]

Option 1 would have introduced legislation similar to that introduced in England and Wales in 1967, while Option 2 would have repealed the 1861 and 1885 laws and introduced an equal age of consent for both heterosexual and homosexual activity. In comments on both options, Geoghegan-Quinn noted that Option 1 'might attract less opposition from people who are opposed to changing the law on homosexuality', while 'it would be strongly criticised by those pressing for change on the ground that it does not go far enough ...'.[106] Option 2, she continued, would find 'most favour with those groups which have been pressing for change', but 'would be strongly criticised by those opposed to change who would see it as marking society's approval of homosexuality as an acceptable or parallel lifestyle'. Geoghegan-Quinn did, however, point out a significant distinction between Option 1 and Option 2: Option 2 conformed to the Law Reform Commission's recommendations.[107]

The introduction of Option 1 would have been a massive disappointment for GLEN, which had been campaigning strenuously for an equal age of consent. While it was not until April 1993 that news broke that Geoghegan-Quinn was considering these two options, GLEN was clearly aware earlier on that consideration was being given to an unequal age of consent. In a letter to Fergus Finlay, Programme Manager at the Department of Foreign Affairs, Suzy Byrne (GLEN) expressed concern about 'the current discussions in relation to the age of consent. We would be alarmed if the Government introduced legislation that was "unequal" when the new Minister for Equality and Law Reform is promising so much in relation to full equality for all citizens'.[108] Byrne had attached a copy of GLEN's latest policy document, 'Equality in Reform of the Criminal Law', which set out the merits and justification for an equal age of consent. The document argued that should British style law reform be introduced in the Republic of Ireland, it would 'mean that the Oireachtas, for the first time in its history, would be legislating to make some Irish citizens less equal than others'.[109] In a subsequent letter to members of the cabinet, Christopher Robson referred to the 1967 Act as a failure, one he said the main political parties in Britain were committed to change. The introduction of antiquated laws would, Robson maintained, be a step backwards and be against the government's own programme for government, which was based on 'equal status to all citizens including those of us of a different sexual orientation'.[110] Three days later, at a specially convened press conference to promote equal law reform, GLEN implored the government to introduce an Irish solution, not a British solution. Speaking to the press, Kieran Rose insisted that the 'programme for government gives priority to the achievement of equality; it would be a travesty of the Government's policy if they were to start by legislating for inequality'.[111]

Those with a personal experience of the 1967 law also sought to encourage the Irish government to avoid its introduction. In a moving letter to Geoghegan-Quinn, Jeffrey Dudgeon sought to stress the hurt and trauma that the 1967 Act had allowed to manifest:

> Quite simply, it is a discriminatory, unfair and antiquated law, which serves neither to protect non-homosexuals, nor to control gay men. It is frequently used in Northern Ireland in an inhumane and cruel fashion, for no useful purpose ... Here in Northern Ireland, as in Britain, there have been a series of local round ups or purges of gay men. These have invariably concerned acts of so-called public

indecency and have had no under-age aspect. For each group, eventually rising to twenty men in the Antrim town case, there is almost always a suicide, as the fear of one's name appearing in the newspapers, even after being fined a trivial amount, is totally devastating – even to gay activists ... In a phrase, I hope that you can accept the concept of not making gay people specially subject to any law that could convict them of a victimless crime.'[112]

Opponents also sought to influence the Minister. In April 1993, Joseph McCarroll wrote to *The Irish Times* repeating Family Solidarity's objections to any law reform, insisting that 'each change made in response to gay pressure enhances the legitimacy of the gay ideology, increases the likelihood of young people, whose developing sexual orientation is ambivalent, being drawn into the gay sub-culture, because it is normalised by such social changes'.[113] This was a view shared by Bridget Randles, a member of the Christian Family Movement, who pleaded with members of the *Dáil* 'to reflect carefully before pushing society in the wrong direction', arguing that 'after the Government has decriminalised homosexual acts for over-17s then it will be too late to make an objection to homosexual information being available in our schools'.[114] Writing in the *Kerryman*, Monsignor Denis O'Callaghan argued that the 'general perception would be that such removal would send the wrong message, particularly to young people, that society has changed its attitudes and now accepts and approves of homosexual activity', insisting that 'It is naïve to proclaim that the gay lifestyle should not be a problem; in simple terms, it is a problem and should be a problem.'[115] The appearance of these letters in and around the same time was not a coincidence, but rather a strategic plan of action by both sides to try to influence Geoghegan-Quinn.

'They're here, they're queer and now they're legal'

On 23 June 1993, nineteen years after the foundation of the Irish Gay Rights Movement, Máire Geoghegan-Quinn rose in *Dáil Éireann* to introduce the Criminal Law (Sexual Offences) Bill. Not only did this Bill decriminalise sexual activity between men but it also introduced an equal age of consent for homosexual and heterosexual activity. Option 2 had won the day. In introducing the Bill, Geoghegan-Quinn argued that 'it is right that we should take the opportunity now of rolling back over 130 years of legislative prohibition which is discriminatory, which reflects an inadequate understanding of the human condition and which we should, rightly, see as an impediment, not a prop, to the maintenance and development of sound social values and norms'.[116] Geoghegan-Quinn's reasoning adopted the same argument that GLEN and gay rights organisations before it had been making for many years, affirming:

> there is nothing revolutionary in having a common age of consent ... If we could raise our sights beyond our nearest neighbour to the European mainland, we would realise that a common age of consent is the norm on the European mainland. For example, in France, the common age of consent is 15 years; in Italy 14 years ... All those countries have a religious heritage similar to ours.[117]

Clearly GLEN's arguments had influenced the Minister, who repeated them in Leinster House. Geoghegan-Quinn's views, however, were supported by a considerable number of TDs and Senators who spoke on the provisions of the Bill. Giving her thoughts, Mary Harney (Progressive Democrats) affirmed that they were about 'freedom, tolerating difference and respecting the rights of other consenting adults – I think 17 is the appropriate age for young people to fulfil their sexual orientation and not be declared criminal in the process'.[118] Echoing this sentiment, Mervyn Taylor (Labour Party) sought to ease the mind of opponents, declaring that 'it is important to recall that what is proposed is the enabling of persons in the gay community to pursue loving relationships. What could be more important, for us as legislators, than to create a climate and a space in which two people who have chosen each other can express and share their love?' Recognising the role of gay and lesbian activists, Joe Costello (Labour Party) paid tribute to their 'well-structured and carefully and calmly reasoned arguments they have made in recent years to promote education and awareness of the normalcy of homosexual orientation ...'.[119] In *Seanad Éireann*, Senator John Dardis described 'the day as highly significant and historic, when we look back at today, we can say with some satisfaction that a good day's work was done ... People have a right to happiness and homosexuals and lesbians have the same right to happiness as heterosexuals and they must not be discriminated against.[120]

The Criminal Law (Sexual Offences) Bill 1993 was passed in *Dáil Éireann* on 24 June without a vote and in *Seanad Éireann* on 30 June, before being signed into law on 7 July 1993 by President Mary Robinson. This was despite a last-minute campaign by Family Solidarity to rally support for a rejection of the legislation, which Denis Coglan reported 'failed spectacularly', and an eleventh-hour statement by the Irish Roman Catholic Church denouncing the proposed provisions of the Bill.[121] In a happy coincidence for those involved in the law reform campaign, the 1993 Dublin gay pride parade weekend coincided with the passage of the Criminal Law Bill. Speaking to the almost 500 individuals who marched, Kieran Rose declared that:

> this is a great achievement for Irish society and its lesbian and gay community. Today we can be here, proud to be Irish citizens and proud to be lesbians and gays. We really believe that Irish people are progressive, that Irish people do support the lesbian and gay community, do support human rights and equality and have no time at all for bigotry. I think we also have to say that this law reform that we have got was not inevitable. It could have been delayed, we could have got the British reform. I think we've got equality because of the Irish tradition of struggling for civil, political and religious freedom. Everyone here did it. Everyone here helped. Everyone who came out to their parents, everybody who said I'm not going to put up with discrimination.[122]

Rose's comment summed up almost twenty years of gay rights activism in the Republic of Ireland. There had been nothing inevitable about the introduction of progressive law reform in 1993. In reality, the particular character of these achievements constituted the work of the many gay and lesbian individuals and their allies who had campaigned for change since the foundation of the IGRM in 1974. This activism and resistance had taken many forms, from those who openly challenged the stigma of homosexuality to those who appeared in the media, wrote letters and articles, to those who marched, to those who had involved themselves behind-the-scenes by providing social spaces for gay and lesbian individuals to meet, or by those who decided to cross the threshold of a gay centre at much personal risk. The successes of 1993 did not result from fortune or luck, but from considerable planning, sacrifice, determination, bravery, debate, and the implementation of considered strategies. At times strategies had to be changed to adapt to the many different obstacles activists encountered. At the heart of their campaign, however, activists had framed their demands in terms of basic human rights, something many in Irish society could relate to. Through their activism they had succeeded in mobilising people from different backgrounds and different organisations. These efforts were paramount to the introduction of progressive legislation. Crucially, there can be no doubt that these efforts had changed the attitudes of many towards gay and lesbian individuals, to such an extent that the government felt it could introduce an equal age of consent and other legislation outlawing discrimination based on sexual orientation. This is not to say that gay and lesbian citizens had achieved a full place in Irish society in 1993; they had not. Rather, Irish society began to acknowledge the many restrictions placed on the citizenship rights of gay/lesbian individuals as unjust. A strong foundation had been put in place for future campaigns to build upon.

While institutional change is significant, alone it cannot change socio-cultural attitudes. By 1993 the efforts of gay and lesbian activists had produced a marked shift in socio-cultural attitudes and, in turn, made the introduction of the laws much easier for politicians. This was clearly evident when Geoghegan-Quinn introduced the Bill and the numerous TDs from the different political parties supported it. At no point did Geoghegan-Quinn seek to hide behind the ECHR and lay the blame for the law at the court's feet. She could have done so for reasons of political expediency. Instead, Geoghegan-Quinn sought to downplay the role of the ECHR, insisting that reform was endorsed by the government. No opposition party sought to profit from an allegedly unpopular issue by condemning the Bill or by calling for a derogation. Like Geoghegan-Quinn, the vast majority welcomed it and saw its introduction as a positive step for the Republic of Ireland. It is worth repeating how small the organised opposition was to the liberalisation of the laws both inside and outside parliament. Whereas well-organised campaigns had developed to oppose the 1986 Divorce Referendum and the 1992 Abortion Referendum, in contrast, the opposition to decriminalisation was much smaller.

In her paper 'Nothing Ventured, Nothing Gained? Conceptualising Social Movement "Success" in the Lesbian and Gay Movement', Mary Bernstein argues that 'shifts in discourse represent important cultural effects of social movements'.[123] Both in the debates on the Criminal Law Bill 1993 and Unfair Dismissals Act 1993, and in the media, it is quite evident that a considerable rhetorical shift had taken place concerning the subject of homosexuality. In this chapter we have seen how individuals from outside the gay community adopted the rhetoric of the gay movement, in particular the adoption of the word 'gay' rather than 'homosexual', the wider usage of 'lesbian', the mainstreaming of the term 'sexual orientation', the greater understanding of homophobia, the acceptance that gay rights were human rights, the recognition that gay and lesbian individuals should have the same right as heterosexuals to engage in consensual sexual activity, and the actual recognition of the existence of an Irish gay community.

In her opinion piece in *The Irish Times* reacting to the Dublin gay pride celebrations in June 1993 and passage of the Criminal Law Bill, Mary Holland also observed a shift in attitudes, remarking that:

> having been in the US for St. Patrick's Day this year and watching as people spat and threw empty beer cans at the young leaders of the Irish Lesbian and Gay Organisations in New York, I was quite fearful that an ugly incident or some abusive jeers would ruin the atmosphere of last Saturday's march [in Dublin]. Instead, middle aged women, laden with shopping bags smiled indulgently and caught pink carnations.[124]

This was a view confirmed by her colleague Edward O'Loughlin, who wrote that:

> some people believe in opinion polls, but experienced march-watchers can read a lot from what happens when a procession draws up at the crucible of Irish politics, the busy crossing where North Earl Street and Henry Street join O'Connell Street. On this occasion, the loiterers seated around the Floozie in the Jacuzzi, eyed the boisterous procession for a moment and then gave a round of ragged but unprecedented applause.[125]

Outside of Dublin, change of a kind was also evident. One month after the Dublin gay pride parade, almost seventy people marched in Galway's gay pride parade.[126] This was the largest group ever to march in a gay pride parade in Galway and demonstrated its growth in the space of just three years.[127] Earlier that year, PLUTO (People Like Us Totally Outrageous), the gay and lesbian society at University College Galway, had received official recognition from the UCG college authorities.[128] In Limerick, during an Easter vigil, the parish of Dooradoyle heard from Joan, a lesbian, who told her story of growing up as a lesbian woman in Ireland.[129] Perhaps, however, the participation of gay and lesbian individuals in St Patrick's Day parades throughout Ireland highlighted the advance that had occurred. While the Ancient Order of Hibernians (AOH) banned the Irish Lesbian and Gay Organisation (ILGO) from marching in New York's 1992 St Patrick's Day parade, back in Ireland, in response to events in New York, members of the Cork Lesbian Group secured permission to march in the 1992 Cork St Patrick's Day parade, with the organisers describing the actions of the AOH as 'totally unacceptable'. In explaining their reason for granting the Cork Lesbian Group permission to march, Kieran Murphy (Cork Junior Chamber of Commerce) remarked that:

> I suppose you could say we are fairly progressive down here in Cork. The junior chamber as the organisers of this parade recognise that this group are a part of our society and have as much right to march as anybody else. We do want to demonstrate to the people in the US that not everybody in Ireland agrees that marchers from gay and lesbian groups should be banned from taking part in parades in US cities.[130]

During the 1992 Cork St Patrick's Day Parade, members of the Cork Lesbian Group, together with the Cork Gay Collective, marched through Cork City singing Tom Robinson's 'Sing if you're Glad to be Gay' and carrying placards saying, 'Hello New York'.[131] Orla Egan, one of the marchers, described the reaction from spectators as 'amazingly positive ... all along the route there were people shouting, clapping and waving in support ... We had reason to celebrate. We brought the words lesbian, gay and bisexual into people's vocabulary and consciousness and we had made ourselves visible in a proud, happy and positive way.'[132] Not only was the reaction of the crowd reason to celebrate but so too was awarding the prize for best new entrant to the gay and lesbian float.

The participation of a gay and lesbian float in the Cork St Patrick's Day parade set a precedent and led to the National Lesbian and Gay Federation (formerly National Gay Federation) requesting permission to march in Dublin's St Patrick's Day parade in 1993 and for PLUTO to do the same for the Galway parade that same year – both requests were successful.[133] The presence of gay and lesbian floats in St Patrick's Day parades in Ireland led Nuala O'Faolain to comment that it is 'all the more surprising then, that in the matter of accepting gay and lesbian Irish people, it is Ireland that is progressive and New York not'.[134] As an event which is synonymous with Irish identity, the presence of gay and lesbian individuals openly marching in St Patrick's Day parades throughout Ireland reinforced the claim that one could in fact be Irish and gay/lesbian; they were no longer mutually exclusive. This, in many respects, symbolised that a shift in attitudes had taken place by 1993.

One incident, however, which suggests the degree to which positive change had occurred, and that stood out during the course of researching this book, was a letter I found in the personal papers of David Norris. In this letter, written in October 1989, Norris responded to a student from Sligo Grammar School who had written to him about an assignment she had been given. The assignment concerned the subject of homosexuality and gay rights for her school's magazine. Recognising just how significant this student's assignment was, Norris responded by saying that he was not at all offended by her request, noting that 'such a subject would have been quite taboo in my own days in school, but that of course was twenty-five years ago and things I am glad to say have changed since then'.[135] The fact that homosexuality and gay rights was not only topical within a secondary school, but actually the subject of an assignment marked, as Norris noted, a considerable shift from his own time in school. The vast majority of Irish schools may have been under the patronage of the Irish Roman Catholic Church, yet in Sligo a young student carried out research on homosexuality and gay rights for her school magazine. It was no longer the terrible taboo subject it once was within Irish society, something Norris acknowledged in his response.

Writing after the passage of the Criminal Law Bill, David Norris explained why he believed he had acquired such a high profile:

> Because of my personal circumstance, I had an unusual freedom of manoeuvre. I was employed by the University of Dublin, a liberal environment; and both my parents were dead, so that neither family nor employer could bring undue pressure to bear. For this reason I was able, as many others were not, to speak out publicly

early on. As a result I have received a disproportionate amount of praise for the tenacity with which we have fought for our rights, but I should like to place on record my gratitude to the very many courageous people in the various organisations, such as the Irish Gay Rights Movement, National Lesbian and Gay Federation, Campaign for Homosexual Law Reform and the Gay and Lesbian Equality Network who selflessly, and for the most part anonymously, dedicated themselves to the task of social reform.[136]

To understand the changes of 1993, we must recognise the degree to which gay rights in the Republic of Ireland were not fought for and achieved by one gay man, not fought simply through the courts and not fought only in Dublin. The fight for gay rights was much more complicated than a simple victory at the European Court of Human Rights. It resulted from the collective endeavour of many, many individuals both inside and outside Dublin and Ireland. It was a collective of gay and lesbian individuals who formed social movements and social connections throughout Ireland and who fought for their human rights. In the space of twenty years, they had made significant progress. Their efforts laid a solid foundation from which activists in more recent years have been able to continue the fight for greater diversity within Irish society and LGBT equality. In the last six years Ireland's international reputation as a socially conservative country has been shattered with the passage of the 2015 marriage equality referendum and the 2018 referendum that repealed the 8th Amendment. For many, these two moments heralded the dawn of a new Ireland. These changes, however, are rooted in the grassroots activism which began in the twentieth century. To understand these dramatic changes, we must recognise the considerable efforts of often marginalised groups in society who have fought to make the Republic of Ireland a more tolerant, diverse and inclusive society in the twenty-first century. Speaking after the passage of the 2015 referendum on marriage equality, the Archbishop of Dublin, Diarmaid Martin, described it as a social revolution.[137] Irish gay and lesbian individuals were central to this revolution and to many others in Irish society. Their contribution, however, to the wider history of modern Ireland has yet to be fully acknowledged. It is hoped that this book will contribute to expanding Ireland's rich queer history.

Notes

Introduction

1 Lise Hand, 'Troubles melt like lemondrops on a day of sunshine, happiness and rainbows', *Irish Independent,* 25 May 2015, 19.
2 'Ban Ki-moon praises Ireland on marriage equality vote', *Irish Examiner*, 24 May 2015. http://www.irishexaminer.com/breakingnews/ireland/ban-ki-moon-praises-ireland-on-marriage-equality-vote-678570.html (accessed 3 October 2020).
3 Cormac McQuinn, 'MEP hits back at former Polish Prime Minister's attack on Ireland for improving LGBT rights', *Irish Independent*, 17 September 2020. https://www.independent.ie/irish-news/politics/mep-hits-back-at-former-polish-prime-ministers-attack-on-ireland-for-improving-lgbt-rights-39539647.html (accessed 3 October 2020).
4 It is important to note that the Sexual Offences Act 1967 did not fully decriminalise sexual activity between men. The Act only decriminalised sexual activity in private between men over the age of 21. According to Jeffrey Weeks, it 'absurdly restricted the meaning of "private": for the sake of the Act, "public" was defined as meaning not only a public lavatory but anywhere a third person was likely to be present.' As a result, the number of prosecutions under the Act actually increased following its passage. Jeffrey Weeks, *Coming Out: Homosexual Politics in Britain, from the Nineteenth Century to the Present* (London: Quartet Books, 1977), 176.
5 See: Sonja Tiernan, *The History of Marriage Equality in Ireland: A Social Revolution Begins* (Manchester: Manchester University Press, 2020); Gráinne Healy, Brian Sheehan and Noel Whelan, *Ireland Says Yes: The Inside Story of How the Vote for Marriage Equality was Won* (Kildare: Merrion Press, 2016); Charlie Bird, *A Day in May: Real Lives, True Stories* (Kildare: Merrion Press, 2016); Gráinne Healy, *Crossing the Threshold: The Story of the Marriage Equality Movement* (Kildare: Merrion Press, 2017).
6 Miriam Lord, 'Some puffing out of the Norrisonian chest', *The Irish Times*, 27 May 2015. http://www.irishtimes.com/news/politics/oireachtas/miriam-lord-some-puffing-out-of-the-norrisonian-chest-1.2227038 (accessed 27 May 2015).
7 Kieran Rose, *Diverse Communities: The Evolution of Lesbian and Gay Politics in Ireland* (Cork: Cork University Press, 1994); Íde O'Carroll and Eoin Collins (eds), *Lesbian and Gay Visions of Ireland towards the Twenty-first Century,* (London: Cassell, 1995); Paul Ryan, 'Coming Out: Gay Mobilisation, 1970–1980', in Linda Connolly and Niamh Hourigan (eds), *Social Movements and Ireland* (Manchester: Manchester University Press, 2006); Diarmaid Ferriter, *Occasions of Sin: Sex and Society in Modern Ireland*, (London: Profile, 2009); David Kilgannon, 'How to survive a plague': AIDS activism in Ireland, 1983–1989' (MA dissertation, School of History, University College Dublin, Dublin, 2015); Orla Egan, *Queer Republic of Cork* (Cork: Onstreams Publications, 2016); Páraic Kerrigan, 'Out-Ing AIDS: The Irish Civil Gay Rights Movement's Reponses to AIDS Crisis, 1984–1988', *Media History*, 25, no. 2 (2019): 244–258;

Maurice Casey, 'Radical Politics and Gay Activism in the Republic of Ireland, 1974–1990', *Irish Studies Review*, 26, no. 2 (2018): 217–236; James Grannell, 'Gay Health Action and the Fight Against AIDS in 1980s Ireland', *History Workshop*, 24 July 2019. http://www.historyworkshop.org.uk/gay-health-action-and-the-fight-against-aids-in-1980s-ireland/ (accessed 6 August 2019); Daryl Leeworthy, 'Rainbow Crossings: Gay Irish Migrants and LGBT Politics in 1980s London', in *Studi Irlandesi: A Journal of Irish Studies*, 10 (2020): 79–99.

8   Diarmaid Ferriter, *Transformation of Ireland 1900–2000* (London: Profile, 2004), 749.
9   Ed Madden, 'Queering Ireland, In the Archives', *Irish University Review*, 43, no. 1 (Spring/Summer 2013): 184.
10 Ferriter, *Occasions of Sin*, 9.
11 Weeks, *Coming Out*, 173.
12 Chrystel Hug, *The Politics of Sexual Morality in Ireland* (New York: Palgrave Macmillan, 1999), 1.
13 Lindsey Earner-Byrne and Diane Urquhart, *The Irish Abortion Journey, 1920–2018*, (London: Palgrave Pivot, 2019), 11.
14 Ibid.
15 Under Section 61 & 62 of the 1861 Act anyone convicted of buggery could be sentenced to penal servitude for life, while anyone found to have attempted to commit buggery, or anyone guilty of any assault with intent to commit the same, or of any indecent assault upon any male person, could be kept in penal servitude for any term not exceeding ten years. http://www.irishstatutebook.ie/eli/1861/act/100/enacted/en/print.html (accessed 8 October 2020). Under Section 11 of the 1885 Act, any male person who, in public or private, commits or procures the commission by any male person of any act of gross indecency with another male person could be sentenced to prison for any term not exceeding two years, with or without hard labour. http://www.irishstatutebook.ie/eli/1885/act/69/enacted/en/print (accessed 8 October 2020).
16 Averill Erin Earls, 'Queering Dublin: Same-sex Desire and Masculinities in Ireland, 1884–1950' (PhD thesis, Faculty of the Graduate School of the University of Buffalo, State University of New York, New York, 2016), xi.
17 Hug, *Politics of Sexual Morality*, 208.
18 National Archives of Ireland (henceforth NAI), 2019/101/1171, 'The European Court of Human Rights Norris Case, Memorial of the Government of Ireland, Appendix 2: Tabular Statement of updated statistics of prosecutions for homosexual offences in Ireland from 1979 to the end of August 1987'.
19 Terence Brown, *Ireland: A Social and Cultural History 1922–1985* (London: Fontana, 1985), 68.
20 Ibid., 76.
21 National Library of Ireland, Irish Queer Archive (henceforth NLI, IQA), MS 46,051/1, Campaign for Homosexual Law Reform, 'Homosexual Legislation in Ireland: A Case for Reform', January 1978.
22 To read more about the Catholic Church and the 1937 constitution see: Dermot Keogh, 'The Catholic Church and the writing of the 1937 constitution', *History Ireland*, 13, 3 (May/June 2005). https://www.historyireland.com/20th-century-contemporary-history/the-catholic-church-and-the-writing-of-the-1937-constitution/ (accessed on 15 February 2021).
23 Niall O'Dowd, *A New Ireland* (New York: Skyhorse Publishing, 2020), 139.
24 Ibid.

25 'Religion', Article 44.1.2 A referendum in 1972 subsequently removed this article. http://www.legislation.ie/eli/1972/act/23/enacted/en/print.html (accessed 9 August 2020).
26 Nathalie Rougier and Iseult Honohan, 'Religion and Education in Ireland: Growing Diversity – or Losing Faith in the System?', *Journal of Comparative Education*, 51, no. 1 (2015): 71–86.
27 *Bunreacht na hÉireann*, 'The Family', Article 41.2.2. http://www.irishstatutebook.ie/eli/cons/en/html (accessed 9 August 2020).
28 Department of Justice and Equality, 'Report of the Inter-Departmental Committee to establish the facts of State involvement with the Magdalen Laundries', 5 February 2013. https://www.gov.ie/en/collection/a69a14-report-of-the-inter-departmental-committee-to-establish-the-facts-of/ (accessed 9 August 2020); 'Final Report of the Commission of Investigation into Mother and Baby Homes', 12 January 2021. https://www.gov.ie/en/publication/d4b3d-final-report-of-the-commission-of-investigation-into-mother-and-baby-homes/ (accessed 14 February 2021).
29 Lindsey Earner-Byrne, 'Reinforcing the family: The role of gender, morality and sexuality in Irish welfare policy, 1922–1944', *The History of the Family*, 13, no. 4 (2008): 363.
30 For the most part throughout this book I use the terms gay and lesbian. I do so because these were the terms most commonly used by activists to describe individuals who were emotionally and sexually attracted to members of the same sex during the period of focus in this book. Like their international counterparts, Irish gay and lesbian individuals adopted these terms to move away from what was perceived as the more clinical term, homosexual. While gay was used to refer to gay men and gay women, Irish women began to use lesbian in the late 1970s to move away from using gay, which was perceived as overwhelmingly associated with men. This was also part of efforts to increase the visibility of lesbian women and the issues that directly affected them. In saying that, I use the term gay community to refer to gay men and lesbian women, and gay rights to refer to the demands of gay men and lesbian women to advance their civil rights. Again, this is how they were used during this period. In Chapter 1, however, I use homosexual, rather than gay and lesbian individuals, as this was the term most commonly used during the period in focus in Chapter 1. This is not to suggest that gay and lesbian were not known or used in the mid-1970s – they were – but rather to reflect the more common use of homosexual, rather than gay and lesbian, which became more common from the late 1970s and early 1980s onwards. Homosexual refers to both homosexual men and women. Exceptions to these rules will appear throughout the book, depending on the context or individual/organisation being quoted, referenced or discussed. It is worth noting, however, that some often used homosexual and gay interchangeably.
31 Martin Duberman, *Has the Gay Movement Failed?* (California: University of California Press, 2018); Barry D. Adam, *The Rise of a Gay and Lesbian Movement* (Boston: Twayne Publishers, 1987).
32 Suggested reading: Brian Lacey, *Terrible Queer Creatures: Homosexuality in Irish History* (Dublin: Wordwell Ltd., 2008); Éibhear Walshe, *Oscar's Shadow: Wilde, Homosexuality and Modern Ireland* (Cork: Cork University Press, 2011).
33 Dublin Gay and Lesbian Collective, *Out for Ourselves: The Lives of Irish Lesbians and Gay Men* (Dublin: Women's Community Press, 1986), 122.
34 NAI, 2019/101/1171, 'The European Court of Human Rights Norris Case, Memorial of the Government of Ireland, Appendix 2: Tabular Statement of updated statistics of prosecutions for homosexual offences in Ireland from 1979 to the end of August 1987'.

35 'Seminar on Homosexual Problems', *The Irish Times*, 19 May 1975, 13.
36 'Calls for Help Increase by 17%', *The Irish Times*, 25 July 1978, 11.
37 'More People Seek Aid from Samaritans', *The Irish Times*, 24 July 1979, 11.
38 Theresa Blanche interview with Edmund Lynch, 14 June 2013 (Edmund Lynch Irish LGBT Oral History Project).
39 Tonie Walsh interview with Edmund Lynch, 6 April 2013 (Edmund Lynch Irish LGBT Oral History Project).
40 NLI, IQA, MS 45, 990/2, unsigned and undated letter sent to *OUT*. *OUT* was a gay magazine published in Ireland from 1984 to 1988.
41 'Don't Jail them, pleads doctor', *Irish Independent*, 6 November 1973, 7. https://www.irishnewsarchive.com (accessed 20 September 2020).
42 Ibid.
43 'Laws against homosexuality "an open incitement to hatred"', *The Irish Times*, 8 March 1977, 5.
44 Brendan Kelly has explored this issue somewhat in 'Homosexuality and Irish psychiatry: medicine, law, and the changing face of Ireland', *Irish Journal of Psychological Medicine*, 34, 3 (2017): 209–215.
45 David Norris, *A Kick Against the Pricks* (Dublin: Transworld Ireland, 2012), 113.
46 Ibid.
47 See Leeworthy, 'Rainbow Crossings', 79–99.
48 Johanne Devlin Trew and Michael Pierse, 'Introduction: Gathering Tensions', in *Rethinking the Irish Diaspora: After the Gathering* (Palgrave Macmillan, 2018), 1.
49 Ibid., 20.
50 Leeworthy, 'Rainbow Crossings', 83–85.
51 Colm O'Clubhán, 'Other Dimensions', *Out for Ourselves*, 90–91.
52 Ibid.
53 For more information on the Irish LGBT community in New York, see: Katherine O'Donnell & Sally R. Munt, 'Pride and Prejudice: Legalizing Compulsory Heterosexuality in New York and Boston's St Patrick's Day Parades', *International Journal of Social Spaces*, 10, 1 (2007): 1–21.
54 Róisín Ryan-Flood, 'Sexuality, Citizenship and Migration: The Irish Queer Diaspora in London', in *Sexuality, Citizenship and Belonging*, eds. Francesca Stella, Yvette Taylor, Tracey Reynolds, Antoine Rogers (New York: Routledge, 2016), 52.
55 The launch of Maurice Casey's exhibition 'Out in the World: Ireland's LGBTQ+ Diaspora' at EPIC: The Irish Emigration Museum in June 2021 is an important and welcome development in this regard.
56 See Ferriter, *Transformation of Ireland*; Linda Connolly, *The Irish Women's Movement: From Revolution to Devolution* (Dublin: Palgrave Macmillan, 2002); Mike Chinoy, *Are You With Me?: Kevin Boyle and the Rise of the Human Rights Movement* (Dublin: Lilliput Press, 2020).
57 Connolly, *The Irish Women's Movement*, 113.

1 Irish Homosexuals are Revolting, 1973–1978

1 Public Record Office of Northern Ireland (hereafter PRONI), Northern Ireland Gay Rights Association Archive (hereafter NIGRA), D/3762/1/3/2/1, 'News from Ireland', newspaper clipping from *Gay News* (May 1973).

2   Crossley's visit was reported in *The Irish Times*, P.M., 'Homosexual Law Reform', *The Irish Times*, 21 November 1972, 6. *The Irish Times* reported that Crossley's visit to Dublin was 'at the request of CHE members in Ireland'.
3   'Problems discussed', *Irish Independent*, 14 April 1970, 10. https://www.irishnewsarchive.com (accessed 20 September 2020).
4   Paddy, 'News from Ireland'.
5   John Grundy interview with Edmund Lynch, 27 April 2013 (Edmund Lynch Irish LGBT Oral History Project).
6   Paddy, 'News from Ireland'.
7   NLI, Personal Papers of David Norris, Acc. 6672, Box 25, 'Guides to gay pubs in Ireland', *A Newsletter from IGRM – Irish Gay Rights Movement*, 19 February 1975.
8   Theresa Blanche interview with Edmund Lynch, 17 June 2013 (Edmund Lynch Irish LGBT Oral History Project).
9   Edmund Lynch interview with John Early and Karl Hayden, 9 February 2013 (Edmund Lynch Irish LGBT Oral History Project).
10 NLI, Personal Papers of David Norris (henceforth PPDN), Acc. 6672, Box 25, *In Touch: the Newsletter of the Irish Gay Rights Movement*, 1 no. 5, October 1977, 4.
11 Ibid.; I use the Irish Inflation Calculator throughout this book to calculate today's value. http://www.hargaden.com/enda/inflation/calculator.html (accessed 15 February 2021).
12 Kieran Rose interview with author, 12 January 2016.
13 Cathal Kerrigan interview with author, 14 January 2016.
14 'Dublin pubs listed as 'gay bars', *Sunday Independent*, 11 May 1975, 4. https://www.irishnewsarchive.com (accessed 20 September 2020).
15 Ibid.
16 Paddy, 'News from Ireland'.
17 PRONI, NIGRA, D/3762/1/3/2/1, 'Irish Gay Beginnings: Full Report on First Ever Irish Gay Conference', newspaper clipping from *Gay News* (November 1973). Part of this chapter was previously published in Patrick McDonagh, 'Homosexuality is not a problem – it doesn't do you any harm and can be lots of fun': Students and Gay Rights Activism in Irish Universities, 1970s–1980s, *Irish Economic and Social History*, 46, no. 1 (2019): 111–141 – Reproduced with kind permission by SAGE and *Irish Economic and Social History*.
18 NLI, Ir 360 p 24, Peter Hughes, 'The Aims of GLS', *Gay Forum: seven essays on homosexuality*, published by Belfast Gay Liberation Society (1974), 4.
19 The National Union of Students (NUS) is a United Kingdom-wide organisation representing university student unions. The Union of Students in Ireland is the all-Ireland equivalent of the NUS. Together, they jointly represent student unions in Northern Ireland. https://nus-usi.org/who-we-are/ (accessed 21 July 2019).
20 PRONI, NIGRA, D/3762/1/3/2/1, 'Irish Gay Beginnings: Full Report on First Ever Irish Gay Conference', newspaper clipping from *Gay News* (November 1973).
21 Ibid.
22 'Students Back Gay Liberation', *The Irish Times*, 5 April 1973, 15.
23 David Malcom, 'A Curious Courage: The Origins of Gay Rights Campaigning in the National Union of Students', *History of Education*, 47, no. 1 (2018): 80.
24 PRONI, NIGRA, D/3762/1/3/2/1, 'Irish Gay Beginnings', *Gay News*, 1973.
25 PRONI, NIGRA, D/3762/1/3/2/1, 'Gay rights – History & Emergence of IGRM', newspaper clipping from *Gay News* (August 1974).

26 Mary Dorcey interview with Edmund Lynch, 8 June 2013 (Edmund Lynch Irish LGBT Oral History Project).
27 Ibid.
28 Edmund Lynch interview with John Early and Karl Hayden, 9 February 2013 (Edmund Lynch Irish LGBT Oral History Project).
29 Christina Murphy, 'Homosexuals – An Oppressed Minority', *The Irish Times*, 16 February 1974, 6.
30 NLI, Ir 360 p 24, Jeffrey Dudgeon, 'Featurette', *Gay Forum: seven essays on homosexuality*, published by Belfast Gay Liberation Society (1974), 8.
31 Ibid.
32 Ibid.
33 Christina Murphy, 'Homosexuals Set Up Organisation', *The Irish Times*, 18 February 1974, 6.
34 Email correspondence with Edmund Lynch, 20 November 2020.
35 Conor McAnally, 'I Changed My Mind about Homosexuals', *Sunday Independent*, 17 February 1974, 3; Angela Nugent, 'Different is not dangerous', *Irish Farmers Journal*, 45. https://www.irishnewsarchive.com (accessed 20 September 2020).
36 Edmund Lynch (director), *Did They Notice Us? Gay Visibility in the Irish Media 1973–1993*, 2003. Copy courtesy of Edmund Lynch.
37 NLI, IR 369 I 23, *In Touch*, 2, no. 7 (August/September 1980), David Norris, 'Homosexuals are Revolting: A history of the gay movement in Ireland', 9.
38 Ibid.
39 PRONI, NIGRA, D/3762/1/3/2/1, 'David Norris: gay lecturer', newspaper clipping from *Gay News* (August 1974).
40 Norris, 'Homosexuals are Revolting', 9.
41 Ibid.
42 PRONI, NIGRA, D3762/1/3/5/5, 'Norway takes up Irish cause', *Gay News*, no. 51 (1974), 4.
43 Norris, *A Kick Against the Pricks*, 84.
44 NLI, PPDN, Acc. 6672, Box 25, Meeting in the South County Hotel, 7 July 1974.
45 NLI, PPDN, Acc. 6672, Box 21, Edmund Lynch letter to David Norris, 19 April 1975.
46 NLI, IQA, MS 45, 951/2, Constitution of the Irish Gay Rights Movement.
47 NLI, PPDN, Acc. 6672, Box 25, *IGRM Circular*, 14 October 1975.
48 PRONI, NIGRA, D3762/1/10/1, 'Eire', newspaper clipping from *Gay News* (c. Autumn/Winter 1975).
49 NLI, PPDN, 'General Information', *A Newsletter from IGRM – Irish Gay Rights Movement*, 19 February 1975.
50 PRONI, NIGRA, D3762/1/10/1, 'Dublin Toast', newspaper clipping from *Gay News* (c. Autumn/Winter 1975).
51 NLI, PPDN, Acc. 6672, Box 25, *In Touch*, 'Income and Expenditure Account for the period 1 September 1976 – 27 May 1977', 1, no. 4 (September 1977).
52 NLI, PPDN, Acc. 6672, Box 25, *In Touch*, 'Review of the Year', January 1978, 6.
53 Ibid.
54 Anthony Redmond, 'A visit to a gay disco in Dublin', *Sunday Independent*, 7 December 1975, 14. https://www.irishnewsarchive.com (accessed 20 September 2020).
55 Mary Maher, 'An end to the isolation', *The Irish Times*, 21 February 1977, 11.
56 NLI, IQA, MS 45, 951/9, Letter from Anna from Cavan to Theresa Blanche (IGRM), May 1977.
57 NLI, PPDN, Acc. 6672, Box 25, *IGRM Circular*, 14 October 1975.

58 NLI, PPDN, Acc. 6672 Box 25, 'Sappho in Dublin', *Phoenix Review*, April 1977, 3.
59 Ibid.
60 NLI, PPDN, Acc. 6672, Box 25, *IGRM Newsletter*, December 1975.
61 Gale Primary Sources, Archives of Sexuality and Gender, Theresa Blanche, 'Irish Action', *Sappho*, 5, no. 2 (1976), 25, https://go.gale.com/ps/i.do?p=AHSI&u=tlemea_ahsi&v=2.1&it=r&id=GALE%7CBAVOKD185905362&asid=1600574400000~817d916c (accessed 8 March 2016).
62 NLI, PPDN, Acc. 6672, Box 25, 'Women's Group', *In Touch*, 1 no. 4 (September 1977), 5.
63 NLI, PPDN, Acc. 6672, Box 25, 'Income and Expenditure Account for the period 1 September 1976 – 27 May 1977', *In Touch*, 1, no. 4 (September 1977).
64 NLI, IQA, MS 45, 951/1, IGRM newspaper clipping, Hugh Lambert, 'Gay Rights: the good news and the bad', *Sunday Press*, 10 August 1975.
65 PRONI, NIGRA, D3762/1/2/6/1, 1974 Committee of Northern Ireland Gay Rights Association to Trevor Phillips, University of London Union, 28 April 1976.
66 Edmund Lynch interview with Des Fitzgerald, 18 July 2013 (Edmund Lynch Irish LGBT Oral History Project).
67 NLI, IQA, MS 45, 949/4, Report of the operation of TAF for the period April 1979 to April 1980.
68 NLI, PPDN, Acc. 6672, Box 25, *IGRM Newsletter*, no. 9 (1976).
69 Orla Egan, 'Cork Irish Gay Rights Movement', 27 July 2014. http://corklgbthistory.com/2014/07/27/cork-irish-gay-rights-movement/ (accessed 9 August 2020).
70 NLI, PPDN, Acc. 6672, Box 25, Michael Bergin, 'Cork Report', *IGRM Newsletter*, no. 1/76, January 1977.
71 Ibid.
72 NLI, PPDN, Acc. 6672, Box 25, Bert Meany notice, 9 January 1977.
73 Ibid.
74 Orla Egan, 'Cork Irish Gay Rights Movement', 27 July 2014. https://corklgbthistory.com/2014/07/27/cork-irish-gay-rights-movement/ (accessed 17 September 2020).
75 Cathal Kerrigan interview with author, 14 January 2016.
76 NLI, PPDN, Acc. 6672, Box 22, Bert Meany, 'Report', *Corks Crew*, 1, no. 4 (December 1977), 3.
77 'Woman.......', *Sapphire*, 1, no. 1(January/February 1978), 18. https://corklgbtarchive.com/items/show/183 (accessed 16 March 2021).
78 Orla Egan, *Queer Republic of Cork*, 13.
79 NLI, PPDN, Acc. 6672, Box 25, *In Touch: the newsletter of the Irish Gay Rights Movement*, January 1978, 2.
80 'Annual General Meeting 1978', *Sapphire*, 1, no. 1 (January/February 1978), 13. https://corklgbtarchive.com/items/show/183 (accessed 16 March 2021).
81 Oliver Cogan, 'Comment', *Sapphire*, 1, no. 1(January/February 1978), 2. https://corklgbtarchive.com/items/show/183 (accessed 16 March 2021).
82 Ibid., 3.
83 Ibid., 2.
84 For further reading on LGBTQ visibility in the Irish media see: Páraic Kerrigan, *LGBTQ Visibility, Media and Sexuality in Ireland* (Oxfordshire: Routledge, 2021).
85 Norris, *A Kick Against the Pricks*, 86.
86 RTÉ Archives, *Last House*, 24 July 1975. http://www.rte.ie/archives/2014/0212/503805-david-norris-chairman-of-the-gay-rights-movement-1975/ (accessed 18 April 2018).
87 Kerrigan, *LGBTQ Visibility*, 34.

88. RTÉ Archives, *Last House*, 24 July 1975. http://www.rte.ie/archives/2014/0212/503805-david-norris-chairman-of-the-gay-rights-movement-1975/ (accessed 18 April 2018).
89. NLI, IQA, MS 45, 951/1, IGRM report on the interview between Aine O'Connor & David Norris on *Last House*, 24 July 1975.
90. Ibid.
91. 'Complaint against RTE is upheld', *Irish Press*, 3 February 1976, 3. https://www.irishnewsarchive.com (accessed 20 September 2020).
92. Ibid.
93. Tony Wilson, 'It was just a matter of fact', *Evening Herald*, 2 August 1975, 7. https://www.irishnewsarchive.com (accessed 20 September 2020).
94. Pearse Hutchinson, 'The Great Fiddler', *The Irish Times*, 4 August 1975, 8.
95. NLI, IQA, MS 45, 951/1, IGRM report on the interview between Aine O'Connor & David Norris on *Last House*, 24 July 1975, IGRM newspaper clipping, Val Mulkerns, *Evening Press*, 2 August 1975.
96. Peter Cleary, 'Pap for people is politicians' delight', *Sunday Independent*, 27 July 1975, 2. https://www.irishnewsarchive.com (accessed 20 September 2020).
97. Ibid.
98. Sean Connolly, 'A clout at critic Cleary', *Sunday Independent*, 3 August 1975, 10. https://www.irishnewsarchive.com (accessed 20 September 2020).
99. Ibid.
100. John Donlon, 'Beyond the Fringe', *Longford Leader*, 3 October 1975, 16. https://www.irishnewsarchive.com (accessed 20 September 2020).
101. 'More Gays', *Longford Leader*, 10 October 1975, 8. https://www.irishnewsarchive.com (accessed 20 September 2020).
102. 'Rights for the gays!' *Longford Leader*, 10 October 1975, 8. https://www.irishnewsarchive.com (accessed 20 September 2020).
103. John Donlon, 'Beyond the Fringe', *Longford Leader*, 14 November 1975, 16. https://www.irishnewsarchive.com (accessed 20 September 2020).
104. 'Gay secretary replies', *Longford Leader*, 24 October 1975, 8; 'Gay rights', *Longford Leader*, 14 November 1975, 16. https://www.irishnewsarchive.com (accessed 20 September 2020).
105. NLI, IQA, MS 45, 951/5, Press Release, Project Arts Centre, 10 November 1976.
106. NLI, IQA, MS 45, 951/5, IGRM newspaper clipping, 'Gay Theatre Group for Dublin', *Scene Magazine*, November 1976.
107. Gus Smith, 'Crowded Project see Gay Show', *Sunday Independent*, 21 November 1976, 15. https://www.irishnewsarchive.com (accessed 20 September 2020).
108. NLI, IQA, MS 45, 951/5, IGRM newspaper clipping, Jim Farrelly, "'Gay' show may end the theatre grant', *Irish Independent*, 17 November 1976.
109. Ibid.
110. Desmond Rushe, 'Gay group's propaganda offensive', *Irish Independent*, 16 November 1976, 7. https://www.irishnewsarchive.com (accessed 20 September 2020).
111. Ibid.
112. Elgy Gillespie, 'Gay Sweatshop at Project Arts Centre', *The Irish Times*, 17 November 1976, 9.
113. Nial MacDara, 'Fighting pornography', *Irish Press*, 15 December 1976, 10. https://www.irishnewsarchive.com (accessed 20 September 2020).
114. 'War of words on theatre aid', *Irish Press*, 20 January 1977, 7. https://archive.irishnewsarchive.com/Olive/APA/INA/Default.aspx☒nel=document (accessed 10 October 2020).

115 'Gay Sweatshop to return to Dublin', *The Irish Times*, 24 January 1977, 4.
116 "'Gay' mag raps Dublin", *Sunday Independent*, 27 February 1977, 5. https://www.irishnewsarchive.com (accessed 20 September 2020).
117 'Irish Gay Rights in Euro-aid campaign', *Evening Herald*, 24 January 1977, 4. https://www.irishnewsarchive.com (accessed 20 September 2020).
118 John O'Shaughnessy, 'Sweatshop for City Theatre? I don't think ratepayers can object: Bourke', *Limerick Leader*, 5 February 1977, 1. https://www.irishnewsarchive.com (accessed 20 September 2020).
119 NLI, IR 650 R 1, Cathal O'Shannon, 'Homosexuals – their view', *RTÉ Guide*, 1, no. 7 (18 February 1977), 3.
120 Ibid.
121 'Homosexuality in Ireland', *Tuesday Report* (RTÉ) 22 February 1977. Copy of this programme provided by Edmund Lynch.
122 Ibid.
123 Fr. Colm Kilcoyne, 'Homosexuals', *Western People*, 18 September 1976, 13. https://www.irishnewsarchive.com (accessed 20 September 2020); It was later revealed that Cleary, along with another high-profile priest, Eamonn Casey, had fathered children, leading Professor Diarmaid Ferriter to describe him as an 'obnoxious hypocrite': Diarmaid Ferriter, 'Fr Cleary, the obnoxious hypocrite, wasn't half the man his son is', *Irish Examiner*, 6 September 2007. https://www.irishexaminer.com/opinion/commentanalysis/arid-20041770.html (accessed 19 February 2021).
124 NLI, IQA, MS 45, 943/2, Transcript of calls to RTÉ following *Tuesday Report*.
125 NLI, IQA, MS 45, 943/2, Letter from Margaret Kegley to Cathal O'Shannon, 23 February 1977.
126 Peter Cleary, 'The Gay people "come out" of the shadows', *Sunday Independent*, 27 February 1977, 25. https://www.irishnewsarchive.com (accessed 20 September 2020).
127 Val Mulkerns, 'Candid Report on difficult subject', *Evening Press*, 26 February 1977.
128 'Cleary's comments drew readers' fire', *Sunday Independent*, 6 March 1977, 8. https://www.irishnewsarchive.com (accessed 20 September 2020).
129 Ibid.
130 'Complaints by Telefís viewer rejected', *Irish Press*, 6 January 1978, 7. https://www.irishnewsarchive.com (accessed 20 September 2020).
131 NLI, IQA, MS 45, 948/1, USI Welfare Policy March 1981: Adopted motions on Welfare from 15th-23rd Congresses Unions of Students in Ireland, 28.
132 NLI, IQA, MS 45, 948/2, Sexual Freedom: A Discussion Document presented to 16th Annual Congress, 10–13 January 1974; Report of Coleraine Conference on Sexual Freedom.
133 Ibid.
134 'USI Plea for Birth Law Change', *Irish Independent*, 12 January 1974, 9; Gerry McMorrow, 'Homosexuality laws "barbaric"', *Irish Press*, 12 January 1974, 3. https://www.irishnewsarchive.com (accessed 20 September 2020).
135 Robert Rhoads, 'Student Activism as an Agent of Social Change: A Phenomenological Analysis of Contemporary Campus Unrest', paper presented at the Annual Meeting of the American Educational Research Association, published online by The Educational Resources Information Centre, March 1997, https://files.eric.ed.gov/fulltext/ED407902.pdf (accessed on 29 January 2019); Valerie Korinek, 'The Most Openly Gay Person for at least a Thousand Miles': Doug Wilson and the Politicization of a Province, 1975–83', *Canadian Historical Review*, 84, no. 4 (2003): 517–550; Brett Beemyn, 'The Silence is Broken: A History of the First Lesbian, Gay, and Bisexual

College Student Groups', *Journal of the History of Sexuality*, 12, no. 2 (2003): 205–223; T. Evan Faulkenbury and Aaron Hayworth, 'The Carolina Gay Association, Oral History, and Coming Out at the University of North Carolina', *Oral History Review*, 43, no. 1 (2016): 115–137.
136 'Protest by "Gay Lib" chairman', *Irish Press*, 2 May 1976, 5. https://www.irishnewsarchive.com (accessed 20 September 2020).
137 NLI, IQA, MS 45, 951/10, Peter Davies to IGRM, 20 September 1977.
138 'Gay article protest by students', *Irish Press*, 18 March 1976, 3. https://www.irishnewsarchive.com (accessed 20 September 2020).
139 Ibid.
140 'Gay Letter for Bishops', *Catholic Standard*, 17 January 1975, 3.
141 Ibid.
142 NLI, IQA, MS 45, 951/1, Archbishop of Dublin Alan Buchanan to David Norris, 4 February 1975.
143 NLI, IQA, MS 45, 951/1, Church of Ireland Social Service to David Norris, 28 February 1975.
144 NLI, IQA, MS 45, 951/1, James Young to David Norris, 19 September 1975.
145 NLI, IQA, MS 45, 951/1, James Young to David Norris 'Re: Sub-Committee of the Board for Social Responsibility', date not specified but sometime in late 1975.
146 NLI, IQA, MS 45, 951/4, *IGRM Newsletter*, February 1976.
147 Ibid.
148 NLI, LB 05 03, 'General Synod 1976', *Church of Ireland Gazette*, 21 May 1976, 4.
149 John Cooney, 'Support for Law Reform after plea on homosexuality', *The Irish Times*, 13 May 1976, 14.
150 'Statement on sex maligned by media – Bishop Daly', *Catholic Standard*, 30 January 1976, 3.
151 David Norris letter published in *Catholic Standard*, 6 February 1976.
152 NLI, IQA, MS 45, 954/1, Diocesan Secretary of the Archdiocese of Armagh to James Malone, 21 September 1976.
153 *Seanad Éireann* debate, 'Law Reform Commission Bill', 80, no. 2 (10 April 1975).
154 'Gay Movement seeks "rights"', *Evening Herald*, 11 March 1975, 2. https://www.irishnewsarchive.com (accessed 20 September 2020).
155 NAI, 2012/21/582, Office of the Attorney General, Louis Renkin to Ireland's Permanent Representative Brussels, 25 April 1975.
156 Ibid., André Baudry letter to Irish Ambassador to France, 7 September 1976.
157 'Changes in homosexual law sought', *The Irish Times*, 17 January 1977, 11.
158 'Senators in homosexual law move', *Irish Press*, 25 January 1977, 6. https://www.irishnewsarchive.com (accessed 20 September 2020).
159 *Dáil Éireann* debate, 'Homosexuality Laws', 302, no. 8 (13 December 1977).
160 NLI, PPDN, Acc. 6672 Box 21, David Norris to National Executive of IGRM, 7 January 1977.
161 Ibid.
162 NLI, PPDN, Acc. 6672 Box 21, Report of Letter of Resignation of Sean Connolly as General Secretary, 10 March 1977.
163 Ibid.; IGRM special committee meeting on finance, 13 March 1977.
164 NLI, PPDN, Acc. 6672 Box 21, Notice of extraordinary general meeting, 6 April 1977.
165 PRONI, NIGRA, D3762/3/5/1, Profile of Candidates seeking election to the National Executive of IGRM, 28 May 1977.
166 Ibid.

167 NLI, PPDN, Acc. 6672 Box 17, 'Normal Service will be resumed as soon as possible', *Gay News*, no. 137 (23 February – 18 March 1978).
168 NLI, PPDN, Acc. 6672, Box 21, David Norris to Frank Ryan, General Secretary of IGRM, 24 November 1977.
169 TCDA, Personal Papers of Noel Browne, 11067/6/4/1, CHLR meeting, 23 January 1978.
170 European Court of Human Rights, 'Case of Norris v. Ireland', Judgement, 26 October 1988. https://hudoc.echr.coe.int/fre#%7B%22itemid%22:%5B%22001-57547%22%5D%7D, (accessed 18 September 2020).
171 NLI, Personal Papers of David Norris, ACC 6672 Box 17, 'Normal Service will be resumed as soon as possible', *Gay News* No. 137 (23 February – 18 March 1978).

2 Social Life as Resistance in 1980s Dublin

1 Maurice Haugh, 'Life revives in a dying part of Dublin', *The Irish Times*, 30 July 1984, 13.
2 NLI, IR 650 S 1, Niall O'Dowd and Mary Kavanagh, 'Going for the Top: Chasing the Pink Pound', *Success*, November 1984, 19.
3 Ibid., 21.
4 'The Struggle for LGBT rights in Ireland: Interview with Ailbhe Smyth', *Irish Marxist Review*, 3, no. 11 (2004): 29. http://irishmarxistreview.net/index.php/imr/article/viewFile/136/138 (accessed 10 August 2020).
5 To read more about spaces and sexuality see: Nancy Duncan, 'Renegotiating Gender and Sexuality in Public and Private Spaces', *Destabilizing Geographies of Gender and Sexuality*, ed. Nancy Duncan (London: Routledge, 1996); Anne Enke, *Finding the Movement: Sexuality, Contested Space, and Feminist Activism* (Durham & London: Duke University Press, 2007).
6 Ciaran McKinney interview with Edmund Lynch, 9 February 2013 (Edmund Lynch Irish LGBT Oral History Project).
7 '"Gay" group opens new headquarters', *The Irish Times*, 25 April 1979, 7; Anthony Redmond, 'A new centre for counsel and friendship', *Irish Press*, 1 May 1979, 9. https://www.irishnewsarchive.com (accessed 20 September 2020).
8 Norris, *A Kick Against the Pricks*, 102.
9 WhatsApp conversation with Tonie Walsh, 13 February 2021.
10 Anthony Redmond, 'A new centre for counsel and friendship', *Irish Press*, 1 May 1979, 9.
11 Bill Hughes interview with Edmund Lynch, 9 February 2013 (Edmund Lynch Irish LGBT Oral History Project).
12 NLI, IQA, MS 45, 936/3, NGF Constitution.
13 Gale Primary Sources, Archives of Sexuality and Gender, 'New Group Set to Open Old Wounds in Ireland', in *Gay News*, no. 173 (23 August – 5 September 1979), 8. https://go.gale.com/ps/i.do?p=AHSI&u=tlemea_ahsi&v=2.1&it=r&id=GALE%7CAFZUKM862867393&asid=1600574400000~66ce8315 (accessed 19 September 2020).
14 Ibid.
15 'Fire stops the dancing', *Evening Press*, 7 July 1979, 3. https://www.irishnewsarchive.com (accessed 20 September 2020).
16 Gale Primary Sources, Archives of Sexuality and Gender, 'New Group Set to Open Old Wounds in Ireland', in *Gay News*, no. 173 (23 August – 5 September 1979), 8. https://

17 Ibid.
18 NLI, PPDN, Acc. 6672 Box 19, *Gay News* no. 176 (October 4 – 17 1979).
19 Ibid.
20 NLI, IR 369 I 23, 'Comment', *In Touch*, 2, no. 1 (January 1980), 1.
21 NLI, IQA, MS 45, 951/8, Gallagher, Shatter and Co. letter to David Norris, 23 January 1980.
22 NLI, PPDN, Acc. 6672, Box 40, Chris Kirk, 'How the Dubliners got it together!', *Gay News*, 222 (20 August – 2 September 1981), 13.
23 NLI, IQA, MS 45 951/8, IGRM Press Release, 9 September 1979.
24 Norris, *A Kick Against the Pricks*, 106.
25 NLI, IR 369 I 23, *In Touch*, 1, no. 2 (October 1979), 'I.G.A.', 10.
26 Irish Gay Rights Movement advertisement, *In Dublin*, no. 97 (7–20 March 1980), 14.
27 NLI, Ir 94133 I 2, Lynn Geldof, *In Dublin*, 117 (12 December 1980 – 8 January 1981), 45; NLI, ILB 780, 'Hirschfeld: Solidarity Centre', *Hot Press*, 4, no. 12 (7 – 12 November 1980)
28 Brian Black, 'Hirschfeld Centre home of Gay Liberation', *Ireland's Eye* (RTÉ), 24 November 1981. http://www.rte.ie/archives/2016/1123/833947-hirschfeld-centre-national-gay-federation/ (accessed 10 August 2020).
29 Ibid.
30 NLI, IQA, MS 45, 946/1, Flikkers disco attendance figures.
31 Haugh, 'Life revives in a dying part of Dublin', 13.
32 NLI, IQA, MS 45, 998/6, Johnny McEvoy, 'The Hirschfeld Biograph', January 1990.
33 NLI, IR 369 07, 'Hirschfeld Biograph', *OUT*, *NGF News*, 1, no. 1 (December 1984/January 1985).
34 Ibid.
35 NLI, IR 94133 I 2, Donal Hounam, 'In Dublin RECOMMENDS', *In Dublin*, no. 214 (4–17 October 1984), 58; Ray Comiskey, 'A Mixed Bag', *The Irish Times*, 1 October 1984, 10.
36 Ciaran Coleman interview with Edmund Lynch, 8 November 2013 (Edmund Lynch Irish LGBT Oral History Project).
37 NLI, IR 369 I 23, Bernard Keogh, 'NGF Youth Group', *In Touch*, 1, no. 3 (November/December 1979), 10–11.
38 Ibid.,10. Parts of this chapter appear in Patrick McDonagh and Páraic Kerrigan, '"Cherishing all the Children of the Nation Equally": Gay Youth Organisation and Activism in Ireland (Basingstoke: Palgrave Macmillan, forthcoming). Reproduced with kind permission by Palgrave Macmillan.
39 The NGF Administrative Council consisted of 18 elected members who took over the running of the NGF for a twelve-month period.
40 NLI, PPDN, Acc. 6672, Box 36 – NGF Gay Youth Group Report, September 1979.
41 Ibid.
42 Keogh, 'NGF Youth Group', *In Touch*, 1979.
43 NLI, IQA, MS, 45, 956/1, Bernard Keogh, NGF General Secretary to Anne Keogh, Student Counsellor, Trinity College, 4 March 1980.
44 Keogh, 'NGF Youth Group', *In Touch*, 1979.
45 NLI, IQA, MS 45, 943/3, Maurice Devlin, Liaison Officer (Comhairle Le Leas Óige) to Pat McGrath (NGF Youth Group), 28 September 1982.

46 Tom Rowley, 'Row over gay group's grant', *Irish Independent*, 14 October 1982, 3. https://www.irishnewsarchive.com (accessed 20 September 2020).
47 'Grant to gay group attacked', *The Irish Times*, 14 October 1982, 5.
48 Ignorance and prejudice', *OUT*, no. 8 (March/April 1986), 4.
49 NLI, IQA, MS, 45, 956/1, Bernard Keogh, NGF General Secretary to Anne Keogh, Student Counsellor, Trinity College, 4 March 1980.
50 Derek Moloney interview with Edmund Lynch, 31 August 2013 (Edmund Lynch Irish LGBT Oral History Project).
51 'The gay with parents', *The Irish Times*, 5 September 1980, 10.
52 Marianne Heron, 'New support group for parents in Dublin', *Irish Independent*, 26 June 1980, 12. https://www.irishnewsarchive.com (accessed 20 September 2020).
53 Phil Moore interview with Edmund Lynch, 18 July 2013 (Edmund Lynch Irish LGBT Oral History Project).
54 'I hadn't realised I had so many prejudices in my mind', *Evening Herald*, 1 November 1983, 19. https://www.irishnewsarchive.com (accessed 20 September 2020).
55 Ibid.
56 Walt Kilroy interview with Edmund Lynch 17 May 2013 (Edmund Lynch Irish LGBT Oral History Project).
57 NLI, IR 369 I 25, 'Welfare Service', *Identity*, no. 7 (October – December 1983), 24.
58 NLI, IR 369 I 23, 'Report from the International Lesbian Conference, 27–30 December 1980', *In Touch*, 3, no. 2 (March/April 1981), 19–23.
59 NLI, IQA, MS 46, 005/3, Report of the Second National Gay Conference held in Dublin between June 18–20. The first National Gay Conference took place in Cork in 1981 and will be discussed in Chapter 3.
60 Ibid.
61 NLI, PPDN, Acc. 6672, Box 25, 'LIL is five', *NGF News*, 6, no. 2 (September 1983).
62 NLI, IQA, MS 45, 964/7, 'LIL News – Tribute to Ireland's Only Lesbian', *NGF News*, 8, no. 2 (December 1983).
63 Gale Primary Sources, Archives of Sexuality and Gender, 'Irish Lesbians', *GPU News*, 8, no. 8 (July 1979), 8. https://go.gale.com/ps/i.do?p=AHSI&u=tlemea_ahsi&v=2.1&it=r&id=GALE%7CPNXKAI155553709&asid=1600574400000~fd234ff2 (accessed 8 March 2016). Joni Sheerin and Joni Crone refer to the same individual. I use both interchangeably, depending on how Joni is referred to in the material.
64 NLI, IQA, MS 45, 936/10, Manifestos of the candidates for election to the 5th administrative council of the NGF.
65 NLI, IQA, MS 45, 936/4, Breakdown of Membership of the National Gay Federation 17 March 1979 to 31 March 1980.
66 NLI, IQA, MS 45, 938/2, NGF leaflet on Lesbian Women.
67 NLI, IQA, MS 45, 949/4, TAF 1981–1982.
68 Caroline Walsh, 'Women who love women', *The Irish Times*, 12 October 1984, 11.
69 'The Silent Majority', *Out for Ourselves*, 126.
70 NLI, Ir 369 I 23, Joni Sheerin, *In Touch*, 2, no. 3 (March 1980).
71 NLI, Ir 369 I 23, 'SITA-LIL Affiliation', *In Touch*, 2, no. 6 (June/July 1980), 13.
72 Pauline O'Donnell interview with Edmund Lynch, 13 May 2013 (Edmund Lynch Irish LGBT Oral History Project).
73 Grainne Healy interview with Edmund Lynch, 15 November 2013 (Edmund Lynch Irish LGBT Oral History Project).
74 Joni Crone interview on *The Late Late Show* (RTÉ) 9 February 1980. Copy provided by Edmund Lynch.

75 Ibid.
76 NLI, Ir 369 I 23, Majella Breen, 'Our women in the Public Eye', *In Touch*, 2, no. 3 (March 1980).
77 Joni Crone interview on *The Late Late Show* (RTÉ) 9 February 1980.
78 Ibid.
79 NLI, IQA, MS 45, 940/4, 'Summary of Telephone Reaction received on Friday 9 February 1980'.
80 Ibid.
81 Caroline Walsh, 'No room for Jehovah Witnesses?', *The Irish Times*, 25 February 1980, 11.
82 'Late Late Attacked', *Evening Herald*, 11 February 1980, 7. https://www.irishnewsarchive.com (accessed 20 September 2020).
83 Ibid.
84 NLI, Ir 369 I 23, Majella Breen, 'Our women in the Public Eye', *In Touch*, 2, no. 3 (March 1980).
85 'Marriage and Children', *Out for Ourselves*, 81.
86 Joni Crone, 'Lesbians: The Lavender Women of Ireland', *Lesbian and Gay Visions of Ireland: Towards the Twenty First Century*, ed. Íde O'Carroll and Eoin Collins (London: Cassell, 1995), 62.
87 NLI, IQA, MS 45, 955/2, Extra Event – Lesbian Conference, 28 June 1980.
88 NLI, IR 369 I 23, 'Report from the International Lesbian Conference, 27–30 December 1980', *In Touch*, 3, no. 2 (March/April 1981), 19–23.
89 'Children: Whose Right to Choose?', *Out for Ourselves*, 82.
90 NLI, IQA, MS 45, 940/10, Steering Collective Report on Second National Gay Conference, Trinity College Dublin, 1982 – Women's Report.
91 NLI, IQA, MS 45, 964/3, Mary Kinnane, 'Lesbian Mothers', *NGF Newsletter*, no. 4 (July 1982).
92 'Lesbian seminar', *The Irish Times*, 30 October 1982, 7; NLI, IQA, MS 45, 964/5, LIL, 'Irish Lesbian Conference', *NGF Newsletter*, Christmas Edition 1982, 5.
93 NLI, IQA, MS 45, 936/10, Manifestos of the Candidates for election to the 5th Administrative Council of NGF; Pauline Cronin, 'Lesbians: Ireland's Sexual Exiles', *Sunday World*, 7 November 1982, 6.
94 Ibid.
95 Jacqui Dunne, 'The election partners', *Sunday Independent*, 21 February 1982, 31. https://www.irishnewsarchive.com (accessed 20 September 2020).
96 Ibid.
97 Caroline Walsh, 'Women who love women', *The Irish Times*, 12 October 1984, 11.
98 Ibid.
99 NLI, PPDN, Acc. 6672, Box 36 – NGF Administrative Council meeting, 14 September 1979.
100 NLI, PPDN, Acc. 6672, Box 40 - Chris Kirk, 'How the Dubliners got it together!', *Gay News*, 222 (20 August – 2 September 1981), 12.
101 NLI, PPDN, Acc. 6672, Box 46, letter from Women's Group, NGF Minutes, 27 November 1981.
102 Ibid.
103 The Women's Right to Choose Campaign campaigned for the legalisation of abortion in Ireland. Parts of this chapter have appeared previously in Patrick McDonagh, 'Abortion, Gay Rights, and the National Gay Federation in Ireland, 1982-1983', in

Journal of the History of Sexuality 29 no.1 (January 2020): 1–27. Copyright 2020 by the University of Texas Press. All rights reserved. Used by permission.
104 NLI, PPDN, Acc. 6672, Box 46, NGF Minutes 9 July 1982.
105 NLI, PPDN, Acc. 6672, Box 22, Bernard Keogh letter to editor, *NGF News* (March/April 1983), 6.
106 NLI, PPDN, Acc. 6672, Box 25, 'Secretary's Report: Women's Right to Choose Ballot', *NGF News* (June 1983), 4.
107 NLI, IQA, MS 45, 966/5, 'Women's Right to Choose Campaign', *NGF News* (May 1983), 15.
108 Crone, 'Lesbians: The Lavender Women of Ireland', 68.
109 Una Mullally, 'The Brutal Killing of Charles Self', *The Irish Times*, 24 June 2017, 3.
110 NLI, IR 32341 G 24, Melissa Murry and Charles Kerrigan, 'Gays step up the pace', *Gralton*, no. 3 (Aug/Sep 1982), 5.
111 Ibid.; NLI, IQA, MS 45, 940/10, Steering Collective Report on Second National Gay Conference, Trinity College Dublin, 1982. For further information on the Dublin Gay Collective see Casey, 'Radical politics and gay activism in the Republic of Ireland, 1974–1990'.
112 Peter Murtagh, 'Claim for gay rights attacked', *The Irish Times*, 3 April 1982, 8.
113 'Suspended sentences for killing man in park', *Irish Independent*, 9 March 1983, 9; Hugh Leonard, 'I'll not be moved from Mr. Dukes' Ireland', *Sunday Independent* 13 March 1983, 11. https://www.irishnewsarchive.com (accessed 20 September 2020).
114 Mary Rice, 'Political forum on homosexuality', *Irish Press*, 25 June 1979, 7. https://www.irishnewsarchive.com (accessed 20 September 2020).
115 NLI, IQA, MS 45, 955/2, National Gay Federation, Gay Pride Week 1979.
116 NLI, IQA, MS 45, 955/2, 'Gay Pride Week 1981'; Paul Murray, 'March planned as part of Gay Pride Week', *The Irish Times*, 22 June 1981, 6.
117 Paul Murray, 'March planned as part of "Gay Pride Week"', 22 June 1981, 6.
118 NLI, IR 369 I 23, Tonie Walsh, 'Gay Pride Week', *In Touch*, 2, no. 7 (August/September 1980), 5.
119 NLI, IQA, MS, 45, 964/3, 'Gay Pride Week Pub Zap', *NGF Newsletter*, no. 4 (July 1982).
120 Gale Primary Sources, Archive of Sexuality and Gender, 'Dubliners welcome families and friends', *Gay News*, no. 172, (26 July–22 August 1979), 14. https://go.gale.com/ps/i.do?p=AHSI&u=tlemea_ahsi&v=2.1&it=r&id=GALE%7CBYFQHF055333140&asid=1600574400000~d098a9c8 (accessed 19 September 2020).
121 NLI, IQA, MS 45, 964/3, 'Gay Pride Week Pub Zap', *NGF Newsletter*, no. 4 (July 1982).
122 Carl Berkeley, 'Equal Rights for Gays', *The Irish Times*, 25 June 1981, 12. Other examples can be seen in: Kerry McCarthy, 'A week of coming out for the gays', *Evening Herald*, 25 June 1980, 6. https://www.irishnewsarchive.com (accessed 20 September 2020); Michael Riordan, 'A question of rights for a different minority', *Irish Independent*, 26 June 1980, 12. https://www.irishnewsarchive.com (accessed 20 September 2020).
123 Marina Forrestal interview with Edmund Lynch, 6 December 2019 (Edmund Lynch Irish LGBT Oral History Project).
124 NLI, IR 369 I 25, 'Fairview Park', *Identity*, no. 5 (April–June 1983), 20.
125 Ibid., 17–20.
126 NLI, IQA, MS 46, 053/3-4, 'The March to Fairview Park', *Quare Times*.
127 Ibid.

128 Patrick O'Byrne interview with Edmund Lynch, 15 November 2013 (Edmund Lynch Irish LGBT Oral History Project).
129 Noel Walsh, 'Gay Rights Protest March', *The Irish Times*, 24 June 1983, 11.
130 NLI, IQA, MS 45, 955/1, Noel Walsh letter to Superintendent, Pearse Street Garda Station, 31 May 1983.
131 Tonie Walsh interview with Edmund Lynch, 6 April 2013 (Edmund Lynch Irish LGBT Oral History Project).
132 '2nd International Gay Youth Congress', *OUT*, 1, no. 4 (June/July 1985), 5.
133 '2nd International Gay Youth Congress', *OUT*, 1, no. 5 (August/September 1985), 25.
134 NLI, IR 369 07, Carol Laing, 'LIL Report', *NGF News* in *OUT*, 1, no. 3 (April/May 1985).
135 Nicole E. Roberts, 'The Plight of Gay Visibility: Intolerance in San Francisco, 1970–1979, *Journal of Homosexuality*, 60, no. 1 (2013): 105–119.
136 NLI, IR 3991 C 30, 'Address by Most Rev. Dr. Brendan Comiskey at A.G.A, 1984', *Christian Family Movement Newsletter*, 13.
137 Ibid.
138 NLI, IR 2805 O 13, Thomas McFadden, 'Gay Rights? Why not', *Our Family*, 1, no. 1 (March/April 1984), 11.
139 NLI, 1A 2099, *Love is for Life*, Irish Bishops Pastoral, 1985.
140 Ibid.
141 'The late Bishop Eamonn Casey took a lover and fathered a son he then rejected … but now even darker allegations have emerged', *Belfast Telegraph*, 30 March 2019. https://www.belfasttelegraph.co.uk/life/features/the-late-bishop-eamonn-casey-took-a-lover-and-fathered-a-son-he-then-rejected-but-now-even-darker-allegations-have-emerged-37965209.html (accessed on 16 February 2021).
142 'Gay Group Attacks Bishops', *The Irish Times*, 6 March 1985, 7.
143 NLI, K365, Rhona McSweeney, 'The Gay Generation', *In Dublin*, no. 234 (26 July – 7 August 1985), 6.
144 NLI, IR 94133 I 2, 'Gay', *In Dublin*, no. 189 (6–20 October 1983), 10.
145 NLI, IR 369 I 23, Bernard Keogh, 'New book service for NGF members', *In Touch*, 3, no. 3 (June/July 1981), 10.
146 NLI, ILB 305 G 2, *Gay Community News*, no. 15, February 1990.
147 NLI, IR 369 07, 'Classified', *OUT*, 13 (September/October 1987), 57.
148 NLI, IQA, MS 45, 993/1, Edmund Lynch for *OUT*.
149 NLI, IR 369 07, 'Side One', *OUT*, 8 (March/April 1986), 7.
150 NLI, ILB 305 G 2, 'Hooray Henries', *Gay Community News*, no. 9 (November 1988).
151 NLI, IQA, MS 45, 936/17, NGF letter sent to members, 31 August 1989.
152 *Seanad Éireann* debate, 'Hirschfeld Centre', 121, no. 4 (2 November 1988).
153 Edmund Lynch interview with Gerard Lawlor, 23 February 2013 (Edmund Lynch Irish LGBT Oral History Project).

3 1980s Provincial Activism: Cork and Galway

1 'Community Workers Cheered', *Galway Advertiser*, 2 June 1988, 1. http://archive.advertiser.ie/pages/search.php (accessed 13 August 2020); Bernie Ní Fhlatharta, 'Organic farmer Patricia wins city achievement award for youth project', *City Tribune*, 3 June 1988, 7. https://www.irishnewsarchive.com (accessed 13 August 2020).

2   'Call to RTÉ', *Connacht Tribune*, '17 February 1984, 27. https://www.irishnewsarchive. com (accessed 20 September 2020).
3   Richard Phillips, Diane Watt, and David Shuttleton, *De-Centring Sexualities: Politics and Representations Beyond the Metropolis* (London: Routledge, 2000); Larry Knopp and Michael Brown. 'Queer diffusions' in *Environment and Planning D*, 21, no. 4 (2003): 409–424; Orla Egan, *Queer Republic of Cork* (Cork: Onstreams Publications, 2016); Valerie J. Korinek, *Prairie Fairies: A History of Queer Communities and People in Western Canada, 1930–1985* (Toronto: University of Toronto Press, 2018); Daryl Leeworthy, *A Little Gay History of Wales* (Wales: University of Wales Press, 2019).
4   Knopp and Brown, 'Queer diffusions', 422.
5   'Census 1981 Volume 1 – Population' http://www.cso.ie/en/census/ censusvolumes1926to1991/historicalreports/census1981reports/census1981volume1-population/ (accessed 13 August 2020).
6   Ibid.
7   NLI, IQA, MS 45, 948/7, Galway Individual to Bernard Keogh, July 1979.
8   NLI, IQA, MS 45, 948/7, Bernard Keogh to Galway individual, August 1979.
9   NLI, IQA, MS 45, 936/4, Breakdown of membership of NGF, 1980.
10 NLI, IQA, MS 45, 936/3, Denis O' Neill letter to NGF Council Members, February 1982.
11 NLI, PPDN, Acc. 6672, Box 36, NGF Discussion Paper on Provincial Activities, 5 May 1982.
12 Ibid.
13 NLI, IQA, MS 45, 936/3, Denis O' Neill letter to NGF Council Members, February 1982.
14 'Gay Movement for Kilkenny', *Kilkenny People*, 21 May 1982, 4.
15 Brian Looney, 'Platform Three', *Limerick Echo*, 29 August 1981, 3. https://www. irishnewsarchive.com (accessed 20 September 2020).
16 NLI, IQA, MS 46, 951/2-4, 'Report of the Secretary [Stephen Quillinan] of the Munster Regional Council, IGRM, 1980/1981, 4 July 1981.
17 Personal Papers of Kieran Rose (henceforth PPKR), Eric Presland, 'Cruising 121: Cork', *Capital Gay*, 2 December 1983, 14.
18 Author interview with Helen Slattery, 9 March 2016.
19 'Cruising 121: Cork', *Capital Gay*, 2 December 1983, 14.
20 NLI, IQA, MS 46, 051/2-4, Report of the Convenor [Patrick Mahony-Rysh] of the Munster Regional Council of the IGRM, 4 July 1981; NLI, Ir 705 c 10, *The Cork Review* (April – June 1981), 14.
21 NLI, IQA, MS 46, 051/2-4, Report of the Convenor of the Munster Regional Council of the IGRM, 4 July 1981.
22 NLI, IQA, MS 46, 051/2-4, Cork Gay Switchboard, Report for the Annual General Meeting of the Munster Regional Council of the IGRM, July 1981.
23 NLI, IQA, MS 46, 051/2-4, Report of the Secretary of the Munster Regional Council of the IGRM, 1980/1981, 4 July 1981.
24 Personal Papers of Sean Connolly, 'Munster Report', *In Touch*, 4, no. 4 (Winter 1981), 8.
25 Gale Primary Sources, Archives of Sexuality and Gender, Steve Quillinan, 'A call for Help from Irish Gays', *Out Front: Colorado's Premier Gay Magazine*, 7, no. 19 (10 December 1982), 13. The Cork IGRM had contacted international groups to lobby Ireland's ambassadors on the matter. https://go.gale.com/ps/i.do?p=AHSI&u=tlemea_ahsi&v=2.1&it=r&id=GALE%7CIVWTLH846164350&asid=1600574400000~a3363d1d (accessed 8 March 2016).

26 Dick Hogan, 'Gay Rights group claims Cork postal interference', *The Irish Times*, 13 April 1985, 6.
27 NLI, IQA, MS 46, 051/2–4, Report of the Secretary of the Munster Regional Council of IGRM, 1980/1981, 4 July 1981.
28 Ibid.
29 NLI, IQA, MS 45, 951/7, Stephen Quillinan to Eamon Somers (NGF President), 7 April 1982.
30 Ibid.
31 NLI, PPDN, Acc. 6672 Box 40, 'New Irish Gay Alliance?, *Gay News*, no. 238 (15 April – 28 April 1982). In January 1980 the Irish Independent reported on allegations of an official cover-up 'over the recruiting of boys at a Belfast children's home [Kincora] for homosexual prostitution'. This led to an investigation that resulted in the sentencing of three men in December 1981 for sexual offences against a number of boys aged between 15 and 18 in the Kincora home. The handling of this case and earlier reports of abuse resulted in calls for an official enquiry in early 1982 to investigate if there was a cover-up of the abuse. The media coverage and language used surrounding what became known as the Kincora Boys home scandal caused fear amongst the gay community, who felt they were being scapegoated as much of the coverage described it as a result of 'homosexual activities'. The NGF issued a statement in 1982 condemning the coverage, stating that 'there had been a failure to distinguish between homosexuality and pederasty' and also condemned 'the apparent assumption that sexual orientation should affect one's suitability for a job'. 'Sex Racket at Children's Home', *Irish Independent*, 24 January 1980, 1; 'Gays criticise Kincora coverage', *The Irish Times*, 4 February 1982, 13. https://www.irishnewsarchive.com (accessed 20 September 2020).
32 Ibid.
33 NLI, IQA, MS 49,655/1, Cathal Kerrigan, 'Growing up gay in Cork 1971–1981'.
34 'Television Today', *The Irish Times*, 11 February 1980, 17.
35 *Week In* (RTÉ), 11 February 1980.
36 Barbara McKeon, 'Speaking out on a taboo subject', *Irish Press*, 12 February 1980, 4. https://www.irishnewsarchive.com (accessed 20 September 2020).
37 Kieran Rose interview with author, 12 January 2016.
38 Cathal Kerrigan interview with author, 14 January 2016. Kerrigan described himself as a socialist republican who believed that only through national liberation could gay liberation be achieved. He later established a small collective, Gays Against Imperialism, in December 1981. For more on Gays Against Imperialism see: Padraig Robinson, *Gaze Against Imperialism* (Metaflux Publishing, 2019).
39 NLI, IQA, MS 45, 938/2, Cork Gay Collective Manifesto.
40 Ibid.
41 NLI, IQA, MS 45, 936/10, Report of the Political Co-Ordinator, David Norris, to the 3rd Annual General Meeting of NGF, 18 September 1982.
42 NLI, IQA, MS 45, 949/6, Cork Wednesday Night Group (later renamed Cork Gay Collective), 20 November 1980.
43 Ibid.
44 NLI, IQA, MS 45, 949/6, Larry Bond, 'Motions passed by Meeting of Gay Activists at Glencree Centre for Reconciliation on Sunday, 30 November 1980'.
45 NLI, IQA, MS 46, 051/2-4, Bert Meaney (IGRM Secretary) letter to Cork Gay Collective, 4 December 1980.
46 NLI, IQA, MS 45, 940/9, Report on National Gay Conference 1981.

47 NLI, PPDN, Acc. 6672 Box 33, Letter from Bernard Keogh to Michael Woods, Minister for Health, 3 February 1981.
48 Ibid.
49 NLI, IR 369 I 23, Tom McClean, 'Editorial Comment', *In Touch*, 3, no. 3 (June/July 1981), 3.
50 PPKR, 'Cork Gay Pride Week', 23 June 1981.
51 Ibid.
52 'Gay Pride Week 20:28 June 1981' leaflet handed out by Cork IGRM and Cork Gay Collective. https://s3-eu-west-1.amazonaws.com/corklgbtarchiveomeka/original/5248 d7b59024e7660f7e3f2ff65a1ff3.pdf (accessed 7 September 2020).
53 Stephen Quillinan, 'Gay Pride Week', *The Irish Times*, 7 July 1981, 9.
54 Margaret Rossiter, 'Pink Triangle', *The Irish Times*, 18 July 1981, 17.
55 Ibid.
56 Author interview with Marese Walsh, 4 April 2016.
57 NLI, IQA, MS 45, 948/7, Galway Gay Collective Announcement 1980.
58 Author interview with Marese Walsh, 4 April 2016.
59 NLI, IQA, MS 45, 948/6, Marese Walsh to Bernard Keogh, 15 December 1981.
60 Ibid.
61 NLI, IQA, MS 45, 948/7, Marese Walsh to Bernard Keogh, 29 April 1980.
62 NLI, IQA, MS 45, 948/7, Edmund Lynch to Marese Walsh, 9 June 1980.
63 Author interview with Marese Walsh, 4 April 2016.
64 NLI, IQA, MS 45, 948/7, John Porter to Tonie Walsh, 8 September 1980.
65 NLI, IQA, MS 45, 948/7, Bernard Keogh to John Porter, 1 November 1980.
66 NLI, IQA, MS 45, 948/6, John Porter to Bernard Keogh, 19 January 1982.
67 NLI, IR 369 I 23, 'Galway Gay Group', *In Touch*, 2, no. 5 (May 1980), 6.
68 Ibid.
69 Author interview with Marese Walsh, 4 April 2016.
70 NLI, IQA, MS 45, 948/6, John Porter to Bernard Keogh, 3 May 1981.
71 NLI, IQA, MS 45, 948/6, John Porter to Walter, 20 April 1983.
72 NLI, IQA, MS 45, 948/7, Marese Walsh to Bernard Keogh, 21 October 1980.
73 NLI, IQA, MS 45, 948/6, John Porter to Bernard Keogh, 19 January 1982.
74 NLI, IQA, MS 45, 948/6, Sean Rabbitte notice/letter (undated), Galway IGRM.
75 Author interview with Marese Walsh, 4 April 2016.
76 NLI, IQA, MS 45, 948/6, Marese Walsh to Bernard Keogh, 15 December 1981
77 Ibid.
78 NLI, IQA, MS 45, 948/7, Galway Gay Collective Announcement December 1980.
79 NLI, IQA, MS 45, 948/6, John Porter, Galway Gay Collective, to NGF, 1 December 1983.
80 NLI, IQA, MS 45, 948/6, Mary Kinane informing NGF members that John Porter called informing her about a Galway Gay Collective social on 17 November.
81 NLI, IQA, MS 45, 948/6, John Porter to Bernard Keogh, October 1981.
82 NLI, IQA, MS 45, 948/6, John Porter to Walter, 20 April 1983.
83 Ibid.
84 NLI, IQA, MS 45, 948/6, Sean Rabbitte notice/letter (undated), Galway IGRM.
85 Arthur Leahy interview with Edmund Lynch, 2 October 2017 (Edmund Lynch Irish LGBT Oral History Project).
86 'Cruising 121: Cork', *Capital Gay*, 2 December 1983, 14.
87 Vincent Power, 'Quay Co-Op Denies Subversive "Haunt" Claim', *Evening Echo*, 26 March 1984, 17. https://www.irishnewsarchive.com (accessed 20 September 2020).
88 'Gardaí raid co-op in Cork', *Irish Times*, 26 March 1984, 8.

89　*Quare Times*, Spring 1984, 11. http://corklgbtarchive.com/items/show/79 (accessed 21 January 2016).
90　PPKR, 'Development of Cork Gay Collective'.
91　NLI, IQA, MS 46,002/4, Booklet on the Quay Co-Op: Women's Place, 5.
92　'Cork Women's Place Support Group Proposal'. http://corklgbtarchive.com/items/show/130 (accessed 21 February 2016).
93　'Cork Women's Place Definitions and Directives' 1982. http://corklgbtarchive.com/items/show/129 (accessed 21 February 2016).
94　'Quay Co-Op Newsletter', 1984. http://corklgbtarchive.com/items/show/99 (accessed 21 February 2016).
95　Author interview with Helen Slattery, 9 March 2016.
96　'Quay Co-Op Newsletter', 1984. http://corklgbtarchive.com/items/show/99 (accessed 21 February 2016).
97　Caitlin Ni Houlihain, 'A lesbian in Cork?!!', *Munster Women's Newsletter*, c. 1985. http://corklgbtarchive.com/items/show/81 (accessed on 22 February 2016), 23–25.
98　Author interview with Deirdre Walsh, 9 March 2016.
99　'1984 Report Cork Women's Place'. http://corklgbtarchive.com/items/show/137 (accessed on 21 February 2016).
100　Joan McCarthy interview with Edmund Lynch, 28 September 2015 (Edmund Lynch Irish LGBT Oral History Project).
101　Louise Walsh, 'Artist-Activist', *Lesbian and Gay Visions of Ireland*, 172.
102　Edmund Lynch interview with Mary Flanagan, 15 June 2015 (Edmund Lynch Irish LGBT Oral History Project).
103　Author interview with Helen Slattery, 9 March 2016.
104　Jo, 'Creating a New Tradition: 5th Annual Cork Women's Fun Weekend', *Women's Place Newsletter*, no. 3 (July/August 1988), 6. http://www.corklgbtarchive.com/items/show/61 (accessed 9 January 2018). Loafer's Pub opened in 1983 and continued to be a popular gay bar until it closed in 2015.
105　Author interview with Deirdre Walsh, 9 March 2016.
106　Egan, 'Cork Women's Fun Weekend'. https://corklgbthistory.com/2014/07/18/cork-womens-fun-weekend/ (accessed 22 February 2016).
107　Churchfield Women's Group, 'Class', in *Quare Times*, Spring 1984, 6. https://s3-eu-west-1.amazonaws.com/corklgbtarchiveomeka/original/537df67d1ed16d2e77fd9c005283e479.pdf (accessed 8 September 2020).
108　PPKR, 'Minutes of Cork Lesbian and Gay Community Project', 16 April 1984.
109　'Cruising 121: Cork', *Capital Gay*, 2 December 1983, 14.
110　Ibid.
111　PPKR, 'Cork Collective News', 1984.
112　*Quare Times*, Spring 1984, 2–5. https://s3-eu-west-1.amazonaws.com/corklgbtarchiveomeka/original/537df67d1ed16d2e77fd9c005283e479.pdf (accessed 8 September 2020).
113　PPKR, 'Minutes of Cork Lesbian and Gay Community Project', 16 April 1984.
114　Author interview with Helen Slattery, 9 March 2016.
115　Author interview with Deirdre Walsh, 9 March 2016.
116　Author interview with Helen Slattery, 9 March 2016.
117　Author interview with Deirdre Walsh, 9 March 2016.
118　T.E. Crosbie, Chief Executive *Cork Examiner*, to Kieran Rose, 18 June 1985. http://corklgbtarchive.com/items/show/41 (accessed 22 February 2016).
119　'Lesbians in the Examiner?' http://corklgbtarchive.com/items/show/98 (accessed 22 February 2016).

120 Ibid.
121 Author interview with Helen Slattery, 9 March 2016.
122 '1985 Notes Cork Lesbian Line'. http://corklgbtarchive.com/items/show/96 (accessed 22 February 2016).
123 'National Lesbian Line Conference', *Women's Space Newsletter*, no. 5 (December 1988/January 1989), 6. http://corklgbtarchive.com/items/show/63 (accessed on 14 August 2020). Co-Operation North is a private, non-political organisation dedicated to the development of good neighbourliness between the people of Northern Ireland and the Republic of Ireland.
124 Constance Short, Programme Manager, to Geraldine McCarthy, Cork Lesbian Line, 11 January 1990. http://corklgbtarchive.com/items/show/124 (accessed on 22 February 2016).
125 Orla Egan, 'Searching for Space: Cork Lesbian Community 1975–2000', *Women's Studies Review: Women's Activism and Voluntary Activity*, 9 (2004), 194.
126 Author email correspondence with Nuala Ward, 22 April 2018.
127 NLI, IQA, MS 45, 948/6, Galway Gay Collective, 20 May 1985.
128 NLI, IR 369 07, Rory Murray, 'ONCAMPUS', *OUT*, 1, no. 3 (April 1985), 5.
129 Collegian, 'Let's get the Record Straight Mr. President!', *Connacht Sentinel*, 2 June 1981, 5. https://www.irishnewsarchive.com (accessed 20 September 2020).
130 'Gay society a first at U.C.G.', *Connacht Sentinel*, 16 October 1984, 6. https://www.irishnewsarchive.com (accessed 20 September 2020).
131 'Advertisement for Gayline', *Galway Advertiser*, 29 November 1984, 13. http://archive.advertiser.ie/pages/home.php?login=true (accessed 20 September 2020).
132 NLI, UCC LGBT Society Archive, 49,655/4.
133 Author interview with Marese Walsh, 4 April 2016.
134 Paul Gouldsbury (director), *Bród: Out in the Streets*, 2008. https://www.youtube.com/watch?v=wEGClLPlJ5Yandlist=PLKKnW9AnvAmCjIegw9GbAoQs5gqjyK4e- (accessed 23 February 2016).
135 Author email correspondence with Nuala Ward, 22 April 2018.
136 Nuala Ward interview with Edmund Lynch, 2 October 2017 (Edmund Lynch Irish LGBT Oral History Project).
137 Paul Gouldsbury (director), *Bród: Out in the Streets*, 2008. https://www.youtube.com/watch?v=wEGClLPlJ5Yandlist=PLKKnW9AnvAmCjIegw9GbAoQs5gqjyK4e- (accessed 23 February 2016).
138 'Galway March for International Gay Pride Day', *Galway Advertiser*, 9. http://archive.advertiser.ie/pages/home.php?login=true (accessed 20 September 2020).
139 Nuala Ward interview with Edmund Lynch, 2 October 2017 (Edmund Lynch Irish LGBT Oral History Project).
140 Ibid.
141 Paul Gouldsbury (director), *Bród: Out in the Streets*, 2008. https://www.youtube.com/watch?v=wEGClLPlJ5Yandlist=PLKKnW9AnvAmCjIegw9GbAoQs5gqjyK4e- (accessed 23 February 2016).
142 Ibid.

4 Gay Rights are not Extravagant Demands

1 'David Norris against Ireland'. https://hudoc.echr.coe.int/eng#%7B%22itemid%22:%5B%22001-45392%22%5D%7D (accessed on 13 October

2017). Parts of this chapter have appeared previously in Patrick McDonagh, '"It's Poppycock to Say Homosexuals Can be Excused": Rethinking the Gay and Lesbian Movement in the Republic of Ireland, 1970s–1990s', eds Sean Brady and Mark Seymour, *From Sodomy Laws to Same-Sex Marriage: International Perspectives since 1789* (London: Bloomsbury Academic, 2019), 183–200.
2. 'It's unconstitutional. Gay Rights leader says', *Irish Independent*, 25 June 1980, 3. https://www.irishnewsarchive.com (accessed 20 September 2020).
3. 'Case against homosexual acts argued', *Evening Press*, 1 July 1980, 5. https://www.irishnewsarchive.com (accessed 20 September 2020).
4. Ibid.
5. 'Judge holds laws on homosexuality not unconstitutional', *The Irish Times*, 11 October 1980, 8.
6. NLI, IQA, MS 45, 952/4, Judgement of the Supreme Court on David Norris V. Attorney General, 22 April 1983.
7. NLI, IQA, MS 45, 955/2, Gay Pride Week 22–29 June – Gay Rights: It's Time.
8. Hubert Mannion, UCD Welfare Officer, 'Rights of Homosexuals', *Irish Press*, 12 July 1982, 8. https://www.irishnewsarchive.com (accessed 20 September 2020).
9. NLI, IQA, 45, 948/2, 'USI Conference on Gay Rights', Trinity College Dublin, 12 May 1979.
10. NLI, IQA, MS 45, 948/1, USI Welfare Policy March 1981.
11. NLI, 9A 212, UCC Welfare Handbook 1980–1981, 36.
12. 'Come as a Shock to Parents', *Evening Echo*, 30 October 1980, 1. https://www.irishnewsarchive.com (accessed 20 September 2020).
13. Ibid.
14. University College Cork Archives (henceforth UCCA), Minutes of UCC Governing Body, Minute Book, no. 54, 'Letter from Student Health Officer', 23 June 1981.
15. UCCA, Minutes of UCC Governing Body, Minute Book, no. 53, 'Students' Union Welfare Book', 18 November 1980. UCCA, Minutes of UCC Governing Body, Minute Book, no. 53, 'Students' Union Welfare Book', 20 January 1981.
16. Ibid.
17. UCCA, Minutes of UCC Governing Body, Minute Book, no. 55, 'Students' Union Welfare Book', 19 January 1982.
18. NLI, IQA MS 45, 948/2, 'USI: The Need to Form a Gay Society'.
19. Ibid.
20. NLI, IQA MS 45, 949/5, 'David Norris to UCD Academic Council', 9 November 1982.
21. University College Dublin Archives (henceforth UCDA), Minutes of the UCD Academic Council Meeting, 5 March 1990.
22. UCDA, Minutes of the UCD Academic Council Meeting, 16 November 1983.
23. NLI, IQA, MS 49, 655/3, The Philosophical Society, Main Debates of the 131st Session.
24. NLI, UCC Cork LGBT Archive, MS 49, 655/3, 'Gay Soc', *The Sage*, 3 (February 1981).
25. Maurice Gubbins, 'Gay Society Refused Recognition by U.C.C.', *Cork Examiner*, 10 February 1981, 3; UCCA, University College Cork Minutes of Governing Body, Minute Book, 24 March 1981; 'Gay Society Accuses UCC', *Sunday Tribune*, 15 February 1981, 2. https://www.irishnewsarchive.com (accessed 20 September 2020).
26. NLI, IR 369 0 7, Andrew Jackson, 'Gays are an embarrassment to Maynooth College', *OUT*, no. 14 (February/March 1988), 12–14.
27. Fionnuala Egan, 'Q Soc on Providing Constant Support for Trinity's LGBT community', in *University Times*, 27 February 2017, http://www.universitytimes.

ie/2017/02/q-soc-on-providing-constant-support-for-trinitys-lgbt-community/ (accessed on 3 June 2019).
28 NLI, Ir 369 h 6, John Ryan, 'Gays on Campus', *Hermes*, 1, no. 1 (December 1978), 11.
29 NLI, Ir 3784105 b 1, 'Gay Soc', *Bulletin* (January 1979), 9.
30 Paul Yeats, 'Election Fever in the Air', *Irish Press*, 4 March 1981, 17. https://www.irishnewsarchive.com (accessed 20 September 2020).
31 NLI, IQA MS 45, 964/7, 'UCD Gay Soc Refused Recognition', *NGF News* (1983).
32 UCDA, Minutes of the UCD Academic Council Meeting, 10 March 1988.
33 NLI, IQA MS 45, 964/7, 'UCD Gay Soc Refused Recognition', *NGF News* (1983).
34 UCDA, Minutes of the UCD Academic Council Meeting, 10 March 1988.
35 Ibid.
36 Colette Sheridan, 'Campus Crusade', *Hot Press*, 12, no. 5 (24 March 1988), 7.
37 NLI, UCC Cork LGBT Archive, MS 45, 655/4, 'Letter from UCC Gay Society members Josephine O'Halloran, Sandra Buckley, Emmett Flynn and Mick Quinlan to UCC Clubs and Societies'.
38 NLI, UCC Cork LGBT Archive, MS 45, 655/4, Letter from Secretary of the Sociological Society to UCC Governing Body.
39 'Cork Pulls It Off', *Gay Community News*, no. 15 (February 1990), 3.
40 UCCA, University College Cork Minutes of Governing Body, Minute Book, no. 68, March/April 1989.
41 Ibid.
42 Pat Brosnan, 'Gay Group Gets UCC Recognition', *Cork Examiner*, 26 April 1989, 1. https://www.irishnewsarchive.com (accessed 20 September 2020).
43 Ibid.
44 Lance Pettitt, 'A Positive Success: UCD Week', *Gay Community News*, no. 16 (March 1990), 3.
45 UCDA, Minutes of the UCD Academic Council Meeting, March 1990.
46 Ibid.
47 UCDA, Minutes of the UCD Academic Council Meeting, March 1990; John Walshe, 'UCD Academics Warn on Gays', *Irish Independent*, 17 March 1990, 3. https://www.irishnewsarchive.com (accessed 20 September 2020).
48 Anne-Marie Smyth, 'Gay Students "Come Out" in UCD Victory', *Sunday Tribune*, 11 March 1990, 13.
49 Michael Foley, 'ICCL urges referendum on divorce', *The Irish Times*, 9 June 1980, 11; NLI, IQA, MS 45,949/9, David Norris to G.M.H. Byrne, ICCL Secretary, 12 May 1980.
50 NLI, IQA, MS 45, 949/10, 'Campaign for Gay Rights', *Bulletin*, 6, no. 2 (March 1981), 6–7.
51 Ibid.
52 NLI, IQA, MS 45, 949/9, 'Minutes of the meeting of the ICCL Gay Rights Committee', 12 October 1981; NLI, IQA, MS 45, 949/9, 'Bernard Keogh to Michael Kelly', 3 October 1981.
53 NLI, IQA, MS 45, 949/10, 'Gay Rights', *Bulletin*, 7, no. 2 (May 1982), 4.
54 'Gay News to be banned by censors', *Irish Press*, 16 August 1982, 7. https://www.irishnewsarchive.com (accessed 20 September 2020).
55 NLI, IQA, MS 45, 949/10, 'Gay News', *Bulletin*, 7, no. 3 (September 1982), 15.
56 Ibid.
57 Conor Lally, 'Former garda sacked in 1982 for being gay sues State', *The Irish Times*, 4 March 2020, 1.
58 Ibid.

59 'Out at Work', *Out for Ourselves*, 177.
60 'Lesbians fear sacking', *Sunday Independent*, 12 April 1987, 2. https://www.irishnewsarchive.com (accessed 20 September 2020).
61 Genevieve Carbery, 'Eileen Flynn, teacher sacked in 1982, dies', *The Irish Times*, 11 September 2008, 8.
62 NLI, K365, Rhona McSweeney, 'The Gay Generation', *In Dublin*, no. 234 (26 July – 7 August 1985), 9.
63 NLI, IQA, MS 45, 948/9, Employment Protection Appeal leaflet on John Sanders Case, Bulletin No. 1, 1980.
64 NLI, IR 369 I 23, 'Foreign Guests', *In Touch*, 2, no. 6 (June/July 1980), 12.
65 NLI, IQA, MS 45, 936/9, Report on Trade Union Activity presented to the Second Annual General Meeting of the NGF, 27 June 1981.
66 Ibid. The ten unions that replied to the questionnaire were: Amalgamated Transport and General Workers Union (ATGWU), Association of Scientific, Technical and Managerial Staffs (ASTMS), Local Government and Public Services Union (LGPSU), Irish Federation of University Teachers (IFUT), Association of Higher Civil Servants (AHCS), Electricity Supply Board Officers Association (ESBOA), Union of Professional and Technical Civil Servants (UPTCS), National Graphical Association (NGA), Federated Works Union of Ireland (FWUI), Post Office Workers Union (POWU). Four of the ten that did not return a completed questionnaire were the ESBOA, FWUI, NGA and POWU.
67 Ibid.
68 'Teachers oppose sex discrimination', *The Irish Times*, 22 November 1980, 5.
69 Niall Kiely, 'IFUT Split on sexuality ruling', *The Irish Times*, 27 April 1981, 5.
70 Ibid., NLI, IQA, MS 45, 936/9, Report on Trade Union Activity presented to the Second Annual General Meeting of the NGF, 27 June 1981.
71 NLI, IQA, 45, 949/6, Kieran Rose to Secretary of ICTU, 26 March 1981.
72 PPKR, letter titled 'Gay Rights are Workers' Rights', sent to ICTU, 9 July 1981.
73 NLI, IQA, MS 45, 948/3, Harold O'Sullivan to the Secretary of NGF, 26 January 1981.
74 Ibid.
75 Motion proposed by Kieran Rose and seconded by Tricia Treacy at Cork Branch of LGPSU, 30 March 1982. https://s3-eu-west-1.amazonaws.com/corklgbtarchiveomeka/original/1842a8765fe63d17ed48aa84c5870b11.jpg (accessed 15 August 2020).
76 NLI, IQA, MS 45, 949/6, Kieran Rose speech on gay rights motion no. 35 at Cork branch of LGPSU meeting, 30 March 1982.
77 Ibid.
78 'Union supports change in law on homosexuality', *Cork Examiner*, 14 May 1982, 12. https://www.irishnewsarchive.com (accessed 20 September 2020).
79 Ibid.
80 ICTU Annual Report 1982, copy obtained from ICTU.
81 PPKR, 'Gay Rights Leaflet'.
82 Bernard McCartan speech moving motion 106, 'Job Discrimination on Sexual Grounds', ICTU Annual Report, 1982.
83 Ibid.
84 ICTU Annual Report for 1982; Vivion Kilfeather, 'ICTU backs gay rights and divorce', *Irish Examiner*, 10 July 1982, 14. https://www.irishnewsarchive.com (accessed 20 September 2020).
85 NLI, Ir 32341 g 24, Kieran Rose and Arthur Leahy, 'Gay Rights at Work', *Gralton*, no. 4 (October/November 1982), 6.

86 Sebastian Buckle, *The Way Out: A History of Homosexuality in Modern Britain* (London: I. B. Tauris, 2015), 99; John Sweeney, 'The Growing Alliance between Gay and Union Activists', *Social Text*, no. 61 (Winter 1999): 31–38.
87 NLI, IQA, MS 46, 005/3, Report of the Second National Gay Conference held in Dublin between June 18–20.
88 NLI, IQA, MS 45, 948/3, Bernard Keogh of Social Justice Committee of Electricity Supply Board Officers Association to Tonie Walsh, 5 September 1983.
89 PPKR, ESBOA Information Leaflet on Gay Rights, 1984.
90 NLI, IQA, MS 45, 949/6, Kieran Rose to ICTU secretary, 1984.
91 PPKR, Discrimination against lesbian and gay workers: report of discussion at workshop at ICTU conference, 3 July 1984.
92 Ibid.
93 ICTU's Women Charter 1985.
94 NLI, IQA, MS 45, 952/6, Summary Report of Seminar on Discrimination in Employment in Relation to Sexual Orientation, ICTU, 29 November 1985.
95 Ibid.
96 Ibid.
97 PPKR, report of meeting held in LGPSU head office Dublin on 3 May 1986.
98 PPKR, Donal Nevin General Secretary to John Mitchell, 15 September 1986.
99 PPKR, John Mitchell to Donal Nevin, 14 July 1986.
100 NLI, IQA, MS 45, 938/2, *Lesbian and Gay Rights in the Workplace Guidelines for Negotiators*, 1987.
101 NLI, ILB 306 G 2, 'Continuing Progress for Lesbian and Gay Workers', *Gay Community News*, 3/4 (April/May 1988).
102 Department of Finance circular, 'Civil Service Policy on AIDS', 22 June 1988. https://circulars.gov.ie/pdf/circular/finance/1988/12.pdf (accessed 15 August 2020).
103 TCDA, Personal Papers of Noel Browne, 11067/6/1/2, David Norris to Noel Browne. 29 July 1978.
104 Ibid.
105 *Dáil Éireann* debate, 'Law Reform Commission', 308, no. 1 (11 October 1978).
106 NLI, IQA, MS 45, 955/2, 'Gay Pride 80 – Dublin', 22–29 June 1980.
107 NLI, IQA MS 45, 948/9, NGF Press Release, 24 July 1980.
108 Ibid.
109 NLI, IQA, MS 45, 959/5, 'Ireland', *IGA Newsletter*, 80-3 (September 1980), 3.
110 NAI, 2015/51/1575, Department of Foreign Affairs, Jackie Boeykens, President of Federation of Working Groups Homophily to Irish; document is not dated nor does it specify who it was addressed to. It was likely sent in late 1980 or early 1981 to one of Ireland's Permanent Representatives, likely in Brussels.
111 NAI, 2014/32/928, Department of Foreign Affairs, Kevin C. Griffin to Sean P. Kennan, 5 January 1981.
112 NAI, 2012/59/442, Department of Foreign Affairs, Sam Staggs, Editor-in-chief MANDATE to Noel Dorr, Permanent Representative to the United Nations for the Irish Republic, 28 September 1982.
113 Ibid.
114 NLI, IQA, MS 45, 948/9, Ian Christie to the Director of the Office of Censorship of Publications, 4 October 1982.
115 Ibid.
116 Ferriter, *Occasions of Sin*, 479.

117 David Norris, 'Reform Campaign', *Irish Press*, 20 July 1978, 8. https://www.irishnewsarchive.com (accessed 20 September 2020).
118 Liz Doran, 'Kieran seeks rights for gays', *Cork Examiner*, 3 August 1983, 10. https://www.irishnewsarchive.com (accessed 20 September 2020).
119 'Dutch Attack law here on homosexuals', *Irish Press*, 8 May 1980, 4. https://www.irishnewsarchive.com (accessed 20 September 2020).
120 Patrick Murray, '"Gay" laws: we "won't bow" to outside pressure', *Irish Independent*, 9 May 1980, 9. https://www.irishnewsarchive.com (accessed 20 September 2020).
121 Ibid.
122 NLI, IQA, MS 45, 940/2, Young Fine Gael Press Release on Motion 106, 1 April 1979.
123 Ibid.; 'Establishment of law reform group sought', *The Irish Times*, 2 April 1979, 10.
124 'Parliamentary Assembly of Council of Europe, Discrimination against homosexuals', Recommendation 924 (1981). http://assembly.coe.int/nw/xml/XRef/Xref-XML2HTML-en.asp?fileid=14958&lang=en (accessed 15 August 2020); 'Discrimination against homosexuals', Resolution 756 (1981), Parliamentary Assembly of Council of Europe. http://semantic-pace.net/tools/pdf.aspx?doc=aHR0cDovL2Fzc2VtYmx5LmNvZS5pbnQvbncveG1sL1hSZWYvWDJILURXLWV4dHIuYXNwP2ZpbGVpZD0xNjE2NyZsYW5nPUVO&xsl=aHR0cDovL3NlbWFudGljLGFjZS5uZXQvWHNsdC9QZGYvWFJlZi1XRC1BVC1YTUwyUERGLnhzbA==&xsltparams=ZmlsZWlkPTE2MTY3 (accessed 15 August 2020).
125 NAI, 2012/21/582, Office of the Attorney General, handwritten note from a J. Liddy (assuming a legal advisor within Department of Foreign Affairs) dated 17 December 1981.
126 NAI, 2015/51/1577, Department of Foreign Affairs, David Norris to Minister of State for Law Reform, Mr Dick Spring, 23 October 1981.
127 NAI, 2015/51/1577, Department of Foreign Affairs, Munster IGRM Press Release, 12 February 1982: Survey results of political parties' views policy on gay rights.
128 Ibid.
129 Ibid.
130 Fergus Pyle, 'Homosexual vote', *The Irish Times*, 14 March 1984, 4.
131 Ibid.
132 Report drawn up on behalf of the Committee on Social Affairs and Employment on sexual discrimination at the workplace, 13 February 1984. http://aei.pitt.edu/63768/1/B1930.pdf (accessed 15 August 2020).
133 NAI, 2014/107/76, Department of Labour, Stephen Quillinan (IGRM) to Minister for Labour, 28 June 1983.
134 NAI, 2014/107/76, Department of Labour, Freda Nolan (Private Secretary to Minister for Labour) to Stephen Quillinan, Irish Gay Rights Movement, 17 November 1983.
135 NAI, 2014/107/76, Department of Labour, D. Horan (assuming this is the name, signature hard to figure out) to Mr J. O'Brien, 26 September 1983.
136 'Unfair Dismissals Act, 1977', ICTU 1985 Annual Report, 135.
137 NAI, 2014/107/76, Department of Labour, John Mitchell (IDATU) to Ruairí Quinn, 11 September 1986; Lesbian and Gay Rights at Work to Ruairi Quinn, 22 September 1986; Sylvia Meehan to Ruairí Quinn, 8 October 1986; Sylvia Meehan to Ruairí Quinn, 2 December 1986; Patricia O'Donovan (ICTU) to Department of Labour, 26 November 1986.
138 PPKR, Lesbian and Gay Rights at Work, November 1986.
139 NAI, 2014/107/76, Department of Labour, Lesbian and Gay Rights at Work to Ruairí Quinn, 22 September 1986.

140　Ibid.
141　NAI, 2014/107/76, Department of Labour, Ruairí Quinn to John Rogers Attorney General, 6 October 1986.
142　NAI, 2014/107/76, Department of Labour, John Dunne, director of the Federated Union of Employers, to Department of Labour, 6 January 1987.
143　NAI, 2014/107/76, Department of Labour, Patricia O'Donovan to Department of Labour, 26 November 1986.
144　NAI, 2014/107/76, Department of Labour, Sylvia Meehan to Ruairí Quinn, 2 December 1986.
145　Ibid.
146　NLI, IR 369 07, Walter Kilroy, 'Political Parties Reply', *OUT*, no. 12 (March/April 1987), 18.
147　Ibid.

5　Ireland was Ill-Equipped to deal with the AIDS Epidemic

1　Joe Carroll, 'Hierarchy plans to set up task force on AIDS', *The Irish Times*, 12 March 1987, 1.
2　Ibid.
3　Ann Nolan, 'AIDS, Sexual Health, and the Catholic Church in 1980s Ireland: A Public Health Paradox?', *American Journal of Public Health*, 108, no. 7 (July 2018): 908–913.
4　'Bishops' task force on AIDS established', *The Irish Times*, 27 March 1987, 8.
5　Anne Flaherty, 'AIDS campaign overdue, says new church task force', *Irish Press*, 3 April 1987, 3. https://www.irishnewsarchive.com (accessed 20 September 2020).
6　Des Hickey, 'AIDS – finding ways to help the helpless', *Irish Independent*, 19 February 1987, 16. https://www.irishnewsarchive.com (accessed 20 September 2020).
7　NLI, IR 610 F 6, Derek Freedman, *AIDS: The Problem in Ireland* (Dublin: Townhouse, 1987), 68.
8　Health (Family Planning) (Amendment) Act, 1985. http://www.irishstatutebook.ie/eli/1985/act/4/enacted/en/html (accessed 8 February 2017).
9　*Dáil Éireann* debate, 'Health (Family Planning) (Amendment) Bill, 1985', 356, no. 2 (20 February 1985).
10　Censorship of Publications Act, 1929. http://www.irishstatutebook.ie/eli/1929/act/21/enacted/en/html (accessed 8 February 2017); Indecent Advertisements Act, 1889. http://www.irishstatutebook.ie/eli/1889/act/18/enacted/en/print (accessed 8 February 2017).
11　'Killer disease is here', *Irish Press*, 13 May 1983, 7. https://www.irishnewsarchive.com (accessed 20 September 2020).
12　NLI, IR 369 07, 'The OUT Interview', *OUT*, 1, no. 2 (February/March 1985), 18.
13　Ibid., 28.
14　'Desmond moves estimate of £978.6m for health', *The Irish Times*, 3 June 1983, 5.
15　Nathalie Rougier and Iseult Honohan, 'Religion and education in Ireland: growing diversity – or losing faith in the system?', *Journal of Comparative Education*, 51, no. 1 (2015): 71–86.
16　J. Farrell letter to the editor, *The Irish Times*, 22 February 1985, 11.
17　'Family at risk – Dr McNamara', *The Irish Times*, 1 January 1985, 8.
18　'"Gay disease" hits children', *Evening Herald*, 13 December 1982, 7; 'Killer disease is here', *Irish Press* 13 May 1983, 7; 'Death lurks in blood bank', *Evening Herald*, 26

September 1984, 10; 'AIDS may be widespread', *Irish Examiner*, 11 December 1984, 9. https://www.irishnewsarchive.com (accessed 20 September 2020).
19 Elgy Gillespie, '"New" disease reaches Ireland', *The Irish Times*, 13 April 1983, 14.
20 David Nowlan, 'Desmond asks for AIDS inquiry', *The Irish Times*, 3 June 1983, 6.
21 William Dillon, 'Screening ordered as Irish AIDS victim dies', *Irish Independent*, 25 May 1983, 3. https://www.irishnewsarchive.com (accessed 20 September 2020).
22 Elgy Gillespie, '"New" disease reaches Ireland', *The Irish Times*, 13 April 1983, 14.
23 Christopher Robson, 'Out of the Clinical Closet', *NGF News*, 2, no. 1 (January/February 1983), 2.
24 Ibid., 1.
25 Donal Sheehan, 'Health Matters', *Quare Times*, Spring 1984, 7. http://corklgbtarchive.com/items/show/79 (accessed 15 August 2020).
26 Ibid.
27 NLI, IQA, MS 45, 964/7, Edmund Lynch, 'I.G.A. AIDS Conference in Amsterdam', *NGF News*, 3, no. 1 (January/February 1984), 6.
28 NLI, IQA, MS 45, 966/5, Walter Kilroy, 'AIDS: Reducing the Risk', *NGF News* (date and issue unknown, but most likely from 1984): 4.
29 NLI, IR 369 07, 'AIDS "SCARE" RESPONSE', *OUT*, 1, no. 2 (February/March 1985), 4.
30 NLI, IR 369 07, 'Gay Health Action', *OUT*, 1, no. 3 (April/May 1985), 5.
31 NLI, IQA, MS 45, 936/14, GHA meeting, 8 February 1986.
32 Ibid.
33 NLI, PPKR, Acc. 6672, Box 21, 'Smash AIDS Blitzkrieg' leaflet.
34 NLI, PPKR, Acc. 6672, Box 21, Christopher Robson to David Norris, 24 November 1988.
35 GHA, 'AIDS information leaflet', 1 May 1985. http://www.corklgbtarchive.com/items/show/42 (accessed 16 August 2020).
36 Ibid.
37 Kevin Moore, 'Quinn in AIDS leaflet rumpus', *Sunday Independent*, 25 August 1985, 3; Des Rushe, 'A public misuse of our money', *Irish Independent*, 23 August 1985, 20. https://www.irishnewsarchive.com (accessed 20 September 2020).
38 Ibid.
39 Alison Wightman, Regional Administrator of The Family Planning Association: Northern Ireland Region, to Cork branch of Gay Health Action, 7 November 1985. https://s3-eu-west-1.amazonaws.com/corklgbtarchiveomeka%2Foriginal%2Fc939eca8f8c993bf4d6fa904647c4b46.pdf (accessed 1 February 2018).
40 NLI, IQA, MS 46, 001/1, Christopher Robson to Minister for Health, Barry Desmond, 14 February 1986.
41 Interestingly, and a sign of the many contradictions evident in Irish society during this period, GHA's application to Manpower was successful in mid-1985. As a result, Mick Quinlan and Ciaran McKinney received £70 per week for twenty hours a week. Manpower came under the Social Employment Scheme run by the Department of Labour. Those looking to be in receipt of a Manpower payment had to be over 25 and in receipt of unemployment assistance. NLI, IR 369 07, 'Gay Health Action', *OUT*, 1, no. 5 (August/Septmber 1985), 5.
42 NLI, IR 369 07, 'Gay Health Action', *OUT*, 1, no. 6 (October/November 1985), 11.
43 NLI, IQA, MS 45, 943/8, Dr Glen Margo to Tonie Walsh, 8 August 1985.
44 NLI, IQA, MS 45, 943/8, Michael Bergin to Director of TAF, 26 August 1985.
45 NLI, IR 369 07, 'Gay Health Action', *OUT*, 1, no. 7 (December/January 1986), 6.
46 NLI, IQA, MS 45, 949/3, Reg Deane, Honorary Secretary of TAF (date unknown, but sometime in 1986).

47 NLI, IQA, MS 45, 949/3, TAF Honorary Secretary's Report 1985–1986.
48 NLI, IR 369 07, 'Gay Health Action', *OUT*, 1, no. 7 (December/January 1986), 6.
49 NLI, K561, 'AIDS Diary: HIV Positive', *Magill* (July 1989), 33.
50 NLI, IR 369 07, 'Cairde', *OUT*, 1, no. 9 (May/June 1986), 13.
51 NLI, IQA, MS 45, 936/14, GHA meeting, 8 February 1986.
52 'AIDS Action Alliance' leaflet. https://s3-eu-west-1.amazonaws.com/corklgbtarchiveomeka/original/0c1cb63d95a793e3289ab517a5e3da08.pdf (accessed 16 August 2020).
53 Maureen Fox, 'Sexual harassment in the workplace an ongoing problem', *Irish Examiner*, 13 March 1987, 11. https://www.irishnewsarchive.com (accessed 20 September 2020).
54 'Aids hotline as death toll rises', *Evening Herald*, 10 April 1987, 11. https://www.irishnewsarchive.com (accessed 20 September 2020).
55 GHA, 'AIDS information leaflet', 1 May 1985. http://www.corklgbtarchive.com/items/show/42 (accessed 16 August 2020); GHA, 'AIDS Information leaflet', February 1986. https://s3-eu-west-1.amazonaws.com/corklgbtarchiveomeka/original/093ad73555cccc7f01889702612932ff.pdf (accessed 16 August 2020).
56 Ibid.
57 RTÉ, 'AIDS Information Book', 17 December 1986. https://www.rte.ie/archives/collections/news/21235617-aids-information-book/ (accessed 16 August 2020).
58 *Dáil Éireann* debate, 'AIDS Disease', 369, no. 9 (12 November 1986).
59 David Nowlan, 'One new case of AIDS each week forecast by gay group', *The Irish Times*, 18 December 1986, 8.
60 NLI, 8A 2194, Gay Health Action, *AIDS Information Booklet* (Dublin: Gay Health Action, 1986), 5.
61 Ibid., 6.
62 Liam Ryan, 'AIDS toll "far worse" than admitted', *Irish Independent*, 18 December 1986, 10. https://www.irishnewsarchive.com (accessed 20 September 2020).
63 Ibid.
64 Joan Brady, 'Better late than never, minister', *Evening Herald*, 19 December 1986, 15. https://www.irishnewsarchive.com (accessed 20 September 2020).
65 Ibid.
66 David Nowlan, 'Gay groups see prejudice in AIDS response', *The Irish Times*, 25 June 1986, 5.
67 NLI, 8A 2194, Gay Health Action, *AIDS Information Booklet*, 1986, 13.
68 NLI, IR 369 07, 'Gay Health Action', *OUT*, 1, no. 5 (August/September 1985), 5.
69 Chris Dooley, 'RTE refuse AIDS fund ad', *Irish Press*, 22 November 1986, 1.
70 'International AIDS Weekend', RTÉ, 4 April 1987. https://www.rte.ie/archives/collections/news/21244421-international-aids-weekend/ (accessed 16 August 2020).
71 NLI, IR 369 07, Carl McManus, 'Father Bernard Lynch's Ministry to the Lesbian & Gay Community', *OUT*, 1, no. 12 (March/April 1987), 20–23.
72 NLI, IQA, MS 45, 943/8, NIGRA letter to the 'Gay Press' (date unknown).
73 Ibid.
74 Randy Shilts, *And the Band Played On. Politics, People, and the AIDS Epidemic* (New York: St Martin's Press, 1987).
75 NLI, IQA, MS 45, 936/15, GHA meeting, 17 February 1986.
76 NLI, IR 369 07, *OUT*, 1, no. 5 (August/September 1985), 'General Secretary's Report', *NGF News*.
77 NLI, IQA, MS 45, 936/14, GHA meeting, 8 February 1986.

78 Ibid.
79 NLI, IR 369 07, Ciaran McKinney, 'Gay Health Action', *OUT*, 1, no. 9 (May/June 1986), 8.
80 Joan Brady, 'Born of fear and ignorance', *Evening Herald*, 4 February 1986, 15. https://www.irishnewsarchive.com (accessed 20 September 2020).
81 David Nowlan, 'Gay Group Issues Explicit Posters on AIDS', *The Irish Times*, 30 August 1986, 8.
82 John Murray, 'AIDS show: RTE inundated with calls', *Evening Echo*, 26 March 1987, 2. https://www.irishnewsarchive.com (accessed 20 September 2020).
83 Anne Marie Hourihane, 'More than the gay plague', *Irish Press*, 6 May 1987, 9. https://www.irishnewsarchive.com (accessed 20 September 2020).
84 Mark Hennessy, 'AIDS Who is at risk', *Irish Examiner*, 21 January 1987, 7. https://www.irishnewsarchive.com (accessed 20 September 2020).
85 NLI, IR 610 F 6, Derek Freedman, *AIDS: The Problem in Ireland*, 85.
86 NLI, ILB 780, Helena Mulkerns, 'The Gay Area', *Hot Press*, 11, no. 2 (12 February 1987), 6.
87 NAI, 2015/51/1574, Department of Foreign Affairs, John Rogers, Attorney General to Barry Desmond, Minister for Health, 19 April 1985.
88 NAI, 2015/51/1574, Department of Foreign Affairs, Barry Desmond, Minister for Health to John Rogers, Attorney General, 14 May 1985.
89 Jerome Reilly, 'Desmond Pledge on control of AIDS', *Irish Independent*, 26 October 1985, 1. https://www.irishnewsarchive.com (accessed 20 September 2020).
90 NLI, IQA, MS 46,001/1, Chris Robson to Barry Desmond, 14 February 1986.
91 'Pamphlet on AIDS launched', *Irish Examiner*, 1 August 1986, 5. https://www.irishnewsarchive.com (accessed 20 September 2020).
92 John Armstrong, 'AIDS Details Cut from Health Booklet', *The Irish Times*, 14 August 1986, 8.
93 Dermot Hayes, 'AIDS book omits safe sex guide', *Irish Press*, 2 August 1986, 4. https://www.irishnewsarchive.com (accessed 20 September 2020).
94 David Nowlan, 'AIDS Booklet to Clarify Risk', *The Irish Times*, 11 September 1986, 7.
95 'Campaign to combat AIDS', *The Irish Times*, 12 November 1986, 8.
96 NLI, IQA, MS 45, 999/4, Department of Health press release, 'Launch of AIDS Public Information Programme', 1 May 1987.
97 NLI, IQA, MS 45, 999/14, Rory O'Hanlon, Minister for Health, at the launch of the AIDS Public Information programme, 1 May 1987.
98 Catholic Bishops Statement on AIDS, Statement by the Standing Committee of the Bishops' Conference from its meeting of 12 January 1987. Copy provided by the Dublin Diocesan Archives.
99 Ibid.
100 'AIDS the Facts', *Irish Independent*, 14 May 1987, 3. https://archive.irishnewsarchive.com/Olive/APA/INA/Default.aspx#nel=document (accessed 8 October 2020).
101 'AIDS The Dangers', *Today Tonight*, 2 February 1989. https://www.rte.ie/archives/2019/0131/1026675-the-spread-of-aids/ (accessed 7 October 2020).
102 Ibid.
103 NLI, 8A 1297, Health Education Bureau, 'Safer Sex', *AIDS Information Booklet* (Dublin: Health Education Bureau, 1987), 8.
104 NLI, IQA, MS 45, 997/10, GHA press release, 14 November 1986.
105 NLI, IQA, MS 45, 999/14, GHA press release, 1987.
106 NLI, IR 3318 L 20, 'Social Services under attack from New Right coalition', *Liberty News*, 3, no. 3 (Summer 1987).

107 Ibid.
108 Nuala O'Faolain, 'AIDS campaign short on street credibility', *The Irish Times*, 11 May 1987, 12.
109 Ibid.
110 'Group launches AIDS guide', *The Irish Times*, 29 April 1987, 6.
111 NLI, Personal Papers of David Norris, Acc. 6672, Box 31, 'GHA Condom Card'.
112 Ibid.
113 Bernie Ni Fhlatharta and Cathy Halloran, 'AIDS Programmes become crash sex education shows', *Connacht Sentinel*, 19 May 1987, 8. https://www.irishnewsarchive.com (accessed 20 September 2020).
114 'That is the dreaded object', *The Late Late Show*, RTÉ, 15 May 1987. https://www.rte.ie/archives/2017/0504/872557-condom-controversy/ (accessed 16 August 2020).
115 Ibid.
116 'AIDS Programmes become crash sex education shows', *Connacht Sentinel*, 19 May 1987, 8. https://www.irishnewsarchive.com (accessed 20 September 2020).
117 'Yes to condoms', *Sunday World*, 8 February 1987, 2.
118 NLI, PPDN, Acc. 6672, Box 31, 'GHA Joys of Sex Poster'.
119 Ibid.
120 NLI, IQA, MS 45, 999/1, NGF newspaper clipping, 'Hire Gay to work on AIDS campaign', *Evening Press*, 14 September 1988.
121 *Dáil Éireann* debate, 'AIDS Campaign', 383, no. 6 (2 November 1988).
122 Ibid.
123 'O'Hanlon says his plan is working', *The Irish Times*, 1 December 1989, 17.
124 '30% still believe myths on AIDS', *Irish Press*, 1 December 1989, 13. https://www.irishnewsarchive.com (accessed 20 September 2020).
125 NLI, PPDN, Acc. 6672, Box 21, 'GHA Survey Results', *AIDS Action News* (August 1989).
126 Ibid.
127 *Seanad Éireann* debate, 'Information and Education Programme on AIDS', 118, no. 14 (25 February 1988).
128 NLI, PPDN, Acc. 6672, Box 21, 'GHA Survey Results', *AIDS Action News* (August 1989).
129 'Red light for AIDS survey', *Evening Herald*, 17 March 1988, 10. https://www.irishnewsarchive.com (accessed 20 September 2020).
130 NLI, PPDN, Acc. 6672, Box 21, 'GHA Survey Results', *AIDS Action News* (August 1989).
131 Ibid.
132 NLI, ILB 305 G 2, 'GHA News', *Gay Community News*, no. 20 (July 1990), 9.
133 Ibid.
134 *Seanad Éireann* debate, 'European Court of Human Rights Judgment: Statements', 127, no. 1 (2 December 1990).

6 Gay Rights: It's Time

1 *Dáil Éireann* debate, 'Criminal Law (Sexual Offences) Bill 1993: Second Stage', 432, no. 7 (23 June 1993).
2 Ibid.

3   Case of Norris v. Ireland, ECHR judgement, 26 October 1988. https://hudoc.echr.coe.int/eng#{"fulltext":["David%20Norris"],"itemid":["001-57547"]} (accessed 13 October 2017).
4   Ibid.
5   NLI, IQA, MS 45, 976/2, Unite for Change: Seminar on Lesbian and Gay Law Reform, 17 September 1988.
6   Ibid.
7   Ibid.
8   Chris Robson, 'Anatomy of a Campaign', in *Lesbian and Gay Visions of Ireland*, 50.
9   NLI, ILB 305 G 2, 'From Closet to Equality', *Gay Community News*, no. 54 (August 1993), 6.
10 Denis Coghlan, 'Government to act on ruling in Norris case', *The Irish Times*, 27 October 1988, 6.
11 Ibid., 1.
12 *Seanad Éireann* debate, 'Prohibition of Incitement to Racial, Religious or National Hatred Bill, 1988', 121, no. 8 (24 November 1988).
13 *Dáil Éireann* debate, 'Homosexuality Laws', 302, no. 8 (13 December 1977).
14 *Seanad Éireann* debate, 'Prohibition of Incitement to Racial, Religious or National Bill, 1988', 121, no. 9 (30 November 1988).
15 *Dáil Éireann* debate, 'Prohibition to Racial, Religious or National Hatred Bill', 389, no. 2 (26 April 1989); NLI, IQA, MS 45, 940/2, Tonie Walsh to Anne Colley, Progressive Democrats, 7 March 1989.
16 Ibid.
17 NLI, IQA, MS 45, 976/3, GLEN manifesto, 1989 General Election.
18 Dick Ahlstrom, 'Three to stand on gay equality', *The Irish Times*, 5 June 1989, 2.
19 Yvonne Galligan, 'The report of the second commission on the Status of Women', *Irish Political Studies*, 8, no. 1 (1993), 125.
20 NLI, Y 29, *Second Commission on Status of Women* Report, 1993.
21 *Seanad Éireann* debate, 'Prohibition of Incitement to Hatred Bill, 1988', 123, no. 6 (22 November 1989); Ann-Louise Gilligan and her wife Katherine Zappone later became prominent leaders in Ireland's marriage equality campaign.
22 Ibid.
23 NLI, PPDN, Acc. 6672, Box 33, Cathal Kerrigan to David Norris, 23 September 1989.
24 Ibid.
25 NLI, IQA, MS 45, 979/5, Kieran Rose to ILGA conference delegates, 12 December 1989.
26 NLI, IQA, MS 45, 979/5, Proposed letter to be sent in support of Irish law reform campaign, January 1990.
27 Ibid.
28 Ibid.
29 NLI, IQA, MS 45, 944/6, Philip Bockman to Charles Haughey, *Taoiseach*, 19 October 1989.
30 NLI, IQA, MS 45, 944/6, Arthur Leonard to Charles Haughey, *Taoiseach*, 21 October 1989.
31 *Seanad Éireann* debate, 'European Court of Human Rights Judgment: Statements', 127, no. 1 (12 December 1990).
32 Edmund Lynch interview with Cathal Kerrigan, 28 September 2015 (Edmund Lynch Irish LGBT Oral History Project).

33 Christopher Robson, 'Homosexual acts should not be crimes', *The Irish Times*, 19 July 1991, 12.
34 Nuala O'Faolain, 'Bringing homosexuality out of the closet', *The Irish Times*, 4 February 1991, 10.
35 Law Reform Commission: Report on Child Sexual Abuse, September 1990. http://www.lawreform.ie/_fileupload/Reports/rChildSexAbuse.htm (accessed 17 October 2017).
36 NLI, IQA, MS 45, 976/5, Frank Ryan, secretary to the Law Reform Commission, letter to Kieran Rose, 23 October 1989.
37 Law Reform Commission: Report on Child Sexual Abuse, September 1990. http://www.lawreform.ie/_fileupload/Reports/rChildSexAbuse.htm (accessed 17 October 2017). Although the Law Reform Commission's Report was officially published in September 1990, they had issued provisional recommendations in August 1989, hence GLEN using their provisional recommendations in their letters drafted for ILGA members.
38 Jackie Gallagher, 'Child sexual abuse report gets mixed reception', *The Irish Times*, 26 September 1990, 2; Kieran Rose, 'Gay Rights', *The Irish Times*, 5 October 1990, 11.
39 'Complaint over delays in legalising homosexuality', *The Irish Times*, 12 March 1990, 10.
40 NLI, IQA, MS 45, 949/9, Irish Council for Civil Liberties, *Equality Now for Lesbians and Gay Men*, 1990, iii.
41 'Complaint over delays in legalising homosexuality', *The Irish Times*, 12 March 1990, 10.
42 Ibid., preface.
43 Ibid., 26.
44 Ibid.
45 Ibid., 52.
46 Ibid.
47 NLI, IB 799, GLEN Resource material on lesbian/gay law reform, 175.
48 Ibid.
49 Paul O'Neill, 'EEA dealing with tip of iceberg', *The Irish Times*, 7 September 1991, 2.
50 Ibid.
51 NLI, IB 799, GLEN Resource material on lesbian/gay law reform, 6.
52 NLI, IQA, MS 45, 974/10, GLEN, 'After the Parade: Report Back 1992'.
53 Ibid.
54 NLI, ILB 305 G 2, Frank Thackaberry, 'Archbishop comes out', *Gay Community News*, no. 35 (November 1991), 1.
55 'Decision deplored by family group', *The Irish Times*, 27 October 1988, 6.
56 NLI, IQA, MS 45, 978/11, Family Solidarity, *The Homosexual Challenge: Analysis and Response* (Dublin: Family Solidarity, 1990), 11.
57 Ibid., 15.
58 Ibid., 62.
59 Ibid., 18.
60 Ibid., 20.
61 Ibid.
62 Ibid., 21.
63 Joseph McCarroll, 'Why homosexual acts should not be legalised', *The Irish Times*, 30 May 1991, 10.
64 Ibid.

65 Ibid.
66 Christine Newman, 'Booklet described as inciting hatred', *The Irish Times*, 22 August 1990, 10.
67 Ibid.
68 'Councillors attack on Family Solidarity', *Munster Express*, 24 August 1990, 1. https://www.irishnewsarchive.com (accessed 20 September 2020).
69 Ibid.
70 Michael Foley, 'Anti-gay laws complaint', *The Irish Times*, 17 April 1992, 2.
71 *Dáil Éireann* debate, 'Written Answers – Unfair Dismissals Act Amendment', 418, no. 6 (9 April 1992).
72 NLI, IQA, MS 46, 005/12, 'National AIDS Strategy Committee report and recommendations', 13 April 1992, 73.
73 Sean Flynn, 'Homosexuality law reform pledge', *The Irish Times*, 16 May 1992, 1.
74 *Dáil Éireann* debate, 'Legislation on Homosexuality', 420, no. 6 (3 June 1992).
75 Deaglán de Bréadún, 'Taoiseach not to meet Hierarchy on poll', *The Irish Times*, 11 September 1992, 1.
76 Fintan O'Toole, 'The law is the law-unless it is not on the priority list', *The Irish Times*, 16 September 1992, 10.
77 NLI, IQA, MS 45, 979/ 7, Kieran Rose to the Director of Human Rights Directorate, Council of Europe, 30 September 1992.
78 Catherine Foley, 'Gays protest at inaction on change in laws', *The Irish Times*, 29 October 1992, 5.
79 Sean Flynn, 'Delay in altering gay law criticised', *The Irish Times*, 11 November 1992, 3.
80 NLI, IQA, MS 45, 979/7, Campaign for Equality, signatories.
81 Irish Election Manifesto Archive, 1992 Labour Party Manifesto. http://michaelpidgeon.com/manifestos/docs/lab/Labour%20GE%201992.pdf (accessed 13 November 2017).
82 NLI, IQA, MS 45, 977/2, GLEN proposal for an agreement for government, 2 December 1992; ICCL proposals for inclusion in a programme for government, 12 December 1992.
83 Uinsionn Mac Dubhghaill, 'Gay and lesbian group received by President', *The Irish Times*, 14 December 1992, 5.
84 Edmund Lynch interview with Mary Robinson, 28 April 2016 (Edmund Lynch Irish LGBT Oral History Project).
85 Uinsionn Mac Dubhghaill, 'Gay and lesbian group received by President', *The Irish Times,* 14 December 1992, 5.
86 *Evening Herald*, 15 December 1992, 18. https://www.irishnewsarchive.com (accessed 20 September 2020).
87 Mary Holland, 'Afraid to be identified', *The Irish Times*, 17 December 1992, 12.
88 'Gays demand Irish reform', *The Irish Times*, 31 December 1992, 8; NLI, IQA, MS 45, 979/1, ILGA 14th European Regional Conference, Brussels, 27–31 December, 1992, Draft Report.
89 NLI, IQA, MS 45, 979/7, ILGA to the Director, Human Rights Directorate, Council of Europe, 30 December 1992.
90 'Gays demand Irish reform', *The Irish Times*, 31 December 1992, 8.
91 'Council Supports Gays', *Evening Herald*, 5 January 1993, 7. https://www.irishnewsarchive.com (accessed 20 September 2020).
92 Irish Election Manifesto Archive, Fianna Fáil and Labour Programme for a Partnership Government, 1993–1997. http://michaelpidgeon.com/manifestos/docs/pfgs/PfG%201993%20-%201994%20-%20FF-Lab.pdf (accessed 13 November 2017).

93 NLI, IQA, MS 45, 977/4, Christopher Robson to Máire Geoghegan-Quinn, 18 January 1993.
94 NLI, IQA, MS 45, 977/1, Tobias Wikström, Swedish Federation for Gay and Lesbian Rights, to Irish Ambassador to Sweden, Paul Dempsey, 13 January 1993.
95 NLI, IQA, MS 45, 977/1, Landsforeningen for Lesbik og Homofil Frigjøring-Bergen to the *Taoiseach* and *Tánaiste*, Norwegian Foreign Minister and Norwegian ambassador to the Council of Europe, 20 March 1993.
96 NLI, IQA, MS 45, 977/1, *Die Andere Welt* to GLEN (date not stated – most likely early 1993).
97 NLI, OPIE Y/29, Report to government from Second Commission on the Status of Women, January 1993, 175.
98 Ibid., 176.
99 NLI, IQA, MS 45, 977/4, Brian Fitzpatrick, Department of Equality and Law Reform, to Kieran Rose, 24 February 1993.
100 Edmund Lynch interview with Máire Geoghegan-Quinn, 9 February 2016 (Edmund Lynch Irish LGBT Oral History Project).
101 Ibid.
102 *Seanad Éireann* debate, 'Unfair Dismissals (Amendment) Bill', 135, no. 6 (10 March 1993).
103 Ibid.
104 Edmund Lynch interview with Máire Geoghegan-Quinn, 9 February 2016 (Edmund Lynch Irish LGBT Oral History Project).
105 Geraldine Kennedy, 'Gay Law change is defined in Victorian moral terms', *The Irish Times*, 23 April 1993, 12.
106 NLI, IQA, MS 45, 977/8, Draft Memorandum for the government: the decriminalisation of homosexual acts, April 1993.
107 Ibid.
108 NLI, IQA, MS 45, 977/5, Suzy Byrne to Fergus Finlay, Programme Manager, Department of Foreign Affairs, 1 March 1993.
109 NLI, IQA, MS 45, 977/5, GLEN, 'Equality in Reform of the Criminal Law', February 1993.
110 NLI, IQA, MS 45, 977/1, Christopher Robson to Joe Walsh, Minister for Agriculture, Forestry and Food, 20 April 1993.
111 NLI, IQA, MS 45, 977/8, GLEN press conference, 23 April 1993.
112 NLI, IQA, MS 45, 977/7, Jeffrey Dudgeon to Minister for Justice, Máire Geoghegan-Quinn, 5 April 1993.
113 Joseph McCarroll, 'The case against homosexual law reform', *The Irish Times*, 23 April 1993, 12.
114 Bridget Randles, honorary secretary of Christian Family Movement, 'Legalising homosexuality', *The Irish Times*, 19 May 1993, 15.
115 Monsignor Denis O'Callaghan, 'State has to balance homosexuals' rights with Christian values', *Kerryman*, 7 May 1993, 6. https://www.irishnewsarchive.com (accessed 20 September 2020).
116 *Dáil Éireann* debate, 'Criminal Law (Sexual Offences) Bill, 1993', 432, no. 7 (23 June 1993).
117 Ibid.
118 Ibid.
119 Ibid.
120 *Seanad Éireann* debate, 'Criminal Law (Sexual Offences) Bill, 1993', 137, no. 3 (29 June 1993).

121 Denis Coghlan, 'Government bites bullet on gays issue', *The Irish Times*, 23 June 1993, 12; 'Bishops statement on homosexuality', *The Irish Times*, 23 June 1993, 19.
122 Edward O'Loughlin, 'Carnival atmosphere pervades Gay Pride celebrations', *The Irish Times*, 28 June 1993, 2.
123 Mary Bernstein, 'Nothing Ventured, nothing gained? Conceptualising Social Movement 'Success' in the Lesbian and Gay Movement', in *Sociological Perspectives*, Vol. 46, No. 3, (Autumn 2003): 358.
124 Mary Holland, 'They're here, they're queer, and now they're legal', *The Irish Times*, 1 July 1993, 10.
125 Edward O'Loughlin, 'Carnival atmosphere pervades Gay Pride celebrations', *The Irish Times*, 28 June 1993, 2.
126 NLI, ILB 305 G2, 'We Were Proud!', *Gay Community News*, no. 54 (August 1993).
127 Eibhir Mulqueen, 'Celebration march for Galway gays', *City Tribune*, 2 July 1993, 9. https://www.irishnewsarchive.com (accessed 20 September 2020).
128 NLI, ILB 305 G 2, 'News from PLUTO', *Gay Community News*, no. 52 (June 1993).
129 NLI, ILB 305 G 2, 'Church Welcomes Limerick Gays', *Gay Community News*, no. 52 (June 1993).
130 'Gay Group to march in Cork Parade', *The Irish Times*, 16 March 1992, 2.
131 NLI, ILB 305 G2, 'Historic Victory', *Gay Community News*, no. 39 (April 1992).
132 Ibid.
133 NLI, ILB 305 G 2, 'St. Patrick's Day Parade WILL Include Us!', *Gay Community News*, no. 49 (March 1993).
134 Nuala O'Faolain, 'New York could learn a lesson from St. Patrick's Day in Cork', *The Irish Times*, 15 March 1993, 12.
135 NLI, PPDN, Acc. 10, 345, Box 111, Norris letter to Sligo student, 27 October 1989.
136 David Norris, 'Decriminalising homosexual act an historic event', *The Irish Times*, 25 June 1993, 12.
137 Henry McDonald, 'Ireland becomes first country to legalise gay marriage by popular vote', *The Guardian*, 23 May 2015. http://www.theguardian.com/world/2015/may/23/gay-marriage-ireland-yes-vote (accessed 25 May 2015).

Appendix: Glossary of Terms

An Garda Síochána Irish police force.
Ard Fheis Annual political party conference.
Áras an Uachtaráin Irish president's residency.
Bunreacht na hÉireann Constitution of Ireland.
Dáil Éireann Lower house of the Irish parliament.
Éire Irish for Ireland.
Leinster House Parliament of Ireland where *Dáil Éireann* and *Seanad Éireann* meet.
Oireachtas Legislature of Ireland consisting of the President of Ireland, *Dáil Éireann* and *Seanad Éireann*.
Seanad Éireann Upper house of the Irish parliament.
Senator Member of *Seanad Éireann*.
Tánaiste Deputy Prime Minister of the Republic of Ireland.
Taoiseach Prime Minister of the Republic of Ireland.
Teachta Dála Member of *Dáil Éireann*.

Bibliography

Archives

National Library of Ireland

Irish Queer Archive
Personal Papers of David Norris
University College Cork LGBT Archive

National Archives of Ireland

Department of Foreign Affairs
Department of Justice
Department of Labour
Office of the Attorney General

Public Record Office of Northern Ireland

Northern Ireland Gay Rights Association Archive

Gale Primary Sources

Archives of Sexuality and Gender

Cork LGBT Archive

http://corklgbtarchive.com

***Dáil Éireann* Debates**

https://www.oireachtas.ie/en/debates/find/

University College Cork Archive

Minutes of UCC Governing Body Meetings

University College Dublin Archive

Minutes of UCD Governing Body Meetings

Trinity College Dublin Archive

Personal Papers of Noel Browne

Dublin Diocesan Archives

Irish Roman Catholic Bishops Statement on AIDS, Statement by the Standing Committee of the Bishops' Conference from its meeting of 12 January 1987

Irish Election Manifesto Archive

http://michaelpidgeon.com/manifestos/

Irish Times Archive

https://www.irishtimes.com/archive

Irish Newspaper Archive

https://www.irishnewsarchive.com

Seanad Éireann Debates

https://www.oireachtas.ie/en/debates/find/

Personal papers

Personal Papers of Kieran Rose.
Personal Papers of Sean Connolly.

Newspapers, periodicals, religious publications

AIDS Action News
American Journal of Public Health
Belfast Telegraph
Bulletin
Capital Gay
Catholic Standard
Christian Family Movement Newsletter
Church of Ireland Gazette
City Tribune
Connacht Sentinel
Connacht Tribune
Cork Examiner
Cork Review

Corks Crew
Evening Echo
Evening Herald
Evening Press
Galway Advertiser
Gay Community News
Gay News
Gay Star: Belfast Bulletin of the Northern Ireland Gay Association
GPU News
Gralton
Hermes
Hibernia
Hot Press
Identity
IGA Newsletter
IGRM Newsletter
In Dublin
In Touch
Irish Examiner
Irish Farmers Journal
Irish Independent
Irish Marxist Review
Irish Press
Journal of Comparative Education
Kerryman
Kilkenny People
Liberty News
Limerick Echo
Linc: Cork's Lesbian Magazine
Longford Leader
Magill
Mayo News
Munster Express
Munster Women's Newsletter
NGF News
Our Family
OUT
Out Front: Colorado's Premier Gay Magazine
Phoenix Review: Magazine of the Irish Gay Rights Movement
Quare Times
Reporter
RTÉ Guide
The Irish Times
The Sage
Sapphire
Scene Magazine
Sociological Perspectives
Success
Sunday Independent

Sunday Press
Sunday Tribune
Sunday World
University Times
Western People
Women's Space Newsletter

Visual sources & oral interviews

'AIDS Information Book' (RTÉ), 17 December 1986.
'International AIDS Weekend' (RTÉ), 4 April 1987.
Bród: Out in the Streets, 2008.
Edmund Lynch Irish LGBT Oral History Project.
Edmund Lynch, *Did They Notice Us? Gay Visibility in the Irish Media 1973–1993* (2003).
Ireland's Eye (RTÉ), 24 November 1981.
Last House (RTÉ), 24 July 1975.
The Late Late Show (RTÉ), 15 May 1987.
The Late Late Show (RTÉ), 9 February 1980.
Today Tonight (RTÉ), 2 February 1989.
Tuesday Report (RTÉ), 22 February 1977.
Week In (RTÉ), 11 February 1980.

Council of Europe resolutions and recommendations

Parliamentary Assembly of Council of Europe. 'Discrimination against homosexuals', Recommendation 924 (1981).
Parliamentary Assembly of Council of Europe. 'Discrimination against homosexuals', Resolution 756 (1981).

European Parliament

Vera Squarcialupi, report drawn up on behalf of the Committee on Social Affairs and Employment, European Parliament Working Document, 13 February 1984.

European Court of Human Rights

'Case of Norris v. Ireland', Judgement of European Court of Human Rights, 26 October 1988. https://hudoc.echr.coe.int/fre#%7B%22itemid%22:%5B%22001-57547%22%5D%7D

Interviews/email correspondence (conducted by author)

Cathal Kerrigan (14 January 2016)

Edmund Lynch (Email correspondence 20 November 2020)
Kieran Rose (12 January 2016)
Helen Slattery (9 March 2016)
Deirdre Walsh (9 March 2016)
Marese Walsh (4 April 2016)
Tonie Walsh (WhatsApp conversation 13 February 2021)
Nuala Ward (Email correspondence 22 April 2018)

Unpublished theses

Earls, Averill Erin. 'Queering Dublin: Same-sex Desire and Masculinities in Ireland, 1884-1950'. PhD thesis, Faculty of the Graduate School of the University of Buffalo, State University of New York, New York, 2016.
Kilgannon, David. 'How to survive a plague': AIDS activism in Ireland, 1983-1989', MA dissertation, School of History, University College Dublin, Dublin, 2015.

Books/academic articles

Adam, Barry D. *The Rise of a Gay and Lesbian Movement*, Boston: Twayne Publishers, 1987.
Beemyn, Brett. 'The Silence is Broken: A History of the First Lesbian, Gay, and Bisexual College Student Groups', *Journal of the History of Sexuality*, 12, no. 2 (2003): 205-223.
Bernstein, Mary. 'Nothing Ventured, Nothing Gained? Conceptualising Social Movement 'Success' in the Lesbian and Gay Movement', *Sociological Perspectives*, 46, no. 3 (Autumn 2003): 353-379.
Bird, Charlie. *A Day in May: Real Lives, True Stories*, Kildare: Merrion Press, 2016.
Brown, Terence. *Ireland: A Social and Cultural History 1922-1985*, London: Fontana, 1985.
Buckle, Sebastian. *The Way Out: A History of Homosexuality in Modern Britain*, London: I. B. Tauris, 2015.
Casey, Maurice. 'Radical Politics and Gay Activism in the Republic of Ireland, 1974-1990', *Irish Studies Review*, 26, no. 2 (2018): 217-236.
Chinoy, Mike. *Are you with me?: Kevin Boyle and the Rise of the Human Rights Movement*, Dublin: Lilliput Press, 2020.
Connolly, Linda. *The Irish Women's Movement: From Revolution to Devolution*, Dublin: Palgrave, 2003.
Coogan, Tim Pat. *Ireland in the Twentieth Century*, London: Hutchinson, 2003.
Crone, Joni. 'Lesbian Feminism in Ireland', *Women's Studies International Forum*, 11, no. 4 (1988): 343-347.
Devlin Trew, Johanne and Michael Pierse. 'Introduction: Gathering Tensions', in *Rethinking the Irish Diaspora: After the Gathering*, Palgrave Macmillan, 2018.
Duberman, Martin. *Has the Gay Movement Failed?*, California: University of California Press, 2018.
Dublin Lesbian and Gay Men's Collective. *Out for Ourselves: The Lives of Irish Lesbians and Gay Men*, Dublin, 1986.
Duncan, Nancy. 'Renegotiating Gender and Sexuality in Public and Private Spaces', *Destabilizing Geographies of Gender and Sexuality*, ed. Nancy Duncan, London: Routledge, 1996.

Earner-Byrne Lindsey. 'Reinforcing the Family: The Role of Gender, Morality and Sexuality in Irish Welfare Policy, 1922–1944', *The History of the Family*, 13, no. 4 (2008): 360–369.

Earner-Byrne Lindsey, and Diane Urquhart. *The Irish Abortion Journey, 1920–2018*, London: Palgrave Pivot, 2019.

Egan, Orla. 'Searching for Space: Cork Lesbian Community 1975–2000', *Women's Studies Review: Women's Activism and Voluntary Activity*, 9 (2004): 186–210.

Egan, Orla. *Queer Republic of Cork*, Cork: Onstreams Publications, 2016.

Enke, Anne. *Finding the Movement: Sexuality, Contested Space, and Feminist Activism*, Durham & London: Duke University Press, 2007.

Family Solidarity, *The Homosexual Challenge: Analysis and Response*, Dublin: Family Solidarity, 1990.

Faulkenbury, T. Evan and Aaron Hayworth. 'The Carolina Gay Association, Oral History, and Coming Out at the University of North Carolina', *Oral History Review*, 43, no. 1 (2016): 115–137.

Ferriter, Diarmaid. *Occasions of Sin: Sex and Society in Modern Ireland*, London: Profile, 2009.

Ferriter, Diarmaid. *Transformation of Ireland 1900–2000*, London: Profile, 2004.

Freedman, Derek. *AIDS: The Problem in Ireland*, Dublin: Townhouse, 1987.

Galligan, Yvonne. 'The Report of the Second Commission on the Status of Women', *Irish Political Studies*, 8, no. 1 (1993).

Gay Health Action, *Information AIDS Booklet*, Dublin: Gay Health Action, 1986.

Gay Liberation Society, *Gay Forum: Seven Essays on Homosexuality*, Belfast: Gay Liberation Society, 1974.

Grannell, James. 'Gay Health Action and the Fight Against AIDS in 1980s Ireland', *History Workshop*, first published online 24 July 2019, http://www.historyworkshop.org.uk/gay-health-action-and-the-fight-against-aids-in-1980s-ireland/ (accessed 6 August 2019).

Health Education Bureau, *AIDS Information Booklet*, Dublin: Health Education Bureau, 1987.

Healy, Gráinne. *Crossing the Threshold: The Story of the Marriage Equality Movement*, Kildare: Merrion Press, 2017.

Healy, Gráinne, Brian Sheehan and Noel Whelan. *Ireland Says Yes: The Inside Story of How the Vote for Marriage Equality was Won*, Kildare: Merrion Press, 2016.

Hug, Chrystel. *The Politics of Sexual Morality in Ireland*, New York: Palgrave Macmillan, 1999.

Irish Bishops Pastoral, *Love is for Life: Pastoral Letter Issue on behalf of Irish Hierarchy*, Dublin, 1985.

Irish Congress of Trade Unions, *Lesbian and Gay Rights in the Workplace Guidelines for Negotiators*, 1987.

Irish Council for Civil Liberties, *Equality Now for Lesbians and Gay Men*, Dublin: Irish Council for Civil Liberties, 1990.

Kelly, Brendan. 'Homosexuality and Irish Psychiatry: Medicine, Law, and the Changing Face of Ireland', *Irish Journal of Psychological Medicine*, 34, 3 (2017): 209–215.

Kerrigan, Páraic. *LGBTQ Visibility, Media and Sexuality in Ireland*, Oxfordshire: Routledge, 2021.

Kerrigan, Páraic. 'OUT-ing AIDS: The Irish Civil Gay Rights Movement's response to the AIDS crisis (1984–1988)', *Media History*, 25, no. 2 (2019): 244–258.

Kerrigan, Páraic. 'Projecting a Queer Republic: Mainstreaming Queer Identities on Irish Documentary Film', *Studies in Documentary Film*, 13, no. 1 (2019): 1–17.

Knopp, Larry. 'Queer Diffusions', *Environment and Planning D: Society and Space*, 21 (2003): 409–424.

Korinek, Valerie J. *Prairie Fairies: A History of Queer Communities and People in Western Canada, 1930–1985*, Toronto: University of Toronto Press, 2018.

Korinek, Valerie J. 'The Most Openly Gay Person for at least a Thousand Miles': Doug Wilson and the Politicization of a Province, 1975–83', *Canadian Historical Review*, 84, no. 4 (2003): 517–550.

Lacey, Brian, *Terrible Queer Creatures: Homosexuality in Irish History*, Dublin: Wordwell Ltd., 2008.

Lavelle, Paul, *Understanding AIDS: A Christian Approach*, Dublin: Irish Messenger, 1989.

Leeworthy, Daryl. 'Rainbow Crossings: Gay Irish Migrants and LGBT Politics in 1980s London', *Studi Irlandesi: A Journal of Irish Studies*, 10 (2020): 79–99.

Madden, Ed. 'Queering Ireland, In the Archives', *Irish University Review*, 43, no. 1 (Spring/Summer 2013): 184–221.

Malcom, David. 'A Curious Courage: The Origins of Gay Rights Campaigning in the National Union of Students', *History of Education*, 47, no. 1 (2018): 73–86.

Mullally, Una. *In the Name of Love: The Movement for Marriage Equality in Ireland*, Dublin: The History Press Ireland, 2014.

McDonagh, Patrick. 'Abortion, Gay Rights, and the National Gay Federation in Ireland, 1982–1983', *Journal of the History of Sexuality*, 29, no. 1 (January 2020): 1–27.

McDonagh, Patrick. 'Homosexuality is not a problem – it doesn't do you any harm and can be lots of fun': Students and Gay Rights Activism in Irish Universities, 1970s–1980s, *Irish Economic and Social History*, 46, no. 1 (2019): 111–141.

McDonagh, Patrick. '"It's Poppycock to Say Homosexuals Can be Excused": Rethinking the Gay and Lesbian Movement in the Republic of Ireland, 1970s–1990s', eds Sean Brady and Mark Seymour, *From Sodomy Laws to Same-Sex Marriage: International Perspectives since 1789* (London: Bloomsbury Academic, 2019), 183–200.

McDonagh, Patrick. 'Homosexuals are Revolting – Gay & Lesbian Activism in the Republic of Ireland 1970s–1990s', *Studi Irlandesi: A Journal of Irish Studies*, 7 (2017): 65–91.

McDonagh, Patrick and Páraic Kerrigan. '"Cherishing all the Children of the Nation Equally": Gay Youth Organisation and Activism in Ireland', Basingstoke: Palgrave Macmillan, forthcoming.

Nolan, Ann. 'AIDS, Sexual Health, and the Catholic Church in 1980s Ireland: A Public Health Paradox?', *American Journal of Public Health*, 108, no. 7 (July 2018): 908–913.

Norris, David. *A Kick Against the Pricks: The Autobiography*, London: Transworld Ireland, 2012.

O'Carroll, Íde and Eoin Collins (eds). *Lesbian and Gay Visions of Ireland: Towards the Twenty-First Century*, London: Cassell, 1995.

O'Donnell, Katherine & Sally R. Munt. 'Pride and Prejudice: Legalizing Compulsory Heterosexuality in New York and Boston's St Patrick's Day Parades', *International Journal of Social Spaces*, 10, 1 (2007): 1–21.

O'Dowd, Niall. *A New Ireland*, New York: Skyhorse Publishing, 2020.

Phillips, Richard, Diane Watt, and David Shuttleton. *De-Centring Sexualities: Politics and Representations Beyond the Metropolis*, London: Routledge, 2000.

Rhoads, Robert. 'Student Activism as an Agent of Social Change: A Phenomenological Analysis of Contemporary Campus Unrest', paper presented at the Annual Meeting of the American Educational Research Association, published online by The Educational Resources Information Centre, March 1997. https://files.eric.ed.gov/fulltext/ED407902.pdf (accessed 29 January 2019).

Roberts, Nicole E., 'The Plight of Gay Visibility: Intolerance in San Francisco, 1970–1979', *Journal of Homosexuality*, 60, no. 1 (2013): 105–119.

Robinson, Padraig. *Gaze Against Imperialism*, Metaflux Publishing, 2019.

Rose, Kieran. *Diverse Communities: The Evolution of Lesbian and Gay Politics in Ireland*, Cork: Cork University Press, 1994.

Rougier, Nathalie and Iseult Honohan, 'Religion and Education in Ireland: Growing Diversity – or Losing Faith in the System?', *Journal of Comparative Education*, 51, no. 1 (2015): 71–86.

Ryan, Paul. 'Coming Out: Gay Mobilisation, 1970–1980', in *Social Movements and Ireland*, eds Linda Connolly and Niamh Hourigan, Manchester: Manchester University Press, 2006.

Ryan, Paul. *Asking Angela MacNamara: An Intimate History of Irish Lives*, Dublin: Irish Academic Press, 2011.

Ryan-Flood, Róisín. 'Sexuality, Citizenship and Migration: The Irish Queer Diaspora in London', in *Sexuality, Citizenship and Belonging*, eds Francesca Stella, Yvette Taylor, Tracey Reynolds, Antoine Rogers. New York: Routledge, 2016, 52.

Scott, James C. 'Everyday Forms of Resistance', *Copenhagen Papers*, no. 4 (1989): 33–62.

Shilts, Randy. *And the Band Played On. Politics, People, and the AIDS Epidemic*, New York: St Martin's Press, 1987.

Sweeney, John. 'The Growing Alliance between Gay and Union Activists', *Social Text*, no. 61 (Winter 1999): 1–38.

Sweetman, Rosita. *On Our Backs: Sexual Attitudes in a Changing Ireland*, London: Macmillan, 1979.

Tiernan, Sonja. *The History of Marriage Equality in Ireland: A Social Revolution Begins*, Manchester: Manchester University Press, 2020.

Walshe, Éibhear. *Oscar's Shadow: Wilde, Homosexuality and Modern Ireland*, Cork: Cork University Press, 2011.

Weeks, Jeffrey. *Coming Out: Homosexual Politics in Britain, from the Nineteenth Century to the Present*, London: Quartet Books, 1977.

Index

advertising
   of gay culture 60–1
   parades 84
   personal advertisements 61
   pubs 14
   refusal of 123
   STDs, help for 112–13
   telephone lines 75, 82, 83
age of consent 135, 136, 142–3, 144, 154, 155–6
AIDS Action Alliance (AAA) 120
AIDS epidemic 111–33
   AIDS Action Alliance (AAA) 120
   AIDS Helpline Dublin 120
   AIDS Information Booklet 121–2
   Cairde 119
   education campaigns 116–18, 120–3, 127, 128–30, 132
   Family Solidarity and 147–8
   a 'gay disease' 113–14
   GHA and 111–12, 116–33
   government response to 125, 126–32
   international support 118–19
   media coverage of 114–15, 116, 121–2, 125–6, 127, 128, 129, 130
   other high-risk groups 120–1, 131
   responses to 58, 111
   Roman Catholic Church and 111, 126, 127–8
   sex, discussion of 112–13
   statistics 114, 122, 125, 127, 131, 132
   STD clinic services 116
   threat of 59
   understanding of 121
   volunteers 124–5
alcoholism 48
Ancient Order of Hibernians (AOH) 158
Anna, from Cavan 20, 21
Anti-Amendment Campaign (AAC) 57
archival research 6
Asmal, Kadar 37, 93, 96

Athlone, Westmeath 13
attitudes towards homosexuals 8–9, 18, 102–8
   see also stereotypes
aversion therapy 10, 72
awards 63, 82

Ban, Ki-moon 1
Barden, Garrett 92
Barnes, Monica 131, 145
Barry, Marian 23
bars 13, 14, 21, 61, 80, 82
   see also clubs
Bartley Dunne's, Dublin 13, 14
Baudry, André 35
befriending services 81–2
   see also Tel-A-Friend (TAF) phone line
Belgium 35, 103
Bergin, John 143
Bergin, Michael 124
Berkeley, Carl 48, 56
Bernstein, Mary 157
Black, Brian 44
Blanche, Theresa 9, 14
Bockman, Philip 141
Boekyns, Jackie 103
Bogue, Tom 97
Book Upstairs 60
bookshops 60, 78
Borderline (RTÉ TV) 130
Boyle, Hilary 32
Bradley, Peter 16, 32
Brady, Joan 122
Breathnach, Maire 26, 32
Breen, Majella 51, 53, 72
Brennan, Ned 28
Broadcasting Complaints Commission 32
Broughton, Fred 15, 16
Brown, Michael 63–4
Browne, Noel 31, 35, 36, 102
Bruton, John 142

Bruton, Terry 15
Buchanan, Alan, Archbishop of Dublin 34
Burke, Ray 140, 148
Byrne, Gay 50, 130
Byrne, Suzy 154

Cairde 119
Campaign for Homosexual Equality (CHE) 13, 16
Campaign for Homosexual Law Reform (CHLR) 37
Campbell, Tomas 91
Canada 103
candidates, political 52–3, 139
Cantillon, Jack 125
Capital Gay 66
Carson, Phil 30, 36
Casey, Eamonn, Bishop of Galway 60
Catholic Church *see* Roman Catholic Church
Catholic Standard 31, 33–4, 35
Censorship Board 94
Censorship of Publications Act (1929) 7, 112–13
characterisation of homosexuals 8–9
 see also attitudes towards homosexuals; stereotypes
child molestation 9, 178 n.31
children, custody of 52
Christian Family Movement 155
Christian organisations 60
Christie, Ian 104
Church of Ireland 34
churches *see* Church of Ireland; Roman Catholic Church
Churchfield Women's Group 80
cinema 44–5
Civil Service 101–2, 107
Clancy, Clement 42
Cleary, Fr Michael 31, 169 n.123
Cleary, Peter 27, 31–2
clinics 113, 116
clubs 20, 21, 42, 43, 61
 see also bars
Cogan, Oliver 24, 72
Coglan, Denis 156
Coleman, Ciaran 45
Collins, Gerry 35–6, 138–9

Comhairle Le Leas Óige (Dublin Youth Service) 46
coming out 9–10, 11, 47, 50–1, 54, 153
Comiskey, Brendan, Bishop of Ferns 59
Comiskey, Ray 45
commission on law reform 102, 142–3
commission on the status of women 139–40, 152
community awards 63
condoms 112, 117–18, 122, 128, 129–30, 131
conferences and other meetings
 Discrimination against Lesbian and Gay Workers workshop (1984) 99
 Discrimination in Employment in Relation to Sexual Orientation (1985) 100
 Gay Rights, Coleraine (1973) 14–16
 homosexuality, Church of Ireland (1976) 34
 homosexuality, TCD (1974, 1976) 17–18, 33
 human sexuality, QUB (1977) 33
 IGRM, South County Hotel (1974) 18–19
 IGRM and NGF, Glencree (1980) 71
 International AIDS Weekend (1987) 123–4
 International Gay Youth Congress (1985) 58
 lesbian (1980, 1982) 51, 52
 National Gay Conference, Cork (1981) 72–3
 National Gay Conference, TCD (1982) 48, 52, 98–9
 Women's Conference on Lesbianism, TCD (1978) 48, 50
Connacht Sentinel 83, 130
Connolly, Linda 12
Connolly, Sean 27, 28, 30, 36
constitution of Ireland 1, 8, 26, 39–40, 87–8, 141
contraceptives 112
 see also condoms
Cooney, Tom 136
Cork
 bars and clubs 13, 14
 Cork Gay Collective (CGC) 69–74, 77, 80–1

discos 66
    first National Gay Conference (1981) 72–3
    IGRM local group 23–4, 66–9, 71–2, 106
    lesbian groups and activities 77–82
    Phoenix Centre *see* Phoenix Centre, Cork
    population of 64
    St Patrick's Day parade 158–9
    telephone line 67–8
    University College Cork (UCC) 89–90, 91–2
Cork Examiner 67, 82, 90, 92, 97
Cork Gay Collective (CGC)
    AIDS epidemic 115
    employment rights 96, 98, 99
    lesbians and 77, 80–1
    local group 69–74
    St Patrick's Day parade 159
Cork Lesbian and Gay Community Project 81
Cork Lesbian Group (CLG) 78–9, 80–1, 158–9
Cork Lesbian Line 81–2
Cork Women's Fun Weekends 79–80
Cork-about (radio) 24
Costello, Declan 35, 95
Costello, Joe 156
cottaging 13
Council for the Status of Women (CSW) 139–40, 152
Council of Europe 105–6, 148, 149
counselling services 48
Cowen, Brian 148
Crawley, Harry 127
Crawley, Marie 83
Criminal Law Amendment Act (1885) 7–8, 87, 148–9, 150, 162 n.15
Criminal Law (Sexual Offences) Bill (1993) 135, 155, 156–7
criminalisation of sexual activity between men 7–8, 9, 87, 126, 162 n.15
    see also decriminalisation of sexual activity between men
Crone (aka Sheerin), Joni 21, 49, 50–1, 53, 54, 140
cross-border cooperation 15–16
Crossley, Alan 13

Daly, Cathal, Bishop of Ardagh and Clonmacnoise 35
Dardis, John 156
Darragh, Austin 10
Davern, Noel 105
Davies, Peter 33
Davies, Terence 44–5
De Valera, Eamon 8
decriminalisation of sexual activity between men 1, 103, 135, 144, 148, 155, 161 n.4
Dempsey, Anne 32
Dempsey, Paul 151
Department of Equality and Law Reform 152
Department of Finance 101–2
Desmond, Barry 114, 126
Det Norske Forbundet 18
Devlin Trew, Johanne 11
Die Andere Welt 151
Dillon, Annie 52
discos
    in Cork 66
    Flikkers, Dublin 41, 44, 62
    in Galway 76, 77
    IGRM and 20, 21, 43
    Phoenix Club, Dublin 81
    women's 21, 50
Donnelly, Don 143
Dooney, Roy 105
Dooradoyle, Limerick 158
Doran, Liz 104
Dorcey, Mary 16–17, 18
Dorr, Noel 104
Downey, Garbhan 83
Dublin
    bars and clubs 13, 14, 61
    as 'Gay Paree' 39, 59–62
    gay pride events 56–8, 158
    IGRM and 19–21
    Phoenix Club 20, 21, 42, 43
    population of 64
    Project Arts Centre 28–9
    Second International Gay Youth Congress (1985) 58
    South County Hotel, Stillorgan, Dublin 18–19
    St Patrick's Day parade 159
    Temple Bar 39

Trinity College Dublin (TCD) 16–18,
    33, 48, 51, 52, 90, 98–9
  women's spaces 50
  see also Hirschfeld Centre
Dublin Gay Collective (DGC) 54–5, 56
Dublin University Sociological Society
    33
Dublin Vocational Education Committee
    46
Dublin Women's Centre 52
Dudgeon, Jeffrey 17, 154–5
Duffy, Mickey 99
Dunn, Ian 17, 95
Dunne, John 108
Dupree, John 118–19

Earls, Averill Erin 7
Earner-Byrne, Lindsey 7, 8
Easons 60
education 113, 159
education campaigns, AIDS epidemic
    116–18, 120–3, 127, 128–30,
    132
Educational Matters 33
Egan, Orla 23, 80, 82, 159
electric shock treatment 10, 72
Electricity Supply Board Officers
    Association (ESBOA) 99
emigration 10–11, 30–1
Employment Equality Act (1977) 95, 97,
    107
Employment Equality Authority (EEA)
    107, 108, 145
employment rights 93–101, 106–8
  absence of official cases 107
  dismissal from employment 94–5
  ICCL, support from 93–4
  political attitudes 106–7
  trade unions and 95–101
European Convention on Human Rights
    135, 136, 144, 151
European Court of Human Rights 135,
    136, 147, 148, 153–4, 157
European Economic Community (EEC)
    35, 103, 105
European Parliament 106–7, 151
Evening Echo 67, 77–8, 82, 89
Evening Herald 47, 120, 125, 150, 151
Evening Press 26, 27, 31–2

Fairview Park Protest March 56–8
Family Planning Bill (1979) 112
Family Solidarity 146–8, 155, 156
  The Homosexual Challenge 146, 147
Federated Union of Employers (FUE) 108
Federated Workers Union of Ireland
    (FWUI) 100, 101
Federation of Working Groups
    Homophily (FWGH) 103
Ferriter, Diarmaid 2, 4, 169 n.123
Fianna Fáil 106, 108, 140, 151, 153
film societies 44–5
Fine Gael 105, 106, 108, 125, 147
Finlay, Fergus 154
Finnegan, Peter 33
Fitzgerald, Des 22
Fitzpatrick, Brian 152
Fitzpatrick, John 118
Flanagan, Mary 79
Flikkers disco 44
Flynn, Declan 54, 55, 56
Flynn, Eileen 94–5
Flynn, Phil 100, 145
Forrestal, Marina 56
Forthroll, Deidre 83
Fownes Street, Dublin 39
France 16
Freedman, Derek 112, 113, 125, 130
Friele, Kim 18

Galway
  community awards 63, 83
  discos 76, 77
  Galway Gay Collective (GGC) 74–7, 83
  gay pride events 83–5, 158
  IGRM local group 66, 74–6
  NGF, lack of contacts in 65
  phone lines 83
  population of 64
  St Patrick's Day parade 159
Galway Advertiser 63, 75, 83, 84
Galway Gay and Lesbian Line 83
Galway Gay Collective (GGC) 74–7, 83
Galway Lesbian and Gay Collective 63
Gardaí *see* police
Gay and Lesbian Equality Network
    (GLEN) 136–45
  age of consent 142–3, 144
  Campaign for Equality 145, 149

Council of Europe and 149
EHCR, complaint to 148
equality, principle of 136-8
General Election (1989) 139
General Election (1992) 149-50
The Homosexual Challenge 147
international gay rights movement 140-2, 150-1
and Máire Geoghegan-Quinn 151, 152-3
Prohibition of Incitement to Hatred Bill 138-40
Gay Community News 92
Gay Defence Committee 54-5
Gay Health Action (GHA) 111-12, 116-33
and AAA 120
Cairde 119
Condom Card 129-30
disbanding of 132
education campaign 116-18, 120-3, 132
establishment of 116
funding of 118, 123, 124, 131, 132, 188 n.41
government response to AIDS crisis 126, 128-9, 131
International AIDS Weekend 123
international support 118-19
'Joys of Sex' poster 130
legacy of 125, 132-3
media coverage 125-6
other high-risk groups 120-1
survey 132
volunteers 124-5
Gay Information Cork 81, 82
Gay Liberation Day 18
Gay News
advertising 14
banning of 94, 103-4
centres 43
IGRM reporting 36, 68
letters to 13
NGF interview 42
pub zaps 56
'Gay Paree' of Dublin 39, 59-62
gay pride events 18, 55-8, 73-4, 83-5, 158
gay rights 32-6, 88-108, 135-60
age of consent 135, 136, 142-3, 144, 154, 155-6
court cases 87-8

definition of 88
employment rights 93-101, 153
equality, principle of 136-40, 143-5, 149, 154-5
Europe and 140-2, 148
government movement on 152-4
history of activism 2-5
Law Reform Commission and 102, 142-3
laws, changes in 155-7
legal reforms, campaign for 101-8
Mary Robinson and 150
Norris judgement and 136
opposition to 34-6, 145-8, 155, 156
student unions and 88-93
support for 32-4
see also international gay rights movement; Irish Gay Rights Movement (IGRM)
gay scene (1980s) 39-41, 61-2
gay subculture (1970s) 13-14
Gay Sweatshop 28-9
Geldof, Lynn 43
General Election (1989) 139
General Election (1992) 149-50
Genoa Bar, Athlone 13
Geoghegan-Quinn, Máire 135, 151, 152-3, 153-4, 155-6, 157
George Bar, Dublin 61
Germany 151
Gill, Don 15
Gillespie, Elgy 29, 114
Gilligan, Ann-Louise 140
Gilmore, Eamon 148
government attitudes 102-8
government response to AIDS crisis 125, 126-32
GPU News 49
Griffin, Kevin C. 103
growing up gay 9
Grundy, John 13
Gym, Dublin 124

Halligan, Brendan 106
Halloran, Cathy 130
Harney, Mary 156
Harris, Drew 94
Haugh, Maurice 39, 44
Haughey, Charles 140

Hayes, Dermot 127
Health Education Bureau (HEB) 117–18, 126–7
Healy, Gráinne 50
Heaume, Chris 45
Henn, Tom 97
Hennessy, Mark 125
heterosexual allies 31–2
Higgins, Michael D. 131
Hirschfeld, Magnus 41
Hirschfeld Biograph, Dublin 44–5
Hirschfeld Centre, Dublin
   closure of 61–2
   legacy of 62
   LIL and 49, 53
   NGF and 39, 40, 41, 43–4, 44–5
   Second International Gay Youth Congress (1985) 58
history of gay rights activism 2–5
Holland, Mary 150, 158
Holt, Tom 46
homosexual offences 9
(homo)sexuality in the Republic of Ireland, overview of 6–12
Hooray Henry's, Dublin 61
Horan, Paddy 27–8
Hot Press 43, 91, 125–6
Hug, Chrystel 7
Hughes, Bill 41
human rights, gay rights as 15, 41, 73, 88–9, 93, 97, 102
Hussey, Gillian 111
Hutchinson, Pearse 26–7

Imperial Hotel, Cork 13, 14
In Dublin 43, 45, 60, 95
Incognito, Dublin 124
Indecent Advertisement Act (1889) 112–13
Infor-Homosexualite 35
international AIDS organisations 115, 116
International AIDS Weekend (1987) 123–4
International Gay Association (IGA) 43, 103, 115
international gay rights movement
   AIDS epidemic 115, 116
   condemnation of Ireland by 105
   GLEN and 140–2, 150–1

history of gay rights activism 4, 8
Ireland and 41
support from 35, 103–4
International Lesbian and Gay Association (ILGA) 140–1, 150–1
interviews 6
Ireland's Eye (RTÉ TV) 43–4
Irish Congress of Trade Unions (ICTU)
   age of consent 144
   and gay rights 95, 96, 98, 100–1, 107, 108
   Women's Charter 99–100
Irish Constitution 1, 8, 26, 39–40, 87–8, 141
Irish Council for Civil Liberties (ICCL) 93–4, 138
   Equality Now for Lesbians and Gay Men 143–4
Irish Distributive and Administrative Trade Union (IDATU) 100, 107
Irish Examiner 120
Irish Federation of University Teachers (IFUT) 96, 98
Irish Gay Rights Movement (IGRM) 19–37
   churches and 33–5
   establishment of 18–19
   Gay Sweatshop controversy 28–9
   laws and 35–6
   leadership of 19, 36–7
   lesbians and 21, 23
   letters to 20
   local groups 22–4, 66–9, 74–6, 77
   media coverage of 25–32
   negative comments, responses to 27–8
   and NGF 42–3, 65–6, 69, 71
   objectives of 19
   rights, search for support 32–6
   running costs 20
   rural outings 22
   social activities 19–20
   students and 32–3, 89
   survey of political parties 106
   Tel-A-Friend (TAF) 21–2, 23–4
Irish Gay Switchboard 43
Irish Independent 28, 46, 112, 114, 118, 122
Irish Lesbian and Gay Organisation (ILGO) 158

Irish Municipal, Public and Civil Trade Union 145
Irish Press
  advertising, refusal of 123
  AIDS epidemic 125
  Catholic Church, influence of 89
  draft Bill on sexual activity 35
  Gay News, banning of 94
  Gay Pride Week 55
  Hirschfeld Centre 41
  Maynooth University 33
  Soviet Union, Ireland compared to 104
  UCC gay society 91
Irish Queer Archive (IQA) 2
Irish Times, The
  AIDS epidemic 111, 113, 125, 127, 129
  Alan Buchanan speech 34
  Catholic countries 142
  ECHR judgement, options for 153–4, 155
  'Gay Paree' of Dublin 39
  gay pride events 55–6, 158
  Gay Sweatshop controversy 29
  Hirschfeld Biograph 45
  Hirschfeld Centre 41
  homosexual ideology 147
  ILGA 150–1
  Last House, appearance of David Norris on 26–7
  Law Reform Commission 143
  Lesbian Line 49
  letters opened in Cork 68
  letters to 51
  Liz Noonan and Ruth Jacobs interview 53
  parents, support for 47
  Phoenix Club 20
  police raids 77–8
  protest march announcement 57
  reception of President Robinson 150
  sex education 113
  Unfair Dismissals Act (1977) 145
isolation of homosexuals 9

J. J. Smyth's, Dublin 50
Jacobs, Ruth 52–3

Kaczynski, Jaroslaw 1
Kameny, Franklin 25

Kavanagh, Mary 39
Keating, Michael 105
Keenan, Paula 82
Kegley, Margaret 31
Kennan, Sean P. 103
Keogh, Bernard
  CHLR and 37
  on contacts in the West of Ireland 65
  ESBOA and 99
  GGC and 74, 75–6
  LIL and 53
  on medical treatments for homosexuality 72
  Sean Connolly, resignation from IGRM 36
  Soviet Union, Ireland compared to 104
  under 18s, support for 45–6
  WRTCC affiliation 54
Kerrigan, Cathal
  and CGC 70, 72
  and Cork IGRM 23, 69
  on gay bars 14
  gay rights 140, 142
  ILGA and 150
  on violence 57
Kerrigan, Páraic 25
Kerryman 155
Kilkenny 66
Kilkenny People 66
killings of gay men 54, 55, 56, 94
Kilroy, Walt 47–8, 115
Kincora Boys' Home scandal 99, 178 n.31
Kinnane, Mary 52
Kirk, Chris 43, 53
Knight, Pat 15
Knopp, Larry 63–4

La Chateau, Cork 14
Labour Party 106, 108, 139, 150, 151
Lacey, Aidan 20
Lacey, Tom 101
Lambert, Hugh 21
Landsforeningen for Lesbik 151
language 102, 103, 146–7, 157
Last House (RTÉ TV) 25–6
Late Late Show, The (RTÉ TV) 17, 50–1, 123–4, 130
Lavelle, Rev Paul 111, 112
Law Reform Commission 102, 142–3

Lawlor, Gerard 62
laws
   Censorship of Publications Act (1929) 7, 112–13
   Criminal Law Amendment Act (1885) 7–8, 87, 148–9, 150, 162 n.15
   Criminal Law (Sexual Offences) Bill (1993) 135, 155, 156–7
   Employment Equality Act (1977) 95, 97, 107
   Family Planning Bill (1979) 112
   Indecent Advertisement Act (1889) 112–13
   Offences Against the Person Act (1861) 7, 87, 148–9, 150, 162 n.15
   Prohibition of Incitement to Hatred Bill 138–40
   Sexual Offences Act (1967) (England and Wales) 1, 154–5, 161 n.4
   Unfair Dismissals Act (1977) 95–8, 107, 144–5, 148, 150, 153
League of Decency 51
Leahy, Arthur 69–70, 72, 80, 98
Leeworthy, Daryl 11
Legion of Mary 13
Lenaboy Arms Hotel, Salthill 75, 76, 77
Lenihan, Brian 138
Leonard, Arthur 141
Lesbian and Gay Rights at Work (LGRW) 100, 107–8
Lesbian and Gay Rights in the Workplace: Guidelines for Negotiators 101
Lesbian Lines 49, 59, 81–2
lesbians
   and alcoholism 48
   conferences and other meetings 48, 50, 51, 52, 99
   Cork groups and activities 77–82
   Cork Women's Fun Weekends 79–80
   employment rights 99–101
   at gay bars 14, 21
   and the IGRM 21, 23
   LIL group 49–50, 53–4, 58–9
   media coverage 50–1
   mothers 51–2
   National Lesbian and Gay Federation 159
   phone lines 49, 59, 81–2
   political candidates 52–3
   publicly declared relationships 53
   relationship with men 48
   Second Commission on the Status of Women 152
Liam Nolan Show (radio) 17
Liberation for Irish Lesbians (LIL) 49–50, 53–4, 58–9
Liberty News 129
Liddy, J. 105–6
Limerick 66, 158
Limerick Echo 66
Limerick Leader 29
Liz, LIL member 52
Loafer's Pub, Cork 80, 82
Local Government and Public Services Union (LGPSU) 96–8, 100, 101
Loftus, Sean D. 28
London, England 11
loneliness of homosexuals 9
Longford Leader 27–8
Looney, Brian 66
Lynch, Fr Bernárd 123–4
Lynch, Edmund
   AIDS epidemic 115
   on bars 14
   and CHE 16
   and CHLR 37
   conference speech 33
   IGA, Dublin home of 43
   interviews by 6
   and media coverage 25
   OUT magazine 61
   and SLM 17
   South County Hotel meeting (1974) 18–19
   television coverage 17
Lynch, Jack 102

McAnally, Conor 17
McCarroll, Joseph 147, 155
McCartan, Bernard 98
McCarthy, Joan 79, 80
McClean, Tom 73
McCormack, Inez 99
MacDara, Nial 29
MacDonagh, Fr Enda 17
Mac Dubhghaill, Uinsionn 150
McEvoy, Johnny 44
McGee, Michael 46

McKeon, Barbara 70
McKinney, Ciaran 40, 111, 124–5, 188 n.41
McMahon, Larry 46
MacManus, Hugo 17
McNamara, Kevin, Archbishop of Dublin 113
McQuaid, Fr John Charles 8
McSweeney, Rhona 60
McWilliam, Margaret 16, 17
magazines *see* media coverage
Magill 119
Mannion, Hubert 89
Margo, Glen 118–19
marriage, same-sex 1–2, 160
Marrinan, Jack 55
Martin, Diarmuid, Archbishop of Dublin 160
Mary, LIL member 52
Maynooth University 33, 90
Mayo News 75
Meany, Bert 23, 24
media coverage
　1970s TV, radio and newspapers 17–18, 24, 25–32, 33
　1980s newspapers and magazines 43, 47, 51, 52, 56, 57, 60–1, 67, 73
　1980s TV and radio 43–4, 50–1, 52, 69–70
　1990s newspapers and magazines 142, 143, 145, 147, 150–1
　of AIDS epidemic 114–15, 116, 121–2, 125–6, 127, 128, 129, 130
　see also advertising
medical facilities 113, 116
medical treatments 10, 72
Meehan, Sylvia 107, 108
meetings *see* conferences and other meetings
Mitchell, John 100–1, 107
Molloy, Maura 107
Moloney, Derek 47
Moore, Phil 47, 153
Moore's Hotel, Cork 80
mothers, lesbian 51–2
Mulkerns, Helena 125–6
Mulkerns, Val 26, 27, 31–2
Munster gay pride (1981) 73–4
Munster Gay Switchboard 67–8, 81
Munster Women's Newsletter 78

Murphy, Christina 17
Murphy, Kieran 158

National AIDS Strategy Committee 148
National Gay Conference Organising Committee (NGCOC) 96
National Gay Federation (NGF)
　AIDS epidemic 114–15, 115, 118–19
　Book Upstairs and 60
　employment rights 95–6, 99
　establishment of 42
　Flikkers disco 44
　gay pride week 55–6
　Hirschfeld Biograph cinema 44–5
　Hirschfeld Centre 39, 40, 41, 43–4, 44–5, 61–2
　The Homosexual Challenge 147
　ICCL and 93
　and IGRM 42–3, 65–6, 69, 71
　Law Reform Commission 143
　LIL and 49, 53, 54
　local groups 74
　Love is for Life, response to 60
　objectives of 41–2
　OUT magazine 60–1
　Prohibition of Incitement to Hatred Bill 139
　regional membership and local groups 65–6
　Second International Gay Youth Congress (1985) 58
　sexual activity, decriminalisation of 103
　as a 'single-issue organisation' 71
　under 18s, support for 45–8
　Welfare and Counselling Service 48
　WRTCC and 53–4
National Lesbian and Gay Federation 159
National Library of Ireland (NLI) 2
National Socialist Party 117
National Union of Public Employees (NUPE) 116
National Union of Students (NUS) 15, 16
National Youth Council of Ireland 144
Netherlands 105
Nevin, Donal 100–1
New University of Ulster (NUU) 14–15
New York, USA 158
newspaper coverage *see* media coverage

Ní Bheagliach, Máire 51, 52
Ní Fhlatharta, Bernie 130
Ní Mhurchú, Padraigín 99
Nolan, Freda 107
Nolan, John 61
Noonan, Liz 52–3
Norris, David
   address to Church of Ireland seminar 34
   aims of the SLM 18
   article in student magazine 33
   and aversion therapy 10
   campaign for law reform 37
   on conferences 18
   court cases 87–8, 136
   on discrimination 33
   employment rights 96
   Equality Now for Lesbians and Gay Men 143
   European community and 140, 141–2
   Gay Sweatshop controversy 29
   health of 10
   Hirschfeld Centre, opening of 41
   ICCL and 93
   IGA, Dublin home of 43
   IGRM, leadership of 36–7
   Last House, appearance on 25–7
   LIL, affiliation to NGF 49
   NGF, foundation of 41
   NGF as a 'single-issue organisation' 71
   Noel Browne, letter to 102
   on *Persona Humana* 35
   profile of 159–60
   Prohibition of Incitement to Hatred Bill 138, 139
   role of 1–2
   school assignment, reply to letter about 159
   South County Hotel meeting (1974) 18
   Soviet Union, Ireland compared to 104
   Tuesday Report, appearance on 30
Northern Ireland 15, 116, 154–5
Northern Ireland Civil Rights Association (NICRA) 15
Northern Ireland Family Planning Association (NIFPA) 118
Northern Ireland Gay Rights Association (NIGRA) 124
Norway 18, 151

O'Byrne, Patrick 57
O'Callaghan, Denis 89, 155
O'Clubhán, Colm 11
O'Connell, Tony 36, 37
O'Connor, Áine 25, 69
O'Donnell, Pauline 50
O'Donovan, Patricia 108
O'Dowd, Niall 8, 39
O'Faolain, Nuala 129, 142, 159
O'Flaherty, Bridie 63
O'Halloran, Gary 147–8
O'Halloran, Josephine 92
O'Hanlon, R. J. 87
O'Hanlon, Rory 127, 131
O'Loughlin, Edward 158
O'Mahony-Rysh, Pat 67, 72
O'Neill, Denis 65, 66
O'Rourke, Mary 148, 151, 153
O'Shannon, Cathal 30
O'Shaughnessy, John 29
O'Shea, Brian 62
O'Sullivan, Harold 96–7
O'Toole, Fintan 93, 149
offences, homosexual 9
Offences Against the Person Act (1861) 7, 87, 148–9, 150, 162 n.15
opposition to gay rights 34–6, 59, 145–8, 155, 156
Our Family 59
Oral Interviews 6
OUT 10, 60–1, 83, 90, 108, 115, 123, 124–5
Out for Ourselves 11, 52, 94
Out Front 68

Paddy, from Galway 13–14
paedophilia 9
Paisley, Ian 104
parents 47, 51–2, 89
Parents and Friends of the Mentally Handicapped 51
Parents Enquiry 47–8
Paris, France 16
Parliament Inn, Dublin 50
Peader O'Donnell Achievement Awards 63, 83
People Like Us Totally Outrageous (PLUTO) 158, 159
Persona Humana 35

personal advertisements 61
Pettit, Lance 93
Philip, NGF youth group member 47
Philpott, Anne 24
Phoenix Centre, Cork 23, 66–7, 71–2
Phoenix Club, Dublin 20, 21, 42, 43, 81
phone lines *see* Lesbian Lines; Munster Gay Switchboard; Student Gay-line; Tel-A-Friend (TAF) phone line
picnics 56
Pierse, Michael 11
pink economy 39, 61, 80
pink triangles/carnations 55–6, 73, 76, 84
P.O. box numbers 23–4, 75, 83
police
    discrimination in 94
    distrust of 54–5, 76, 94
    raids by 77–8
    response to National Socialist Party leaflet 117
political candidates 52–3, 139
political parties 105, 106, 108
Porter, John 74, 75–6, 77
Presland, Eric 66–7, 77, 81
Pritchard, Bob 84
privacy, issue of 74, 76
Prohibition of Incitement to Hatred Bill 138–40
Project Arts Centre, Dublin 28–9
protest marches *see* gay pride events
provincial regions 63–4
    see also Cork; Galway
pub zaps 56
pubs and clubs 13, 14, 20, 21, 42, 43, 61, 80, 82

Quay Co-Op, Cork 77–82
Queen's University Belfast (QUB) 15, 33
Quelch, Leslie 51
Quillinan, Stephen 66, 68, 107
Quinlan, Mick 188 n.41
Quinn, James 9
Quinn, Ruairí 35, 107, 108, 148
quizzes 80

Rabbitte, Sean 76, 77
Radio City Cork 67
radio coverage 17, 24, 67

Raidió Teilifís Éireann (RTÉ) coverage
    Borderline 130
    Ireland's Eye 43–4
    Last House 25–6
    Late Late Show, The 17, 50–1, 123–4, 130
    Tuesday Report 29–30
    Week In 69–70
Randles, Bridget 155
Recommendation 924, Council of Europe 105–6
Reg, migrant to England 30–1
religion, influence of *see* Church of Ireland; Roman Catholic Church
research methods 6
Reynolds, Albert 148–9
right to choose 53–4
Rigney, Liam 148
Roberts, Nicole E. 59
Robertson, Rose 17, 31, 47
Robinson, Mary 87, 150
Robson, Christopher
    AIDS epidemic 114–15
    on Catholic countries 142
    Civil Service Policy on AIDS 101
    on equality 154
    GHA's *AIDS Information Booklet* 121
    on GLEN campaigns 137, 138
    letter to Máire Geoghegan-Quinn 151
    report of National Socialist Party leaflet 117
Rockland's Hotel, Salthill 76, 77
Rogers, John 126
Roman Catholic Church
    AIDS epidemic, response to 111, 126, 127–8
    Catholic countries, gay rights in 141–2
    and IGRM 33–4, 34–5
    influence of 7–8, 31
    Love is for Life 59–60
    on marriage equality 160
    opposition of 59, 145–6, 156
    sex education 113
Rose, Kieran
    address to President Robinson 150
    advertising in Cork 82
    CGC and 69, 70
    on Criminal Law (Sexual Offences) Bill (1993) 156

employment rights 96, 97, 98, 99, 107
on equality 154
gay pride celebrations 73
human rights 149
ILGA letter campaign 140–1
on Imperial Hotel, Cork 14
Law Reform Commission 143
Soviet Union, Ireland compared to 104
talk at Churchfield Women's Group 80
on winning over the doubtful 137
Ross, Shane 132–3
Rossiter, Margaret 73
RTÉ Guide 123
rural homosexuals 9–10, 21–2
Rushe, Desmond 28–9
Russia 104
Ryan, Frank 36–7
Ryan-Flood, Róisín 11

safer sex 115, 117–18, 121, 126–7, 128, 130
Salthill, Galway 13, 75, 76, 77
Samaritans 9
same-sex marriage, legalisation of 1–2
Sanders, John 95, 98
Sappho 16
saunas 60, 124
Scene Magazine 28
school assignments 159
schoolteachers 94–5
Scottish Homosexual Rights Group (SHRG) 95, 104
Scottish Minorities Group (SMG) 15
Sebald, Natalie 84
Second Commission on the Status of Women 139–40, 152
secret symbols 76
Self, Charles 54, 94
seminars *see* conferences and other meetings
sex
    discussion of 112–13
    safer 115, 117–18, 121, 126–7, 128, 130
    unsafe 117, 126–7, 128
sex education 113
sexism 48
sexual acts with minors 9
Sexual Liberation Movement (SLM) 16–17, 18

Sexual Offences Act (1967) (England and Wales) 1, 154–5, 161 n.4
Sexual Reform Movement (SRM) 15
sexually transmitted diseases (STDs) 112–13, 116
Sheehan, Donal 78, 115, 122
Sheerin, Joni *see* Crone, Joni
SIDES, Dublin 61
Sinn Féin 106, 108
Slattery, Helen 66, 78, 80, 81–2
Smyth, Ailbhe 39
Smyth, Freddie 48
social activities *see* bars; clubs; discos; Hirschfeld Centre; picnics; quizzes
Somers, Eamon 44, 68
South County Hotel, Stillorgan, Dublin 18–19
Soviet Union 104
Spring, Dick 106
Squarcialupi, Vera 106–7
St Patrick's Day parades 158–9
Staggs, Sam 104
state officials, difficulties with 67–8
statistics
    AIDS epidemic 114, 122, 125, 127, 131, 132
    prosecutions 7, 9
Steele, Laurie 69–70
stereotypes 9, 25, 30, 89
    see also attitudes towards homosexuals
Stewart, Alastair 15, 16
sticker campaign 82
Student Gay-line 83
student unions 32–3, 88–93
    see also Union of Students in Ireland (USI)
students 16, 83
Success 39
Sunday Independent
    criticism of RTÉ coverage of homosexuality 27, 31–2
    dismissal from employment 94
    Gay Sweatshop controversy 28
    GHA leaflet 118
    IGRM discos 20
    on Liz Noonan 52
    pubs in *Gay News* 14
    TCD symposium (1974), effect of 17–18

Sunday Press 21
Sunday Tribune 90, 93
Sunday World 52, 130
Swedish Federation for Gay and Lesbian Rights 151
symposia *see* conferences and other meetings

Talbot, Jane 84
Tavern Bar, Galway 76, 77
Taylor, Mervyn 156
teachers 94–5
Tel-A-Friend (TAF) phone line 21–2, 23–4, 43, 49, 115, 119, 120
  see also Lesbian Lines; Munster Gay Switchboard; Student Gay-line
television coverage *see* Raidió Teilifís Éireann (RTÉ) coverage
Temple Bar, Dublin 39
terminology 8, 163 n.30
Terrence Higgins Trust (THT) 116, 118
threat of homosexuality 59–60
Todd, Babs 17
Tóibin, Colm 2
trade unions 95–101
Treacy, Tricia 97
treatments for homosexuality 10, 72
triangle symbol *see* pink triangles/carnations
Trinity College Dublin (TCD) 16–18, 33, 48, 51, 52, 90, 98–9
Trinity News 33
Tuesday Report (RTÉ TV) 29–30

under 18s, support for, by NGF 45–7
Unfair Dismissals Act (1977) 95–8, 107, 144–5, 148, 150, 153
Union of Professional and Technical Civil Servants (UPTCS) 100, 101
Union of Students in Ireland (USI) 16, 32–3, 89, 90

United States of America 104, 158
universities 14–15, 33, 83, 89–93, 158
  see also Trinity College Dublin (TCD)
University College Cork (UCC) 89–90, 91–2
University College Dublin (UCD) 90, 91, 92–3
University College Galway (UCG) 83, 158
unsafe sex 117, 126–7, 128
Urquhart, Diane 7

Walsh, Caroline 53
Walsh, Deirdre 78, 80, 81
Walsh, Louise 79
Walsh, Marese 74, 75, 76, 83, 84
Walsh, Noel 57
Walsh, Tonie 9–10, 41, 56, 58, 99
Ward, Nuala 83–4
Waterford 22, 67
Week In (RTÉ TV) 69–70
Weeks, Jeffrey 6
Wightman, Alison 118
Wikström, Tobias 151
Wilson, Tony 26
women
  commission on the status of 139–40, 152
  constitution of Ireland, implications of 8
  see also lesbians
Women Today 52
Women's Fun Weekends 79–80
Women's Place, Quay Co-Op, Cork 78
Women's Right to Choose Campaign (WRTCC) 53–4
Woods, Michael 72
Workers' Party 106, 108, 139
workshops *see* conferences and other meetings

young people 45–7

Plate 1 Members of the Sexual Liberation Movement protesting outside the Department of Justice on 27 June 1974 as part of Gay Pride. Top photo from left to right: Hugo MacManus (holding placard saying 'Homosexuals are Revolting'). Directly behind Hugo is Michael Kerrigan who is wearing a hat. Behind Michael is Edwin Henshaw who is also carrying a placard. The bottom photo from left to right: Joseph Leckey and Margaret McWilliam. Photograph by Gareth Miller. Reproduced with kind permission of David Norris.

Plate 2 Picture of five of the founding members of the Irish Gay Rights Movement. Kenneth F. Jackson is the sixth person. From left to right: David Norris, Martin Barnes, Edmund Lynch, Clement Clancy, Kenneth F. Jackson and Sean Connolly at the end. Photograph reproduced with kind permission of David Norris.

Plate 3 Dublin's Gay Pride Protest March, June 1983. Photo courtesy of Kieran Rose.

Plate 4 Arthur Leahy and Tony O'Regan of Cork Gay Collective handing out leaflets during Gay Pride Week on Princes Street, Cork, c. 1982/83. Photo courtesy of Kieran Rose.

Plate 5 The Quay Co-Op, Sullivan's Quay, Cork. Photo c. 1984 during Lesbian and Gay Pride Week. Photo courtesy of Kieran Rose.

Plate 6 Laurie Steele of Cork Gay Collective lobbying delegates as they arrived for the Irish Congress of Trade Unions annual general congress at Cork City Hall, July 1981. Photo courtesy of Kieran Rose.

Plate 7 GHA AIDS Information Leaflet, May 1985. Arthur Leahy Collection part of Cork LGBT Archive. Photo courtesy of Orla Egan, Cork LGBT Archive.

Plate 8 GHA Play Safe Card, 1986. Arthur Leahy collection part of Cork LGBT Archive. Photo courtesy of Orla Egan, Cork LGBT Archive.

www.ingramcontent.com/pod-product-compliance
Lightning Source LLC
Chambersburg PA
CBHW062214300426
44115CB00012BA/2053